One of the main objects of
is to argue that the *right kind*
economy can be an instrume... ...
human freedom and a way of
satisfying wants superior to collectivist alternatives.

The subject is approached from a
variety of angles. There is a provo-
catively written prologue, free of
technicality or jargon, which points
out the similarities between the values
of competitive capitalism and those
of the 'permissive society', and
discusses the paradoxical hostility of
so many young radicals to freedom
in the economic sphere. The first and
longest of the subsequent essays is
entitled 'A Restatement of Economic
Liberalism', a concept which is carefully
distinguished from *laissez-faire*.
The standard economic case for
market forces is examined critically
and in the end the argument is seen
to hinge on the excessive and
incompatible expectations from
political activity now prevalent.
A great many subjects, ranging from
utilitarian ethics to equality, the rule of
law, individual freedom and the
economics of socialism are covered.
The analysis in this essay should be
of value to anyone seriously interested
in these issues, irrespective of
political belief.

Subsequent essays cover a wide
variety of issues. They range from a
discussion of 'Jobs, Prices and Trade
Unions' to an essay on the economics
of an alternative and less materialistic
society, which still retains market
institutions. There is a careful study of
Conservative economic policy,
which is often wrongly identified
with the pursuit of a market economy.
Other essays cover issues such as

the Common Market, monopoly policy, economic growth and the balance of payments. There are also excursions into foreign policy and shorter pieces dealing with contemporary political leaders, as well as some fresh thoughts on the difficult concepts of 'left' and 'right'.

Capitalism and the Permissive Society

Capitalism and the Permissive Society

SAMUEL BRITTAN

MACMILLAN

First published 1973 by
THE MACMILLAN PRESS LTD
London and Basingstoke
Associated companies in New York Dublin
Melbourne Johannesburg and Madras

SBN 333 12464 2

Printed in Great Britain by
NORTHUMBERLAND PRESS LIMITED
Gateshead

TO THE MEMORY OF MY FATHER

Contents

If men were actuated by self-interest, which they are not – except in the case of a few saints – the whole human race would co-operate. There would be no more wars, no more armies, no more navies, no more atom bombs ...

I do not deny that there are better things than selfishness, and that some people achieve these things. I maintain, however, on the one hand that there are few occasions upon which large bodies of men, such as politics is concerned with, can rise above selfishness, while on the other hand, there are a very great many circumstances in which population will fall below selfishness, if selfishness is interpreted as enlightened self-interest.

And among those occasions on which people fall below self-interest are most of the occasions on which they are convinced that they are acting from idealistic motives. Much that passes as idealism is disguised hatred or disguised love of power.

Bertrand Russell, *Human Society in Ethics and Politics*

Note to the Reader

The case for competitive markets, as a superior way of co-ordinating human activities to decisions arrived at by political means, has been frequently put forward over several centuries and just as frequently disputed. There is nevertheless, a great presentational difficulty in stating this case. It is usually understood to mean something like *laissez-faire*: that governments should not bother with business or commercial activities unless perhaps there are glaring monopolies or cartels. Stated in this form it is plainly wrong, on almost any prevalent set of value judgements. One only has to think of Public Health regulations or the disadvantages of free and unrestricted parking in a busy street, without going into anything more controversial or subtle, to see that this is so.

Yet, if an attempt is made to make the arguments more convincing and set out the conditions which have to be fulfilled – the necessary background of laws, and of financial and other policies – if market forces are to yield a reasonably satisfactory result, the reader is likely to feel cheated. The simplicity of a simple slogan that we can accept or reject has gone. If the necessary conditions are stated in detail, the result is a series of textbooks (which are far from being in perfect agreement with each other); and the question seems too expert for the normal educated citizen or elected politician. Alternatively, if one tries to simplify and summarise, the result can seem so vague and general that it may seem compatible with almost any policy.

Yet it is highly dangerous to give up the attempt. For there is a connection, however difficult to state, between economic, personal and political freedom. It is also paradoxical and worrying that so many of the young and the radical, who rightly put great emphasis on personal freedom and who are sceptical of the claims of authority, should be so intolerant of private initiative in the so-called economic sphere.

One of the objects of this book is to persuade the open-minded reader that the *right kind* of market economy can be an instrument of human freedom and a way of satisfying human wants rather than a hollow dogma to quiet business-men's consciences. The greater part of the space is, however, devoted to the difficulties and problems that have arisen in the various attempts to expound such a 'liberal' economic philosophy – 'liberal' in the sense that it welcomes market forces and the price mechanism as *potential* forces for good. To do this will require venturing well outside the area con-ventionally regarded as 'economic'.

It is hoped that a few guidelines, which will be neither oversimplified slogans nor impossible technicalities, will emerge. But the main emphasis is on the underlying argu-ments. There is more chance of arousing the interest of the sceptical reader if he is invited to listen to, and participate in, debates inside the 'liberal' camp, than if he is presented with a fixed doctrine that claims to solve all problems; and arous-ing interest is half the battle. The main enemy of the econo-mic liberal is not reasoned opposition, but bored hostility, whether that of the businessman or politician who thinks his attitude 'unrealistic', or of the radical student who thinks that 'it isn't where it's at'.

An authoritative study of the whole area would be a full-time labour of many years, involving highly technical studies of areas ranging from academic philosophy to mathematical welfare economics and the empirical analysis of modern busi-ness. Even then it is doubtful if any one person could under-take it, or whether if he did, the result would be coherent and convincing. Instead, I have attempted to tackle the sub-ject from a variety of different angles in the hope of shedding a little light. The aim of the following essays is to open up some lines of discussion rather than to formulate watertight theories; but I am immodest enough to hope that those who specialise in more formal or mathematical models, or in the statistical testing of hypotheses, will find in this quarry some material worth further development.

The fairly long Prologue, 'Capitalism and the Permissive Society', which provides the title essay, is a deliberately pro-vocative statement of my main conclusions. It is written with the minimum of qualification and is designed to be comprehensible to people who do not normally look at writings on political economy. For this reason it inevitably depends more than the other essays on personal judgement; and those whose main interest is in analysis may be able to see it in better perspective if they look beforehand at some of the subsequent essays.

The principal arguments are developed in Part I. The first, and by far the longest, of the essays is entitled 'A Restatement of Economic Liberalism'. After stating certain fundamentals, this goes on to examine the traditional arguments for market forces. Although these retain a kernel of validity, if stated with sufficient care, some of the most important considerations lie in a different area: in the excessive and incompatible expectations from political activity now current, not least among those who are most cynical about individual politicians. The title of the second essay 'Jobs, Prices and Trade Unions' is self-explanatory. It is a very summarised treatment of endlessly debated matters relevant to a modern market economy; its aim is not novelty, but to penetrate the mists with which political tactfulness and peripheral technical controversies have obscured the essentials of the subject. The third essay, 'The Economics of the Alternative Society' seeks to raise its sights from the immediate squabble of interest groups and to analyse the role of economic freedom in a less materialistic environment than the present. It attempts to take a little further some of the issues raised by the Prologue, with which it has a natural link, and is the one essay which makes some very modest claim to originality. It is also one of the very few whose opening quotation is not taken from David Hume.

The whole of Part I, together with the fresh thoughts on 'left and right' at the end of Part III, are entirely new and between them make up the greater part of the book. In between I have sandwiched a number of self-contained essays most of which have appeared before, but in varied, and not always very accessible, places. The desire to give these studies a more permanent home is not, however, the only reason for their inclusion here. Several friends have impressed on me the need to provide specific and concrete policy applications of my more general arguments. These contributions, which range from economic growth, monopolies, the E.E.C. and the balance of payments to the activities of contemporary political leaders, should help supply this link. I have also included a hitherto unpublished and very early attempt to apply a similar individualist-liberal outlook to the realm of foreign policy.

In the reprinted and revised essays, I have tried where possible to cut out repetition of what is already said in other parts of the book, although this cannot be done everywhere if the thread of the argument is to be maintained. I have also tried to eradicate material that is out-of-date in an uninterest-ing way, without striking out misjudgements, false predic-tions, or views which I have had subsequently to modify. The original dates of these essays are given, as this is an area where one can learn from one's mistakes as well as from one's successes; and to blot out the former would be no service to reader or author.

An empirical survey that I have made of the approach of economists, politicians and commentators to policy questions, entitled *Is There An Economic Consensus?*, is being pub-lished alongside the present volume; and its results may shed some additional light on the questions discussed here. In both books I have attempted to present the arguments in a form which will still be useful to those who do not share my judgements, and impart a certain amount of information as well as analysis and advocacy.

As already indicated, I have made no attempt to be gratui-tously original; the footnote references are accordingly no mere formalities, but indicate a number of distinguished works in which some of the themes touched upon here are more fully developed and elaborated. If there is a difference of emphasis between what is presented here and the principal writers of the 'economic liberal' school, it is that some of the latter have tended to see the main threat to freedom as coming from the 'left', whereas I tend to see both threats and oportunities from many different points of the political compass.

One of the main concerns of this book is to stress the liberal alternative as a valid, and in my view, superior ideal to the collectivist one, and not just to knock the latter. If we are, in

Professor Hayek's words, 'to free the process of spontaneous growth from the obstacles and encumbrances that human folly has erected', our hopes 'must rest on persuading and gaining the support of those who by disposition are "progressives", those who, though they may now be seeking change in the wrong direction, are at least willing to examine critically the existing system and to change it wherever necessary'.[1]

It may strike some readers that the 'liberal utilitarianism' presented in Chapter 1 is such a heavily qualified form of utilitarianism that it is closer to some modern version of the social contract doctrine, such as that recently put forward by Professor John Rawls, than to any recognised form of utilitarianism. Fortunately the question does not have to be resolved at the ultimate philosophical level. The starting-point of any assessment of institutions and policies for the economic liberal is the goals and desires of individual human beings rather than some supposedly superior conception of the public good. This individualistic element is common to both utilitarian and contract doctrines, in contrast to those of a more perfectionist or paternalist kind.

It would have strengthened my case if I could have incorporated Professor Rawls's argument for the 'priority of liberty'. This attempts to 'rule out' any sacrifice of basic liberties in exchange for economic and social gains, however large the latter. My failure to do so reflects, I am afraid, more than the unfortunate fact that Rawls's path-breaking book *A Theory of Justice* appeared after my own manuscript went to press. The arguments he provides for the priority of liberty, while persuasive and appealing (and pointing in a similar direction to some of the more informal reflections in the early part of my own Prologue) do not seem to me entirely conclusive. There still seems no alternative to a political pluralism in which different goals have to be balanced against each other; and, although reasoned discussion of the relative weights to be given to each of these in different situations is possible, there remains an irreducibly subjective element in the choices made.

The most controversial part of the present book may well

be found in Chapter 10, a very early and almost-undergraduate piece, written before I had acquired even such limited prudential experience of how to guard my flank as I may have since attained. In that chapter I draw attention to the 'successive circles of obligation' that people have, which are strongest towards those who are personally closest to them, somewhat less strong to those with whom they have national, racial, religious or cultural affinities, and weakest of all towards the human race in general. I argue that a frank recognition of these facts would be preferable – and lead to more humane results – than the customary proclamation of universal benevolence as the ideal to which all should aspire.

The real difficulty of this concept is not that it is reprehensible, but that it relates to a private code of morality in which the weights will differ from person to person, and is therefore not easy to translate into a set of public rules on which all, or most, can agree. For this purpose some impartial guide such as Rawls's 'veil of ignorance', in which we ask ourselves what criteria we would accept if we did not know what our own particular station in society was to be, is clearly more suitable. But it still leaves open the question of the reference group; that is of the exact society in which we are to imagine ourselves to be ignorant of our station. It is far from obvious that this should be the whole human race. The idea of a weighting system in which we attach smaller, but non-zero, weights to people outside our own country still seems to me a helpful one for traditional types of foreign policy questions. It may even give us some clue in our present confused situation where there is strong and emotional disagreement about the relative degrees of obligation to British subjects, fellow members of the E.E.C. and members of the Commonwealth of varying degrees of 'kinship'. But I can scarcely claim to have scratched the surface of the whole question of 'reference groups' which is one of the most neglected areas of both moral philosophy and of empirical political analysis.

When it comes to the domain and content of economic policy, the position reached in this book is very similar to that of US theorists of the 'public choice' school. This is that the dissection of 'failures' or 'imperfections' in the market place does not automatically set up a presumption in favour of political intervention; nor does it provide an easy guide to the form that such intervention, when it is desirable, should take. For the political as well as the market process is subject to 'failures' and 'imperfections' in satisfying and reconciling the desires of citizens; and it is illegitimate to argue that people who are guided by self-interest (however defined) in their role as producers or consumers, will act totally differently when they shift from the economic to the political arena. (This point is made very well by Professor James Buchanan in his introduction to *Theory of Public Choice* (ed. J. M. Buchanan and R. D. Tollison).)

The fact that, in the course of my own observations as an economic journalist, I arrived at conclusions remarkably similar to those which had been worked out on a deductive basis by scholars on the other side of the Atlantic, may have more than a personal interest. For too long economists have based their policy prescriptions on the assumption of a benevolent (and sometimes even omniscient) despot. The pressures, constraints and incentives affecting politicians, civil servants and their advisers, should be subjected to the same analytical scrutiny as are those affecting business firms, trade unionists and consumers. If this were done, public debate on economic topics might well take on a much less crudely interventionist form than it does at present.

If it were the custom to dedicate books to one's contemporaries, this one would undoubtedly be dedicated to Nigel Lawson and Peter Jay. I have discussed the central problems of this book with the former over a long period and with the latter over what is also now a number of years. Many of the ideas discussed in the following pages are either developments of points first made by one or other of these friends, or attempts to cope with criticisms that they have made. As it is mainly a certain fastidiousness of standards which has prevented them from going into print first on some of the central logical and philosophical problems raised, the least I can do is to record my gratitude to them for many enjoyable discussions.

In connection with the new essays presented in this book, I must add a special word of thanks to Professor John Williamson, who commented on the first draft of Chapters 1 and 3, and nobly helped me to straighten out the logic of certain arguments even when he did not share some of the underlying judgements. William Keegan, David Watt and my brother Leon Brittan commented on the draft Prologue, and Professor Richard Lynn on Chapter 13, which he did so much to stimulate, as did Professor Anthony King. Andrew Best was an invaluable counsellor on general problems of construction.

A great many other friends and colleagues have discussed with me directly or indirectly both the new material and the reprinted essays. Although it would not be feasible to list all their names, I can at least record my gratitude in general terms. They are responsible for my opinions only to the extent that they failed to argue me out of them.

Although he was not involved in this book, I cannot omit from these acknowledgements a special reference to Professor Peter Bauer. It was he who first introduced me to economic studies in Cambridge and brought home to me at an early stage that there was no alternative to making up my own mind on key issues. More recently he encouraged me to persist in thinking through certain themes which now feature in Chapter 1.

Last, but far from least, I must thank Mrs Anne Shotts, who not only typed but deciphered the bulk of the manuscript and whose devoted efforts made publication possible.

Finally I must thank the following organisations and publications for permission to make use of material which originally appeared in earlier versions under their aegis: The Institute of Economic Affairs, *The Political Quarterly*, the Department of Trade and Industry, the *Journal of Common Market Studies*, the *Spectator*, the *Financial Times*, and *Crossbow*. I must thank Professor H. J. Eysenck and Routledge & Kegan Paul Ltd for permission to reproduce the diagram on p. 360, from *The Psychology of Politics*, and Professor Richard Lynn and the *Swinton Journal* for the one on p. 366. I am also grateful to George Allen & Unwin Ltd and Simon & Schuster Inc. for the extract from *Human Society in Ethics and Politics* by Bertrand Russell.

Spring 1972   SAMUEL BRITTAN

Prologue: Capitalism and the Permissive Society

> To declaim against present times, and magnify the virtue of remote ancestors, is a propensity almost inherent in human nature...
>
> David Hume, 'Of Refinements In the Arts'

The values of competitive capitalism have a great deal in common with contemporary attitudes, and in particular with contemporary radical attitudes. Above all they share a similar stress on allowing people to do, to the maximum feasible extent, what they feel inclined to do rather than conform to the wishes of authority, custom or convention. Under a competitive system, the businessman will make money by catering for whatever it is that people wish to do – by providing pop records, or nude shows, or candyfloss. He will not make anything by providing what the establishment thinks is good for them. An individual citizen is free to maximise his income by using his abilities (and his capital if he has any) to cater for public tastes. But he does not have to. He can go for the easiest or most congenial job, or the one with the most leisure; or, like most of us, he can find some compromise between these alternatives. In any case his life-style is his own. He can concentrate on personal pleasure, social service at home, the relief of poverty abroad, or any combination of these and numerous other activities.

Competitive capitalism is far from being the sole or dominating force of our society and Galbraith is right to force this on our attention. But to the extent that it prevails, competitive capitalism is the biggest single force acting on the side of what is fashionable to call 'permissiveness', but what was once known as personal liberty. Business enterprise can, of course, thrive and prosper alongside a great deal of 'moral' prohibitions and prescriptions, whether enforced by law or public opinion. But the profit motive will always be kicking against such restraints and seeking to widen the range of what is permissible – whether it is a 19th century publisher launching an attack on orthodox religion or a 20th century theatrical or film producer challenging conventional concepts of decency and decorum. The profit motive will act both to stretch the existing law and as a force for its liberalisation.

As against these advantages it is often alleged that competitive capitalism is based on the false values of the 'consumer society'. Critics of this sort often forget that the great virtue of the consumer society is that no one is forced to consume. There may be middle class, or middle age pressures in that direction (and plenty of 'trendy' pressures of other sorts among the young); but social pressures are not the same as edicts enforced by the police, and the rise of the 'counterculture' has itself set up pressures of an opposite kind, and the range of effective choice has been extended. To the extent that the competitive element prevails, a citizen can be equally indifferent to right-wing attacks on the self-indulgence of modern youth and to the traditional left-wing demand that all economic activity be channelled into some higher national purpose. The ethos of the market economy can be summed up in the vernacular as 'doing your own thing'. A capitalist market economy is not, of course, an equal society. But it is a powerful agent for disrupting existing class barriers and official hierarchies. Indeed, commercial societies are notorious, among those who dislike this aspect, for bringing new people and families to the fore and undermining traditional status barriers.

The expression 'competitive capitalism' is used here in its broadest possible meaning. It does not exclude the existence of a substantial public sector; nor does it prevent the state from carrying out a great many functions which are required if the market is to transmit people's preferences effectively – and this includes a great many measures in the anti-pollution field. But the emphasis is on the profit motive, consumer choice and competition. The conditions required for these activities to lead to tolerable results will be discussed in greater detail in later essays. The aim of this introductory chapter is to state the issue in its simplest terms; and rather than take refuge in terms such as 'mixed economy' or 'social market economy', I shall stick to the more provocative term 'competitive capitalism'. I would add, however, that 'competitive capitalism' is not a partisan slogan. When it comes to the test of practical application, it has at least as many opponents among Conservatives as among Labour supporters, and among businessmen as among trade unionists.

The Historical Context

The reasons why people hold certain beliefs have no bearing on their validity; to suppose otherwise would be to fall into the same intellectual trap as the worst Marxist or Freudian camp followers (it is not a trap that Marx, and above all Freud would have been guilty of themselves). Examination of the roots of widely held views can, all the same, be useful in explaining why people persist in holding them, despite rational arguments to the contrary, and why the latter fail to make a sufficient impression.

In the discussion that follows I shall begin with a reference to the historical background, go on to the features of the contemporary behaviour of businessmen and others in authority, which seem to confirm the worst suspicions of their critics, and then describe some of the other causes of the rise of anti-capitalist sentiment. With these matters out of the way, the path will be clear for a discussion of the New Left critique of capitalism and of the prospects of dealing with evils such as poverty and 'alienation' under alternative systems. This may seem a reversal of the logical order; but the treatment adopted may be more illuminating for the non-specialist reader who wants to put the economic arguments into a broader context.

Modern ideals of personal freedom, and the accompanying political, economic and legal beliefs, emerged from the religious writers of the 17th century and the political and economic philosophers of the 18th and 19th centuries. Yet, during the period when these ideals formed part of the public philosophy of the country, they were both less important to human welfare and more hedged around with stultifying qualifications than they are today when their credentials are so widely challenged. The period of English history when the capitalist ideal of freedom was most widely acknowledged was the mid-19th century – the age of Peel and Gladstone. Yet, in many ways and for many people, it must have been a very unattractive time in which to live; and economic liberals would do well to acknowledge this fact.

The point most frequently made is, of course, that although living standards were rapidly improving, the mass of people were too poor to enjoy their freedom. This stricture needs to be more carefully stated than it often is. Freedom is not the same as absence of poverty; and to say that a labourer in the 1870s, or an Egyptian peasant today is 'not really free' is a confusion of thought. If freedom is defined so that the absence of poverty is a necessary condition of its existence, two different values become confused, distinctions which exist in real life are obliterated, and language is impoverished. It is better to stick to the negative concept of freedom, but say that where the majority of the people hardly earn enough to cover their bare physical requirements, freedom may be less important as a goal than an increase of wealth.

The above, however, is well-trodden ground. What is less often pointed out is the limited number of people to whom even the legal freedoms of the 19th century applied. Personal liberty was effectively limited to male heads of households over twenty-one. Women and children had as few rights as the subjects of the Eastern despots so much condemned in the Liberal literature of the period; and the same applied to anyone who had once volunteered for the Army or Navy. If freedom is defined as the absence of coercion, there was precious little for a schoolboy or soldier of the period, both of whom were also victims of the passion for flagellation which was (and to some extent still is) the real English sickness. Even for adult heads of households, freedom was carefully circumscribed. There was freedom to start up a business enterprise, freedom to emigrate and freedom to move money over frontiers (all freedoms which we despise at our peril). But in view of the very great powers still in the hands of local J.P.s, and the ferocious maximum penalties on the statute book, there was far more discretionary power of one individual over another than nostalgic admirers of the Victorian era would admit.

Apart from this, the prohibitions in the law and custom of the land were numerous and oppressive. Whether E. M. Forster's novel *Maurice* is good or bad as a work of literature, one can only recoil with horror at the revelations of the weight of the legal and the social penalties – and above all the burden of guilt – imposed on those whose impulses were not in keeping with the official sexual mores. Among those with 'normal' tastes promiscuity abounded, and was tolerated provided that it was not publicly admitted and the pretences were maintained.

The important point, however, is that both the political and economic philosophy and the capitalist practices of a century ago set in motion a train of events and ideas which eventually undermined the status-ridden conventional society of the time and brought into being the more tolerant England of today. Indeed, the basic arguments for the so-called 'permissive' morality were developed by thinkers in the 19th-century liberal tradition from John Stuart Mill onwards (one has only to think of his lifelong campaign against the subjection of women – the genuine article before which 'Women's Lib' groups pall). Many of the classical ideas of 19th century liberalism did not come on the statute book until the 1960s. The battle is still far from won, as can be seen from the sentences still passed on 'obscene publications' or the hysterical and vindictive attitude adopted by so many authority figures towards the problem of drugs.

Growing prosperity and leisure have meanwhile increased the importance and desirability of individual freedom for the mass of the population. The paradox is that just when personal liberty is beginning to govern the life-style of a generation, the economic system which makes it possible has become intensely antipathetic to a great many of that generation's most articulate members. The old opposition to competitive capitalism from the puritan Left that instinctively felt (even when it denied this) that the Fabian state *did* know better, has been succeeded – just when it seemed about to fade away

– by fresh opposition from the 'New Left',* which is rightly suspicious of all authority, has no lingering affection for Joseph Stalin (and is Marxist only because that seems a far-out thing to be), but which identifies 'capitalism' with 'the system' and, in its headier movements, has brought back semi-serious talks of 'the revolution'. (To take 'the revolution' seriously is acceptable at many expense account lunches. It is equally 'trendy' to discuss it semi-facetiously; the one thing that is out-and-out 'square' is to be seriously opposed to it.)

Reasons for Suspicion

Among the middle classes and the establishment generally, adherence to competitive capitalism is, even where it exists, largely a matter of lip-service. Most middle class voters, who are not business leaders hardly ever mention competitive capitalism, or any of its synonyms, except as dirty words. 'Less government' is a popular cry, not to promote freedom of any sort, but because those who utter it believe that it would lead to a transfer of income from other classes to themselves. The favourite subjects of older middle class conversation are in a different area altogether – capital punishment, abortion

* Like most such expressions, 'New Left' is used by different people in different ways. The term is sometimes used for those radicals who glorify violence, support movements such as Black Power and identify with the 'Third World' as the main hope of revolution now that the Western proletariat has failed them. The prophets or 'modern masters' of such goals are analysed in a highly critical survey entitled *The New Left* edited by Maurice Cranston (Bodley Head, 1970), which deals with figures such as Che Guevara, the latter-day Sartre, Marcuse, Fanon and Laing.

The term 'New Left' is used in this and subsequent essays in a wider sense for the much larger body of people who are against the 'system' which they believe to be capitalist, but have lost the faith of the Old Left in state socialism, and insist on the individual's right to his own life-style. Their positive ideas for reform are varied and often vague, ranging from a watered-down version of the slogans of the 'modern masters' to the very different ideas of pacifism, universal love, mysticism and 'dropping out from society' and schemes for workers' control, 'participation' and opposition to techno-logical advance. To call this very diverse group of people 'hippies' would give a misleading impression of the life-styles of many of those involved. The term that best describes the highest common factor among their beliefs is probably that of 'The Alternative Society', but this is too cumber-some as a shorthand descriptive term; and in both this and in subsequent essays the term New Left is used instead – but always in the very wide sense explained.

or sympathy with Southern Rhodesia. These are the land-mines that aspirant Conservative candidates, or those who manage the annual conference of the Party, have to avoid.

If one looks at the attitudes of leading figures of industry, commerce and finance, their support for capitalism is rarely part of any wider libertarian outlook. Such people are not notable for their championship of libertarian causes outside the economic field. Prominent businessmen have the views that one would very much expect on 'permissiveness', the indiscipline of modern youth, drugs, the prosecution of obscene publications, and so on.

Even in their own professional sphere, the devotion of many in the business community to the competitive aspects of capitalism is usually conspicuous by its absence. While they may proclaim the virtues of competition in the abstract, their own industry is very often a special case qualifying for protective restriction, subsidy or regulation; and the organised leaders of business are often in the forefront of the drive for Government intervention, provided that their own financial interests do not appear to suffer (and sometimes even when they do, so great is the failure of nerve).

To come down to a slightly more technical level: the minority among the intellectual classes who bother to read the standard defences of capitalism by writers such as Friedman or Hayek, soon find that the contemporary business leader not merely has seldom heard of the key points emphasised by them such as the rule of impersonal law, consumer sovereignty and the separation of politics from business. On the contrary, his ideal is often that of negotiated deals with government officials on a 'power game basis' for projects for which the consumer would not be willing to pay and which have negative 'spillover' effects. No wonder that capitalism on closer investigation seems no more attractive to our hypothetical inquisitive radical than he had earlier imagined and that thus his New Left views are only further confirmed.

None of this is any cause for surprise and was long ago described by Adam Smith. The typical businessman is, after all, more often an administrator or manager than an entrepreneur. The virtues of capitalism have little to do with the intentions of capitalists; and if there is far more competition in the longer run than the more *simpliste* critics suppose, it is because of the difficulty of keeping out new entrants, products and ideas, rather than because of any lack of desire to do so.

The logic of the system makes the capitalist a two-faced animal. When he faces outward in his business life he is, whether he likes it or not, in a permissive society. However much he spends on advertising, he must in the end persuade people to take his wares; and however much he dislikes the process, he must either influence or serve the public taste; he cannot use the weapon of coercion or the sanctity of tradition. Indeed, much of the business history of the post-war period consists of the replacement of the long-established Anglo-Saxon upper middle class managerial dynasties by immigrants or newcomers of 'non-U' stock, who had no fastidious scruples about catering for the requirements of a more affluent working class.

Yet, although he operates within a libertarian framework in his outside dealings, and he must also have some regard to the preferences of his work force in conditions of high employment, within his organisation the capitalist manager operates by authority and not via commercial forces. Within the wider community the business executive is on the side of authority, he identifies with the governors rather than the governed and expects their support in his difficulties, and he seems to have more in common with unambiguous authority figures such as judges, senior civil servants, generals, or headmasters than with the representatives of permissive culture, whether pop stars or 'trendy left' journalists. Yet, in his own business life, especially if he is a successful innovator, he is engaged in undermining accepted ways and destroying established values and practices.

He is sandwiched between two worlds. He cannot identify himself with radical protest or with anti-authoritarian sentiment of any kind, for he realises that these forces, if unleashed, would sweep away his own position. There was an important exception to this in the heady triumphant phase of the Anti-Corn Law agitation of the 1830s and 40s, when the capitalists had sufficient confidence to rally the masses in a crusade against the established order. But this phase did not last very long; and once their immediate free trading objective had been achieved, the business classes gave Cobden little further support in his dream of world peace through enlightened self-interest. Within ten years of the repeal of the Corn Laws he and Bright lost their seats as a result of their opposition to the Crimean War. The capitalist did not apply the utilitarian calculus he used in his own business decisions to issues of war and peace in which he remained as jingoistic as any other Victorian.

Yet if he cannot thrive as a radical, or 'dove', or apostle of the permissive society, the capitalist – whether entrepreneur or business manager – is unimpressive as a leader in the authoritarian, paternalistic mode. As Schumpeter observed, a bourgeois ruling class completely lacks the glamour of an aristocracy. With neither the trappings of tradition, nor the heroic qualities of the great war leaders or generals, middle class business leaders cannot excite the identification or hero worship which reconcile other people to their wealth and position.

Indeed, the more that other members of the governing classes, such as politicians, civil servants or college heads, model themselves on the successful business manager, the less deference they are likely to attract and the more their authority is likely to be resented. Moreover, the more 'merito-cratic' the process of selection, the less the governing classes are differentiated by special accents or special clothes, and the more 'they are just like us' (only luckier, or cleverer or more given to 'swotting'), the more 'they' will be resented. Even the pretence at aristocratic superiority and genteel dowdiness of the governing politicians of the Macmillan-Butler era were more appealing than the habits of their meritocratic successors. The hostility of the latter's opponents is not one whit less, while this is in no way compensated for by a sneaking or deferential respect among the population at large. At most they are tolerated on the strict condition that they bring results.

The Rise of the Word Man

Another characteristic of capitalism is that it tends to nourish in its own midst an anti-capitalistic culture. This was explained many years ago by Joseph Schumpeter in *Capitalism, Socialism and Democracy*, a work largely written before and at the beginning of the Second World War, and which is more up-to-date than most works currently off the press.[1] His basic thesis was that capitalism was killing itself by its own achievements.

Capitalist civilisation is above all rationalist. It is anti-heroic and anti-mystical. The spirit that animates it is the very opposite of 'Theirs not to reason why, theirs but to do or die'. The successful capitalist is forced by circumstances to query the way everything is done and endeavour to try and find a better way. If he relies on a traditional, mystical or ceremonial justification of existing practices, he will be over-taken by someone else and may well sink into oblivion. The breakdown of theological authority, the rise of the scientific spirit and the growth of capitalism were interrelated phenomena. A new ethic arose in the 17th century and had grown to fruition by the 19th, which blessed empirical and logical enquiry, denigrated the claims of authority and legitimised the profit motive (*inter alia* by removing the mediaeval restraints on usury and the notion of the 'just price').

So long as the capitalist and the scientific segments were contained within an essentially aristocratic order, which preserved many traditions, superstitions and entrenched customs and, above all, deferential attitude towards a traditional ruling class – as was the case throughout most of the 19th century – capitalism could flourish. But in time the sceptical enquiring attitude was bound to turn on established institutions, and not only on kings or the restricted franchise, but on capitalism itself.

Unfortunately – and here Schumpeter makes no attempt to flatter his probable readers – a refusal to take on trust the customs and institutions of society (which is the negative part of the rational critique) does not itself bring a willingness to accept or understand rational arguments. It requires an intellectual and imaginative effort to understand the allocative function of the price mechanism, to see how a high (relative) price will set in motion forces that will remedy a shortage, how the shift of workers from bankrupt to expanding enterprises can increase prosperity, and eventually benefit even the workers who are transferred. Above all, it takes considerable insight or powers of analysis – and a rare freedom from envy – to see the harmful implications of paying people according to presumed merit rather than market values, or to see the advantages as well as disadvantages of the private ownership of capital and the dangers of simply trying to suppress it. The hostile reaction to some of the features of capitalism just mentioned would be shared not only by collectivists, but by many conventional Tory voters of the middle class, who would simply exhort capitalists not to behave too selfishly, cite instances of bad trade union behaviour and fall back on anti-nationalisation prejudices – in other words, respond with anything but a reasoned defence of capitalism.

Not only does a capitalist civilisation engender a skin-deep rationalism, but growing wealth and the accompanying educational expansion encourage a great expansion in the demand for the spoken and written word and in the supply of those able to produce it. This argument has been elaborated further by F. A. Hayek,[2] who points out that those who gain the public ear consist of two elements: the communicators, who are expert at putting other people's ideas or information across, but are amateurs in the substance; and professional people theorising outside their own field – doctors reforming the political system, engineers putting the economy to right and so on. In both cases they will go for the more plausible rather than the more profound ideas; and failing to understand the logic (or for that matter the real weaknesses) of the capitalist system, they are easily tempted to utter the cheap gibe or go for the state-imposed solution to every problem.

A great deal of press and especially television comment is based on a vague mixture, sometimes watered down, of the Old and New Left. A survey by Jeremy Tunstall shows that 54–59 per cent of specialist journalists writing for Conservative quality and popular publications describe themselves as 'to the left' of their organisations – and 'Conservative' papers are defined to include *The Times* and *Sunday Times*. Only 4–11 per cent describe themselves as 'to the right'. For those working for Labour papers the deviations are much more even, while for the media as a whole, including broadcasting and agencies, there are 44 per cent of left-wing deviationists compared with 12 per cent of right wing ones.[3] For the vast majority of those involved, 'to the left' means *unfortunately,* 'more opposed to the market economy'.

The detailed analysis of specialist categories is even more interesting. There is a strong Conservative bias among fashion and motoring correspondents – just the areas where the attitude to commercial products usually associated with Labour sympathies would be most helpful. On the other hand, a strong Labour bias was evident among trade union correspondents. In view of the harmful effects of union monopolies on employment, personal freedom and prosperity, this is just the area where a left bias is least required.

The Dilemma of the Economic Liberal

The economic liberal, who is prepared to justify certain aspects of capitalism, has to face many drawbacks. Unless he is an apologist for business interests, or a party politician, he is bound to be highly critical of the particular forms of capitalism which prevail and of the policies of Conservative and Republican Governments. To them he will appear as a far-out radical or, at best, an impractical theorist. Yet, among students and communication media which act as the middlemen for ideas, he will appear as a timid apologist for the 'system'.

A further difficulty is that the type of intellectual professionally qualified to explain the case for capitalism is the economist. Businessmen can usually be relied upon to defend the indefensible aspects of their activities while giving in to their collectivist opponents on all essentials. Nor is this a criticism; businessmen are paid to operate the system rather than to understand or expound it, and nothing is more pathetic than to see politicians of either party coming cap in hand to industrialists or bankers for advice that the latter are not qualified to give.

Unfortunately, partly as a result of growing specialisation and technicality within the subject, there has been, as Stigler has pointed out,[4] a retrogression in the ability of economists to communicate with other intellectuals. The difficulty is not just that economists are bad popularisers or that their message is unwelcome. It goes much deeper. The real trouble is that economists are no longer sure what it is that they wish to communicate to a wider public. Individual economists feel passionately on particular subjects in opposition to other economists. But they are far less sure of what it is that they can put forward which would both reflect a professional consensus and also convey a relatively simple message to the educated layman.

The New Left Attack

So much for the climate of opinion in which capitalism now operates. What, however, are the main objections to competition and the profit motive actually put forward by the new generation of radicals? The New Left critics differ from both their Marxist and their Fabian forerunners in being equally distrustful of market forces and of central planning or bureaucracy in any form. This revival of the more utopian and anarchic strain is a welcome change from the paternalism and emphasis on state power which have for so long characterised socialist movements. Indeed, it ought to make a dialogue between the New Left and the market economists possible in a way it was not possible with either the Webbs or the Stalinist Communists. (Professor Lindbeck cites the case of a pseudonymous writer of the Chicago free market school who, by using a flamboyant style sprinkled with four letter words, at first reading gives the impression of being somewhere on the anarchist wing of the New Left.)

Unfortunately, the fatal flaw in the economic outlook of the New Left is the belief that one does not have to choose between a market and a command economy or between varying mixtures of the two; and that there is a third ethically preferable system which would rely on more spontaneous and less unselfish motives. A large part of Assar Lindbeck's *The Political Economy of the New Left*[5] is taken up with a sympathetic but relentless analysis of this fallacy; and I find it strange that Paul Samuelson should give the impression in his

polemical foreword that the book will make an impartial or
hostile observer take New Left economics more seriously. The
opposite effect seems to me far more likely.

Lindbeck conveniently summarises the standard problems
of any society which have caused generations of economists
to doubt that one can have an economy dispensing with both
markets and bureaucratic commands. These are the needs:

(1) to obtain information about people's preferences;
(2) to allocate men, machines, land, building and other
resources in accordance with these preferences;
(3) to decide which production techniques to use;
(4) to create incentives to avoid unnecessarily costly
methods, to invest, to develop new technologies and
products; and
(5) (and perhaps most important) to co-ordinate the
desires of millions of individuals, firms and households.

This list is provided not by Friedman or Hayek, but by a
Swedish Social Democrat whose book is offered to us by
Samuelson as an antidote to the former writers. I would only
add that four at least of these requirements do not depend
on selfishness but on the need for co-ordinating and signalling
devices which would still exist even if we could rely more on
people's goodwill. Remarks such as Adam Smith's about
addressing ourselves not to the 'humanity' but to the 'self-
love' of others and Alfred Marshall's about men's motives 'in
the ordinary business of life' give a misleading impression.
Even if people were actuated by benevolence, they would
still need to know what jobs to do and what methods to use
to satisfy other people's desires most efficiently, and a co-
ordinating mechanism would be required. At most we could
dispense with the fourth item on the list – incentives. Even
then the profits or opportunities for high earnings would still
be indispensable as *signals,* although any excess wealth
gained by following them might eventually be given away to
charitable organisations.

Galbraith's influence on the New Left has, as Lindbeck
has pointed out, strengthened its temptation to ignore the
inconvenient problem of co-ordination. Galbraith fails to

explain how the few large firms on which he concentrates – let alone millions of householders and individuals – co-ordinate their activities. He concentrates on planning within firms, and many readers overlook the fact that he has said nothing about relations between firms, except by quasi-mystical references to the 'technostructure'.[6]

Lindbeck also lays to rest the illusion that computers could take over from markets the functions just listed. This belief is more characteristic of the old technocratic Left than of the New Left; but the latter might be inclined to clutch at it as a straw. Complicated messages about preferences, product qualities and information on production processes cannot be coded onto a computer. This is more than a practical impossibility. Even if consumers could immediately translate into computer language their preferences between an indefinitely large set of alternatives made possible by technology, they do not themselves know how they would react to new kinds of goods or changes in quality or innovation in general, for the simple reason that people do not always know how they themselves will react in hypothetical circumstances. Even when it comes to communicating details of production processes it is difficult to envisage how the specifics of 'knowing how' could be put into a computer. Moreover, all this effort, even if successful, would simply reproduce the data already presented by prices, profits and sales figures.

A dominant feature of New Left thinking, again powerfully stimulated by Galbraith, is a denial that the market does allow people to 'do their own thing'. Consumer wants, it is alleged, are artificially fabricated by advertising and other sales techniques. The art of salesmanship has never been regarded as quite respectable. It has, of course, always been disliked by conservative traditionalists and strictures here are no monopoly of the New Left. E. J. Mishan has argued strongly against advertising from the premises of conventional economic theory; and Charles Carter, the Secretary General of the Royal Economic Society and notable university administrator, has outlined a complex scheme excluding from tax-deductable expenses most marketing expenditure, including sales staff and packaging, as well as promotion and advertising, and imposing a prohibitive tax on such expenditure when it exceeds a certain proportion of turnover.[7]

Such writers do not, however, go to the lengths of the New Left and some of its prophets in asserting that firms can create a demand for whatever goods they choose to produce. As Lindbeck has pointed out, the latter is a new form of 'Say's Law' – so much attacked by Keynes for giving too *favourable* an impression of the capitalist system – which asserted that supply created its own demand and which thereby denied the possibility of a depression. The new form of the law seems to assert that this is true, not merely for the economy as a whole, but for each individual firm or product.

The belief is quite false. Simply because firms do not limit themselves to supplying demands felt by the human race when it left the Garden of Eden, but actively build up a market for their products, this does not mean that they can impose whatever they like on a defenceless public. The British motor industry has not been able to prevent consumers from buying more imported cars; Cunard has been unable to prevent a fall in demand for passenger shipping lines; the Coal Board has been unable to prevent a switch to other fuels; and there are countless other examples.[8] Marketing studies suggest that among products regarded as 'technical successes' only perhaps 10–20 per cent survive market and pre-launching studies, while of those that are launched one-third to one-half are withdrawn as failures within one year.[9]

There are two extreme and equally absurd prevalent models of the role of the consumer. There is, on the one hand, the view that people have innate tastes which firms exist to satisfy. Hardly any reputable economist, however orthodox, has ever explicitly held this view; but there are incautious statements, particularly in American textbooks, which give credence to this allegation of Galbraith's.[10] At the other extreme is the view, to which Galbraith himself comes perilously close, that sees consumers as plastic clay on which the advertisers can impose any shape they like. In fact, salesmanship is part of the process of increasing the range of alternatives of which people are aware. Like many other technological and cultural techniques, it develops desires of which people were not aware before and – the point must be conceded – causes some people to be more dissatisfied with their lot than they otherwise would be. This is part of the price of freedom of communication. Nearly all the products of civilisation – arts, sports and recreations, just as much as running water, telephones or labour-saving gadgets – have been invented and sold to people who were not spontaneously asking for any of them, but were glad to have them when they arrived. It is part of the function of a market economy to suggest new possibilities to people which they are then free to accept or reject. It may be that commercial advertising increases demand for consumer goods relative to 'public goods', leisure or a pleasant environment. But politicians, writers and journalists can and do propagandise in the opposite direction; the activities of the New Left are themselves part of the free market in ideas, and by no means the least successful part of it.

None of this means that the situation in regard to advertising or consumer information is incapable of reform. If advertisers really discovered and used forms of subliminal advertising, which exercised a literally hypnotic effect which people were powerless to resist, the case for legal prohibition of these forms would be strong. On the positive side, much more could be done to encourage the provision of information and views on products from points of view other than the producer's. The case for state encouragement and financial support of consumer bodies is discussed on pp. 247–9. It is still too difficult to organise or finance anything analogous to the political 'Opposition' in the commercial sphere.

Another objection to markets, which does not fit very easily with a belief in a 'permissive' morality, but which is sometimes heard from the same camp, is that the exercise of choice itself involves costs and inconvenience which some people do not wish to bear. In many aspects of life an attempt to survey the total range of options would be impracticable, because the consumer lacks the knowledge to make it, or irrational, because the benefits are too trivial in relation to the time and effort expended; and there may be advantages in voluntarily delegating the choice to others. Investment and unit trusts spare the investor the bother of selecting his own securities; organisations such as the *A.A.* and *The Good Food Guide* select hotels and restaurants and group them into convenient grades. Travel agents offer both package and individual tours for people who cannot be bothered to make their own arrangements. There are excellent 'flower clubs' which, for a fixed annual subscription, arrange a weekly delivery of the flowers that happen to give the best value for money at the time of year. This gives access to both expertise and to economies of bulk purchasing which most individuals could not hope to have acting on their own. Every encouragement should be given to such methods of delegating choice; and we can all exercise our own preferences about which purchases to delegate, and to whom.

It is true that we still have to choose between investment trusts, or between advisers on investment trusts, between hotel guides and so on. A resurrected and expanded Consumer Council or similar body could publish lists of organisations fulfilling minimum standards. The appropriateness of the standards and their application to particular instances will always be open to argument and there will be nothing sacrosanct about the lists; but they would, at least, provide reassurance to those instinctively afraid of being cheated by commercial enterprises. In the social service area, no one need be forced to 'shop around' for private education and health services, however much such private provision is encouraged, so long as state services of the present standard or higher continue to exist side by side.

Poverty and Equality

Another common objection to competitive capitalism reflects a renewed outburst of egalitarian sentiment. It is certainly possible to go a long way towards 'levelling up' the conditions of the poorest section of the population under capitalism. A legitimate charge against modern industrial society, which applies to both the 'capitalist' and the Communist countries, is the amount of poverty that continues despite average levels of real income per head which are very high by all past standards. Poverty usually means an income below that required to maintain an adequate standard of living for the family or individual concerned. Although the notion of an adequate standard rises with average income levels, it is not meaningless to speak of a whole society being poor – for example, when the *average* standard of living, however defined, is insufficient to prevent starvation or gross malnutrition. But as society becomes richer, it becomes more and more reasonable to regard the poor as those with less than some given minimum proportion of average post-tax real income (adjusted for family size and other complications). The size of this minimum is necessarily arbitrary. But it is perfectly possible to set up as a goal that no household of average size should have an income of less than, say, a third of the national average. The best available estimate for 1972 is that there are 17 million households with, on average, disposable incomes approaching £2,600. The proposed minimum would then be nearly £900 – more for families with several children, less for smaller households. (For comparison, the supplementary benefit rates amounted to nearly £660 for a married couple plus about £100–£150 per child according to age.) This figure will rise in future years both with real income and inflation. By guaranteeing an income of this kind, there is a limited sense in which the poor need not always be with us. Poverty is partly an absolute and partly a relative phenomenon. A family, which earns a given and small proportion of the national average, is not poor in the same sense when this involves having only one car and having to share a swimming pool as when it involves infants dying of starvation.

In Chapter 3 a suggestion is made for a guaranteed income, to be provided at first in the form of a negative income tax, but eventually to be distributed as a social dividend to all, whether at work or not. It is presented there as a way in which those who did not wish to participate in a consumption-oriented, work-obsessed society could 'opt out' of it, without imposing an unwanted revolution on the rest of the population. The main object of such a scheme would, however, be to provide guarantees against extreme poverty for everyone. Yet we would be wise not to expect too much from it, especially in the early years. As Professor Harry Johnson has pointed out,[11] there are limits to the degree of earnings transfer, whether in guaranteed incomes or other forms that the bulk of the population will tolerate; and there are many poor people who do not share the anti-consumption ethos and who would be glad of the opportunity to earn more than any feasible income guarantee is likely to provide.

The most promising, although most difficult, way of helping such people is to increase their opportunity to acquire the skills that are demanded in the market place. Lack of knowledge of technical trends and opportunities leads children to follow their parents' occupation into what Professor Johnson has called 'perpetual pockets of poverty'. While the provision of 'free' or subsidised information or training would help, the inclination of those who are hostile to market forces is to conserve the population of existing districts and industries by a variety of make-work devices, which hinder the geographical and occupational mobility which would, in the long run, provide the victims of change with their best opportunities.

Many kinds of discrimination make for poverty. Racial discrimination is a less important factor in Britain than in the U.S.A., but there is plenty of discrimination against the old, by compulsory retiring ages, and against the young, by forcing children to stay on at school for longer and longer periods. It is worth noting that the more profit-seeking and less bureaucratic a firm, and the less hamstrung it is by unions or staff associations, the more incentive it will have to provide work for elderly people who may not be worth a normal wage but who may still be able to render some productive service.

In his discussion of the forces which could improve opportunities for the poor, Professor Johnson rightly gives pride of place to the general level of employment. A high demand for labour exercises a perennial effect to 'upgrade labour skills', and to find suitable opportunities for people of impaired mental or physical capacity. The scarcer that labour is in general, the more incentive there is 'to devise square holes in the economic system to accommodate the square pegs available'.

If anyone still believes that the pressure of demand for labour and the overall unemployment percentage can be fixed by the Treasury at any level it chooses by manipulating some financial levers, then the remedy is clear. But if, as becomes more and more obvious each year, the ability of the authorities to do this is limited by union exercise of monopoly power, the implication is rather different.

Apart from their overall economic effects, trade union monopolies – by raising relative wages in a few supposedly skilled or semi-skilled trades, such as the motor industry or printing – reduce the welfare of other workers. Trade unions on both sides of the Atlantic have also raised unemployment by insisting on above market wage rates and/or minimum wage laws for the less skilled occupations. Those particularly hard hit have been the untrained, or less easily employable, who could have found a niche at wages corresponding to their productivity, but have now been pushed out of the labour market and onto relief, to the applause of the bogus humanitarians.

To many critics, however, egalitarianism involves not only a 'levelling up' in the conditions of the poor, but also an elimination of all major disparities of income so that no one is much above some general average. How far it is either possible or desirable to go in this direction will be discussed in some detail in the next essay. It is certainly possible to modify the distribution of income and wealth without destroying a market economy, if appropriate methods of redistribution are used. But there are limits to the process. Despite the achievements of capitalism in breaking down class barriers, any viable capitalist system does involve the existence of individuals many times wealthier than average. The same applies to non-capitalist economies where market forces are allowed a role. This can be seen, for example, in the tendency in some Eastern European countries to pay bonuses out of profits to managers of state undertakings, which has obvious analogies to capitalist practices.

If all material differentials are intolerable, then the only alternative is centralised direction of labour. This is a lesson of Western economic theory and Communist economic practice which will not be refuted by any number of 'demos' or vituperative outbursts. There comes a point at which radicals of all hues have to choose between their commitment to freedom of choice of occupation and life-style, and extreme egalitarianism. With those to whom equality of material award is the single absolute value to which everything else must be subordinated, no further argument is possible. But I doubt very much if this is the ultimate position of most of today's young radicals. If they could understand that the single-minded pursuit of equality would lead to the sacrifice of other valued goals most of them would probably modify their attitude. Too much New Left writing seems to assume that it is *necessarily the case* that the wealth of some individuals is the *cause* of the poverty of others. As Lindbeck has put it, economic activity is seen as a zero-sum game, where what is gained by one person is lost by another. This ties in all too well with the distaste for patient analysis which is one of the less attractive features of 'the movement'.

The New Left has a much better case when it attacks the concentration of power in the hands of what President Eisenhower called the 'military-industrial complex', or the scandalous ability of interest and pressure groups of all kinds to obtain special favours, ranging from import controls to tax exemptions, tariffs and subsidies. Although these influences may be specially noticeable in the U.S.A., they are not exactly absent in Britain. Tempting though it may be to quote the stock example of the special tax depletion allowances, production controls and import quotas for American oil producers, I am not persuaded that the tax privileges for British home owners – which redistribute income from the poor to the better off – are on an altogether higher plane of virtue.

What the radical critics so frequently fail to realise is that many of these abuses are the result of the absence of competitive market pressures, not their presence; and this is, in turn, due in most cases to extensive paternalistic intervention of the kind for so long preached by a dominant section of the Old Left. It is too easy to persuade politicians and officials whose own money is not at stake that journeys to the moon, ever more advanced aircraft, or home-based computer industries, should be subsidised from the public purse. Governments find it notoriously difficult to separate genuine defence needs from the inevitable desire of the military-industrial complex for elaborate, ever more expensive forms of hardware. It is not an accident that the danger of the 'New Industrial State' is greatest in just the area where government involvement with business is at its closest and most specific. Professor Galbraith is so intent on ridiculing market-oriented economists (for the benefit of a mass readership that will accept on trust his account of their views) that he accepts a quite unnecessarily fatalistic attitude to the trends about which he is supposed to be worrying, and dismisses all remedies that do not involve even more frequent and personalised involvement between government and business.[12]

The remedy for these evils lies in the direction of more competition, more reliance on markets and more reliance on the price mechanism, adjusted to take into account 'social' costs and benefits at present unpriced. It does not lie in the 'suppression' of capitalism and greater concentration of power at the centre. To cite Lindbeck yet again: would Concorde be less likely to have been built if the British and French Governments not only co-operated with the aircraft producers but also entirely owned them (as they partially do already)? The valid elements in the New Left objection to the cult of technology and growth of measurable G.N.P. arise from the intervention of governments to impose on the community more hardware of every sort, whether computers, satellite systems or common-or-garden machinery benefiting from 'investment incentives', than would be provided if firms interested in these areas had to compete unaided for the customer's purse.

'Alienation'

One early Marxist concept now back in fashion as a basis for anti-capitalist sentiment is that of 'alienation'. I wish I could think of a less ungainly name for the relation between many workers and their employment but it does refer to a real and undesirable phenomenon. It can be used, not just rhetorically, but to refer to a sense of powerlessness which many people feel within large organisations, a feeling of meaninglessness about the operations performed and of a lack of any intrinsic satisfaction outside the wage packet. The archetypal example is that of the car assembly-line worker who performs identical repeat operations of a nature and at a pace over which he has no control.

Again, however, although the complaint is correct, the diagnosis and remedy offered are frequently wrong. As Edwin G. Dolan has remarked in a penetrating analysis of the concept, published interestingly enough in the Chicago-based *Journal of Political Economy*,[13] alienation arises not so much from the system of property relations – whether capitalism or Soviet-style Communism – as from a particular stage of industrial and technological development involving the combination of an extreme division of labour with the wage system in large impersonal institutions. The individual can, of course, in present-day capitalism choose to avoid jobs with such characteristics, at the expense perhaps of less take-home pay; and the greater the place of competitive forces in the system the greater this choice is likely to be.

Nevertheless, the habit of deference to authority – alternating perhaps with bloody-minded rebellion against it – that grows up when the majority of the population have jobs characterised by the alienation syndrome, affects the whole character of society. The key variables are probably the proportion of the population in paid employment and the nature of the jobs they perform. After sadly quoting figures showing the decline in the proportion of the self-employed, one perceptive author speaks of the dangers that arise 'if society is progressively turned into one great hierarchy of employment'. As many exercises of freedom are of little direct interest to the employed, 'they cannot see the need for them, and they attach little importance to opportunities for action which hardly ever occur in their lives'. If the reader is wondering which neo-Marxist I am quoting, it is F. A. Hayek in *The Constitution of Liberty*.[14]

Characteristically, but correctly, Hayek believes that these dangers are aggravated by tax and other legislation which discourage the independent businessmen or professionals in the supposed interests of the employed. He emphasises the need to preserve a body of men of independent means and to avoid replacing the present number and variety of employers by public corporations all dependent on the state.

There is, however, more to be said. Just as the extreme division of labour and movement away from self-employment is an expression of one phase of technological development, future technological advance may make possible a movement in the reverse direction. It is already a commonplace that the development of both factory and office automation should reduce drastically the number of routine jobs and increase the demand for jobs involving the discretionary use of varied skills.

Another less obvious aspect of the growth of potential output that advancing technology makes possible is that it will become sensible to work in ways that are, in the technical (although not economic) sense, inefficient. The deservedly famous passage in Marx's *German Ideology* where he speaks of a society in which it is possible for anyone to 'hunt in the morning, fish in the afternoon, rear cattle in the evening, criticise after dinner' was, as he knew, not possible in his own day. But it should be possible to take out some of the fruits of the much higher level of productivity we may expect in the future in the form of a deliberately 'wasteful' and pleasanter pattern of work and/or in shorter hours, rather than in more and more material goods.

There is already an incipient tendency for a rise in the ratio of self-employed. A number of jobs, especially in the building and catering trades are shifting from an employee to a quasi-entrepreneurial basis – a development that is held back by various kinds of government intervention and by the hostility of organised unions. During the period in which the majority are bound to remain paid employees in the strict sense, there are two ways in which their influence over their working environment can be increased. One is 'workers' control' or 'industrial democracy'. The other is freedom of choice of occupation, or voting with one's feet.

The two approaches are not incompatible. By all means let us experiment with every sort of choice for giving people more say in the organisations in which they work – although my own feeling is that what people most want is, in the first place, to be informed in advance so that decisions are not sprung upon them and secondly, to be consulted so that they can express their views before it is too late, rather than to attempt themselves the tasks of management.

Another point, not generally realised, is that to the extent that workers really want to have a say in management, those firms who are responsive will find it easier to attract workers. Thus, if there is a real demand for greater workers' participation (although not for expropriating the owners), this too can be brought about by the market.

If the above remarks seem a little removed from reality, the main reason lies in the part played by the restrictionist activities of the trade unions themselves. Catering for minority tastes in, say, hours of work, or in preference for a more relaxed tempo of work, is a costly business. It can be costly because of the kind of preferences involved, or simply because they are minority tastes and an employer who caters for them will have to do more searching around for staff. These are real costs, which would exist in a non-capitalist society; and an employee who wishes to be treated in this way must expect smaller take-home pay. Unfortunately the insistence of union activists on levelling up all wage differentials between workers of comparable skills would soon discourage any employer who tried to cater for such minority tastes or attitudes. It will also not have escaped attention that the possibilities of shopping around depend on the state of the labour market. They were not worth much in the interwar period and they were of only limited use in the early 1970s in high unemployment areas like Scotland. Here again trade union monopoly activity has, as already noted, a key role in reducing the overall demand for labour that can be maintained without provoking an inflationary explosion.

Student Dissent

The remarks made about the advantages of 'voting with one's feet' compared with control from below are particularly relevant to student dissatisfaction. One characteristic of university education is that it is provided at below market-clearing prices. Government grants create an excess of demand over supply for places. Thus, not having to compete for custom, academic institutions are under no market pressures to take into account student preferences. This enables them to run universities to suit their own tastes, whether paternalistic or self-centred.

This inability to vote with his feet – increased by the extreme difficulty of transferring grants from one university to another – makes the student-consumer dependent on a monopoly supplier, a situation guaranteed to create tension and animosity. Although any specific student protest may be misplaced, it is a safe prediction that there will always be some justified grievances arising from the built-in incentives that exist for university administrators and senior staff to suit their own convenience and taste rather than that of students. This explains many of the arrangements for faculty tenure, the priority given to research and publication over teaching, common pay scales linked to seniority rather than ability, minimal student-staff contacts and privileged access of senior staff to the more convenient parking spaces, lifts, common rooms, lavatories and so on. Hence, too, the attempts to enforce arbitrary rules of personal conduct or compulsory residence requirements.

These examples and quotations are taken not from any protest manual but from a paper by Professor Alan Peacock and Anthony Culyer, published by the pro-capitalist Institute of Economic Affairs.[15] It is when they come to remedies that the authors differ from the New Left. The conventional remedy of the latter, 'student participation', is likely to erode the gains from the specialisation of labour among students, teachers and administrators and thus lead to 'dissipation of effort' which 'might be better spent on the main objective: learning and research.' There is also the long term probability that 'student power' will be 'effectively nullified by the complexity of the administrative machine and the expertise of the professionals in its use.' The authors might have also added the danger of disproportionate influence by the professional organiser or 'barrack room lawyer' type of student over colleagues who prefer to spend their time in other ways.

The market alternative proposed by Peacock and Culyer is that 'universities should receive their main financial support through the medium of student choice of university and not directly from the state'. This would involve payments to students to cover fees and living expenses, and ease of transfer of such payments from one institution to another free of the quirks of local education authorities.

The chances of such a use of taxpayers' or ratepayers' money to increase effective student power under the present grant system are almost nil. The only way that students could acquire larger sums to spend at their discretion would be if part or the whole of these sums were in the form of student loans, with repayment obligations related to future earnings. Such a switch from grants to more generous loans would achieve two objects which student radicals claim to have at heart: an increased say in conditions affecting their own life and work, and an egalitarian influence over the general distribution of incomes. For, looking at lifetime, rather than immediate earnings, non-repayable grants from taxpayers to students are a transfer from a lower to an upper income group. It is a sign of the poverty of much progressive thought that the loan idea should be regarded as a reactionary proposal to be opposed at all costs.

The present system provides the worst of all worlds. On the one hand, the grant system is a net transfer to those who can expect to earn more than the average income over their working lives. On the other hand, *during their period at university* students (most of whom do not have the degree of parental support that they did in earlier generations) belong for the time being to the poorest section of their age group. This fact goes a long way to explain a new element in student radicalism.

Students have often tended to be severe critics of the existing order. The novel feature of recent years has been the identification of considerable numbers with the proletarian side in a class war which they have tried to whip up to the best of their ability. This comes out in pathetic attempts to show solidarity with every strike and in participation in militant trade unionism, efforts which often meet a decidedly cynical response from the objects of their affections. Professor Harry Johnson is right to draw a direct link between these attitudes and the large private cost to the student of university education, which he defines as 'the difference between his grant and the earnings he could obtain in commercial employment.' It is not surprising that 'cheeseparing in grants leads the student to identify emotionally with the poorer classes of the community – a great help to sincere protesting'.[16] But the remedy lies not in a losing battle for better grants but in finding new forms of student (and perhaps university) finance.

These problems do not, however, end at university. One result of the great expansion of higher education is that the number of graduates has exceeded the growth in the number of jobs of sufficient status to meet their expectations. The latter is admittedly a highly subjective notion; but many graduates now do jobs for which a degree was formerly neither necessary nor usual. While it remains true that most graduates will belong to the upper quartile of the income distribution, they are no longer the elite group they were in the first post-war decade.

Schumpeter foresaw this problem somewhat prematurely on the basis of the Interwar Depression when he wrote of the graduate failing to find a job worthy of his years of education and spoke of people who were 'literally unemployable' and fodder for the critics of capitalism. It is not, however, necessary to put the point so maliciously. Many of the young people in question have been forced through the examination rat race as the result of an overemphasis on formal education by the more paternalistic forces in society of which they and their employers alike are victims; and the limitations on their initial career prospects are, in part, due to the encouragement given to large corporations and the discouragement of small enterprises and independent professional activity by would-be egalitarian systems of tax.

Contemporary Radicalism

These economic influences, although important, are not the whole story. There are certain ideological and cultural aspects of contemporary radicalism which deserve at least a brief examination. The collectivist movements, about which Schumpeter and Hayek wrote, stretch from Marxism of various sorts to the 1945–50 Labour Government – although the arguments were later extended by Hayek to the conscious pursuit of egalitarian policies in the 'Welfare State' of the 1950s and 1960s. Even Friedman, whose work on the subject is of most recent vintage, directs his fire against schemes for increasing the authority and the role of the U.S. Federal State.

The latest outbreak of radical fervour, after a period in which ideological conflict was supposed to have died down, is, in many respects, different. The emphasis is on personal freedom and not on the state. The apostles of the 'Alternative Society' do not see salvation through the boards of state corporations; and they do not believe that a mixture of Old Etonians, professional managers, governments, generals and retired trade unionists become agents of radical change by means of the magic word nationalisation. Nor do they set much store by state economic plans; and they are repelled rather than attracted by many aspects of the technocratic dream of transforming society by means of science. All this is a change for the better.

Associated with this is a great stress on personal sensual gratification and on giving free reign to instincts, emotions and feelings. The older socialist movements had their roots in the puritan tradition and were nourished by a moral or aesthetic disapproval of the conspicuous consumption of the rich; and many people who were attracted by socialist theories felt, like Mr Harold Macmillan, that the right wing was much more fun. Today the position is reversed. The leaders in consumption, the film makers, and the leaders of fashion tend to be on the left; and although they may be economically better off under a Tory Government, there is little love lost on either side.

Of course reality is far more complex. The puritan tradition lingers on amidst the new hedonism – this is the kindest explanation of the otherwise hypocritical campaign against the Macmillan Government at the time of Profumo, in which so many people, from Bow Group sympathisers to *Private Eye*, worked themselves up into such a state of delighted indignation. The early 20th century British Labour Movement comprised the beery heartiness of the trade unionist as well as Mrs Webb's sense of sinful indulgence in the occasional cup of tea or coffee after a meal. The establishment, whether Whig or Tory, always contained a respectable aldermanic element as well as the more hedonistic 'society' figures. Moreover, the technocratic passion for quantification and 'hard facts' is, if anything, still a growing force in the professions and among the generation of academics now coming to the fore – and it is still a religion among politicians of the generation of Wilson and Heath and even those slightly younger, although it reflects a set of values that is now passing. Such cultural lags are among the platitudes of history. But nothing at all can be said on social trends if one is not prepared to simplify or generalise; and the contemporary New Left – and even more the less overtly political 'youth culture' – is both hedonistic and suspicious of authority.

The removal of inhibitions and barriers, so evident in the more casual and comfortable style of contemporary clothes, is highly desirable. It is the end road of the libertarian and utilitarian ideals professed by the bewigged philosophers of the 18th century and the Victorian political thinkers in their frock coats. The artificiality and conventionalism of the 18th century and the repressive respectability of the 19th century did produce the tensions and anxieties discussed, for example, by Freud in *Civilisation and Its Discontents* (although Freud carefully refrained from prescription).

Unfortunately, although perhaps inevitably, the emphasis on instinctual gratification has been associated with a revolt against rational thinking – whether of the empirical or the logical type – in favour of 'thinking with the belly'. Bertrand Russell rightly remarked that 'reason is and should be the servant of the emotions'; and it was necessary to dethrone reason from the exaggerated point of esteem in which it was then held. The trouble is that reason has been dismissed even as a servant and many apostles of the 'Alternative Society' are impatient of it in any role. This leads to a total sweeping aside of any but the most superficial and short-term approaches to, say, bad housing conditions or poverty; and it is not a climate in which belief in a market economy – or any other rational approach to policy – is likely to flourish.

Anyone who believes these observations exaggerated should turn to that extremely useful publication, Nicholas Saunders' *Alternative London*.[17] Its second longest chapter is entitled 'Mystical' (coming behind 'Crafts' but in front of 'Drugs' in terms of length). This opens with a lament that the Christian churches have lost the essence of religion, which is 'to let the pure light inside flow out freely rather than ooze out discoloured'. Another analogy is to see oneself 'as God suppressed by being encased by layers of shit'. We read of Meher Baba who promised in 1935 to give his disciples the secret of the world after 35 years. He died after 34, 'yet his following is growing still'.

The present reaction against the artificialities of civilisation in favour of the instinctive, the physical, the sensual and the mystical, has been foreshadowed for a very long time. The immediate predecessors of the present romantic sensualists were, in fact, the New Right that grew up, especially in Continental countries, towards the end of the 19th century, and which openly proclaimed 'thinking with the blood'. This New Right may have drawn inspiration from the myth of an uncorrupted past, but it vied with the Marxists in demanding a sweeping overhaul of national life. It was an attempt to escape from the frustrations of urban and industrial life and to move to a more emotional and physical plane of existence, usually accompanied by intense nationalist feelings. It can be traced in writers such as Nietzsche, Kipling, d'Annunzio or D. H. Lawrence. It would be absurd to identify these men with the perversion of the gas chambers, even though the Nazi period is a warning of the direction in which these ideas can lead in unscrupulous or unsophisticated hands.

The perennial argument on the connection between Wagner's music dramas and Nazism illustrates the essential point. It is *because* they appeal to basic emotions, instincts or archetypal patterns, that his works have their strange power and fascination – even for those who think that they are responding to the music only and ignoring the Nordic myths. These very deep-seated human drives are capable of producing both the worst and the best in the species – the sublimest love, the greatest heroism, and also the lowest depths of cruelty and lust for death.

We have, of course, moved away from Lawrence and Wagner. The more extreme beliefs and practices of present-day opponents of the 'system' were perhaps foreshadowed by much that went on in the late Roman Empire. The third century writer Plotinus, far and away the leading philosopher of the age, is described by as level-headed a senior historian as Professor Michael Grant, as 'the pioneer of psychedelic experience for the West'.[18] Nevertheless, Plotinus represented a rational extreme, by the standard of the age, trying to achieve his ends 'by purely cerebral, intellectual discipline – not by schizophrenia and not by drugs and not by religion.'

More characteristic was the mode of life of the early Christian monks as described by Gibbon. Like many modern hippies, who have rejected private property and the consumer society, 'the candidate who aspired to the virtue of evangelical poverty, abjured at his first entrance into a regular community the idea, and even the name, of all separate or exclusive possession.' Gibbon remarks:

> The aspect of a genuine anachoret was horrid and disgusting: every sensation that is offensive to man was thought acceptable to God; and the angelic rule of Tabenne condemned the salutary custom of bathing the limbs in water, and of anointing them with oil. The austere monks slept on the ground, on a hard mat, or a rough blanket; and the same bundles of palm-leaves served them as a seat in the day; and a pillow in the night.... Thirty or forty brethren composed a family of separate discipline and diet; and the great monasteries of Egypt consisted of thirty or forty families.

It could almost be a description of a hippy commune. One cannot resist quoting Gibbon's remark about the more 'savage saints' of both sexes who 'contemptuously cast away all superfluous encumbrance of dress' and 'whose naked bodies were covered only by their long hair' (*Decline and Fall*, Chapter 37). Just as Gibbon's description was unfair as a description of many of the monasteries, which 'transmitted by their indefatigable pens' the 'monuments of Greek and Roman literature' through the Dark Ages, and many of whom suffered a natural descent from 'powerful and dangerous virtue' to 'the common vices of humanity', it would be equally unfair as a description of many of those who affect a hippy-type style. But as far as the extremes of both ideal and practice are concerned, the analogy is convincing. *Alternative London* presents us with a rich variety of communes, many far from the metropolis. One of the more notable contains about 20 people – the men young, the women old. Orders are given daily to one member and imposed by her husband, the founder. Nature spirits help them produce their own food, despite the R.A.F. base next door, and everywhere are cards saying 'Expect a miracle'.

Of course there are differences as well as similarities compared with the phenomena about which Gibbon was writing. Above all, the early Christians were ascetics who took a masochistic delight in mortifying the flesh, while their modern descendants make a cult of sex and promiscuity. We must, however, remember that the early Christians were only one of many rival cults which 'withdrew from the world' in the later Roman Empire. There were others who did emphasise promiscuity in the modern style. Moreover when one passes from a mere lifting of conventions and inhibitions into a cult of promiscuity, irrespective of the great variety of human inclinations and nuances of feeling, we are very near to a new sort of asceticism, or puritanism in reverse.

The external environment in which these practices grow up has uncanny resemblances to that of several Western countries in recent years. There was a very heavy level of military expenditure to guard against the external threat, resulting in hitherto unprecedented levels of government expenditure and taxation; the collection of the necessary funds prompted, according to Professor Grant, a tendency towards a levelling-down egalitarianism; and there were attempts to solve the problems by expanding the monetary circulation with periods of runaway inflation and currency collapse.

The late Roman Emperors were also pioneers in prices and incomes policy and state regulation of trade. Guilds and corporations established closed shops for most trades and crafts. The emperor became the greatest landowner and industrialist and this large public sector was run by an important Ministry in Rome. By the time of Diocletian and Constantine most workers 'were under permanent and inherited obligation to remain at their job'.[19] The saving grace of the system was the inefficiency of its law-enforcement. Nevertheless, the controls, taxes and economic policy of the late Roman Empire eventually paved the way not to meta-phorical, but to literal serfdom in the strict feudal meaning of the term.

A Turn of the Tide?

Yet, although these parallels are ominous, the comparison with the late Roman Empire shows only one of several roads along which we might travel. There are also more hopeful possibilities. The great advance of technology brings with it an immense range of options which were quite unknown to most societies before the 20th century. For all the excesses cited on previous pages, the spirit of most of those who 'opt out' is more critical, less submissive to some mystical fate than that of the Manichaeans, neoplatonists or early Christian monks.

The instinctive revolt against a life grimly devoted to work and promotion is soundly based. There is a healthy mean be-tween the superstitious worship of the Gross National Pro-duct and a belief in the sanctity of poverty. Behind the clichés about the 'quality of life' and 'the environment' is a well-founded suspicion of false goals which we are free not to follow.

The mistake of too many radicals is (a) to underestimate the forces working against the cosy 'New Industrial State' that many business leaders would admittedly love to establish and (b) to overrate the potentialities and gravely under-estimate the risk of political accountability as a check on economic power. But their rejection of all the many arrange-ments and institutions which are neither responsible to the consumer through the market, nor politically accountable, nor subject to known laws, is sound and admirable.

In time they may come to see that the remedy is neither to indulge in nostalgia for a pre-industrial age, nor to talk about 'the revolution', but to promote an effective market in which all costs and benefits are properly priced and which are regulated by deliberately impersonal processes. More simply and crudely, there is a need to restore the entrepreneurial and even buccaneering element in capitalism at the expense of the managerial one. Then, given a proper framework of laws, taxes and subsidies, we shall have no more Concordes or other loss-making home-based technological industries and produce more of the things that people actually want, whether these be leisure, peace and quiet, or a less hectic pattern of living, more consumer goods, or some combination of all of these.

The 'guerrilla capitalist' battling against the monopoly of the Post Office or broadcasting authorities is a small sign of a change in the direction of youthful energy and dissent. There are signs that some of those who 'opt out' are trying their luck at small scale entrepreneurial activities of their own, supplying many services on a personal, flexible basis impossible to the large public and private bureaucracies. Certainly the time is ripe for a realignment in which the more thoughtful members of the New Left and the more radical advocates of competitive free enterprise realise that they have a common interest in opposing the corporate industrial state.

There are built-in forces in modern society providing a ready audience for specious anti-capitalist propaganda which I have repeatedly emphasised in this prologue. But in optimistic moods I am impressed by the limits to human gullibility. There is a chance – how large I cannot predict – that the modern mixed economy will develop in a less materialist direction through the development of the attitudes and of institutions of a free society rather than through coercion from above or below. The revolt of young people against the pattern of their lives being decided by others or by impersonal forces they cannot influence is fundamentally justified. Precisely the same arguments are to be found in the classical defences of free markets, private property and limited governments. Until recently technological limitations were such that freedom could be important only in the lives of a fortunate minority. It is now possible for all who are not afraid of it.

Part One

*Freedom, Prosperity
and the Market*

1 A Restatement of Economic Liberalism

The chief benefit which results from philosophy...
proceeds more from its secret insensible influence,
than from its immediate application.

David Hume, *The Sceptic*

Synopsis

1. Fundamental Judgements

A liberal is someone who attaches special value to personal freedom. He desires to reduce the number of man-made obstacles to the exercise of actual or potential choice.

The concept of 'freedom' involved is what Sir Isaiah Berlin has called 'negative freedom'.[1] A man is said to be free to the extent that no other human being interferes with his activity. Freedom is not the same thing as equality, self-government, prosperity, stability or any other desirable state of affairs.

There is no need to derive all public policy from any one central goal. There is a plurality of goals which most of us, including liberals, seek to satisfy. These goals may sometimes be complementary, but at other times are competitive with each other.* A liberal attaches a specially great importance to freedom compared with other goals, but he need not give it total priority and ignore other goals. Absolute freedom is not even a possible objective, as one man's freedom must be limited to the extent that it interferes with the freedom of another, and there may have to be a choice between different types of freedom. All that a liberal can hope to do, as Hayek explains in *The Constitution of Liberty*,[2] is to minimise the

* There are some who argue that the weight given to particular goals, when there are conflicts between them, is, or should be, derived from some overriding principle such as utility or happiness. But any such overriding principle is likely to be of such a highly generalised and abstract kind that it will have to be broken into a number of sub-goals for even the most theoretical discussion of actual policy. The concept of a trade-off between goals is, in my view, more useful for the issues discussed in this essay irrespective of whether or not one believes that these goals are final ends or that they are derivable, in conjunction with empirical judgements, from some overriding ultimate criterion.

role of coercion in human affairs. He cannot eliminate it completely.

The term liberalism has become so extended in contemporary discourse that for many people it means nothing more than a vague 'do-goodism'; indeed, in the U.S.A. 'liberal' is often a label for those who wish to extend the authority and role of the central government. Unfortunately, there is no good modern term which will convey the emphasis on personal freedom associated with the traditional meaning of liberalism. 'Individualist' conveys misleading associations. 'Libertarian', which has been used in the U.S.A., is too ungainly. There can be no harm in using 'liberal' in its old-fashioned English meaning so long as this is made clear from the start. The important point is that liberalism in this sense represents a set of priorities with which it is possible for men of goodwill to disagree vehemently. It is not a synonym for some vague form of general enlightenment.

Liberalism, so defined, as has frequently been pointed out, is not identical with democracy. It can exist under a variety of political regimes. There can be personal freedom, both of expression and in economic decisions, under a dictatorship. The temptations the other way round are obvious; but the Enlightened Despots of the 18th century such as Joseph II of Austria, consciously tried to increase personal freedom, for example, by abolishing serfdom. A democracy on the other hand can – and too often does – insist on a high degree of conformity by its citizens.

The question with which a liberal is concerned is not so much 'Who is to govern?', but rather 'How much government is there to be, and of what kind?' At one extreme is a liberal regime, in which people are given the maximum freedom to make their own decisions. Next on the scale comes an authoritarian regime, which decides what is good for them (or the regime) over a wide area. But even under an authoritarian system people may have considerable choice in their own private and professional lives, provided that they keep quiet on certain topics and avoid clashes with the positive and negative injunctions of the authorities. Further on the scale is a totalitarian regime, which insists on making every aspect of personal life, including as far as possible thoughts and beliefs, conform to an ideological pattern – 'Big Brother is watching you'.

These distinctions are matters of degree. The most liberal society is likely to have certain restraints on personal conduct (e.g. on the taking of drugs or on dress in public places) while in practice, even under the most totalitarian regime, a large part of life in peacetime for a large number of people, will consist of working, sleeping, eating, drinking and sex, in forms very little different to what would occur in a freer society.

What is the particular relevance of *economic* liberalism? The most obvious is an emphasis on the importance of freedom in the economic sphere. The bearing of liberalism on such issues as free speech, artistic censorship or non-interference in sexual activities between consenting adults is clear enough. But many of those who stress such matters do not realise that a commitment to freedom and personal choice also involves freedom to spend one's money in the way one chooses and to select one's own occupation; and this in turn has implications for the organisation of production, pay, prices and all other staple items of economic controversy.

One can make the further claim that the development of economic reasoning has provided insights into aspects of liberty, and perhaps even suggestions for extending it in practice, which go well beyond the realm of material goods. This should make political economy of particular interest to any liberal who can overcome any initial revulsion to its mundane subject matter or the minimum of formal reasoning involved.

The main argument does not, however, depend on this speculative and controversial assertion (which will be taken up further on p. 144). We can provisionally regard economic liberalism as a combination of certain basic views about ends with certain characteristic opinions about how these ends can be best achieved, even though the distinction between means and ends is not nearly as clear-cut as is popularly supposed, and the analysis of possible ways of achieving certain goals is bound to lead to further reflection on the nature of the goals themselves.

Freedom and Coercion

It is worth pointing out that a large weight can be attached
to freedom on a number of different grounds. The classical
exponent of 'negative freedom', John Stuart Mill, devoted the
main part of *On Liberty* to a pragmatic defence of freedom
as a means of achieving other ends: discovering truth, fostering independence of character, variety of life styles and so
on. Hayek's more recent restatement in *The Constitution of
Liberty* rests on very similar grounds. Great stress is laid on
men's ignorance of the factors on which the achievement of
their ends depends and on the danger of the state enforcing
one path or blocking others. Hayek's argument is dependent
on the case for progress, especially progress in the discovery
of new knowledge. He does not say that progress leads to a
better or happier state of affairs. Since human wants change
in the process he doubts whether the question is a meaningful one. What matters, he believes, is successful or hopeful
striving. It is in the 'living in and for the future in which
human intelligence proves itself. Progress is movement for
movement's sake.'[3]

'Arguments for freedom' are a risky business. The ultimate
value, explicitly or implicitly involved, may be less appealing
than freedom as an end in itself. It is perfectly possible for
someone to value freedom despite, not because of, the
'progress' it is likely to bring. While it is true that zealous
striving for new truths, deep and original thought about
human values, imaginative and penetrating literature, and
all the other goals with which liberals have identified, will
certainly suffer in an efficiently regimented society, they may
flourish quite well under an inefficient despotism. Czarist
Russia is, of course, the obvious example; and one can also
cite Habsburg Austria, which was hardly an ideal liberal
society. The existence of obstacles, which are not insurmount-
able, are often an excellent creative spur. But even in the
most favourable cases it would be best to argue that there is,
as J. W. N. Watkins has put it, 'a happy coincidence' between freedom as a value in itself and these other benefits,[4]
and not to identify them.

A good pragmatic argument for freedom is in terms of an implicit bargain. As Milton Friedman has pointed out,[5] if the case for free speech were considered on its merits and a separate vote were taken on whether the advocacy of communism, birth control, atheism, vegetarianism and other controversial views were to be permitted, the result in a great many cases would be 'No'. It is only by grouping all these cases in a bundle that one can hope for widespread support for freedom of expression. This is because the individual voter is likely to give so much weight to his desire for his own free speech on a favourite issue, where he may be in a minority, that he will in return be prepared to concede free speech to others, as the only feasible way of achieving his object. The argument might well apply to a great deal of personal conduct and not just the written or spoken word.

The best way to put the matter is that freedom lies, as Brian Barry has stated, 'at the *confluence* of a number of different considerations'.[6] Some people would regard negative freedom as an end in itself. Others will value it as a means for achieving other ends. In many cases there will be a mixture of considerations. Different considerations may come to the fore in different cases; and very often people will not have analysed their reasons for valuing it. The vital point for the liberal is that importance is attached to free personal choice, not why this is so.

There are innumerable different ways of classifying the constraints on individual action, related to the many meanings of the word 'can', which have given philosophers so many happy hours. Fritz Machlup has selected from them three different types of constraint which are frequently confused in political and economic discussion: (a) 'I am physically or mentally incapable of doing something', (b) 'I have not enough money to do it' and (c) 'I shall be prevented from or punished for doing it.'[7] This last type of constraint is the coercion which believers in freedom try to minimise. Nevertheless, it is not a precise concept; and it is all too easy to think of borderline cases between the three categories. The purest case of coercion would be where a person's hand is taken in a vice-like grip by some powerful human or automaton and physically forced to take action. But between this and the raised eyebrow of an admired friend there is an infinite series of gradations.

How about, for example, the power of an employer over an employee in a period of high unemployment and inadequate dole? The employee is free to depart and starve, just as a man can choose to be shot rather than do something at gun-point. Thus, although it would be highly dangerous to accept a concept of 'positive' freedom, which would be identified with employment, prosperity or any other popular policy aim, the borderline between 'positive' and 'negative' freedom is far from easy to draw. I should myself be inclined to say that there is more freedom, even in the negative sense, in a fully employed than an underemployed economy, everything else being comparable.

Borderline cases, which always exist, are not, however, a reason for obliterating distinctions. In general, coercion implies limitations imposed on a person's actions by his *fellow men*. Those on the 'left' are often inclined to argue that poverty – especially if it reflects remediable defects in social organisation – is a form of coercion. This makes the term so wide as to render it useless. Poverty is one evil and interference with a fellow man's activities another. Hayek, on the other hand, in *The Constitution of Liberty*, is inclined to go to the other extreme and limit the concept of coercion to *discretionary* control of one man's activities by another. He tends to regard hindrances to actions arising from *general* rules, which do not reflect the will of any particular human being, as akin to the hindrances imposed by nature, in being impersonal.

The distinction between the two kinds of restraint is certainly well worth making. A prohibition is felt more keenly if it is due to the arbitrary exercise of power by another human being, in whose power one is, than if it comes from known laws applicable to everyone placed in similar situations. Nevertheless, Hayek is narrowing the concept of coercion too far in limiting it (as Berlin does not) to the *discretionary* use of political power. A general rule made by human beings, and in principle repealable – for example, banning foreign travel for non-business purposes – is clearly coercive in character.

There is indeed a trade-off between severity and arbitrariness. It is well known that a strict regime in institutions such as schools or armies is resented less if it arises from known rules fairly enforced without favouritism than if the same degree of severity arises from unpredictable *ad hoc* actions of teachers or N.C.O.s. On the other hand, it would be worth accepting some degree of unpredictability, capriciousness or even favouritism in an environment that is on average tolerant of a wide range of behaviour, if the only alternative is an extremely repressive system of prohibitions and sanctions imposed with scrupulous fairness on all concerned.

Coercion is best regarded as the presence of man-made restrictions on the range of actions one may undertake – whether these prohibitions come from restrictive laws, or the discretionary exercise of power by one individual over another. But it is not a one dimensional concept; both the severity and the degree of arbitrariness of the restraints imposed are relevant to assessing the degree of coercion to which a person is subject in any particular situation.

If someone insists on saying that a man's inability to fly to Australia, when he cannot afford the fare, reflects coercion – because the inability is due to man-made rules requiring monetary payments and human institutions which affect the amount of money a person has – then there is no *a priori* way of ruling his definition out of order. Definitions are a matter of convenience. As J. W. N. Watkins has pointed out,[8] there is a scale of restraints from physical limitations, imposed by nature at one extreme, going on to limitations imposed by the state or society such as the size and distribution of incomes (which may themselves reflect physical or technological constraints as well as social institutions), prohibitions and duties laid down by general rules, and ending up at the other extreme with the arbitrary use of force to impose one man's intentions on another. The argument for drawing the boundary so that a prohibition on foreign travel counts as coercion, while inability to travel due to shortage of cash does not, is at bottom subjective. Low income is one sort of evil and prevention by one's fellow men of choosing one's own way of life within one's income, is another. The only argument I can offer to someone who is not conscious of this

distinction is that we are more likely to advance both knowledge and policy if we distinguish between different evils and
different desirable aims than if we put every kind of limitation on man's activities into one undifferentiated whole.

Coercion can take a positive form – a law or command
requiring a person to do something, such as joining the army
– or a negative form – such as proscribing certain activities
such as the consumption of liquor, drugs or candyfloss. It
would be generally agreed that positive coercion is a greater
infringement of liberty; for negative coercion does leave open
all the courses not officially proscribed. But negative coercion
is coercion nonetheless; and, if the number of prescribed
courses is sufficiently large or extensive, it can be highly
oppressive. Indeed, in the limiting case a person can be
forced to carry out a specific course of action by forbidding
every feasible alternative (for example, a man without independent means can be forced to join the armed forces by
being forbidden to take a civilian job). Thus, the distinction
between positive and negative coercion is one of degree,
rather than stark opposition.

An interesting unresolved question, among those who
share the concept of freedom outlined above, is whether it is
related to the range of alternatives or number of choices open
to an individual. Granted that there are no coercive laws
preventing one travelling where one wishes, does the opening
up of new forms of transport, the railways in the 19th century,
the airlines in the 20th century or interplanetary travel in the
21st, increase personal freedom in the relevant sense? I am
inclined to argue with those liberal writers who reply 'No',[9]
on the grounds that this would be to confuse freedom with
power or physical opportunity.

The negative form of coercion has, nevertheless, a bearing
on the definition of the kind of prosperity that it is worth
trying to maximise. Freedom should never be identified with
prosperity or want-satisfaction of any kind. But someone
who attaches importance to personal freedom of choice is
likely to say that a person is 'worse off' (not necessarily more
unhappy) if his range of choice is deliberately narrowed by
some authority claiming to know his own interests better
than he does himself. A paternalist or authoritarian might

legitimately take a very different view. A moderate paternalist might say that he is saving the consumer from the adverse effects of candyfloss which he will discover for himself if allowed free choice. A more extreme Hegelian might argue that even if the consumption of candyfloss were not subsequently regretted by individuals, some mysterious organism known as the state or society would nonetheless suffer. Such 'philosophical' differences can be reflected in apparently highly technical discussions on, for instance, the way to measure 'real income'. One of the hallmarks of liberalism of particular relevance to economic policy is a reluctance to justify restrictions imposed upon a person for what someone else regards as his own good.

2. Liberal Utilitarianism

How does liberalism relate to utilitarianism? The latter was defined by a whole series of writers, from Epicurus to Bentham and Mill, as the doctrine that 'actions are right in proportion as they tend to promote happiness' or that 'pleasure and freedom from pain are the only things desirable as ends'.[10] Defined in this way utilitarianism and liberalism are different social philosophies, which can often conflict, despite Mill's attempt to prove the contrary.

But in the century since Mill, the emphasis in utilitarian doctrine has shifted from the psychological intangibles such as 'happiness' or 'pleasure' to the satisfaction of wants or desires actually exhibited by people in their behaviour. The early 20th century English 'welfare economists', who were the intellectual heirs to the utilitarian tradition, reinterpreted it in this way; and this reinterpretation is probably accepted by the majority of practising economists in their analysis of policy problems. If utilitarianism means satisfying the desires that individual people actually have rather than what some authority or mob think would be good for them, there is then much less conflict with liberalism.

The traditional economist's case for a form of market economy has been based on what might be called *liberal utilitarianism*. This is a belief that individual desires should normally be satisfied to the maximum degree possible without interfering with the desires of others. The utilitarianism involved is a highly qualified one. As already mentioned, it seeks to satisfy the people's preferences as shown by their behaviour and not to measure or promote happiness in any direct way. It proceeds on the presumption that the individual should *usually* be regarded *as if* he is the best judge of his own interests. This presumption can be regarded as an inference from a fundamental belief in the importance of individual freedom; or it can be justified pragmatically as Mill and Hayek attempt to do by pointing out that, however badly an individual will make his own choices, anyone else acting on his behalf is likely to make them even worse, and that the resultant increase in governmental power is likely to block many paths to progress and knowledge that might have remained open if people had been left more to their own devices. *Anti-paternalism* is a useful synonym for the doctrine in many contexts.

The economic expression of liberal utilitarianism is sometimes known as *consumer sovereignty*, but this gives too narrow an impression. It is not only the types of goods and services produced, and the relative amount of each that should depend on the expressed preferences of individuals and families. The same should apply, as far as possible, to the choice between extra earnings and extra leisure, between more take-home pay and more congenial working conditions, and between present consumption and investment for future needs. It is not enough for the liberal that some sort of majority judgement should prevail on these questions; he seeks an economic system in which the great variety of individual preferences in these matters can be gratified to the greatest feasible extent rather than one which imposes some sort of average taste to which all have to conform.

Anti-paternalism is a matter of degree. There is no mysterious logical force which compels someone who favours a free choice between domestic and imported cars to commit himself to the general availability of hard drugs on demand.

He does not have to be committed to anti-paternalism to the exclusion of all other values, but he believes that the onus is heavily on the paternalist to prove why any particular set of choices should be governed by the decisions of authority. (There is a distinction, emanating from Mill, between those forms of paternalism which are 'a preparation for freedom' and those which are not. This is too schoolmasterly a justification for restriction. But it would be useful if all paternalist measures, whether anti-drug laws or high taxes on tobacco, could be regarded as under permanent scrutiny and the question of their removal or relaxation considered at regular intervals.)

An additional qualification must be added before any doctrines of providing as many opportunities as possible for people to satisfy the wants they happen to have can be described as 'liberal'. The wants that a liberal will seek to satisfy exclude what Brian Barry, writing as a political philosopher, terms 'publicly oriented wants' and which economists call 'interdependence effects'. In plain English, a preference for butter over margarine or extra leisure over work, would be respected by a liberal. But he would not take into his calculations the 'want' felt by many respectable citizens for compulsory haircuts for long-haired youth, or the want of other citizens for compulsory restrictions on the number of villas or foreign trips that the wealthy can have. Wants of this type are disguised forms of coercion which arise from a desire to regulate the way in which other people spend their lives. The liberal form of utilitarianism is thus a heavily circumscribed form of the doctrine.

E. J. Mishan has, in his role as an economic theorist, explicitly suggested that 'interdependence effects', which are a polite way of describing 'resentment or envy of the achievements or possessions of others' should be sharply distinguished from 'external diseconomies such as smoke, noise and pollution.' The latter should emphatically be a matter of public concern; the former may merely 'elicit sympathy and require psychiatry.'[11] Mishan explicitly suggests, in an excellent textbook on project appraisal, that we should exclude 'interdependence effects' from consideration.[12] Mishan justifies his position on the basis of a supposed 'virtual consti-

tution' containing a number of unwritten ethical propositions which are supposed to command widespread assent.
Unfortunately, there is little evidence that this liberal desire
to exclude prohibitions and deterrents justified by resentment, does command all that much support. Even some economists wax eloquently about 'interdependence effects' and
treat them on all fours with other 'externalities' such as the
pollution of rivers. Fortunately such economists have found
it almost impossible to evaluate such effects in practice, and
this is one of many reasons why the bias of the subject is more
liberal, in the excellent negative sense, than many practi-
tioners would personally like it to be.

One of the most fiercely debated topics among economic
liberals is the role of changes in tastes, whether spontaneous
or 'artificially' induced. From a strictly utilitarian point of
view even a spontaneous change of tastes may seem a waste.
Demand for commodity X is replaced by commodity Y;
capital becomes obsolescent and investment which could have
been used to raise real income (i.e. supply a greater proportion of expressed desires in the first situation) now has to
be devoted to replacing X. Therefore total satisfaction, as
Mishan argues, is less than it might have been if God had
prevented this change from occurring. *A fortiori*, the deliberate diversion of resources to advertising is wasteful, because
it brings about changes of taste which might never have taken
place, as well as subtracting resources which might have been
used to satisfy existing tastes.

The validity of this argument, even on its own grounds,
depends on the assumption that the total capacity for satisfaction remains unchanged. It is undeniable that changes in
tastes, whether artificial or spontaneous, reduce the *proportion* of desires that can be satisfied. But if the total capacity
for satisfaction increases because human imagination has
been stimulated, a person may be better off with a smaller
proportion of his desires satisfied after the changes than
with a larger proportion satisfied in the original situation.
On the other hand, if his total capacity for satisfaction
declines – say, because he becomes restless and disturbed –
then his welfare is reduced even further than Mishan's
formal argument suggests.

To argue this way would, however, be to push utilitarian ethics further than they will go and brings us perilously near to suggesting not only an empirical enquiry into the causes of human satisfaction, but state action to enforce its findings. We would then have the paradox of a form of individualistic ethics apparently leading to Huxley's totalitarian *Brave New World*.

It is best to be frank and say that, in such cases, there might be a conflict between utilitarianism and freedom. To be allowed to attempt to change other people's tastes by non-violent means is an aspect of a free society. If this were banned, or regulated, it would be difficult to justify confining the restriction to advertising. Much political activity, virtually all the arts, and a good deal of philosophical speculation are an attempt to change tastes, and involve a diversion of resources from meeting existing tastes. Unchanged consumer tastes is a useful simplifying assumption in dealing with many practical problems, for example, in cost-benefit analysis, where it is reasonable to assume that changes in taste (e.g. in noise aversion) are either slow or less important than the other factors involved. But it is not a valid long-term policy goal. *A free non-paternalist society may thus require a state of affairs which at any time is less than optimal from the point of view of meeting individual desires as they exist at any one time.* There is here yet another way in which liberal utilitarianism is a very qualified form of utilitarianism and why it is necessary to distinguish between the pure and the qualified versions. (Further discussion of the ways in which a belief in individual freedom would conflict with conventional utilitarianism will be found in Appendix II to this chapter.)

The Corrected Market Economy

A number of overlapping, but far from identical, terms have been used to label an economic system characterised by markets, decentralised decisions and a wide range of choices for consumer and producer. They include *the market economy, the price mechanism, competition, the profit motive, capitalism, private enterprise and free economy* to name only a few. These differ considerably in the political direction of their sales appeal.

'The market economy' and 'the price mechanism' are, in concept at least, independent of the structure of ownership; and they do not involve a commitment to the capitalist system. Some would argue that competition and even a form of the profit motive could be combined with state- or syndicalist-ownership, as is attempted for example in Yugoslavia. 'Capitalism', of course, indicates the private ownership of the means of production, distribution and exchange; but it will also be used here to describe a mixed economy which has a large capitalist element. 'Private enterprise' is most conveniently regarded as the slogan of those who wish any shift in the frontiers between the state and private sectors to be in favour of the private one. A 'free economy' is a much looser term which perhaps suggests a combination of several of the other elements – a competitive capitalist market economy, making maximum use of the price mechanism.

The 'market economy' is the most fundamental of all the concepts. As a first approximation, it can be said to describe a state of affairs in which those who own the means of production, distribution and exchange, as well as workers and consumers, pursue their own freely chosen ends rather than some supposed national good. The 'price mechanism' refers to an important part of the mechanism by which a market economy (and perhaps also some other types of economy) function and individual decisions are reconciled with each other.

A market economy can consist largely, or even entirely, of state-owned enterprises, provided that those who run them are allowed to respond to consumer demand and do not have to follow some politically determined 'plan'. As managers of such state concerns do not have a personal stake in their success they cannot be left entirely free to pursue their own ends and our provisional definition has to be modified. Some very general instructions such as 'maximise profits' may have to be given; and they may be reinforced by linking managerial remuneration with the results achieved. Managers running private concerns on behalf of shareholders have also to identify themselves artificially with a quest for profits which largely go to others; and similar conflicts of interest may arise. The opposite of a market economy is a *command economy*, in which the decision about what to produce, and how much, depends not on market demand but orders from the centre. The terminology is, interestingly enough, derived from discussion of Communist bloc countries, where elements of a market economy have had to be reintroduced in uneasy combination with the command element.

The basic insight behind the case for the market economy is that *under certain conditions* the self-interest of one human being *can* further the welfare of other human beings. In contrast to much popular belief trade is not a 'zero-sum game' like chess. Both parties to a transaction can benefit. The *profit motive* is a special case of the use of self-interest as a guiding force. The action of workers in seeking the employment with the best available combination of pay, working conditions and leisure is another. As Adam Smith put it long ago, we rely on the self-interest of the baker to provide our daily bread. Moreover, the forces of competition will encourage him to develop new types of bread and cheaper methods of baking, and prevent him from exploiting the consumers by obtaining an above-normal rate of return.

It is well known that the 'invisible hand' will work reasonably well only if certain conditions are fulfilled. There is a fair degree of consensus among economists both about what these conditions are and the kinds of corrective that may be appropriate if they are not fulfilled. A little will have to be said in very summary form about these conditions and the correctives in the next few pages – probably too much for the non-specialist and too little for the expert. (As the main conclusions of this chapter are not dependent on the details that follow, and a summary is provided, the reader with little taste for this sort of thing can safely skip over these pages to the section on Political Freedom starting on p. 83.)

The intricate controversies of 'welfare economics' concern refinements, paradoxes and conundrums within a body of propositions which are common property to most working economists, but are alien to most politicians and educated laymen. The statement of the conditions for a social optimum on liberal utilitarian assumptions fills many textbooks; and there is no point in trying to compress them in this essay.

The basic tautology from which the others are derived is in E. J. Mishan's words that 'the social value of the marginal product of each distinguishable factor is the same in all its existing uses'.[13]

It is unfortunate that so much of the high grade intellectual effort has been devoted first to refining *optimum* conditions, which are never likely to be fulfilled, or to establish that nothing can be said in general terms about the principles of policy unless all the optimum conditions are fulfilled – a proposition which is itself a subject of dispute. It would be Luddite to decry the logical and mathematical exercises which lead to such results. But to use them as a blunderbuss to undermine all policy prescriptions by economists is to leave the field open to any charlatan, demagogue, interest group spokesman, or vote-bidder whose standards of argument are infinitely below those of the average working economist at his shakiest.

For all the difficulties that exist at the most rarefied level, there is in fact a body of 'informal welfare economics', which economists use in discussing real world problems. My *Is There an Economic Consensus?* suggests that two competent economists of different political views are likely to be much nearer in their approach to many problems than either would be to an intelligent layman, innocent of economics, who shared his politics. Indeed, there is probably more agreement among economists on the circumstances in which the profit motive does and does not promote the public welfare than on apparently less political and more technical areas.

The success of a market economy will depend a great deal on a monetary and fiscal framework which will minimise the likelihood of either slumps or runaway inflation. The best efforts of the financial authorities can, however, be undermined by union monopoly power, and this topic cannot be omitted from any economic policy agenda. It is here that economists are under the strongest temptation to abandon the liberal element of the liberal utilitarian tradition. The test, however, is not whether they say they are or are not in favour of an 'incomes policy' but what exactly they propose, and how they would deal with the complications and remoter consequences of any such policy.

The main discrepancies between the interest of individual citizens and the working of the profit motive, even in the absence of monopoly elements, arise from what is called under alternative terminologies, 'external economies' or 'dis-economies' (sometimes referred to as 'externalities'), 'spillover effects' or – most evocatively – 'neighbourhood effects'. These arise as the unintended result of some other activity; their effects are indiscriminate and those responsible can neither charge for them if they are beneficial nor be forced to pay for the damage if they are harmful. Chemical products discharged into a river impose harm on a community downstream which do not enter into the profit and loss account of the firm concerned. An extra car coming into London imposes costs on all other cars and on the passenger transport system, for which the driver does not have to pay.

A great many of these discrepancies can be corrected by general measures without either specific intervention or a 'central plan'. Competition can be encouraged by anti-trust laws or freer trading policies. Changes in the law could make firms liable for some of the 'disbenefits' they cause. Discrepancies between private costs and the 'spillover' costs imposed on others can be corrected by taxes and subsidies. For example, a motorist could be discouraged from coming into London by a congestion tax under which he would equate the marginal convenience of his journey with the marginal increase in congestion costs for everyone concerned and not just himself. This allows greater freedom of choice between motorists of different tastes and needs than does prohibition or licensing. Almost by definition the most important of these neighbourhood effects occur in regard to what is nowadays called 'the environment'.

There is also a category of services known as 'public goods', which cannot be sold in the market because they cannot, for technical reasons, be provided in different quantities to different people in accordance with their preference. One obvious example is defence; another is an urban park, which benefits both those who regard the fresh air and view as worth the cost and those who do not. In all such cases a political decision has to be taken. 'Public goods' are like favourable spillovers which convey indiscriminate benefits. The main difference is that their effects are intended rather than accidental.

The range of pure public goods is narrower than is sometimes supposed. Many services which are treated as public goods, such as health, higher education and social security and parts of housing, are provided collectively, either for frankly paternalist reasons, or as a backdoor method of bringing about some desired redistribution of income. However non-paternalist he is, a liberal utilitarian may still not be satisfied with the distribution of income thrown up by the market. His approach here would, however, be to put the emphasis on social benefits in cash, preferably through a negative income tax, rather than, on 'free' services in kind.

Policy disagreements among economists of an anti-paternalist hue are at several different levels. There are some quite important technical disagreements. A hoary old chestnut is whether one should subsidise industries with declining *long-run* unit cost curves (of which there are fewer than is commonly imagined). Another is whether the rate of interest thrown up by the market really does measure the community's true preference between present and future consumption, whether because of the lack of a fully developed forward market, or other reasons.* An interesting recent controversy concerns the value of what has been given the unfortunate label 'indicative planning'. This can be given a strictly liberal interpretation, as Professor James Meade has done, in the form of providing producers with informed guesses about the consequences of certain possible developments, *which they are then free to follow or not*.[14] The value of such projections and stipulated relationships is an empirical matter depending on the predictablity of the relationships involved and the risks that the project may degenerate under political pressure into either an exercise in wishful thinking or attempted government by interest groups.[15]

---

* The whole 'ecological' controversy about whether the growth of material production should be drastically curtailed to preserve a tolerable planet concerns vast 'neighbourhood effects' posited for some future date. Because these threats are remote in time and the growth of our knowledge of ways of meeting them cannot be predicted, the whole problem is shrouded in enormous uncertainty. The controversies are further compounded, however, by differences of view about how much weight to give to the welfare of generations yet unborn.

The really important disagreements do not in all probability relate to these well-known technical issues, and still
less to discrepancies between 'ideal' growth paths in some
mathematical models and what actually does happen. Just
as it is illegitimate to make out a case for non-intervention
on the basis of some idealised version of a market economy,
it is equally illegitimate to base arguments for intervention
on comparisons between messy, real world markets and some
ideal plan which could be introduced by an omniscient
government free from interest groups and guided solely by
disinterested concern for some non-paternalist conception of
the public interest.

Major differences within the liberal utilitarian camp reflect
much more different beliefs about where the onus of proof
should be placed in deciding when to intervene in practical
instances. As Milton Friedman remarks, some 'neighbourhood effects' can be conjured up to justify almost any con-
ceivable act of intervention. Most economists would favour
taxes and subsidies (and perhaps a few out-and-out prohibitions), when there are large and obvious spillover effects, and
would support cost–benefit studies (hopefully of a more
sensitive and civilised kind than some we have seen) when
large projects with obvious environmental effects are being
considered. But to go beyond this and advocate discretionary
state intervention in every private sector activity involves all
of at least the three following empirical judgements: (a) that
the unpriced spillover effects are likely to be large in relation
to the costs of intervention, (b) that officials will have enough
knowledge of cost conditions and individual preferences, now
and in the future, to improve on the unaided market outcome, and (c) and most important of all, that the Government
action will not in practice be largely influenced by local,
political and industrial pressures (or prestige considerations)
which would lead to a worse result than that of the unaided
market.

Another kind of apparent disagreement is largely a matter
of presentation. To the extent that there is a consensus on
how the market works, it can be summarised for popular
purposes in ways which are equally valid, but which have a
very different political flavour. One economist can say that

the market economy works well given the right environmental policies; another, who holds identical views on actual
issues, can emphasise how much intervention is required to
correct the evils of uninhibited market forces. (We are still at
this stage talking about any market economy and begging the
question whether it has to be capitalist.)

There is indeed an ambiguity about the way the term
'market economy' is used in current political and economic
discussion. A liberal writer may put forward a positive case
for a market economy to emphasise the paternalist and anti-
consumer bias of many interventionist policies, to stress that
'production for profit' *need* not be the evil that is supposed
in Labour Party demonology, and that the alternative slogan
of 'production for use' is, on the most charitable interpretation, a meaningless one. Nevertheless, someone who talks
about a market economy is widely understood to mean *laissez-
faire*. To meet this difficulty, the German neo-liberals have
coined the term 'social market economy'. But, as Hayek has
pointed out, the word 'social' is not only vague and confusing,
but risks giving the impression that there are such things as
higher purposes over and above the purposes of individuals.[16]
It is probably best to avoid misunderstanding and to use the
colourless expression, 'corrected market economy', if one
wants to emphasise that appropriate policies are being followed to provide a suitable environment in which the market
can function, and that discrepancies between private and
social costs and benefits are taken into account.

The Price Mechanism

The influence of prices on economic behaviour in most, if not
all, known societies is a fact of life, in no way dependent on
the political philosophy of the person observing this influence.
Most popular discussion about prices refers to the rate at
which their average level (the cost of living) is rising; and
economists struggling with the inflation conundrum are certainly conscious of this problem. They are also, however, at
least as interested in another aspect of prices – that of prices
of different goods and services relative to each other. Prices
are here very broadly defined to include items such as wages,

rents, interest rates and, indeed, the charge made for any commodity or service that is sold for money or even barter.

Both the demand for and the supply of goods and services are normally assumed to be related to the incomes of those involved in the transactions and to the prices offered or asked, relative to the prices of other goods and services. The effect of price upon supply can be in either direction. An increase in wages for a large category of workers can lead either to more hours being put in, because work is now more attractive relative to leisure, or less hours being put in, because a smaller number now suffice to provide a given target income. The more narrowly the category of work is defined the more likely is a higher price to lead to more effort. A general increase in agricultural workers' wages, relative to other occupations, could lead to fewer hours being put in per worker. It is also likely to lead to more people wishing to become agricultural labourers (or fewer people leaving the land than otherwise); and this may or may not outweigh the effects on hours per worker – the time scale considered being of relevance here. What one can say with great confidence is that an increase in the price expected to be realised for a particular foodstuff, relative to other foodstuffs and to the general price level, will lead to an increase in output of the commodity in question, even if it means switching agricultural labourers from other activities.

The demand for a product or service is normally expected to be smaller the higher the price, relative to the general price level. This relationship of the demand for a commodity to the price charged is a tautology if a person's (or a country's) money income is constant and a particular price varies. After all, if the price rises high enough, expenditure on an unchanged quantity of the commodity in question will absorb the whole of one's income. Although this tautology is interesting in some situations (for example, in the analysis of a devaluation), much more interesting is the sensitivity of the demand for a particular commodity to a change in its price when there is no change in real income (either because other prices move in a compensatory direction or because there are compensatory increases in money income). This pure 'substitution' effect of differences in relative prices is an empirical phenomenon, which can be observed by watching a house-wife in a supermarket. The degree of responsiveness to such relative price changes is a matter for observation rather than armchair reflection.

The above is but the briefest of sketches of relations which are elaborated at considerable length in books on economic principles. The *price mechanism* refers not to just these properties of prices, but the way in which they can be used to bring some form of order and co-ordination into a wide range of human activities. *The expression can refer both to the spontaneous adjustments of the market and to the deliberate manipulation of prices by political authorities to change the working of the market – whether in aid of liberal utilitarian goals or more paternalist ones.*

If we are talking of the major products of an advanced industrial society, and not of a few specialist markets or bazaars, it is mainly in the allocation of resources *in the long run* that the price mechanism has a major role to play. If there is a reasonable degree of competition and entry is free to newcomers, prices will bear a roughly similar ratio to costs, including among costs the going rate of return on capital, in different branches of the economy. Assuming a public policy which charges enterprises for the major 'neighbourhood' or 'spillover' costs which do not appear in their accounts (and if possible rewards them for spillover benefits) and a reasonably high overall employment, the resulting price structure will indicate to people the true alternatives that are open to society – how many refrigerators would have to be forgone to produce an additional motor car, the sacrifice in output of consumer goods that would make possible a given addition to the number of coach tours or National Park wardens, or the sacrifice of goods and services of all kinds required to make possible a given addition to leisure and so on. In other words, the structure of relative prices gives some idea of what economists call the 'opportunity cost' of different goods and services.

Over the time horizon in question there is unlikely to be shortage or surplus. For we have been considering a period long enough for production to be increased to remedy any shortages and reduced to eliminate surpluses. Thus, the relative price structure not only indicates the costs of different items in terms of foregone alternatives, but also represents the valuation that consumers place on their marginal purchases. In this way the market system will produce, in suitable circumstances, the goods that people happen to want, rather than what some authority – or their fellowmen – think they ought to have, in the light of prices that convey information about the true costs of the various alternatives.

For the system to work in this way there must be, in the long run, freedom to compete on all aspects of the service offered. The business apologist cannot be allowed to get away with saying that, despite the existence of a price ring, there is competition in 'quality' or fierce sales rivalry. The consumer is being deprived of the option of paying a lower price with less service by the collusive action of producers. Competition does not presuppose private ownership, although to introduce it into the state sector may require deliberate policies which will go against the grain of those most actively concerned and may run up against the statutory monopoly status enjoyed by industry-wide nationalised undertakings.

This is a convenient place to dispose of the widespread fallacy that the case for the market economy depends on the existence of something called 'perfect competition'. This whole approach is based on an edifice of misunderstandings. 'Perfect' and 'imperfect', when applied to competition, are not terms of praise or blame. 'Perfect competition' is said to exist when a firm faces a 'perfectly elastic' demand for its product. This means that it is responsible for such a small part of total supply, and the product is so standardised and the element of goodwill so small, that the firm can sell all it likes at the going market price. If it raises its prices even slightly it will lose all its customers; if it lowers them, it would be overwhelmed with far more orders than it could supply.

This state of affairs prevails mainly in some produce and financial markets. But the concept of perfect competition was arrived at, not from an observation of such markets, but from an attempt to set out in mathematical form the theory of a competitive economy. Later writers then observed that under certain very restrictive conditions it would produce an 'optimum' pattern of output, with production of goods corresponding to consumer preferences, and each firm would produce on a scale that gave it the lowest possible long-run production costs. The main conditions required for this to occur include static technology and static consumer preferences, and the exhaustion of all economies of scale at a small size of firm. They also include the absence of both direct and indirect taxes, which distort the choice between income and leisure.[17]

The degree of competition in a dynamic economy cannot be measured by reference to the yardstick of perfect competition. As Schumpeter long ago observed, the industries where progress has been most rapid are often dominated by large-scale firms far removed from perfect competition. The most effective kind of competition is from the 'new commodity, the new technology, the new source of supply, the new type of organisation.' The threat of competition of this kind is a powerful influence on existing firms, particularly in oligopolistic situations such as the oil or car industries. At any one time the existing firms are in a privileged position; but prolonged failure to improve products or introduce low-cost methods, or any attempt at monopoly pricing, would attract newcomers which would threaten their hold. This does not mean that the public authorities should just stand aside. But the features to watch are the freedom of entry of newcomers into the industry, and imports into the country, as well as the laws relating to restrictive practices. Perfect competition is virtually useless as a yardstick here.

It is, of course, wrong to suppose that even in the most favourable cases, the self-adjusting price mechanism provides any sort of *optimum* distribution of resources. The most that can be reasonably claimed is that with the aid of the corrective devices repeatedly emphasised in these pages, the price system provides a rough and ready way of making those who take economic decisions pay attention to people's preferences whether as consumers or workers, savers or investors, gamblers or insurers.

Nor does the departure of the pattern of prices from what would be the optimum in a static world, where we were satisfied with the distribution of incomes, matter all that much from the point of view of either prosperity or freedom – the twin goals of the liberal utilitarian. The key influence on either our prosperity or its rate of growth is not whether the price of a specified coach tour relative to a refrigerator is 11 : 8 when it ought to be 8 : 11. (Comparisons of exact cost-price relations are mainly of importance when comparing close substitutes, for example, alternative fuels.) What is important, both for freedom and for want-satisfaction, is that, if an increase in the demand for coach tours makes the activity more profitable, the supply of such tours should be allowed to respond and not be held back because some economic planners regard the manufacturing output as more important. The effectiveness of such responses, and the speed with which businessmen adopt the procedures that would pay them best and are already in use in the most advanced firms, has more bearing on the rate of growth than exactly how far from the ideal the existing pattern of prices, costs and profits happens to be. This kind of responsiveness to a given economic environment has been christened 'x-efficiency' – which is another way of saying that economists can tell us little about it.

In the foregoing summary explanation I have been very careful not to suggest that prices are used to eliminate shortages or surpluses in any but a long period sense. Day-to-day rationing by price is nowadays more the exception than the rule. Economic activity can be largely guided by market demand, yet prices may be fairly inflexible for many months at a time. Car firms may allocate popular models by 'waiting lists' rather than by raising prices, and they may reduce production of an unpopular car without experimenting with relative price changes. Branded products do change in price in response to market conditions. Firms with surplus labour are more likely to cease recruitment or declare redundancies than reduce wages, while those with labour shortages may hope to pick up unemployed labour without bidding against other firms. Thus, in the short run, shortages and surpluses may take the place of price changes as signalling devices.

Free markets can be said to exist in those markets where the price of an article is free to vary from day to day, or at least at very frequent intervals, in such a way as to equate supply and demand and clear the market. Examples include the stock market, the second-hand car market, many of the food and raw material exchanges, and the house market. The perfect markets, already mentioned, are a special case of free markets where the product is standardised and no individual seller or buyer is big enough to exert a perceptible influence on the price. At the other extreme is the house market, or the art market, where the items on sale are differentiated and individual buyers and sellers have an all too perceptible influence on the going rate.

Whereas the case for the price mechanism to allocate resources in an adjusted market economy derives in the last analysis from the liberal utilitarian value judgements outlined at the beginning of this essay (plus one or two elementary observations about human behaviour), the case for free markets depend on much more concrete empirical judgements. Those who dislike free markets would claim that the short term responsiveness of demand and/or supply to price changes is small; and that free prices generate large and disturbing fluctuations which are aggravated rather than smothered by speculative activity.

A perennial example of this controversy is that over exchange rates. The case for using the exchange rate mechanism to balance international payments in preference to controls or otherwise unnecessary deflation, is a matter of principle. But the case for freely floating exchange rates, in place of adjustments of official parities, is a matter in the last resort to be judged empirically. Nearly all the serious studies that have been made suggest that the allegations that genuinely floating rates fluctuate widely and are disturbing to trade are central bankers' or businessmen's myths. Most of the alleged instances have either been of fixed rates under pressure, or (as after 15 August 1971) of disturbances due to interference by the authorities with the functioning of the market, combined with the belief that rates would be fixed again after political haggles of uncertain outcome. Where genuinely free rates have moved rapidly, it has been due mainly to highly inflationary domestic policies which would, in any case, have brought about a devaluation.[18]

The trap to avoid in discussing all such questions is to compare the degree of instability of actual free markets with some imagined, ideal smooth path of adjustment. A debating point sometimes made against floating rates is that share prices do not move smoothly, but exhibit pronounced fluctuations around their trend. There are reasons for expecting freely floating exchange rates to fluctuate less than share or commodity prices;[19] but it is worth asking why those who make this point do not advocate either extensive official intervention to smoothen out share fluctuations or the fixing of share prices by financial institutions, to be changed only where there is clearcut evidence of a 'fundamental' imbalance of supply and demand (as actually happens on some overseas exchanges with lesser securities). Can it be that they are not so confident, after all, that the steplike movements resulting from such arrangements would lead to more stability (however that is defined) than actual stock exchanges with all their faults?

A little reflection suggests, however, that, even outside the purely financial sector, the absence of free markets is only tolerable, from the point of view of either freedom or efficiency, because of the presence of safety valves. Someone on a waiting list for one car model can switch over to a close substitute, often imported; or he can use the second-hand market. Many consumer goods producers aim to have a modest margin of unused capacity in a normal year so that production can be stepped up fairly quickly. The use of bonuses, overtime offers and all the other apparatus of 'wage drift' to entice new workers is well enough known; if some well meaning 'incomes policy' or T.U.C.–C.B.I. agreement were to stop such payments, we should really know the meaning of economic crisis. The relatively free market in furnished accomodation is, of course pushed to very high levels by rent controls elsewhere; but without this safety valve many people would be unable to find rented accommodation at all. Although the text-books may exaggerate the extent to which prices are set on a continuous market-clearing basis in a modern economy, the existence of a number of markets which do work in this way is not a matter of indifference, and they should be encouraged rather than suppressed.

Environmental Effects

So far the price mechanism has been described as a system of automatic adjustment. But, as already mentioned, it can also be used as a weapon of government policy. It can be used by a liberal utilitarian regime to improve the market economy as an instrument for satisfying individual desires. Taxes or subsidies can be imposed where there are spillover costs or benefits which the unaided market does not take into account. Sometimes it may be possible to internalise costs, which are at present external – for example, by imposing an obligation to pay compensation at market values for various kinds of damage to other people's property or amenity. Even where it is impracticable to change the law in this way, a good cost–benefit study will seek to assess the actual value that people affected place on the environmental losses from a proposed new project – either how much they would pay to stop it or how much they would need in compensation to waive their objections. The two approaches can yield very different results, but either is better than ignoring the environmental damage, or abstract debating on 'environment' versus 'growth' which ignores the technical trade-offs and the preferences of those concerned. The effect of a project on property values can also give a clue and, in default of other methods, survey data, properly interpreted, can be of help.[20]

Indeed, state intervention of all kinds, whether motivated by liberal utilitarian considerations or more paternalist ones, can employ the price mechanism. Special depreciation allowances or investment grants are in fact subsidies to investment – which may be justified as an offset to the deterrent against investment provided by the rest of the tax system. The Selective Employment Tax was a price mechanism technique for discouraging the shift from manufacturing to services. The Regional Employment Premium was designed as a subsidy to reduce the cost of labour to the employers in the high unemployment areas.

Clear examples of the use of the price mechanism out of a paternalist desire to encourage certain activities or discourage other include heavy taxes on drink and tobacco and subsidies for sports grounds. (One motive for such taxes may be revenue-raising, but the revenue-raisers could not get away with such heavy discrimination against particular goods if they could not cloak it as paternalist disapproval of 'social vices'.) The interesting point is that the price mechanism is a relatively *liberal means* of carrying out even *illiberal policies*, by comparison with prohibition and orders. State action will impart a bias against smoking and drinking and in favour of sport, compared with the unimpeded action of market forces; but individual behaviour will still vary according to personal tastes.

An interesting example of the use of the price mechanism as a relatively liberal means of control is the proposal by William Baumol and Wallace Oates for the setting up of certain 'environmental standards', for example, to achieve a given level of purification of a river or to halve the level of sulphur dioxide emission into the atmosphere. The justification for imposing these 'arbitrary' standards might be that here is an area where a measure of paternalism is justified – people affected by the widespread application of D.D.T. might lack the technical knowledge to assess its harmful effects and put too low a monetary value on it; or it might be the simple, pragmatic one advanced by Baumol that we do not know the marginal net valuation that people affected would put on the environmental spillover from various industrial activities, and the best we can do is to make a political guess about what the outcome would be if these adverse spillovers could be properly priced.

The interesting aspect of this proposal, which distinguishes it from similar proposals emanating from physical scientists, is that the required environmental standards would be obtained, not by regulations or prohibitions, but by levying a sufficient tax on all effluents poured into a river, which varied according to the organic waste load of the effluent, or a tax on smoke emissions.*

Professor Baumol justifies his use of the price mechanism approach on the grounds that it is the least costly method of

---

* These proposals can be found in Bohm and Kneese (eds), *The Economics of Environment* (Macmillan, 1971). As a spillover benefit the reader will find in the following chapter of that book an interview with Dr Pangloss on the pollution problem.

achieving the required standards. Those firms that can reduce smoke or effluent emission at relatively little cost will bear the bulk of the reductions; those for whom such reductions are very expensive or physically impossible will pay the tax (which may, via its effect on prices, reduce their total output). But the argument could also be put in terms of freedom of choice. Taxes are set at a level which is found sufficient to achieve certain environmental standards; but the individual firm is given the choice how far it should pay the tax and how far it should reduce the quantity of its emissions. Those who cannot bring themselves to attach any value at all to freedom for a firm (even though this is likely to benefit the employees as well as directors) have only to transfer the example to activities performed by individuals – taking cars into city centres, 'over-fishing' in rivers, the use of detergents which create disposal problems, and so on.

An eagerness to use the price mechanism is probably the most important single feature linking the policy views of economists of otherwise very varying persuasions. Many of those who are most sceptical of the workings of unimpeded free markets are strong proponents of correctives which work by influencing prices. Devaluation, the 'crawling peg', the Selective Employment Tax, the Regional Employment Premium, and parking meters are all price mechanism devices – in a way in which price *controls*, prohibitions, restrictions and quotas are not. This liberal bias of economists does not reflect any moral virtue, but the fact that their professional competence lies almost entirely in assessing function relations between supply and demand and prices, income and wealth.

Unfortunately, the allocative functions of the price mechanism have never been understood by the general public, or even the politically conscious section of it. This is due partly to a confusion between the goal of price stability (or minimum inflation), which relates to the general level of *all* prices, and price *relativities* between different goods (or occupations). Understanding has not been helped by the incessant exhortation involved in prices and incomes policies; a genuine difficulty is that the correction of long-overdue price relativities – which in practice often means an increase in the prices of basic services such as fuel or rent – will, when other prices are sticky, not merely lead to a once-for-all rise in the general price level, but may also stimulate a continuous process of cost inflation.

Nevertheless, it is doubtful if the confusion caused by the inflationary issue explains entirely the public hostility to the use of price mechanism and its attachment to the mediaeval idea of a 'just price'. One obvious objection is the distributional point that a change in relative prices always makes some people worse off relative to others. This is rationalised by saying that the poor usually suffer if prices, instead of administrative allocation or queuing is used as a rationing device – rents or school meals being stock examples.

There are, of course, other ways of offsetting any adverse distributional effect of relative price changes by means of the tax and social security system. Moreover, it is doubtful if the price mechanism would gain much in people's affections even if it were clear that its use would not shift the distribution of income against the poor. One did not notice much enthusiasm for the use of metering devices to price scarce road space in towns. (One of the first such meters entered a room in Ernest Marples' house via a broken window.) It is tempting to be patronising and talk about the low level of economic literacy among voters, but I am afraid that hostility to the price mechanism and belief in the just price reflects a deeper illiberalism which is discussed further in later sections and illustrated by the hypothetical example in Appendix II.

Freedom or Prosperity?

Liberal utilitarianism was described as a policy aimed at satisfying wants, with want-satisfaction defined in such a way as to be not identical with but consistent with, personal freedom. The goal of the 'corrected' market economy can very loosely be regarded as aiming to secure a combination of freedom and prosperity. The two are certainly not the same but are not all that easy to disentangle, because once we cease to be mesmerised by the veil of money, prosperity is an even more difficult concept to unravel than freedom; and the problem is not solved by using more technical sounding terms such as 'aggregate real income' or 'economic welfare'. It is worth asking to what extent different types of infringements of the ideals of the correct market economy are infringements of freedom and to what extent they are simply holding down the level of prosperity.

Let us start with an example heavily weighted towards the anti-prosperity side, the subsidisation of one fuel so that its price to marginal cost ratio differs very markedly from that of close substitutes and where there are no discrepancies between private and social costs of a type that justify such different pricing policies. Now, there is an element of interference even with negative freedom in this operation. If one believes that coercion is a matter of degree, the consumer is being pushed by government into buying more of one fuel and less of another than he would like. But even if there are numerous examples of these distortions in the economy, the effects on freedom are relatively trivial; and the issues are to be regarded as ones of industrial policy rather than human liberty. In assessing the degree of freedom that exists in the society, we should give them little weight compared with questions such as whether conscription exists, the degree of coercion practised on minors, the extent of civil liberties and the absence or presence of censorship.

But we should pause a moment before dismissing such instances altogether even if our main concern is with freedom rather than industrial efficiency. Freedom of choice of occupation and freedom to spend one's money in one's own way are vital freedoms of the negative kind. A system in which a 'Control of Engagements Order' was enforced (as Diocletian attempted more successfully than the Labour Government of 1947) or where a great many activities, which did not harm other people, were prohibited or restricted by severe rationing, would take us far on the road to serfdom. As Fritz Machlup points out, a dictator who wished to decide what it was good for people to consume and which occupations they should follow, could, in theory, achieve his aims by an extreme manipulation of the price mechanism. He could set very high prices for products of which he disapproved and very low ones for those he liked; he could ordain very low wages for some 'undesirable' activities and high ones for virtuous activities.[21] The resulting heavy losses in some occupations could be offset by subsidies. This would be a less unfree society than one in which individual people were told which jobs to do, an example of our earlier dictum that the price mechanism can be a liberal means even of carrying out illiberal policies. Nevertheless, the society could hardly be regarded as other than a highly regimented one.

At what stage 'perverse' intervention in the market economy becomes a serious threat to freedom is a matter of fine judgement – and of interest to those who could not care less about the G.N.P. or economic growth. Personally I would attach a good deal of value to the fringe free markets, such as that in furnished accommodation or in the phenomenon of wage drift, where market clearing prices are allowed to operate. Their suppression, which a misguided reforming government might attempt at any time, would be a serious narrowing of the range of choice otherwise open to people, compared with which the muddles over energy prices or the road–rail fare structure are of minor importance.

A clear example of misguided interference with the market economy, which is of more importance for freedom than for prosperity, is foreign travel restrictions. An instance of the blindness of the Left to the economic aspects of freedom was the readiness of the Labour Government to impose in 1966 a travel allowance which virtually confined Britons to this country, except for a two weeks' cheese-paring vacation, as a cheap political gesture. Yet one of the severest restrictions it is possible for Governments to impose on personal liberty in time of peace, which remained in operation for over three years, was greeted with hardly a word of protest from Labour's intellectual camp-followers, many of whom had ample opportunity of travel for official, business or cultural purposes.

Such restrictions on foreign travel have an adverse effect on prosperity, real incomes and living standards; but this is very much a secondary aspect. It is perfectly possible to imagine a situation where there is a political veto on devaluation, or where the adverse effects on the terms of trade of a successful devaluation are believed to be very great, and in which the imposition of a stringent travel allowance makes possible an expansion in output, income and employment, which for most people more than compensates for the travel curbs; and the total package may not have an adverse impact on the relative position of the poor, but even improve it. Yet a severe diminution of personal liberty remains – just as it would if bribes were paid to people to vote for the censorship of political views, resulting in a majority in favour of the measures – a majority who would, by definition, be 'better off' as, given the choice, they had preferred the bribes to free speech.

Both the point and the limitations of liberal utilitarianism, and its derivative, the 'corrected' market economy, can be illustrated by the perennially topical example of 'lame duck' industries. The Conservative Government after the 1970 General Election set out the case for not propping up such industries in the most unconvincing and repellent form possible. Whether intentionally or not, Ministers gave the impression that imposing discomforts on those managing or working in unprofitable industries was almost desirable in itself because it would 'wake people up to their responsibilities'. They seemed to take positive pleasure in the fact that life would be 'less cosy' or 'less comfortable' in activities for which state support was to have been withdrawn.

To an economic liberal these unpleasant effects are drawbacks, not advantages. The real argument against supporting loss-making activities, which cannot justify themselves on the basis of demonstrable spillover benefits, is the harm that such support inflicts on the material welfare and on the freedom of consumers. Protective devices for lame-duck industries force the rest of the population to purchase goods from a particular source, and to make sacrifices in their living standards for the sake of privileged producer groups. Moreover, if there is any mobility of labour or facilities for retraining and opportunities for jobs elsewhere, the gains to the protected group will diminish over time. Given that we are all consumers and anyone may find himself a lame duck, it is probable that a mutual understanding to abjure these make-work policies (as exists in Social Democratic Sweden), together with generous financial assistance for those making the readjustment, would be in the best interests of most people including the lame ducks themselves.

Although the above argument puts the emphasis on the loss of potential material welfare, the freedom aspect is not negligible. All taxation is a form of coercion – albeit of the negative kind – in that it prevents an individual spending a portion of his income in his own way. If taxation approached 100 per cent and people had to depend on supplies provided collectively, the degree of coercion would be very great indeed. But a lesser degree of taxation is a necessary evil if we are to enjoy the benefits of 'public goods'. The relationship between taxation and coercion is probably a non-linear one. A large amount of negative freedom can exist in a society where the average person pays 20 per cent of his income. A significant erosion has taken place if this proportion rises to 40 per cent, but we could still be talking about a largely free society. At 60 per cent rates it would not be hysterical to say that people's choices were being largely made for them by the state; and at an 80 per cent rate the society would be a free one only in name.* Subsidies out of taxation for aerospace products, high technology computers or shipyards for which there is no commercial demand are, other things being equal, a restriction on people's freedom to spend their money in their own way; and if it is superimposed on a state of affairs where tax rates tend to be in the 30–40 per cent bracket in any case, it has to be very carefully justified by some countervailing material benefit either to some deserving group or to the population as a whole.

Compensating the Victims

Reference to 'generous financial assistance' to the victims of change does expose an inherent ambiguity in liberal utilitarian philosophy, as soon as we come to ask 'How generous?' The liberal utilitarian aim is to provide as much as possible of what people say that they want in the light of correct information about 'opportunity costs'. But in real world changes some people will lose and others gain. To overcome this difficulty, the concept of a 'potential Pareto improvement' has

* The percentage should, strictly speaking, be net of cash benefits returned to citizens to spend as they like. For some discussion of actual magnitudes, see my chapter in *Taxation Policy* (Penguin, 1973).

been invented for a change in which the gains *could* be so redistributed so that no one is worse off and some people are better off.

Unfortunately the concept of a potential improvement is very ambiguous. Apart from the numerous scholastic paradoxes that fill the literature, the state of the law can make a very real difference to whether a change appears as a potential Pareto improvement or not. A good example is the construction of a new airport. It is quite possible that the maximum sum that the individuals of the area – if they could be properly mobilised – would be prepared to pay to the airport authority not to go ahead would be insufficient to stop construction on a profit-and-loss calculation. So it would look as if the gains exceed the losses and that the airport represented a potential Pareto improvement. The inhabitants could still be compensated by paying them what they would have been prepared to pay to stop the airport.

Now let us suppose that the airport authority is not entitled to go ahead without the consent of the inhabitants. A very much larger sum might be required; so large that the airport would not be built. It would then look as if the losses exceeded the gains and the airport did not represent a Pareto improvement at all. It is not fanciful to suppose that, even if all the inhabitants could be properly organised and could suppress their sense of outrage at the request, they would be only able and willing to pay, say £20m, to stop an airport being built, while if they themselves had the right of veto even £100m would not be enough to persuade them.[22]

Clearly, the wider the range of legal liability and the greater the number of changes which are allowed to take place only on payment of compensation that the victims consider adequate, the slower will be the pace of material change. The wealthier a society becomes the stronger the case for shifting the onus of compensatory payments on to those who want to make the change. For the harm caused by disturbing people's expectations and patterns of life must loom larger the higher the whole community is above the poverty line and the less urgent the overall growth of output.

There are, nevertheless, difficulties in going the whole hog with Mishan and giving full legal rights to the victims of change. There is the obvious incentive to lie or exaggerate. If I have a veto over the construction of an airport, I would be tempted to ask for far more than the sum of money genuinely required to compensate me for the loss I would suffer. But, even if absolute sincerity could be guaranteed, what would be the situation of an old lady who does not believe in the hereafter, who finds that her life would be shattered either if the airport were built or if she had to move? (Sound insulation would be no use, as she has to sit out in the fresh air). She might rationally regard the whole of the national income of the U.K. as insufficient compensation.

Transfer this example to a shipyard threatened with closure. Imagine a worker unwilling or too old to retrain, but whose pride would be hurt by being out of work and who would prefer to continue in his present job at his present wage, even if offered an immensely large capital sum as an alternative. The principle of compensation to victims of change has to be watered down in some common sense way to what the majority of those concerned could be reasonably expected to accept. It is often said half-jocularly by the officials and executives involved that it might be cheaper to pay each man now employed £1,000 per annum until retired, or a lump sum of £10,000, than to keep a particular mine, shipyard or aircraft project going. If this is really so, it would surely be better to pay compensation and close down the operation.

With large and obvious changes, such as the closing down of a shipyard or an aircraft firm, there will be strong support for actual rather than potential compensation to the victims of change. It is unfortunate that the likelihood of this demand will depend on the publicity generated and emotional appeal of the issue for the media; and one would prefer to see more systematic machinery which could be of help to many victims of smaller changes which do not achieve the same publicity, but which often cause far greater human hardship. Nevertheless, complete compensation of all victims of change would be of doubtful desirability. An anti-interventionist would always be able to argue that the choice of occupation is itself a gamble, and full compensation would involve subsidising high risk activities. His opponent could reply that the ordinary worker cannot choose but take the gamble that is associated with a choice of job, and therefore be confronted with a non-insurable risk. Complete compensation, even as an ideal solution, should apply only to those below a certain income or wealth level, and should not apply to shareholders who are knowingly engaged in providing 'risk capital'.

But, even qualified in this way, full compensation to all victims of change is never likely to be practicable. Differences in attitudes within the liberal utilitarian camp often depend on how far the economist in question insists that there should be an *actual*, as distinct from a *potential*, 'Pareto improvement'. One reason for the hostility to market forces of some unquestionably anti-paternalist economists arises from a preoccupation with income distribution so extreme that changes caused by market forces will not be accepted without cast-iron guarantees that the less well-off will be invariably and fully compensated for any adverse impact they might conceivably suffer. A more middle-of-the-road, and also more reasonable, position is to support market remedies, except where the adverse distributional implications are large and unambiguous and it is clear that compensation will not be paid. In other cases it would be best to favour measures likely to provide prosperity and freedom of choice, while keeping a watch on the overall distribution of income and urging appropriate fiscal changes if this seems to be moving in an undesired direction. One wonders what the position of the less well off would be if the cast iron guarantee approach had been used to block all the changes of the last 150 years.

A Socialist Market Economy

It is time to move on from considering the types of correction a market economy requires to the question, so far left aside, of whether a successful market economy needs to be based on *capitalism*. The converse is certainly untrue: capitalism need not involve a market economy. Not only can a system of private ownership of the means of production be highly uncompetitive, but it can even be a *command economy*. The decisions of individual capitalists can be subject to highly detailed instructions given at the discretion of the country's rulers (as in Nazi Germany) or by some central organisation of the capitalists themselves. Historically, however, capitalism has tended more often than not to be associated with a market economy and there are powerful forces impelling it in that direction.

The opposite of capitalism is, of course, socialism; it will be convenient to define it in the old-fashioned way as state ownership of the means of production, distribution and exchange. (The term 'social democracy' will be used in this essay for concepts of socialism which do not involve an insistence on state ownership.) There was a lengthy debate among academic economists in the interwar and wartime years on whether it was possible to have a socialist market economy. Echoes of that debate have continued in some of the writings on the economics of public enterprise. The conclusions seem to hang on whether a dynamic or static approach is used.

There is no reason why an economy consisting entirely of state-owned enterprises should not provide a known set of goods according to a known technology with known public taste, and according to the signals provided by the market place. Indeed, it could probably improve upon private enterprises by decreeing that managers must ignore any element of monopoly power and relate prices to marginal costs more closely than is likely in existing capitalist concerns. The problems of 'externalities' and spillover would, however, remain, and would have to be dealt with by some combination of price incentives and deterrents and administrative controls, as in capitalist economies.

Where, however, it is a matter of *discovering* what is the lowest cost method (rather than finding a position on a known cost curve) or of inventing products or services for meeting changing needs and tastes, the matter is wholly different. How is a limited amount of investment funds to be allocated among everybody with a bright idea? Or indeed, who are to be the managers and who the managed? It is no use applying a standard discounting technique to future costs and receipts and allocating funds to projects expecting the highest return. For both the receipts and the costs are precisely what are in dispute between the rival claimants.

If all investment funds went through one insurance company and were lent to firms consisting entirely of salaried managers with no personal stake in their concerns, the same problems would arise in a capitalist society. But, fortunately, this is not yet the case. Not only are the lending decisions made by different institutions, but the existence of personal private capital allows people to try out their own pet ideas, either with their own funds, or by using their assets as security for further loans. Even when it comes to reinvestment by existing firms, each management can try to prove the validity of its own ideas, however unorthodox, about the returns from alternative ventures, knowing that it is accountable to its own shareholders and can be thrown out by a takeover bid. Such individual hunches would be more difficult to justify to a National Investment Board, acting as trustee for all the nation's investment funds.

A socialist market economy is still better from the point of view of consumer satisfaction than a socialist command economy, even though it is probably less imaginative than a capitalist one in developing new techniques, products and services. This explains why the economic reforms designed to bring in the profit motive and relate prices more clearly to meaningful costs have led to improvements in Eastern Europe, but why a generally dowdy impression remains and why there is such a great desire to borrow Western techniques.

The nationalised industries in the West, and above all in the U.K., have suffered from their symbolic role in left–right politics. This has led to a campaign of ridicule and denigration on the one side and partisan point-scoring on the other. At the time of writing left-wing politicians and academics are fond of pointing to a large book by R. W. S. Pryke,[23] which claims to have shown that, not only have the U.K. nationalised concerns performed better than private manufacturing industry, but that this is the direct result of nationalisation. Predictably this provoked a rebuttal by George and Priscilla Polanyi of the Institute of Economic Affairs.[24] The argument was partly on the suitability of output per man hour as an indicator of performance, and on whether Mr Pryke had made adequate allowance for the effects of the very much larger input of new capital per head into the state sector.

Also at issue were the effects of the inclusion of the fast growing electricity and airways industries in the state sector. These industries have shown rapid productivity gains relative to manufacturing industry in most countries, irrespective of ownership. It was in the end, difficult to believe that anything had been 'proved' by either side.

The one point that did emerge and that was common to both parties was that there had been a large *relative* improvement in the performance of the state sector between the decades 1948–58 and 1958–68. This was related to two phenomena: (a) the loss of effective monopoly power as other sources of energy and transport emerged to compete with state undertakings, and (b) the adoption of a much more commercial approach to the nationalised industries, in which they were given target rates of return, pressed to relate prices more closely to marginal costs and to use modern techniques of investment appraisal, and, above all, given specific subsidies for any loss-making services that they were expected to run.

Even if one accepts that the nationalised industries are capable of putting up a comparable performance to private business in established industries, this tells us nothing whatsoever about how capital would be allocated between new and untried industries and ventures (and individuals wanting to run them) in a completely state-run economy. It is no accident that this side of the Iron Curtain the industries that tend to be state-run are either old established basic ones, such as the railways, buses or coal, or state-subsidised, prestige technology activities such as aerospace and atomic energy. On the other hand, where change is rapid, but not of a broadly predictable kind, and personal contact with consumers or dispersed local knowledge important – such as the retail trade, travel agencies or the profitable end of electronics – private ownership tends to prevail. In the rare cases where state concerns thrive in such trades, it is under the stimulus of strong competition with privately owned rivals.

In sectors which fall behind the two extremes (notably posts and telecommunications), the performance of state monopolies seems, to put it mildly, undistinguished. Some of the most controversial aspects concern the quality of service given to the customer, which is not easily captured by productivity indices. The personal incentive to try out new ideas and respond flexibly to changing consumer demands is normally less in a state enterprise trying to ape capitalist practice than in the genuine article. Not only is there less to gain from success, but there is less to lose from failure. (Salaried managers in large bureaucratic companies suffer from similar drawbacks, but to a smaller degree.) As Patrick Hutber observed in relation to the Post Office Corporation's attempts in 1970–71 to imitate what it thought was correct commercial behaviour, 'You don't make a bear into a tiger by painting stripes upon its back.'[25]

The stock example, constantly quoted against such generalisations, is the more adventurous spirit shown by the I.R.I. state-holding group in Italy. This has been achieved by removing many of the political constraints which, in a country like the U.K., govern public enterprise. The heads of the Italian organisation are given a degree of power without responsibility, which we should rightly hesitate to let such men have. The situation was made tolerable by the fact that state concerns had, up to the beginning of the 1970s, complete monopoly in very few fields and were usually subject to private competition, especially from imports. Should this situation change, as it shows signs of doing, the character of the Italian state sector would be likely to undergo a corresponding transformation. There have, in fact, been signs in several countries of a new role for public ownership and participation – that of saving from liquidation private concerns such as Rolls Royce that have failed the test of the market, and which can offer no favourable spillovers to justify their subsidisation. This kind of safety net gave the worst of both capitalist and socialist worlds; yet it was welcomed by the less thinking socialists on the grounds that it extended the state sector and showed that 'private enterprise does not work'.

Meanwhile the improvements in the main British nationalised industries have been threatened by a Conservative Government which has been using them as a political instrument in a way that the more crudely interventionist Labour Ministers in the previous Cabinet would have dearly loved, but had been prevented from doing by the Treasury. Examples included arm-twisting to make the nationalised industries conform to the C.B.I. price restraint pledge of 1971, when, unlike private industry, they had not been allowed to rebuild their profit margins and were remote from fulfilling their financial objectives. This was followed by pressure to invest in unprofitable directions as part of the Government's reflationary drive. These and many other weaknesses have been pointed out by Christopher Foster in what is much the most perceptive study of the subject available.[26] Foster seems, however, to regard all these misfortunes as being due to remediable errors of particular Governments, and puts forward excellent proposals for clarifying objectives and returning to the previous emphasis on profitability. Yet what shines out from his own account is that their nationalised status put these undertakings into the political area irrespective of what White Papers are written by Whitehall economists; and sooner or later any Government is going to manipulate them – not to achieve some subtle adjustment between private and social costs or returns, but for short-run political objectives.

Political Freedom

So far this exposition has concentrated on the connection between the capitalist market economy and economic freedom and welfare. But many of its most forceful advocates have prized it at least as much as a precondition for political freedom. The argument is well known. In a capitalist society means are available to advocate socialism (or pacificism or numerous other heresies). Ideas in the forms of books, newspaper articles, plays, films, as well as in more subtle and less obvious forms are sold on the open market; and *the more the profit motive operates* the less a publisher will be influenced by his personal attitudes to the views expressed.

It would be absurd to suggest that there are no obstacles to be faced, especially for someone who wishes to advocate non-trendy heresies (such as opposition to the Race Relations Act) or a cause which has little demagogic appeal but is also outside the gentleman's agreement permitted partisan dispute (such as devaluation in 1964/67). Nevertheless, the thing can be done. In a 100 per cent socialist economy, the problem of finding an outlet becomes much more difficult. Heads of state publishing enterprises could be told to publish anything that will sell. But this is a very ambiguous instruction, and the fact that publishers are state employees must have some influence; and it is not open to anyone who disagrees with their verdict to set up on his own or find a private patron. The argument is explained and developed at length in Friedman's *Capitalism and Freedom*.

One of Friedman's most telling examples is of the victims of McCarthyite persecution, who found refuge in the private sector. The relevant point here is that political freedom depends on the existence of a large capitalist sector – a 'socialist market economy' will not do. A syndicalist society might be one better than a purely socialist one – the smaller the units in which 'workers' control' reigns the better from this point of view. But it is all too easy to imagine the syndicates exercising a common censorship. The refusal of the printers in a London evening newspaper to print an 'anti-union' cartoon was an ominous portent, and attempts have been made by members of the N.U.J. chapels to bar opportunities to 'right wing' journalists.

These political considerations point to the desirability of not only of a 'private sector' with dispersed or institutional shareholders, but of some personal fortunes as well. Indeed, freedom of expression is probably stronger if the egalitarian 'correction' of the market distribution of wealth is not pushed too far. For although many controversial books and plays can be and are financed by publishers with institutional shareholders (who are small savers at one remove), the existence of wealthy patrons willing to go against the corporate philosophy (or artistic fashion) of the day is an important additional safeguard. (It made possible, for example, the launching of *Private Eye*.)

This political argument can, however, easily be pushed too far, or in the wrong direction. It does not rule out the existence of a substantial state sector, nor give much guidance on how large it can safely be; nor does it help on a great many of the issues of economic policy which come up every day in a mixed company. Moreover, it can be persuasively argued that freedom of expression (and choice of types of employment, and many other things, too) will be strengthened if there are not merely a multiplicity of firms within the capitalist sector, but a multiplicity of forms of ownership – large private corporations, state-owned enterprises, one-man firms, producer and consumer co-operatives, and so on. This is particularly so where real or alleged technical factors limit the number of outlets, as in television. While a state broadcasting monopoly would be a monstrosity (one has only to recall how Churchill was prevented from speaking on the B.B.C. before the Second World War), freedom of expression is almost certainly greater as a result of the rivalry between the B.B.C. and the independent channels, than it would be if competition were confined to two or three private networks.

Moreover, the value of either private enterprise, or of a multiplicity of forms of ownership, for free expression depends on competition – not on perfect competition, but on the absence of formal or informal restrictive agreements. Friedman himself points to the Hollywood boycott of 'subversive' writers in the 1950s, which was only possible because of a collusive agreement among film-makers regulating who could be employed.

Forms of Economic Liberalism

The question of the role of capitalism and state enterprise has brought to light several different traditions within the liberal utilitarian approach to economics. There is the static emphasis on supplying a given set of goods and services by means of known technology. From this point of view a competitive market economy will bring about an optimum solution, subject to well-known exceptions, which in turn have well-known remedies which can be found in standard texts. If one wishes to emphasise the general rule, one is a 'market economist'; if one wishes to emphasise the exceptions and remedies one can be described as a 'liberal planner' of sorts. The zebra analogy is useful. The ideal can be regarded as a market economy with numerous corrective interventions, or a regulated economy making a great deal of use of prices and market forces.

Another type of approach is more dynamic. It puts the emphasis on the role of market forces in stimulating new tastes and new methods of meeting both old and existing tastes. The danger of this approach is that it can be vulgarised into an abrasive outlook which takes positive delight in 'shaking people up'. This is, however, a distortion. There is nothing in the logic of the dynamic case for a market economy which causes one to regard a quiet sleepy country with a low measured growth of G.N.P. as inferior to a thrusting industrial state. All that is implied is that there must be freedom in both countries to innovate or propagandise. If, in the first country, people are unresponsive to sales appeals (other than quietist or ascetic gospels) and do not take to new technology, then there is no warrant for condemning that country and putting it lower in some absurd league table.

The conclusion needs, however, to be carefully stated. A country may have rising expectations and people may be prepared to change their habits to meet them; but growth may be held down because the country may have the misfortune to have a deficient supply of entrepreneurial talent (due perhaps to the educational system), or that talent may be discouraged by misguided taxation policies, or irrational official devotion to an arbitrary exchange rate or to the maintenance of a reserve currency role leading to stop–go demand management policies or for numerous other reasons. This was the element of truth in the 'growthmanship' of the 1960s; but it was hopelessly confused by many of its supporters and its opponents with the illiberal value judgement that amenity should be sacrificed without limit for the sake of industrial production.

On the basis of what has been said so far it is possible to subdivide economic liberals on left–right lines (see Table 1).

A whole-hog left-wing economic liberal believes in what was earlier termed a corrected market economy, with special emphasis on the corrections. He has no special interest in the pattern of ownership, but puts great emphasis on redistribution via taxation and social service payments. This will do almost as well as a description of a certain kind of Social

TABLE 1

Left Wing Economic Liberals	*Right Wing Economic Liberals*
Belief in strongly redistributive taxes and benefits	Acceptance of income and property distribution that emerges from the market
No special stress on ownership	Strong insistence on private enterprise
Sensitivity to differences between private and social costs and great readiness to intervene to eliminate them	Readiness to intervene where large, clear and proven discrepancies between private and social costs, but benefit of doubt to non-interference
Onus on those responsible for changes to compensate victims	Change desirable if losers cannot 'bribe' those responsible to desist

Democrat of which Professor Schiller was an obvious example – although it will not unfortunately quite do as a description of even the 'Gaitskellite' wing of the British Labour Party. The right wing economic liberal, on the other hand, has clear affinities with certain strands of Conservative (although not Tory) thought.

The above remarks apply to those who come down consistently on one or other side of the above table. But there is no necessary relation between left- and right-wing attitudes in the different subdivisions. One can, for instance, be highly sensitive to environmental damage and not in the least willing to give the benefit of the doubt to the uncorrected market, yet be an out-and-out inegalitarian. There is probably, however some modest empirical correlation between left- and right-wing attitudes here as in other areas.

3. A Fresh Approach

Enough has been said to demonstrate the many possible conflicts and unresolved issues within the camp of those whom I have termed liberal utilitarians and who espouse the 'corrected market economy'. There is, nevertheless, a very good reason for grouping together the common element in the thinking of many people who almost certainly vote in different ways and have different emotional and group loyalties. The link is the belief that the individual should normally be regarded as the best judge of his own interests.

Liberal utilitarians agree that the profit motive *can* promote the general welfare, however much they may disagree on the likelihood of this happening in particular instances. Those who have pondered the problems of the corrected market economy will also realise that, however many interventions and corrections are necessary, there is no need for politicians, civil servants and their expert advisers to attempt entrepreneurial judgements: there is enough on the government agenda without this unnecessary item. A liberal utilitarian who has thought about economic problems is also likely to be highly suspicious of notions such as the superiority of heavy industry over light, goods over services and exports over imports. He will dislike arbitrary physical targets such as 300,000 or 400,000 homes per annum, although he may occasionally accept them – after much critical scrutiny – as a third or fourth best. He will also feel ill at ease with generalised condemnations of the 'consumer society' as *per se* evil.

Moreover, liberal utilitarianism is the one element in a liberal philosophy that can provide guidance, however fuzzy and uncertain, to an applied economist concerned with specific issues. Hundreds of new problems arise every year – whether a bridge or urban motorways should be built and, if so, where; whether V.A.T. should have been introduced, and so on. If liberal utilitarianism is ruled out or – what comes to the same thing – the possibility of 'welfare economics' is denied *a priori*, as is done by some conservative liberals, then the applied economist will be left either to follow some illiberal form of utilitarianism or to adopt the particular variety of paternalist judgement that he imagines his superiors to have. If, alternatively, the 'expert' is denied status altogether, then we deliberately leave unused human knowledge, both of facts and of logical procedures, in favour of pressure group politics, Ministerial infighting, un-informed hunches and all the rest.

Delightful though this last prospect is to many political writers, these traditional political processes do not satisfy the politicians themselves, and the expert is likely to be sum-moned back after all. But there is a danger that the expert in question will then be the engineer, or business efficiency pundit, or a fanatic for one kind of process or goal at the expense of all others. At least the economist, even if he is not consciously a liberal utilitarian, is concerned to reconcile the different priorities of different human beings. He should know that the concept of efficiency has little meaning apart from human preferences (this is elaborated in Appendix I); and if he is too bemused by his statistical tool kit to be aware of this, it will emerge when he comes to evaluate his results, and when others in his profession come to criticise them.

Although liberal utilitarianism therefore provides an in-dispensable ingredient in the economic philosophy of those who place a high value on freedom, it is on its own inade-quate. It cannot provide much in the way of a simple guide to the non-technician on how he should approach economic problems, or even to the technician when he needs to make assumptions outside the particular problem on which he is working. If the reader glances ahead to the case study of *Conservatism and the Market Economy*, he will find that a great deal of government intervention can be justified with-out paternalistic judgements, either on 'second best grounds' or sometimes even on 'first best grounds' (to the extent that this distinction can really be made).

If one sticks to the liberal utilitarian approach, every issue must be examined separately, the non-economist will be inclined to throw his hand in, and there will be no check on the total effects of innumerable policies decided separately. Moreover, as we have seen, there is ample scope for personal judgements about what is important and what makes things tick. On many problems one could say with fair confidence: 'You tell me the expert and I will tell you his conclusions.' Nor could the relevant judgements be 'fed in' by politicians or public opinion. One has to be heavily involved in the subject to know where the judgements come in, or how to frame them. It is essential to examine other approaches of a less technocratic appeal.

Rules versus Discretion

By far the most distinguished recent attempt to restate the principles of liberalism, as applied to economic affairs without resort to the traditional utilitarian calculus, has been that of F. A. Hayek's, *The Constitution of Liberty*. The reception of this book was an intellectual disgrace. Most of the popular reviews, and even some of the 'learned' ones, pilloried it, either by holding out certain policy conclusions for amazed inspection, or by saying that it went against the trend of the times. There were a few eulogies from those who thought it a good stick with which to beat socialists and planners, but much too little serious analysis – perhaps because it cut across too many academic demarcation lines.

The book came out in 1960 on the eve of a decade of 'pragmatism', when, under Kennedy in the U.S. and both Macmillan and Wilson in the U.K., general principles were at a discount, and the fashion was for 'common sense' intervention by bodies such as I.R.C. or N.E.D.C., which made a virtue of their freedom from all guiding principles, and when all the emphasis was on face-to-face contacts which deliberately blurred the extent to which government coercion was used. After a decade of this sort of pragmatism, the hostile reviews read very badly, even by the narrow criteria of their authors.

Hayek starts with his reasons for valuing freedom, which he defines as the absence of coercion. There must, of course, be some coercion in any state, if only to prevent one man's freedom from clashing with that of another. The practical question is how to minimise coercion and establish as much freedom as possible.

The best guarantee is in his view, not the market economy as such, but 'the rule of law', of which he believes the former to be a corollary. By the 'rule of law' Hayek does not mean any law which has been constitutionally enacted, but government by general, abstract, impartial rules with the minimum of administrative discretion in their enforcement. In other words, government policy should as much as possible take the form of general rules, laid down in advance. Where intervention is necessary, it should, where possible, take the negative form of prohibitions, forbidding certain courses of conduct, but leaving people free to choose from all the variety of permitted actions. (The distinction is, however, not as clear-cut as it may seem, or was explained on p. 48.) Even if positive injunctions are unavoidable, they should be laid down in advance with the minimum of administrative discretion in their application.

There is no hard and fast dividing line between general rules and discretionary power. The most watertight statute needs some judicial interpretation, while the most discretionary acts of Ministers and officials take place against some background of law, convention and precedent. The best practical test is not by any administrative or legal classification, but that of predictability. If, by examining the facts of his own case and the known rules, laws and precedents, the citizen can predict what he will be permitted to do, general rules apply. If a great deal 'hangs in the air' because of uncertainty about how a Minister or official or judge will behave – or if his own bargaining skill is crucial – the regime is one of administrative discretion.

The whole concept of judicial discretion or leaving a great deal open to the 'good sense of the jury' conflicts with Hayek's idea of the rule of law. If the definition of pornography or obscenity (if such offences do have to exist) is wide open and depends entirely on public feeling as interpreted by a particular judge or jury, the whole notion of predictable rules goes by the board. It may be that in this, and other areas, the key terms must inevitably be vague and changeable in interpretation; but at least the interpretation should change slowly over time, and there should be a high degree of certainty over whether any particular action will or will not be found permissible.

Of course, if laws tend to produce a net balance of undesirable effects, they should be changed. But it is essential to the whole idea that they cannot be changed at a moment's notice whenever a particular effect displeases some ruler or some temporary majority. The more fundamental the laws, the more difficult they should be to change; and this implies the existence of some constitution, whether written as in the U.S.A., or 'virtual' as we fondly like to imagine exists in this country.

Taken as an analysis of what is normally meant by 'law' in legal and informed lay discourse, Hayek's conception is probably one-sided. In an 'Oxford philosophy' type analysis, *The Concept of Law*,[27] Professor H. L. A. Hart points out that in any large group it is simply not possible to operate by means of particular directions given to each individual, and therefore 'general rules, standards and principles must be the main instrument of social control.' But this similarity to Hayek's position is deceptive; for by resting his case on such widespread features of all societies, Hart clearly has something much broader in mind. He clarifies the issue later on when he states that all systems compromise between two social needs:

> ...the need for certain rules which can, over great areas of conduct, safely be applied by private individuals to themselves without fresh official guidance or weighing up of social issues, and the need to leave open, for later settlement by an informed official choice, issues which can only be properly appreciated and settled when they arise in a concrete case.

Hayek's concept of 'the rule of law' is basically a judgement that maximum emphasis should be on the first aspect and minimum on the second (although it cannot be eliminated altogether). Hart, on the other hand, rejects even the ideal of a rule whose application to a particular case would always be clear in advance, and never leave open a choice at the point of application. The reason he gives is that 'we are men,

not gods'. Ignorance of future acts and the 'relative indeter-
minacy of aim' of the legislator makes such legal determinacy
undesirable as well as impossible. Hayek would use the very
same argument to reach the opposite conclusion. Because
judges or officials are not gods, they cannot foresee the results
of particular acts of discretion, and would do better, he
believes, to stick to the rules which embody the collective
experience of generations of human beings.

The differences between the two conceptions are brought
out very clearly by one of Hart's examples: the case of a
body set up to regulate an industry according to very general
standards, with discretionary power to fix 'fair rates', perhaps
after an inquiry into the facts and arguments. In some cases
there would be 'no possibility of treating the questions raised
by the various cases as if there were one uniquely correct
answer to be found, as distinct from an answer which is a
reasonable compromise between many conflicting interests.'
Needless to say, all this would be worse than anathema to
Hayek; but there is no reason to dispute with Hart that the
system of regulation he mentions would be a normal Western
legal process. It would, therefore, be better to describe
Hayek's doctrine as a preference for *impersonal general rules*;
the expression 'rule of law' may disguise the very radical
nature of what is a goal or proposal and not a description of
what the major legal systems of the West aim to do and to
exclude. The expression 'rule of law' will, however, occasionally be used in quotation marks in the following pages
for Hayek's concept, when the meaning is clear from the
context.

Much more interesting than whether they are a correct
interpretation of accepted legal principles is the question:
how good a guarantee of freedom are impersonal general
rules laid down in advance in practice likely to be? A pre-
liminary question is: how 'general' do general rules have to
be? It is, of course, necessary to single out categories: traffic
laws must deal with motorists, sales taxes have to make
traders liable, and so on. But can general rules discriminate
between industries and occupations? General rules must be
impersonal; but by framing one's definitions carefully, a
supposedly general law can pick out for specially severe treat-

ment any group or even a single individual. Clearly some further constraint is required.

Hayek is dissatisfied with Mill's proposal that the law should not interfere with purely self-regarding activities, on the grounds that almost all human activities affect others. But, if we are prepared to widen 'self-regarding' to include the activities of 'mutually consenting adults' but not necessarily to cover 'public flaunting', and are prepared to disregard remote and improbable effects, we do have a worthwhile distinction, even though one that yields clear cut results in too limited a number of areas to answer all relevant questions. (For example, my travelling abroad or buying an Italian coat has all sorts of effects on others, if only through its effects on the foreign exchange market.)

Hayek's own proposal is that a general rule should be acceptable to a majority of both those whom it harms and those whom it benefits. Yet, as J. W. N. Watkins points out, in much the most perceptive criticism of *The Constitution of Liberty* that I have read, this qualification is much too strong, as it gives a veto to any minority group in any circumstances.[28] The question whether a law is, or can be, modified so as to be acceptable to both sides is always worth asking. Compulsory third party insurance might be acceptable on these grounds; apartheid would not be. But we could hardly expect a law against banditry (or plain murder!) to be equally acceptable to the Mafia and the rest of the Sicilian population. Or – to take one of Hayek's own illustrations – while a case can be made against policies such as steeply progressive taxation, the mere opposition of the rich to measures from which they would suffer is hardly a convincing argument against them.

More promising is the suggestion that a rule should be acceptable to someone who has not the slightest idea in advance on which side of the distinction he himself will fall.[29] This will often call for a large imaginative effort; but at least it supplies a criterion of disinterestedness. Yet it still leaves open some relevant questions.

In particular, how much 'disinterested' support does a rule require? If it is a bare majority, people would still be able to impose their tastes on others; and there would be no bar to military or industrial conscription and countless other horrors (except for the preference for negative rules – and that would not prevent Prohibition). If, on the other hand, unanimity is required, any obstinate individual would be given a veto on any decision. Moreover, the hypothesis of ignorance of how one might be affected works only for some questions. With sufficient goodwill and imaginative power a person ought to be able to imagine himself ignorant of how he would be affected by proposed laws on property inheritance. He could not simulate such ignorance if the question were one of stricter laws against fast driving. For he would have to imagine his trade-off between safety and speed if his temperament were different to what it is; and to perform the exercise he would have to imagine himself a different person. Further difficulties will be mentioned when we come to discuss 'optimal inequality'.

Consideration of the various suggestions in the field makes one suspect that the quest for a foolproof definition of 'impersonal general rules' is unlikely to succeed. It is, nevertheless, a recognisable ideal. Indeed, the basic concepts of mathematics and formal logic are far from easy to define, let alone those of political and social studies; but this does not mean they are useless. We know that many of the items of the criminal code are as close to impersonal general rules as we can hope to get; we know that the Star Chamber and the Press Gang are at the other extreme. We know, too, if we are frank, that a piece of legislation which defines an undesirable monopoly or restrictive practice – even if only in *prima facie* terms – comes closer to the ideal than one which leaves everything to the discretion of the Minister and his advisers.

Hayek sometimes seems to imply that the connection between impersonal general rules and personal freedom is a necessary one. This makes the whole argument hang on an interlocking set of definitions and does less than justice to his own case. It is better to argue that the connection is a causal one, that there is, in practice, likely to be more personal freedom if maximum use is made of impersonal general rules with the minimum of administrative discretion. This is a more plausible and fruitful line of approach.

In Hayek's own words, 'it is because the lawgiver does not

know the particular cases to which his rules apply, and it is because the judge who applies them has no choice in drawing the conclusions that follow from the existing body of rules and the particular facts of the case, it can be said that "laws not men rule".'[30] If those framing the law do not know to whom it might apply and cannot either curtail it or extend it for the benefit of specific individuals, including themselves, they are much less likely to be of an oppressive kind. But the price we must pay for this benefit is that such general rules 'always be applied irrespective of whether or not the consequences in a particular instance seem desirable'.[31]

A system of general and impersonal rules is hardly a sufficient condition for a free society. For many policies clearly involving a high degree of coercion can be imposed in a bigoted society. Examples extend well beyond the Scottish sabbath conceded by Hayek. A ban on all foreign travel or a £50 travel allowance might be justified by general, impersonal rules, and the exceptions such as business or official travel stated quite impersonally. As we have seen, it is very difficult to narrow down the concept of general rules to avoid such cases.

General rules, laid down in advance, should, nevertheless, be supported as one *influence* in favour of personal freedom, even though they are not by themselves enough. There is no one magic recipe for minimising coercion and we should be foolish to abandon the ideal of impersonal rules simply because it cannot *guarantee* the desired result in all cases.

General impersonal rules can be defended not only as a support for personal freedom, but also from a distrust of the other results of discretionary actions. Less bad results, even from the point of view of those initiating a policy, may come from following some standard procedure than by leaving it to particular individuals to issue arbitrary instructions on the basis of their own hunches, prejudices or bargaining skill. As David Hume, who is one of the main sources of Hayek's thought on this subject, observed:

All general laws are attended with inconveniences when applied to particular cases; and it requires great penetration and experience both to perceive that these inconveniences are fewer than those which result from full discretionary powers in every magistrate, and also discern what general laws are, upon the whole, attended with fewest inconveniences.[32]

In our own day it can be argued that there are 'fewer inconveniences' in laying down in advance a permissible range for the growth of the money supply and the 'full employment' budget deficit as against discretionary variation by the monetary authorities. It is also an argument for floating – or genuinely fixed – exchange rates and against the Bretton Woods system. The results of discretionary fiscal, monetary and exchange rate policies have certainly not been so brilliant that one can dismiss this argument out of hand.[33]

What are the specific applications to the general run of domestic economic policy? The principle of generality does not rule out a vast amount of Government intervention. It would not present any bar to outright prohibition of nightwork for children, nor (unfortunately) to any bar on the consumption of candyfloss. Virtually all actions by means of the price mechanism, such as regional employment premia, investment grants, taxes and subsidies on commodities, and so on, can be stated in highly general and impersonal form; and the degree of official discretion could be made very limited indeed, if we had a government that really believed in the 'rule of law'. Even a complete ban on fresh industrial development in the Midlands or South East, with exceptions for small extensions up to a specific size, would be compatible with this ideal. What it would not permit is the practice of granting development permission by Government officials examining each case on its merits.

There is nothing in the concept of the 'rule of law' to prevent the state from supplying any services it thinks fit, or even from running industries. Professor Hayek's sole proviso is that the state must not have a monopoly in any of these things. Even that stipulation is a borderline case. For a law such as 'No one except the Electricity Generating Board should generate electricity' only fails to be a general impersonal rule if the Generating Board is regarded as a specific person or persons! (Of course many of Hayek's policy views are derived directly from his dislike of coercion and his economic studies rather than via the 'rule of law', and are none the worse for that.)

General non-discretionary rules are mainly applicable to relations *between* individuals and organisations. Specific instructions and discretionary action must play a large role *within* any organisation, whether it is a private company, an army, a hospital or a Government Department, and even in the state sector as a whole. General rules can have some role within organisations; but the main function of general rules is to regulate the relationship of *different* organisations that have no common structure. There is such a command structure within the state sector, vague, loose, and disturbed by feuding barons though it is. This suggests that if the rule of law is to have any flesh and blood meaning, the size of the state sector must be limited. No magic percentage can be given and the detailed composition of the state sector (for example, whether it constitutes a small part of many industries or the whole of a few) matters as well as the percentage of the economy covered.

Because Hayek as an individual has regarded the main threat to liberty as coming from the Left, and because he first came into popular prominence with the *Road to Serfdom*[34] which warned against the totalitarian implications of much fashionable wartime thinking about 'reconstructing society', his emphasis on the 'rule of law' has been too easily dismissed as an attempt to erect one further obstacle to a reforming government. While it is true that 'discretionary intervention' was regarded as the ark of the Socialist covenant by a few misguided Ministers in the 1964–70 Labour Administration, some of the greatest opposition to proceeding by general rules emanates from the conventional establishment. Conservative Ministers, central bankers, senior officials and business organisations loathe the idea of operating according to fixed criteria laid down in advance. 'Flexibility' and 'not being bound in advance' is the theme song of the British practical man, when given his way.

The City of London is a particularly bad example, where nods, winks and arm-twisting have long been preferred to known rules of behaviour. The Bank of England has traditionally preferred to operate by vague requests backed by vague sanctions, rather than by publishing definite rules. The 'new monetary policy' adopted in 1971, providing for a common reserve rule and the abolition of advance ceilings was a step forward, after a rearguard action lasting many years. But even the new arrangements were hedged around with numerous discretionary exceptions and additions (e.g. to prevent excessive competition with building societies); and the Bank was still determined to make admissions to the privileged state of 'merchant banker' depend on discretionary and undisclosed judgements by the Governor and his advisers on no known criteria, and to regulate mergers and new entry among the wider banking community in a similar spirit. It is an explanation, but not an excuse to say that those concerned have transferred methods and procedures which might be appropriate for a private club to the sphere of public policy.

Numerous examples are given in Chapter 4 of the preferences of Conservative Ministers for discretionary intervention rather than fixed rules. They clearly regarded arm-twisting by politicians and officials as a lesser evil than legally enforceable and known restraints – indeed, their main argument against Labour's income policies was that they were 'too rigid'. A spectacular example of the contempt of many right wing governments for known rules, generally enforceable, is the way in which the Nixon Republican Adminstration went round the world in 1971, forcing countries to accept 'voluntary quotas' whose size was determined by the balance of threats, counter-threats and bribes. A believer in the 'rule of law' may dislike any import restrictions; but if there have to be any, it is better that they should take the form of tariffs, which present the same fixed obstacle to everyone, rather than quotas which inevitably discriminate on an arbitrary basis. If there have to be quotas, it is at least better that they should be statutory and known in advance than take the voluntary form, which depends on the sum product of numerous individual attempts at coercion. Nor is it likely that once a Government behaves in this way, it will confine such behaviour to 'foreigners'.

A British example was the C.B.I. voluntary undertaking

of July 1971 that 200 of the largest firms would limit their price increases to 5 per cent or less in the coming 12 months and report to the C.B.I. Director-General, Mr Campbell Adamson, if for any reason they found themselves unable to comply. This undertaking was supposed to be a *quid pro quo* in return for the Government's reflationary measures – although it is in fact extremely doubtful if the C.B.I. undertaking had much effect on the size of the subsequent fiscal package.

The whole undertaking was, of course, nominally a voluntary one. But it was obvious that considerable moral pressure was being put by the C.B.I. on doubters to sign. Any who did not, risked incurring Government displeasure; thus the C.B.I. was transforming itself into an organ of Government policy – partly in the hope that the T.U.C. might undergo the same transformation. If this does not turn out to be a system of private law, it will not have been for want of trying on the C.B.I.'s and Government's part. The C.B.I.'s original defence – that the ceiling was its own idea and not the Government's – missed the whole point of the criticism. A system of discretionary arm-twisting by a private body goes against the principle of impersonal general rules applicable to all, whoever suggested the idea. Moreover, as was quite predictable at the time, it did not take long for the Conservative Government to adopt the concept as part of its own policy; and within a year the C.B.I. was being pressurised by Ministers to renew the price undertaking, which it had then become much more reluctant to do. Thus do 'practical businessmen' embark like lemmings on their own destruction.

One can see how this situation arose. The first preference of a Conservative Government and of industrialists is for non-intervention. But if this is, or appears to be, impracticable, they tend to think that the next best thing is that 'industry should plan itself.' But so far from being a second best, it is the worst course of all. For organisations like the C.B.I. are subject neither to the discipline of the market place nor to political control; and 'industrial self government' is, in the literal sense, irresponsible. If a price ceiling is necessary in an emergency it should be introduced by an elected

Government by means of an Act of Parliament, which states the forbidden courses of action clearly.

Hayek's view is more extreme. It is that the principle of general rules excludes altogether all control over prices and wages. The issue of wage controls is best postponed until we come in the next chapter to the thorny issue of union monopoly power. For the moment we can discuss the issue in terms of prices. Hayek's basic case is that any attempt by the authorities to fix prices would create shortages. For if the prevailing market price is just sufficient to bring supply and demand into line, then the imposition of a different, and presumably lower, price would increase demand, and reduce supply. The resulting shortages would involve allocations of goods by administrative discretion; and, even if supplying firms made the allocation, they would in fact be exercising state powers that had been delegated to them. One need not waste time drawing up allocation schemes which might be general and impersonal, and not involve administrative discretion. The rationing of a few basic consumer goods in wartime cannot be compared to continuous allocation of a wide variety of goods at all stages of a peacetime economy; and whatever casuistry one wished to employ, a society in which people and firms were told how much they could have of different commodities would cease to be a free one.

The more important question is the soundness of the economic inference. Does price control inevitably involve allocation? The reader will recall our discussion of different kinds of market on pp. 65–8. Where prices normally vary from day to day in a market-clearing way, Hayek is plainly right. As far as the consumer is concerned, this applies mainly to non-processed foodstuffs, above all fruit and vegetables. Serious price control would rapidly lead to shortages, black market and under-the-counter dealings. It is no accident that this is the area in which recent attempts at price invigilation, whether in the U.K. in the mid 1960s, or the U.S. in 1971, were largely a charade, designed to maintain support for the system in other sectors.

On the other hand, in a large part of manufacturing industry and services, prices are not adjusted to demand in the short term and variations in demand are met by adjustments in output. Short term costs tend to be either constant or to fall with the volume of output (given the cost accountant's convention in allocating overheads). In this situation most businesses would probably absorb in their gross profit margins the effects of a moderate degree of price control. This would be all the easier as price controls have come back into fashion in periods when there is considerable surplus capacity, but when governments would otherwise be afraid of expanding demand for fear of stimulating inflation.

Obviously one must look beyond the short term. The hope of governments of all political persuasions is that price controls will be reflected back in lower wage increases, because employers will then stand up more firmly to union claims and/or such claims will themselves become more moderate. But to put it mildly, this passing back is unlikely to be 100 per cent effective, if only because of the monetary and fiscal stimulation which tends to accompany such policies.

In some industries the return on capital is likely to be less than it would otherwise be if the controls are kept on for any length of time and do more than permit what businessmen would in any case want to charge. If this is true on average, the share of investment in the national income will fall and that of consumption rise. The Government could try to counteract this by higher personal taxes, combined with lower interest rates; but how successful this would be is doubtful* and the process would be very unpopular politically.

In all probability the controls will work differentially and the squeeze on the rate of return be greater in some industries than in others. These industries are likely to underinvest in relation to the demand for their production. But by this time almost anything might have happened: the price controllers (if they are still there) might find some excuse for changing the rules to adjust price relativities to choke off demand, the gap might be filled by imports, and, if the exchange rate is allowed to move to the equilibrium level, this will lead to a change in the composition of exports and imports of a freakish

---

* Many companies would not regard any feasible reduction in the cost or availability of outside finance as a sufficient substitute for their own reduced cash flow.

and inefficient kind. (If the exchange rate is wrong, the results will be still worse.) Another possibility is the Hayekian spectre of allocation – especially likely if the exchange rate is not adjusted appropriately.

The above sketch can provide no more than a few very rough pointers to the consequences of price control in conditions of surplus capacity and cost inflation. But it is enough to show that the bogey of allocation and rationing is too remote and problematical to put price control out of court on 'rule of law' grounds which the plain man can understand. Price control is undesirable in the liberal utilitarian sense that it may promote a use of resources that disregards individual preferences. But it can only be consistently attacked on straightforward 'rule of law' grounds if a great deal of discretionary power is left to administrators or to boards composed of both sides of industries.

A clear cut published price control formula with the minimum of exceptions is the least open to objection on these grounds, because the rules of the game would then be known and firm; and some individuals would not be given discretionary coercive powers over others for more than a short emergency period. The reason why Hayek may be ultimately right is that no such formula would be likely to work for long, and the government concerned would either have to phase out the controls or take a large step towards giving its agents discretionary power over the livelihoods of millions.

Reward According to 'Merit'

The most controversial application of Hayek's concept of the 'rule of law' is that he regards it as inconsistent with an attempt to redistribute income on social justice grounds.

If this part of the discussion is to generate light rather than heat, it is necessary to disentangle two different propositions from this argument. Hayek is against any attempt to make rewards of different people correspond to some supposed consensus on the relative merits of what they are doing. This would, he believes, lead to pernicious results undreamt of by those who talk in this way.

Secondly, he is against any attempt by progressive taxation

or other means to pursue equality or even 'less inequality' as a deliberate objective. It is a weakness of Hayek's presentation that he intertwines his arguments against payment according to merit so closely with arguments against the state taking *any* view on the distribution of incomes as to make them seem synonymous. The two propositions are separable and it is possible to accept the first without accepting the second. In fact, the first argument against payment by merit is both more important and more firmly based, even though it flies in the face of most respectable thinking, radical and conservative alike, from Plato onwards. It will be most convenient to deal with it now and come back later to the controversy about equality and distribution.

The biggest menace to liberal values is not so much any brand of egalitarianism, but the contention that relative rewards should depend on a political assessment of how much a particular occupation is worth. The objection is not, of course, to selection or promotion 'on merits', particularly in large organisations, where the implied contrast is with nepotism. The objection is to the contention that rewards of different individuals should depend on some sort of collective judgement of society of what they are worth.

Not all Hayek's arguments on the subject are, however, of equal weight. He argues that payment by merit would be a breach of the 'rule of law' because it involves a discretionary judgement by the state on the merits of particular individuals. In practice, however, such judgements tend to be on the relative merit of different occupations rather than individuals. Majority views revealed by the opinion polls show a hierarchy with nurses at the top and politicians at the bottom. But, as we have seen, there can be general, impersonal predictable laws differentiating between categories in this way, and it is very much a borderline issue whether such distinctions are to be regarded as a breach of the 'rule of law' ideal.

Hayek is at his most convincing when he argues in Part I of *The Constitution of Liberty* directly from libertarian principles against reward and merit rather than by the roundabout route of 'the rule of law'. His most persuasive proposition is that 'no man or group of men possess the capacity to determine conclusively the potentialities [the deserts and opportunities] of other human beings and that we should certainly never trust anyone invariably to exercise such a capacity.'[35]

To assess merit presupposes that a man has acted in accordance with some accepted rule of conduct and that someone else can judge how much effort and pain this has cost him. Often, of course, a highly meritorious attempt may be a complete failure, while a valuable human achievement will be due to luck or favourable circumstances. To decide on merit 'presupposes that we can judge whether people have made such use of their opportunities as they ought to have made, and how much effort of will or self-denial it has cost them and how much of their achievement is due to circumstances'. This is impossible in a free society or probably at all. Moreover, only a fanatical ascetic would wish to encourage a maximum of merit in this sense. It is more rational for people 'to achieve a maximum of usefulness at a minimum of pain and sacrifice and therefore a minimum of merit'.

Hayek is also right to insist that in a free society a man's livelihood does not depend on other people's valuation of his merit. It is sufficient that he should be able to perform some work or sell a service for which there is a demand. He concedes that as an organisation grows larger it will become inevitable that ascertainable merit in the eyes of managers (or some conventional seniority structure) should determine rewards. But so long as there is no one single organisation with a comprehensive scale of merit, but a multiplicity of competing organisations with different practices (as well as smaller organisations and a self-employed sector), an individual still has a wide degree of freedom of choice.

There is, in fact, a still stronger argument against reward by merit than those already mentioned which should influence even non-liberals who do not attack any special value to personal choice. This is that there simply does not exist in modern Western states a sufficiently wide consensus on the relative merits or deserts of different occupations and groups. However resentful they are about it, people will, in the last resort accept a relatively low position in the pecking order if it is due to the luck of the market, or even the greater success of other groups in their monopolistic activities. They may retaliate by organising monopolistic associations of their own to engage in industrial stoppages; but they will recognise that no ultimate judgement has been pronounced. If, on the other hand, their low position seems to result from a moralistic evaluation of their merits made by their fellow citizens through some political process – whether by the Government or by boards appointed for the task – they will stop at nothing to get the judgement withdrawn. No one likes being consigned to the rubbish heap by a body of wise men appointed to express the supposed moral evaluations of society. Some evidence for this contention is provided by the much greater political bitterness surrounding public sector than private sector wage disputes, despite the fact that nationalised industries have been careful to rest their case on industrial or national expediency, and to avoid any moral evaluation of the claims made.

An interesting feature of the argument against reward by merit is that it ought to be entirely acceptable to a strict egalitarian. The incompatibility of the two ideals of equality and reward according to merits comes out very clearly in one of the few coherent statements of the egalitarian case to have appeared in recent years, Douglas Jay's *Socialism and the New Society*.[36] There the author clearly states that no man or woman has a greater 'right to happiness' than any other and the fact that people are born 'with an endless variety of character, intelligence, energy and ability, is morally irrelevant to this assertion.

An egalitarian could easily find a full-blown system of merit assessment even more distasteful than the present mixture of market and traditional status-determined differentials.

A society in which it was generally presumed that a high income was proof of merit and a low income lack of it, in which it was universally believed that position and remuneration correspond to merit, in which there was no other road to success than the approval of one's conduct by the majority of one's fellows, would probably be much more unbearable to the unsuccessful ones than one in which it was frankly recognised that there was no necessary connection between merit and success.

This is a quotation from *The Constitution of Liberty*, but it could equally have come from an egalitarian socialist inveighing against the meritocracy and arguing against equality of opportunity as an inadequate ideal.

Hayek argues that payment by merit would mean that market valuations of a man's activities would provide him with no guidance about where to use his talents and what risks to undertake. He would have to be told what to do by someone else: in other words, explicit or implicit direction of labour. Here, however, we must be careful. Direction of labour is a plausible result if the principle is pushed too far. But how far is 'too far', and what exactly happens, will depend on certain policy decisions other than the decision to pay according to merit. If, for example, it was decided that a nurse's merit was greater than her market rate of pay, there would be a surplus of girls seeking to enter the profession, and some who had previously come up to standard would be rejected by a selection procedure, thus increasing the discretionary power of the hospital authorities over the careers of those concerned. The effects on the employment of nurses would, however, probably be less than in other occupations because most nurses are remunerated out of rates and taxes.

In the commercial sector, an increase in relative pay for, say, copper plate workers, would not only increase the number of job applicants but would also reduce employment opportunities. If half the jobs in the country were upgraded on a merit basis and the other half downgraded, there would be an exodus of employees from the high merit occupations, where jobs would be chronically scarce, to the low merit ones, where they would be plentiful but ill-rewarded. The only way of avoiding these paradoxical effects would be for the state to give large and expensive subsidies to the favoured trades and/or put heavy taxes on the least favoured ones, thereby substituting a politically determined pattern of output for that preferred by consumers.

But undesirable although all this is to an economic liberal, and restrictive though it is of freedom of consumer choice, it need not amount to direction of labour. The latter would only be necessary if the state begrudged paying the subsidies and raising the taxes, but was not prepared to accept a redistribution of workers towards the low merit occupations. State action to protect the pay of a particular group that stood high in public esteem from adverse market forces – whether engine drivers facing the rundown of the rail system or teachers when there is a glut of graduates – would not take us along the road to serfdom. But an across-the-board system of merit evaluation (e.g. paying lavatory attendants more than university professors and dustmen more than stockbrokers) would lead to such an unacceptable allocation of resources (involving, for example, great unemployment among the lavatory attendants) and the necessary subsidies would be so unpopular (and themselves another source of distortion of the choice between work and leisure) that widespread compulsion would be an all too likely result. This aspect of the discussion will be taken further when we come to the equality issue.

The alternative to payment by merit is payment according to the market value of a person's activities – *as modified by whatever fiscal action is taken to alter the distribution of income and wealth* (such action is discussed below, pp. 124 et seq.). We do not need to be starry-eyed about the character of this market value. It will be influenced by the attempts of professional associations and trade unions to restrict supply, as well as by traditional views of proper scales. If the supply of clergymen suitable for promotion to archbishop exceeds the demand, the archepiscopal stipend will not, in the short run, be reduced (although it may be less quickly adjusted to compensate for inflation). In other words, it will be a highly imperfect market system in which rewards will not only depend on the mixture of luck, skill, opportunity and monopoly power characteristic of actual markets, but also on arbitrary traditional relativities, which themselves represent the lagged influences of the market relativities of a generation or two ago.

The economic liberal will want to do all he can to remove disparities and inequalities imposed by artificial barriers to entry. He should be extremely sceptical of the monopolistic claims made by the medical or legal profession, as of the restrictive practices of the craft unions. To the extent that there are professional skills involved, which the layman is not qualified to judge, it should be sufficient for the state to establish a register of qualified persons, leaving it to the consumer to decide whether to go by this register or to seek unqualified help.

Above all, the liberal should be suspicious of attempts of more and more occupations, whether advertising, management or journalism, to emulate the professions and to set up obstacle courses in the shape of examination requirements or 'on the job training', confining entry to graduates, or similar limitations of entry. To the extent that these new qualifications and courses produce results, employers, or members of the public using the services, will give preference to those holding them. To restrict the activities in question to those so qualified, by law or collective agreement, is a pure exercise of coercion to establish a monopoly position. Yet at the end of the day, even if he is relatively unsuccessful in fighting off these evils, the liberal should still regard a pattern of awards, determined politically by governmental action or demagogic use of the organs of publicity as a cure far worse than the disease.

The Role of Politics

The argument for payment according to merit is in fact one example of the widespread belief that society as a whole should take decisions now arrived at by separate organisations or individuals, or by impersonal general forces. This claim is much the most dangerous that the economic liberal (or any other kind of liberal) now has to face. He must meet it by an equally strong counterclaim: that in a free society the domain of political action should be limited.

This is a third principle, of comparable importance to non-paternalistic value judgements and a belief in general, impersonal rules, for the contemporary economic liberal. It is also an extremely controversial one and likely to lose me the support of even some of those who have followed the preceding discussion with some sympathy.

The principle is extremely difficult to state, not least because of the ambiguity of the term political. One can legitimately talk about the politics of a family or a school, or a firm or an opera house. But political action, in the sense that is relevant here, involves the coercive power of government. Even this, however, is a necessary and not a sufficient condition. The traffic police are an instrument of governmental coercion; but, except in the case of scandals or controversial change in safety regulations, their operations are not a political issue. For a matter to become political, there must also be conflict and strong feeling. Where free speech is permitted, the conflict is in the open; elsewhere the conflict is either suppressed, or else artificially stirred up against the 'enemies of the people' who do not go along with official requirements. (An alternative formulation is that such countries have no politics, but this has the disadvantage of creating an unrealistic black and white distinction between free and unfree states.)

Hayek has, for many years and in many different terminologies, been trying to draw a distinction between two different strands of the liberal and utilitarian traditions. He has contrasted 'true' with 'false' individualism, 'generic' with 'particularist' utilitarianism, and 'restricted' with 'extreme' utilitarianism. He has contrasted the liberal tradition springing from Hume with that springing in different ways from both Descartes and Jeremy Bentham, and he has erected a chamber of horrors full of things such as 'constructivist rationalism', 'social engineering' and 'scientism'. He has with equal regularity been answered by British writers who maintain that he has created artificial distinctions and misconstrued the English (or Scottish!) tradition.

For a long time my own instincts were on the anti-Hayek side, especially as his distinctions were too often associated with a defence of traditional English public schools against continental libertarian criticism and a defence of the conformist impression made by many young British university-educated men and their continental contemporaries earlier in the century. This was leaning over too far backwards to explain away the more authoritarian aspects of British life.

Yet there remains an uncomfortable feeling that there is something in Hayek's distinctions. The 'social engineers' or 'particularist' utilitarians maintain, in the spirit of Jeremy Bentham, that institutions 'are to be approved and respected only to the extent that we can show that the particular effects they will produce in any given situation are preferable to the effects another arrangement would produce', and, therefore, 'our reason should never resort to automatic or mechanical devices'. Hayek contrasts this with the view stemming from Hume which accepts just as much the test of utility, but insists that no single human intelligence is capable of inventing appropriate rules and institutions which 'have evolved in the process of growth of society' and which 'embody the experience of many more trials and errors than any individual mind could acquire'.[37]

The role played by traditional rules, habits and customs in Hayek's defence of freedom in *The Constitution of Liberty* is indeed an uneasy one. The submission to rules and conventions, whose significance we do not fully understand, jars with the impulse to freedom. There are such things as illiberal institutions, traditions and rules. Above all, Hayek does not really explain the process by which unsuitable traditions should be discarded, except by vague references to trial and error and the variability of the social pressure against individuals who transgress the rules. Yet without Hume's sceptical caution about the powers of human reason, we open the gates to the social engineering approach to politics and society. A particularist utilitarian can always find some defect or 'externality' in every real world activity to justify intervention on the most impeccably non-paternalist grounds. Yet the total effect of a series of such interventions, each decided separately on a discretionary basis, could be to destroy most of the existing avenues of choice with an end result totally different from what was intended, owing to the inability to foresee remoter or less obvious consequences.

There is a genuine dilemma here. The Benthamite, social engineering streak in liberalism can lead to an unlimited profusion of state activity, as one hectic intervention follows another, and one fashionable mathematical model – whether of the determinants of productivity in 1984 or of the ecological balance in 2000 – succeeds a previous favourite. Yet too great a hesitation to intervene, where existing institutions neither provide personal choice nor material welfare, can lead liberalism to ossify into a Burkean conservatism (as hap-

pened with Burke himself). We have already met, in an
earlier more technical context, the two strands of right-wing
and left-wing economic liberalism, both claiming to start
from individual desires and choices, but with radically different approaches to state intervention.

Whatever the weight of inherited lore may decree, there
is no sphere of human activity that can be *a priori* and forever
ruled out of the political domain. In the Depression of the
1930s, the operation of the whole economic system was a
matter of legitimate concern. In a grossly pyramided society
where, say, 1 per cent of the families earned 99 per cent of all
incomes, 'inequality' would be the number one political
problem. If the country became plagued by heroin-addiction,
the most extreme liberals might want to waive the anti-
paternalist presumption to give priority to a sensibly conducted search for treatment – even in a country which had no
tradition of repressive rules on the subject.

The point that the liberal can legitimately make is that,
although the focus of political interest is and should be constantly shifting, it should also be limited. There is all the
difference in the world between having a number of different
spotlights of varying strength gradually shifting in direction,
and floodlighting the whole countryside. Some judgements,
such as that of the claims of defence on resources, have to be
made collectively through the political process. Political
judgements on other matters, such as the allocation of resources between present and future needs, or the distribution
of income, or the aesthetic properties of new towns, or the
amounts to be given to help poorer countries, are in a sense
optional, in that we can choose to take them inside or outside
the political process. The more judgements of this kind that
are made politically, and the greater the detail into which
they go, the greater the threat not only to liberty and prosperity, but also to social harmony. Paradoxically, by attempting
to go too far by state action to remove all conflict and discomfort, we actually increase social tension to danger point.

One of the more striking results of Anthony Downs'
pioneering investigation of *The Economic Theory of Democracy*,[38] was how little incentive the ordinary citizen, or even
individual member of a pressure group, has to make a serious

study of issues. The probability that his vote or voice will turn the scale is so small that neither Downs nor his critics have been able to find a rational argument for voting other than the general duties of citizenship or as an outlet for strong personal feelings. If this is so of voting, it applies *a fortiori* to a detailed study of policy; and any short cut method, such as taking on trust the views of a party with which one has a clear identification, or going by the general impression rival leaders make on a television screen, will be quite rationally taken to avoid time-consuming study, which – even if it were undertaken – would only be feasible over a very tiny range of the total issues. Even individual M.P.s often find it more convenient to follow their particular faction of their party on a great many issues on which they neither feel strongly nor regard themselves as particularly competent.

The gist of the matter was expressed by Schumpeter long ago when he said that, for most people, the great political issues were 'sub-hobbies' to which they devoted less attention than bridge.[39] This is not a criticism. It is perfectly rational, given the likely extent of individual influence, to regard political programmes as a form of show business, to be watched only if they are entertaining. Schumpeter conceded that voters appear to react rationally to issues involving immediate personal and pecuniary profit to identifiable groups. But even here 'it is only short run rationality that asserts itself effectively'. As we move to more general issues of national and international policy, even this short-run rationality goes. Such issues normally take their place 'with those leisure hour interests that have not attained the rank of hobbies'. This rationality leads to a reduced sense of responsibility. 'We need only compare,' as Schumpeter put it, 'the lawyer's attitude to his brief and the same lawyer's attitude to the statements of political fact presented in his newspaper.' In the one case he has the competence and the stimulus to master the material. In the other, 'he does not apply the canons of criticism he knows so well how to handle' in his own sphere. The basic trouble is the lack of the rationalising influences of personal experience and responsibility. In their own private lives people know that more of one thing means less of something else because of the cash constraint. They know that they can improve trade-offs (e.g. between the pleasure of living in the country and the discomfort of a journey to work, by a careful choice of location); but they also know that such improvements are not unlimited and cost effort to find.

The absence of this knowledge in the political sphere explains the frequent tendency of democracies to expect too much from government action. If the rate of economic growth is too low, it is supposed to be the Government's duty to raise it, until we come up near the top of the league tables; and moreover, to do so painlessly, without any sacrifice of immediate satisfaction. The belief never dies that if we only had a clever enough Chancellor, with clever enough advisers, he would find some kind of monetary magic for achieving this. To take any other attitude is defeatist, cynical and so on. The impetus towards political consistency is not very strong. It is too easy to favour all worthy objects at the same time: more of the national income for the old and sick, the lower paid, the skilled craftsman and better pay for those doing important professional jobs. The one group which people always think is too well paid are politicians – from whom omniscience and omnipotence are expected.

The difficulty of the subject is that there *are* in fact always ways in which the Government could, if it were cleverer or more enlightened, improve all these matters. There are mistakes which have held back the rate of growth; there may well be policies which could improve road safety at minimal cost to motorists. Or to put it more generally, better technical or institutional arrangements can always improve the trade-offs, so that we could get more growth for a given sacrifice of personal consumption, or more road safety from a given sacrifice by motorists. It is never wrong to seek for a 'Pareto improvement'. The mistake of the politically orientated is to exaggerate the possibility of improvement, both in the abstract, and in the light of the forces that actually do influence both the electorate and men in positions of power and influence.

The inadequacy of the incentive to make wise decisions applies not only to voters, but to a lesser extent to public officials, whether Ministers, M.P.s, civil servants or judges. Good decisions involve considerable private costs in time and effort; and the incentive to invest in this way is reduced because the benefit largely accrues to others and the effect on the individual's own career is very vague and diffused. The gains from investing energy in understanding the internal politics and hierarchical roles and to play the organisation are often both greater and more tangible.[40] Some of the same considerations apply to officials of large commercial organisations, although individual responsibility is slightly easier to pin down because company profits can be allocated among divisions in a way that votes cannot be allocated among Ministers, policies or Departments. But in any case such diminished incentive does less harm in organisations which are not backed by the coercive powers of government.

Even, however, if voters were highly enlightened and could effectively call their rulers to account, there would still be endemic defects in any known political process. Among the most striking of Downs' results (which he might have made more of) was the lack of protection either of the minority by a bare majority, or the majority by a coalition of minorities with strong views on particular issues. This last point is connected with the concentration of producer interests and the dispersion of consumer ones. The beneficial impact of any one protectionist or restrictionist measure on an individual via his professional or geographical interest is far greater than any loss he may bear along with 50 or 60 million other consumers. Thus he is entirely rational to take a producer's view. Political theorists often make the mistake of assuming that if there is a fair balance of policies or bargains between all producers, all is well. But this is simply untrue, even if we forget people such as pensioners and assume that every consumer is also a producer.

For although he gains far more than he loses from restrictionist measures in his own small sphere, he will often lose out on balance, especially in the long run, from the sum total of restrictive measures encompassing the whole field of economic activity. It might pay him to do a deal whereby he renounces his claim to special producer privileges, provided that every other interest group did the same. Yet it is extremely difficult for such a bargain to be negotiated and enforced in a mass democracy. Without the assurance that it would be enforced across the board with the minimum of exceptions, a producer group would rightly think twice of giving up its protections and privileges. These difficulties are aggravated, although not caused, by the geographical basis of representation in parliamentary bodies.

Just as the workings of the market suffer from certain defects, discussed in earlier sections, so does the political process; it is therefore not enough to make some plausible case for a 'neighbourhood effect' or 'externality' to justify government intervention. The cumulative effect of over-extending the political sector must also be considered. It is this desire to limit the domain of the political that distinguishes the economic liberal from some 'social democrats' who would be willing to go along with a great deal of what was said earlier about anti-paternalism and even about impersonal general rules.

To a liberal the market is not just a device to be manipulated by social engineers in accordance with the latest piece of economic research. It is also a mechanism – imperfect and capable of much improvement – which reduces the number and range of decisions which have to be taken by coercive organs after a struggle for votes, power and influence. *Without some presumption of this kind, the bias in favour of some form of market process cannot be supported on supposed grounds of technical economics, even when allied with non-paternalist value judgements; and liberals would do well to acknowledge this fact.*

The direction of the above argument is bound to be distorted or misunderstood by some people whatever disclaimers I add. But perhaps a few very obvious points should be stressed. For all its many weaknesses, democracy is far and away the best method of changing a government by peaceful means; and it is good that governments should be reminded in the most forceful possible way where the wearer believes the shoe pinches, even though the wearer is not an orthopaedic expert. Democracy will work best, however, if it can resist the temptation to expect too much from political activity and to extend the political sphere indefinitely.

Of course it is possible for people to expect too little as well as too much from governments and to make too few collective judgements, as well as too many. Moreover, even if the general bias is too far in favour of political action, there may remain areas where there is too little. But the inherent bias of a *democracy*, which emerges as the elitist elements fall away, is to expect on balance too much. Political action is likely to be more effective, and government more, not less, efficient if limits are placed on the political sphere. Because Ministers and officials are blamed for everything that goes wrong anywhere, their feelings of responsibility for the sphere that is indisputably theirs is diminished. It is an organisational commonplace that people perform better if given reasonably defined and limited (if changing) duties than if they are made to feel vaguely responsible for everything that happens around them.

The attribution of total responsibility to governments blunts the edge, not merely of government, but of reformist agitation. A public issue at the time of writing is conditions in some prisons, especially for those on remand who are sometimes acquitted. The *prima facie* evidence suggests that not only are conditions appalling, but that part of their horror is due not to material deficiencies, but to harsh regulations which could be changed at the stroke of a Home Office pen. Yet information of this kind loses its power to shock and stir to action, when it appears as simply one of many other revelations of bad conditions, which are not the direct responsibility of the Government, but for which it is made responsible in populist eyes.

The Concept of 'Society'

The danger signal for the unwarranted extension of the political sphere is provided by the word 'society' in conjunction with 'modern society', 'society will not tolerate', 'social needs' and similar phrases and slogans. The concept has an interesting history. It was originally invented by the reactionary, nationalist Right to curb the demands of the liberal utilitarians. Faced with the demand to sweep away outmoded institutions, to do away with the authority of kings and bishops and to leave each individual to pursue his happiness in his own way, the conservative replied that this programme was based on a travesty of human nature, it left out of account all kinds of relations among human beings, feelings of national identity to the point of being willing to sacrifice one's life, habits of reverence and obligation, and countless traditions which had a function not immediately obvious to either a Jeremy Bentham or a Saint-Just.

This argument is neither dead nor easy to resolve. But the idea of 'society' and 'social needs' is only a conservative force if there is general agreement on questions of status and obligation. If people agree on hierarchy, it is not too difficult to maintain it in the face of market forces by limiting entry by some form of rationing. The master tailors could maintain the traditional differentials by insisting on long apprenticeships, limiting the number of newcomers and so on. (Of course market forces have had some influence on relativities in the very long run; our concern here is how social values were made effective for substantial periods.) But whether the coercion came from some public body, or was enforced by the various groups themselves, the resulting order was relatively stable. Traces of this attitude, of course, prevailed among the craft unions with their traditional ideas of their just status.

But once the traditional consensus broke down, and human expectations were increased, the concept of society as an organism with its own demands became a recipe for unlimited political intervention and for interminable strife. It required unlimited political intervention because it was no longer a matter of protecting established practices that had grown up over the centuries, but of conscious political interference to impose a new scale of status and remuneration believed to be in line with the 'real' needs and desires of society.

The programme will never work for at least two reasons. The actual members of society have violently conflicting views of what a right and just order would be like. The fact that a majority can agree in opinion polls on rough grading of occupations proves very little. What is important is that people should accept the relative positions assigned by others *for their own groups*. It is also doubtful if one can have an organised society in which those who have most responsibility are heavily downgraded; in practice they will try to make up in 'bad, dirty power' for what they lose in 'good, clean money'.

As important as disagreement on relativities is the blown-up expectation of how much there is available to distribute. Where expectations are high and values diverse, some kind of market economy, however imperfect, is a way of enabling people to live peacefully together. It does not require either knowledge of the size of the cake by each citizen or agreement on its distribution. The progressive apostle of society tries to have it both ways: he wants the cosy feeling of security and an agreed order of merit characteristic of the hierarchical society, plus the free-for-all in ideas, the radical questioning of all institutions and the levels of aspiration characteristic of a spontaneous, decentralised mercantile society.

Again, it may be impossible to improve the trade-offs. But the total programme is arrogant and authoritarian. Unlike traditional authoritarianism, it is of the busy, interfering variety, seeking fresh reorganisations as one campaign takes over from another; and if it were momentarily fulfilled, fresh dissatisfactions and tensions would immediately arise.

As more and more mutually contradictory 'rights' and 'needs' are invented, the gap between aspiration and reality is likely to grow; and growing frustration can lead to growing violence and disintegration. This in turn will lead to demands for harsher penalties, more power for troops and police, as well as anti-liberal clamp-downs on some of the more harmless activities of the 'alternative society' such as pornography and obscenity. Genuine injustices will then be committed by the forces of law and order, which will further increase the sense of outrage of those on the other side.

To attempt to impose a politically determined set of values on a community leads in the developing countries to third-rate dictatorships, with high-sounding slogans and plenty of prestige projects, and has a retarding effect even on statistically measured growth, let alone on the fulfilment of human needs. In the West the result has more often been an anti-interventionist reaction, involving either the electoral defeat of left-wing government or their settling down into a revisionist programme of marginal trimming.

Inquests are then held and scapegoats found. It was all the fault of Mr X, or 'the balance of payments', or the 'Treasury', or 'the wrong sort of economists', or 'not enough sociologists' or 'Ministers moving too far from their roots in the movement'. Next time, of course it will be 'different' for 'the Party is moving to the left' (as it always does in opposition). Everything was wrong, of course, except the underlying philosophy itself.

There are two main enemies of the liberal outlook rampant at present. One is the widespread view that, instead of emerging from the dispersed actions of millions of individuals, the shape of society should be determined by political decisions which reflect the values of society. It is a sort of totalitarian populism. This is a complicated enemy to nail, as many decisions must be taken politically, and a great deal of government activity is necessary if the interaction of individual decisions is to produce harmonious results. But although it is difficult to define, it is not difficult to recognise. It comes out when one hears expressions such as 'should be banned' or 'everyone should have to...'. In a discussion where one person wants to ban cars from towns and his opponent asserts that people have a right to the benefits of the automobile, both are guilty of it. By contrast, when Dr Mishan in one of his more tolerant moods suggests separate residential areas to suit different preferences, with all manner of arrangements from horse-and-buggies only to Los Angeles type urban motorways, he is at least making a constructive suggestion about a complex problem from a liberal point of view.[42]

A threat from another direction is presented by a body of ideas which has at times been given impressive names such as the Corporate State or the New Industrial State. In essence it amounts to the belief in informal directorship of our affairs by the men who run large organisations. 'Gt. Britain Ltd.' is not a bad caricature and conveys the flavour of people who really know what makes things tick, sorting things out together 'without any ideological nonsense'. The popular image is provided by the Power Game series. The everyday strength of this position lies in the close links of many companies with government departments which buy or heavily subsidise their products. The ideal of those who think this way is to build up the authority of bodies such as the Confederation of British Industry and the Trades Union Congress, so that they have effective powers over their own members on whose behalf they can negotiate with each other and the government. The prophets of this brave new world sometimes assert that it is desirable, sometimes inevitable, and most often blur the distinction.

A particular offender here is Galbraith, who never makes it quite clear whether he regrets the advent of the New Industrial State, or whether he welcomes it as an improvement on competitive capitalism. Nor can he of all authors say that he is simply describing and not evaluating. The ambiguity is, of course, of great advantage. Radicals can approve his general mockery of supposedly conventional principles, while the business establishment can have a sneaking admiration for Galbraith because of his 'realism'. Was he not the prophet of price and wage controls canonised by the 1971 Republican Administration in its New Economic Policy?

The dangers of the New Industrial State and of populist totalitarianism may seem opposed; and perhaps in the last analysis they are. But it would be possible for demagogic politicians to ride both horses at once. It is all too easy to imagine an *ersatz* populism under which a supposedly left-wing government would try to make their world safe for high technology 'Big Business', in which 'Britain must be in the lead'. The representatives of the technostructure might be more than happy to accept the charade of government-appointed directors, or even of worker representatives – and have the Minister of Technology to breakfast – in return for a real insulation from market disciplines and the negative control of the Treasury.

A Provisional Summary

It is time to gather up the threads. What then are the main guidelines with which a liberal should approach economic policy? The vague term 'guidelines' has been deliberately used in preference to 'principles'. No attempt to set out the principles of economic (or any other) policy as a system of deductive inferences from a set of ethical postulates in combination with a set of empirically established regularities has succeeded, or is likely to. Such attempts, when carried out rigorously, have usually led to results of such generality that they are of little use in forming policy.

On the other hand certain general presumptions can be stated. Three main ones have emerged from the preceding pages.

(1) Individuals should be regarded *as if* they are the best judges of their own interests, and policy should be designed to satisfy the desires that individuals happen to have, excluding desires to coerce or downgrade other people. This has been termed *liberal utilitarianism.*

(2) Policy should be governed by a preference for *impersonal general rules* with a minimum of discretionary power by publicly appointed officials – or private bodies engaged in backstage pressure – over their fellow men.

(3) We should try to *limit the domain of political activity* even though we cannot mark out exact boundary lines in advance.

These three guidelines, bringing together strands from rather different liberal traditions, have been put together in this way, because there is no one golden rule of policy which can be guaranteed to promote a society appealing to those who attach a high value to individual freedom. But together they can provide some rough pointers. The three presumptions just summarised are interrelated, but can on occasion conflict with or qualify each other. The second presumption, in favour of general rules, qualifies the liberal utilitarianism of the first presumption; and the third presumption, against overextending the political area, can make one on occasion less keen on general laws than one would otherwise be.

Allied with these presumptions go certain rule-of-thumb maxims, of a lesser status, but still worth mentioning in a summary. These include: 'Look for any self-adjusting mechanisms, whether natural or contrived, wherever possible; if the mechanisms, you find are unsatisfactory, seek to modify their operation rather than to replace them by directives and prohibitions.' Another is: 'It is safer to rely on people's private interests rather than their professed public goals.' This derives from Adam Smith; but the expression 'private interests' has been deliberately used to show that this is not a gospel of selfishness, but rather of relying more on people's private goals, whether personal indulgence, saint-hood, charitable works, the welfare of their friends or an infinite variety of possible motives for action other than their professed public policy goals.

A further useful maxim is: 'Irresponsible bodies exercis-ing power, but subject neither to the disciplines of the market place nor to open, political scrutiny and control, are to be avoided.' This must be used with caution, because it leads to a demand that such bodies be made 'politically accountable'. Accountability of this kind can help to strengthen the elem-ent of known general principles in their operation and make them less paternalistic, but it also risks overextending the political area of life. Select Committees on Economic Affairs and Parliamentary scrutiny of public expenditure and revenue projections (which I continue to support) are a second best for returning some of the decisions involved to the individual citizen.[43]

The statement of the above guidelines inevitably abounds in vague expressions such as 'over a wide area', 'wherever possible' and their equivalent, alien to formal logic. But for all their lack of rigour they may, nevertheless, help to reduce the chances of producing unintended and undesired results through the cumulation of specific policies, each adopted on their own merits. They may also stimulate imagination in the search for policies of which we might otherwise not have thought, or thought less quickly, and they may help to pre-vent the field from being pre-empted by anti-liberals. They have also a persuasive function in showing that economic liberalism need not be bogus, circular, unrealistic, inhuman, excessively idealistic or otherwise wrong-headed.

The whole outlook I have tried to summarise is consumer rather than producer oriented. It tends to favour the indivi-dual or small man and organisation against the big battalions; and it does favour the pursuit of prosperity, provided that that is what people want, and prosperity is interpreted in a non-mechanistic way to include leisure, amenities, congenial working conditions and all the other aspects of living standards which do not show up in G.N.P. figures. It favours the permissive 'do-your-own-thing' aspect of the radicalism of the young, but not its intolerant insistence on reshaping the lives and activities of other people. It seeks a society in which the individual is liberated from oppressive working conditions not so much by participation or workers' control, as by the existence of a large variety of differing institutions, between which the individual is free to choose and between which movement is relatively easy.

4. Special Problems

Equality

There is still some more ground to cover even in a non-comprehensive treatment of the subject. This essay started off by defining a liberal as someone who attaches special importance to individual freedom defined in the negative sense. Where does he stand in relation to someone who attaches a special importance to equality in the material things of life? Earlier on I tried to show that the liberal and the egalitarian *should* have a common interest in fighting the notion of payment according to some political decision on the supposed merits of various individuals and occupations.

What has been left open is the question of how far the two ideals can or should be combined. Can one be an egalitarian liberal or a liberal egalitarian? Hayek, as already mentioned, answers with an uncompromising 'No'; and this has at least the merit of focusing on the difficulties and tensions between the two ideals.

What then are the arguments for regarding equality as incompatible with a free society based on a minimum of coercion? Hayek's main 'rule of law' argument is that an attempt to bring about equality by political means is to single out a body of citizens for discriminatory treatment. This is based on the requirement that a general rule must be acceptable to those adversely affected by it; and if one does not accept the requirement for the reasons previously given, the case for equality cannot be demolished on 'rule of law' grounds. Nor can it be demolished by stressing that the only way to make people equal would be to have laws treating them unequally. Such laws could be of an extremely general abstract and impersonal character, distinguishing between people according to some highly general criteria such as income or wealth. Certainly, the wish of a majority of the population to help the less well off, or achieve any other worthy object, should be taken more seriously if it is prepared to foot the bill itself than if the generosity is exercised at the expense of another group, such as the rich, from whom it is fondly hoped that endless resources can be squeezed. But this is not the same as giving the better off classes a veto over the tax and social security system.

Hayek is on somewhat stronger ground when he objects to enforced equality because people would have to be told what to do, and freedom of choice of occupation would be at an end. If a state were ever to go the whole hog and decree complete equality of incomes, Hayek would indeed be right. In that case there would have to be state compulsion to work a minimum amount of hours with much supervision to prevent slacking. Even then some occupations will be understaffed and others overstaffed, as relative earnings will provide no guide. Therefore the state would have to direct labour. Thus, complete equality of incomes would be incompatible with free choice of occupations, as well as with prosperity and efficiency.

Let us, however, start at the other end. How far can one go from the present state of affairs towards equality without bringing in direction of labour? If a stage-by-stage attempt to diminish inequality takes the form of imposing minimum wages, one of the principal effects will be increased unemployment among those whom the measure is supposed to benefit. So it would be better for the egalitarian case to assume that the effort takes the form of progressive income taxes at the top and negative income taxes, or the equivalent in social benefits, at the bottom.

A full analysis of the implications would be highly complex. But there is a basic distinction to be drawn between people who are, and are not, capable of doing each other's jobs. There is a surprisingly prevalent notion that classical economic theory predicts that the most unpleasant jobs should be the best paid; and that if this is incorrect in practice, levelling upwards presents no problem. Both assertions are wrong. People take unattractive ill-paid jobs, such as that of the street cleaner or sewage worker, because they are not able to do, or eligible for, the more attractive ones. (Whether this inability is innate, or the result of inferior education or family opportunities, is not the issue here – we are dealing with the situation that happens to prevail for whatever reason.)

So long as the minimum income, which a negative income tax or other device seeks to promote, is well below the general level of earnings in such occupations, there need be no serious trouble; and the scheme should help to deal with poverty due to age, illness, large families and so on. But as the guaranteed minimum income approaches and perhaps even exceeds earnings in occupations which are both low paid and inherently unattractive, the supply of workers concerned will seriously fall off. There are then two possibilities. One is that the guaranteed minimum is unconditional. In that case, wages in the low paid, unpleasant occupations will have to rise. This, however, will both reduce the demand for the services in question and stimulate mechanisation and other devices for saving unskilled labour. Thus the level of unemployment and unused resources will rise.

The second possibility is that the minimum income is guaranteed to an able-bodied adult only if he is either working or honestly seeking work. In that case, something very like direction of labour is involved. Without the guaranteed minimum, the relative wages paid to sewage workers, dustmen, hospital porters and countless other unskilled and unpleasant occupations requiring comparable ability, serve in a very rough and ready way to ensure the right distribution between them. If there were too few sewage workers, their wages could be raised relative to the others. But once the guaranteed minimum is above prevailing wages in all such occupations, relative wages have no power to attract or deter, and compulsion is required.

The moral to be drawn from this oversimplified illustration is that an attempt to level upwards beyond a certain point involves a choice between either compulsion, or tolerating semi-voluntary idleness and wasted resources. The further the levelling up goes, the greater the cost in efficiency and the greater the pressure to use compulsion. There are, in fact, disturbing analogies to this model even in some of the present practices of the social security and employment services.

Similar arguments can also apply in the upper ranges. Let us suppose that business executives earn, on average, more than financial journalists, and that the latter are not suitable for business posts. If highly progressive taxation in the relevant bands reduces to vanishing point the difference in take-home pay between the two occupations, then some business executives might prefer to become financial journalists or take up some third occupation. (Business executives will be able to pass on some of their taxes by obtaining higher pre-tax salaries; but this will be by no means a complete offset, as the demand for their services will be sensitive to their *pre-tax* cost.) It is hardly feasible to compel people to become business executives in the way that the late Roman emperors tried to compel people to take up municipal office. The likely result is a lowering of standards in the field of practical business, and an excess supply of financial journalists. Restrictive practices aside, the net result would be a fall in the pre-tax pay of such journalists and an increase in their number (and perhaps their quality). The final equilibrium is likely to involve their being fewer and lower grade business executives and more and higher grade financial journalists than the community required before the tax distortion began.

Let us now make the alternative assumption that a number of financial journalists could have been business executives, but preferred not to, despite the difference in pay. In these circumstances, it is in fact doubtful if levelling downwards is really sound egalitarianism, because for those at the margin of decision, the net advantages of the two professions, pecuniary and other, are already equal. A tax-induced narrowing of differentials will, if it is nevertheless insisted upon, have the same effect as in the last example and lead to an increase in the number of financial journalists relative to business executives.

Finally, let us suppose that the difference of earnings in two occupations calling for similar talents is not due to choices made at the beginning of a career, but is due to a shift in demand for the services in question. It is not easy, either practically or emotionally, for people who have committed their careers to one occupation or industry to make a sudden change. In the absence of equalising taxation a differential would persist for some time, attracting new recruits and the more flexible younger people into the better paid occupation, until eventually supply and demand came into better balance, and the differential would then tend to decrease. A highly egalitarian tax structure will slow down the readjustment. The market price of the service in greater demand would shoot up much higher, and its expansion to meet public demand would be much slower. There would be a loss of efficiency – and the pattern of output would be different from that conforming to consumer requirements – but it would not involve direction of people to specific jobs.

The moral of the various examples is that *general* egalitarian policies need not involve direction of labour, provided the community is willing to tolerate a loss in the efficiency with which its requirements are met. In the limiting case of complete equality, the loss of efficiency would be so great that direction of labour would almost certainly be used in an attempt to limit this loss.

There is thus a three-way trade-off between freedom, equality and prosperity.* Douglas Jay implicitly recognises this when he defines the economic aim of socialism as 'the minimum of inequality that is workable if human beings are actively to use their talents'.⁴⁴ (This is much more satisfactory than his attempt a few pages earlier to equate freedom with equality.) As he also makes the libertarian assumption that

---

* This three-way trade-off seems to me the underlying message of Henry Wallich's interesting book *The Cost of Freedom* (Harper, 1960). Professor Wallich argues, as against Hayek, that attempts at 'democratic planning' may lead not to serfdom, but to 'pressures for avoiding readjustments, shoring up losing situations with subsidies' and generally doing things 'the easier rather than the better way'. (p. 47)

there will be no compulsion or direction of labour, his implied operational trade-off is between property and equality.

One major difficulty about this goal is that 'less inequality' is inherently ambiguous. Is it equally important to level down the rich or level up the poor? And, if not, what weighting does one apply? The difficulties can be brought out by the following example of a community of only three people.

TABLE 2

Income of Individual	First Distribution	Second Distribution
A	28	21
B	12	21
C	11	9
Mean Income	17	17
Average Dispersion from Mean ('degree of inequality')	$7\frac{1}{3}$	$5\frac{1}{3}$

The first distribution would be generally regarded as very unequal. The fortunate A has well over twice as much as both B and C. The average deviation of all incomes from the mean of 17 is $7\frac{1}{3}$. In the second distribution the degree of inequality appears to have diminished. The rich A, who now has only 21, has been reduced to much nearer the mean and the scatter is now much less. The average deviation from the mean is now only $5\frac{1}{3}$. Unfortunately, however, the poorest of the individuals, C, is now 2 points poorer. (This example abstracts completely from incentive effects and assumes that the amount to be shared is constant.)

The most frequently used measures of income are a shade more sophisticated, but suffer from the same inherent definitional problems. A good example is the Lorenz curve showing the proportion of total income received by cumulative percentages of recipients, starting from the least well off. This is normally summarised by the 'Gini coefficient' (which depends on the area between the diagonal and the curve). Yet, such a measure fails to distinguish between changes in distribution due to levelling off in the upper reaches (more equality at the top) from those due to gains at the bottom (more equality at the bottom), or shifts on either side of the middle. Even for the purposes of ordinal comparisons between two countries or two periods, the Gini coefficient is ambiguous if the Lorenz curves intersect. A comparison of the 66 possible comparisons between 12 countries at different stages of development by A. B. Atkinson shows that in 50 of the cases they *do* intersect.[45] Indeed, Puerto Rico and Italy (around 1950) emerged with lower Gini coefficients – which were supposed to indicate more equality – than Sweden, Denmark and, the Netherlands; and India had the same coefficient as West Germany. The truth seems to be that equality tends to be greater towards the bottom in poor countries and greater towards the top in more advanced societies.

Professor Atkinson states that some overall 'social welfare function' must be specified before different distributions can be compared. But one would have to be both very sure of one's ideal choice among hypothetical distributions and highly expert at this branch of mathematics before accepting any such measure. It would be much better to reject any single index and base judgements on the total shape of the income distribution. The kind of egalitarian who prefers the second distribution (shown on p. 129) to the first may be legitimately charged with being motivated more by envy of the rich than desire to help the poor.

Another difficulty with the egalitarian goal, modified à la Jay, is that human beings 'actively using their talents' (or using 'reasonably fully' the productive abilities of the community) is not a state of affairs which either exists or does not. There is a continuous range with no sharp cut-off point. The extent to which it is realised depends both on the extent to which human talent is employed, rather than being left voluntarily or involuntarily idle, and the way in which these talents are used.

The proposed goal would have to be stated more specifically. One suggestion would be to attempt to reduce incomes in the upper ranges until the point is reached where any further reduction would ultimately damage the bottom x per cent of householders via its effect on incentives, efficiency and the utilisation of resources. The percentage x would have to be an arbitrary one; it could be of the bottom 10 per cent, 25 per cent, 50 per cent, or 75 per cent depending on the precise interpretation being put on egalitarianism. An alternative aim would be to seek a distribution of income that would *maximise* the average standard of living of that of the bottom 10 per cent, 25 per cent, 50 per cent or 75 per cent. The latter interpretation, although most helpful to the poor or less well off, has modified the egalitarian goal so drastically as to call the label itself into question.

Once an egalitarian can admit pragmatic departures from his ideal on Jay-type lines to secure a more satisfactory use of the community's productive resources, he cannot refuse to to admit such departures on the consumption side. Hayek's argument in *The Constitution of Liberty*, that the existence of people of independent means was of value to the rest of the population, was predictably received with much scorn by his critics. Yet it is undoubtedly true that wealthy individuals have pioneered new forms of enjoyment in the arts, in sport and in many other fields which have afterwards become available to the majority. This is true whether one thinks of the Esterhazys patronising Haydn, the Medicis nourishing Michaelangelo, or the Victorian leisured class developing cricket and rugby football. The point is even stronger if we extend the concept of consumption activities to cover new ideas in politics, morals or religion. Most of the great campaigns against slavery, or cruelty to children or animals, or for penal reform, depended on the enthusiasm of a minority with means.

There are, of course, many reverse examples in the modern age of working-class consumption styles aped by the smart set; and in the political or campaigning field it is easier in an affluent society to raise funds by numerous small subscriptions. Even so, it is still very useful to have some people of means to supply the initial impetus to get such campaigns off the ground. It would be an extremely bold man who could confidently say that there was no longer a role for the wealthy either in developing new tastes and patterns of living or in supporting good (and bad) causes. The future will probably see a two-way process, with some tastes and activities spreading upwards from the bottom and others downwards from the top.

Those egalitarians who have recognised an element of validity in the above argument have sometimes urged conscious attempts by public authorities to take over the pioneering role of the rich. But such efforts, of which the Arts Council is the obvious model, desirable though they are, inevitably lack the spontaneity arising from private individuals pursuing their own diverse and sometimes eccentric goals. Many of the most useful spillover activities for their fellows have indeed been unintentional results of activities of playboys and *bon vivants*.

Hayek remarks that if no better method were available, one in a hundred or one in a thousand selected *at random* should be endowed with fortunes with which they could do what they liked.[46] This would be worth doing even if only one in a hundred or one in a thousand of those selected used their opportunities in ways that appeared retrospectively beneficial to others. Some egalitarians, if they could be induced to give the argument a hearing, might settle for this method – and it would certainly be better than not having such fortunes at all. The argument for allowing inheritance, as well as other kinds of luck, to play a role is that certain socially valuable qualities will often be formed only in the course of two or three generations.

The real weakness of Hayek's position, which few, if any, hostile reviewers have spotted, is that it is, even in principle, completely and characteristically non-quantitative. There must come a point of concentration of income and wealth when the spillover benefits of the consumption of the rich would be more than counterbalanced by their impoverishing effect on the rest of the population. To allow 1 per cent of households to account for 5 or 10 per cent of total personal consumption may be a price well worth paying for the sake of these spillover benefits (as well as for the incentive effects for the working members of that 1 per cent on the size of the total cake). But if 1 per cent consumed 99 per cent, the price would be clearly too high. Somewhere in between must be a point of balance. (The position in 1970 was approximately that of 1 per cent consuming 5 per cent.)

Strictly speaking, a liberal does not have to go any further. Having made the above stipulations and qualifications in relation to the pursuit of equality, he does not have to express a view on the optimum distribution of income or wealth. His concern is with how far any proposed redistribution affects freedom. He is not concerned with the virtues of equality as a goal, and liberals can and do take different views on the matter.

It is, nevertheless, worth asking whether there is any meaningful goal other than equality, or accepting a distribution that emerges either from the existing market, or from a market in which the anti-competitive elements have been reduced, which will be genuinely impersonal, and not involve political judgements of the merits of individuals or professions. For, in the absence of a third principle, there is a real danger that people will think the two impersonal alternatives too extreme and fall back on the dangerous ideas of reward according to merit, or on the 'specific egalitarianism' which will be discussed below.

The most promising third principle is to be derived from the ideas of Rawls already mentioned: [47] the kind of distribution of income and wealth that people would vote for if they were ignorant of what their own position in the scale was to be. Even apart from the imaginative leap, the principle does raise other difficulties. For the different hypothetical distribution for which people would vote would reveal differences in attitude to risk and uncertainty. Someone with a taste for gambling would be interested in seeing that there were some really big incomes just in case he came out lucky. It is not very satisfactory that a majority should be able to impose its preference on gambling versus insurance on the rest of the population.

Yet it is surely much less unsatisfactory than either the Hayek principle, which would give a veto to the richest of the rich, or the crude democratic formula, which would allow 51 per cent of the population to despoil the other 49 per cent. Indeed, there is a great deal of evidence from poll data and M.P.s correspondence that the majority of the population who fall in the middle income ranges are jealous both of those in upper ranges – they dislike surtax cuts – and of those at the bottom end – for they dislike family allowances at least as much. Indeed, the second distribution shown in the table on p. 129 might actually be *preferred* by the electorate. (One must remember that most of the votes are with the 'B's.) But only a blind or bigoted democrat would wish to bless such vindictiveness towards rich and poor alike by the mass of mediocrity in the middle.

The ignorance formula does at least secure disinterestedness, which straightforward voting does not. Moreover, *if* it were operated, I would guess that a large degree of consensus would then emerge. The first thought of most people would surely be to avoid finding themselves in some sort of 'depressed tenth'. They would be interested to level up enough to make sure that there was no badly depressed poverty-stricken tail of the income distribution in which, with bad luck, they might find themselves. At this end, they would be more concerned with insurance than with gambling. They would also dislike so large a concentration at the top that it heavily depressed the median income.

On the other hand, they would not like to flatten out the top of the distributional diamond so much that the median income was reduced for incentive reasons. Most people, I would hazard, would also like the idea of a few really large prizes for the lucky minority, although there would be disagreement on the exact size and distribution of the prize money.*

Enough has been said to emphasise the very large area over which the thoughtful egalitarian and a radically-minded economic liberal can agree. Both could join in an onslaught on artificial barriers to entry imposed by unnecessary apprenticeship or professional qualifications. Both can support generous payments to the poorer members of the community.

---

* Professor Rawls himself appears to identify the maximisation of the long run welfare of the most disadvantaged representative person as the sole criterion of distribution with the one that people would choose in such a position of ignorance. I do not think that the two can be *identified* in this way. The considerations which would enter into choice in such a position are more complex and would probably vary from one person to another. The deliberately vaguer statements made above indicate the degree of special concern for the least well off which might be reasonably expected in this hypothetical position.

Professor Milton Friedman, who is a rather extreme economic liberal, has rightly stated that the only limitation on this sort of levelling up assistance is the wealth and generosity of the majority of the electorate.[48] Moreover, a thoughtful egalitarian would surely agree that a good deal (although not all) of existing inequality reflects the non-pecuniary aspects of different jobs. The Jay formula of 'an equal right to happiness' cannot mean equality of money income for jobs of varying degrees of discomfort, hazard or opportunities for leisure. There are occupations such as opera singing or professional sport, where high rewards are not just 'rents' for scarce abilities, but are to a large extent compensation for the very large risks run by any new entrant into these fields; and a rational egalitarian ought to allow the legitimacy of such discrepancies.

The egalitarian and the liberal could also go a considerable way together on the taxation of inheritance and wealth. Neither should see any virtue in a system of nominally very high Estate Duties with loopholes that make them a voluntary levy. The introduction of a Gifts Tax, and other reforms would make a lower rate of duty more effective than the present high one. Although such a change might be a second best for an egalitarian to duties which were both high and effective, it would be an improvement for both groups compared with the present system. Liberals can perfectly well support the transformation of Estate Duty into a legacy duty to promote a wider diffusion of inherited wealth – again, a change that would be inferior from an egalitarian point of view to the abolition of inherited wealth, but an improvement on the present.

A liberal utilitarian would also prefer, during a person's lifetime, to tax capital itself rather than the yield from capital, as the latter kind of tax is a heavy deterrent to risk-taking. This would point to an annual wealth tax in *place* of the present differential against unearned income. (The £250 million yield from the differential could have been replaced in 1970 by a wealth tax of 1 per cent on wealth above £20,000 or just over 2 per cent on wealth above £50,000.) The egalitarian inclination to impose the wealth tax *in addition* to the present differential should, however, be checked by reflection on the possible effects of such double taxation on investment, saving and risk-taking. But, even if an egalitarian refuses to be checked by such considerations, the above examples are sufficient to show that there are many reforms which he and the liberal can both advocate which, even if not ideal, are at least an improvement on the present.

The real parting of the ways comes only with the rate of progression on the upper ranges of taxes on income. This does not mean that all economic liberals must share the opposition of Friedman and Hayek to progressive taxation. The expressed sentiments of these economists convey, in fact, a misleading impression; for their attitudes to benefits imply considerable progression in net rates on the lower ranges. What they really mean is that the rate of progression should taper off at a moderate upper limit of well below 50 per cent. Other economic liberals, while wanting to preserve the opportunity for some to achieve high incomes and even found fortunes, would certainly agree that the tax rates should vary with incomes and not only in the lowest ranges. My own personal preference, for what it is worth, would be a gradual climb which levelled out at a marginal rate of 50–60 per cent. One cannot expect egalitarians to like even this in principle; but before they reject it out of hand, they should consider that high nominal rates are, to a notorious extent, avoided or evaded. More effective, if somewhat lower rates, should be at least a second best from their point of view.

There are, in fact, few subjects more conducive to intellectual self-deception, or even dishonesty, than the taxation of personal incomes. Many economists (not to speak of politicians and other commentators) have protested too much about the disincentive effects of high tax rates in the upper income ranges without admitting that they have other grounds for opposition and would be *disappointed* if the disincentive effect were found to be small. This is an unfortunate aspect of the English utilitarian heritage which, on the one hand, asserted that incomes ought ideally to be equal and then, on the other hand, discovered a thousand and one countervailing reasons why they should not in fact be so.

The valuable part of utilitarianism is not the principle of equal weighting for all; but the idea that governments should concern themselves with the satisfaction of people's desires rather than some 'higher' goal such as national honour or prestige, territorial aggrandisement or the enforcement of a divinely sanctioned code of behaviour. Reasons have been given in the preceding pages for believing that equality of incomes would be positively undesirable even if it had a zero effect on the rate of growth of the measured Gross Domestic Product. If both sides openly acknowledged that they were not primarily motivated by the incentives issue, the latter could be analysed more candidly.

The search for debating points affects at least as badly the egalitarian side of the argument. It is easy to scoff at simplistic tax-cutting propaganda by pointing out that taxes on incomes (whether direct or indirect) have a 'substitution' and an 'income' effect, which point in different directions. The substitution effect increases the attraction of leisure over work (and of undemanding work over demanding but better paid work), the higher the rate of tax. The income effect means that people have to work harder to obtain a given income. The two effects work in opposite directions and a tax cut can either be a stimulant or deterrent to effort. But it is disingenuous to pretend that analysis ends at this point. The substitution effect relates to *marginal* tax rates, the income effect to the *average* rate paid by the taxpayer on his whole income (what the Inland Revenue calls the 'effective' rate).

Up to the end of 1970–1, marginal rates were so high relative to average rates on the larger professional and management earnings that the disincentive effect was the one that prevailed (to the extent that the rates were made effective); and it is no rebuttal to point out that equally high marginal rates were to be found at the bottom end of the scale owing to the operation of a series of unco-ordinated means tests.* An egalitarian who accepts the Jay qualification about the minimum inequality required for the effective functioning of the system should not want to return to the pre-1971 situation of marginal rates on earned incomes crossing the 50 per cent threshold at £4,000, 75 per cent at £7,000, and eventually reaching 91¼ per cent. The argument of the agnostic applies with greatest force to those in the income bands above, but

* The problems raised by this phenomenon are discussed on pp. 272 et seq.

not too far above, the average, who paid in 1970–1 a marginal rate of just over 30 per cent. They carried much less conviction in the surtax range, where tax cuts were regarded as more politically controversial.

The whole question is often discussed as if the main issue were the amount of effort expended in a given job, when the main disincentive effects in all probability arise from the choice of one job rather than another. The deterrent effects on risky activities – whether jobs or investment – is a matter of arithmetic and can be worked out for himself by any sceptical reader if he will compare the value of two streams of earnings with different probability dispersions around the same average, under more and less progressive tax systems. Of course, knowledge would be advanced if someone could design a really good empirical test of the total net effects of very high marginal rates at either end of the social scale. The surveys I have seen which purport to refute the disincentive effects do not come anywhere near doing so; few even bear on the question. In the meanwhile, no one has answered Lord Robbins's question: 'If we could not argue that it made no difference if the marginal rate were 20s. in the pound, why should we speak as if the position is so radically changed when the residue from a pound's worth of earnings is 6d or 1s?'[49]

In some ways the most irritating aspect of this whole controversy is the emphasis of *soi-disant* egalitarians on 'non-pecuniary incentives'. It may be possible to create something out of nothing by inventing titles, decorations and orders which will serve as a substitute for take-home pay – although why this should specially appeal to those who claim to dislike social stratification is hard to understand. In any case, this process cannot be carried too far without these badges becoming heavily devalued. For the most part 'non-pecuniary' incentives are the pleasures of accomplishment (or just of passing the time), congenial working conditions, or the desire for power and importance. The first is besides the point, as one of the main functions of giving higher net pay to some people of comparable abilities than to others, is to attract them into jobs which yield comparatively little in pleasures of this kind. As for congenial working conditions, these are an aspect of real income, and there is no particular reason to subsidise them (and we are talking here about company cars, executive suites and dining rooms at the expense of living standards in a person's free time). What there is of the argument rests heavily on a belief that power over others is a lesser evil than high pay and should be encouraged as a substitute. This reverses Keynes's dictum that 'it is better that a man should tyrannise over his bank balance than over his fellow citizens'; and, as he insisted, the two were sometimes alternatives.[50]

Instead of expending effort on trying to restore confiscatory marginal tax rates on earnings from work and capital, those of us who are concerned with the distribution of income would do better to worry about the possible effects of rising land values in a society where land ownership is very highly concentrated. With rising affluence and population, the growing demand for pure space which cannot be increased by human effort could make land very much scarcer relative to labour and capital than it has been in the past; and land rents could come to absorb a higher proportion of the national income. It will be obvious to the reader that I believe that the problem of distribution, as distinct from poverty, has been vastly exaggerated by British egalitarians; and, in particular, that the gain to the rest of the population from eliminating the excess incomes of, say, the top 5 per cent would be negligible or, more probably, negative. But the situation would be very different if 40, 50, 60 or 70 per cent of incomes accrued to a small minority of owners of pure space, the total of which was in no way affected by their work saving or enterprise.

It is too soon to say whether there is anything in this nightmare. The share of the national income going to landowners is still remarkably small for a crowded island. The spectre of a monstrous increase in the landowners' share of the national income has haunted economies since the time of Ricardo. Yet as late as 1969, the share of personal income before tax from property of all kinds was only 12 per cent; and the greater part of this was due to earnings on capital (including home ownership and pension fund income) or interest payments on the national debt rather than to land rents.[51] But the possibility of a virulent attack of the disease of land shortage is high enough to merit contingency planning – more so than many of the other horrors that alarm the prophets of doom.

The very worst cure for such a situation would be the control of land rents. If land were so scarce, it would be particularly important to make the most of it, which could only be done by charging full market rents; and, where land is state-owned, this should take the form of parking charges, road tolls, charges for entry to recreational areas and so on. For private land, the object should be to find some way of combining full market rents with a recovery of some of these rents by the general community of taxpayers. The search for some form of taxing pure land values, such as site value taxation, which would not distort the use of land, should continue. But judging by the discouraging experience of the past, such schemes will not be easy to implement successfully; and in the last resort, even the nationalisation of land, provided that it is vested in many different local authorities and other independent bodies who are encouraged to act on commercial principles and compete with each other, would be a lesser evil to those of below-market rents in the envisaged situation. But a better solution, if only it could be brought into effect, would be to make a reality of the slogan of a property-owning democracy. If either land itself or the financial investments which represented land at one or two removes were more widely distributed, the perverse effects of high rents would be very much reduced.

Specific Egalitarianism

The kind of egalitarianism so far discussed may be termed 'general' egalitarianism. Despite its popularity in certain academic and Whitehall circles and its links with the puritan tradition, it is not a widely held ideal among the public. 'Specific' egalitarianism is more widespread and is a much more important threat to liberty. (Some general egalitarians are also specific egalitarians, but this need not be the case.)

Specific egalitarianism comes in two forms: a mild levelling up form and a strong levelling down one. The mild form is paternalistic, but not viciously so. It is suggested by slogans such as: 'Everybody has a right to a decent home, at a price he can afford, and decent medical treatment and education, irrespective of means.' It can even be justified as a liberal–paternalist compromise on the following lines: 'By all means let people spend their own incomes in their own way, but we are only prepared to be taxed to help the less well-off if we can be sure that the money goes for food, homes, health or the welfare of children and is not free spending money for beer and cigarettes.' One may not like such feelings, but they are not incompatible with a free society, provided that no one is prevented from spending above the state minimum. Indeed, if some variant of the voucher system is used, there is no need for even the provision of the bare minimum to be a state monopoly. The mild form of 'specific egalitarianism' is a misnomer for policies concerned with minima, but the label has already been stuck on such policies in the literature on the subject and it is too late to alter it.

This mild form only becomes a menace to liberty, or to the rational conduct of affairs, when the state explicitly or implicitly takes on a commitment that it cannot or will not fulfil. The most obvious example is housing subsidies and rent controls. If the public authorities were prepared to build up enough houses and flats to supply to the full the extra demand created by their policies, more of the nation's resources would go into housing than citizens desire. But this would be the limit of state coercion and once sufficient accommodation was built, the rent controls could be allowed to wither away. A permanent housing shortage and the power of public officials over individual lives arises when a country has the controls and the subsidies without a public housebuilding programme large enough to meet the implicit commitment. (The elaboration of this example will be left to Chapter 4.) The threat to liberty, and the many anomalies and inequities, arise not from the intrinsic nature of the aims, but from the acceptance by the authorities under public pressure of a series of *ad hoc* policies without an attempt to think through their longer term implications – an illustration of the dangers of over-extension of the political sphere already discussed.

The stronger, levelling down form of specific egalitarianism comes in a different category altogether. It is symbolised by deceptively attractive slogans such as: 'Nobody should be able to buy a privileged education for his child or better medical treatment simply because he has more money.' Despite its demagogic appeal, it is a severe use of state coercion to limit freedom of choice; and if any doctrine is the true road to serfdom, it is this strong form of specific egalitarianism. A fixed travel allowance to 'prevent anyone buying a better holiday for himself simply because he has money', would be an example of the attitude in question. Usually, however, arguments for this form of specific egalitarianism tend to concentrate on social services such as health and education. The three arguments one meets most frequently boil down to the following:

(1)   Use of the same education and health service by the whole population is desirable as a common badge of citizenship which reduces the gulf between different sections of society. (This is sometimes called the 'integrationist' argument.)

(2)   Expenditure on a superior education by better-off families – or even by ordinary families who value education above the average – gives some children an unfair start over others of equal innate ability, and is thus incompatible with equality of opportunity.

(3)   The supply of goods and services may be 'inelastic' and will not therefore respond to market incentives. Some form of rationing may be required in such cases if the poor are not to be deprived of access to them.

Of the above arguments, only the third, based on the supposed inelasticity of supply of some services, deserves a hearing by liberals, and it is the one which James Tobin stresses in his defence of specific egalitarianism.[52] The eventual judgement here must, of course, depend on questions of fact as well as of values. If there is some reason why the output of a product cannot respond to increased demand, then the market will cease to perform its normal functions on the supply side (although it can still ration available supplies in line with relative preferences). The key feature of a war situation, in which price control and rationing are introduced, is that there are physical constraints on the supply of food and consumer goods which cannot be easily increased irrespective of profitability.

Such a situation is very exceptional for most products in time of peace. The view that it exists in the medical field (the one most frequently cited) – and hence that 'queue-jumping' is reprehensible – is plausible only if one considers the purely short-term elasticity of supply. There is ample evidence that the number who train as doctors and other medical personnel (and who remain in this country) respond to prospects of pay and employment. Nor is there any reason to doubt that non-N.H.S. hospitals and nursing homes would be built in response to an upsurge in the private market. It is no coincidence that nearly all Western European countries, which do not possess a fully-fledged state health service, devote a larger proportion of the G.N.P. to health than does the U.K. The short-run inelasticity of supply of medical services may point to a gradualist policy of encouraging private provision, but only an obsessional pre-occupation with the short term would be a reason for a permanent policy of forbidding or restricting it.

The first two of the arguments listed on page 142 leads towards, not merely an egalitarian, but a uniform, society and embodies a set of value-judgements at the opposite pole from that which sets store by individual choice and variety in life styles. There is no justification for the high moral tone sometimes adopted by those who wish education, medical care, insurance, and, in some cases, housing, to be provided exclusively on a comon basis by the state. What is there so elevated about a society in which take-home pay is for food and amusement only, and other essentials are provided communally on a free or subsidised basis, without the individual having taken any responsibility for them?[53]

If top priority is to be given to equality of opportunity, in the sense of preventing one child from acquiring any advantages over any other apart from those resulting from genetic endowments, then, indeed, all discretionary or private expenditure on education must be forbidden; and it must be forbidden even if all parents enjoy the same income. But there are many other types of family activities which give some children advantage over others, including the possession of books, foreign travel, or the provision of a 'good home'. An economic liberal can be enthusiastic about policies for giving more opportunities to those starting at the bottom. But absolute equality of opportunity is a mistaken goal. It points inexorably to Plato's recommendation in *The Republic* (based on an extension of Spartan practices) that children should be taken away from their parents at birth and great care taken to prevent them discovering their identity.[54] As Bertrand Russell remarks, 'Plato possessed the art to dress up illiberal suggestions in such a way that they deceived future ages'.[55] The heritage of this brilliant authoritarian still survives in much would-be 'progressive' contemporary thinking. A modern exemplar is James Tobin who, in the well-argued but fundamentally sinister article just quoted, points to the selective U.S. military draft as an egalitarian ideal, suggests the prohibition of volunteering, and actually toys with the idea of setting soldiers' pay well below effective civilian alternatives to perpetuate the draft. If this is representative of the U.S. progressive establishment, the revolt of the campuses is all too easy to understand.

The Role of Economics

If egalitarianism is the most explosive landmine for the economic liberal to negotiate, the relation of his doctrines to economics as an academic discipline is the most elusive. One orthodox view is that there is no relation at all, as economics ought to be a positive science, with findings which can be used to advance any political or ethical ideal according to the taste of the user. This is much too simplistic a distinction. The word 'ought' in the above formulation is itself revealing. It is strange, to say the least, that although all the varieties of economic liberalism rank as political philosophies, professional economists have been largely instrumental in developing them. There are no collectivist or conservative philosophies with which mainstream professional economists have had a similar association. Indeed, it is remarkable how far the endeavours to develop a 'socialist economics' have consisted of attempts to transplant the liberal ideas of the market economy and the price mechanism to an environment of state ownership. The lack of any conservative economic philosophy has long been well known and is a point of pride with some conservatives.

A large number of economists are, of course, virulently opposed to any form of economic liberalism. But they are exhibiting a reaction to a strong tradition within their own profession. Although they may think that they are opposing a pro-capitalist position, a little investigation soon shows that the actual policies of pro-capitalist governments bear very little relation to the doctrines of economic liberalism – indeed, Galbraith has taken a justified delight in explaining how Nixon has violated all its tenets. The anti-liberals in the economic profession are ranged against a whole line of philosophically inclined economists from Adam Smith down to Hayek and Friedman rather than against a political party or a group of capitalists. Empirical evidence can be produced to show that there is much greater support for liberal policy positions in an advanced Western economy among economists than among politicians and commentators, and that economists of differing political beliefs often hold common policy positions which distinguish them from other educated laymen interested in public affairs.

This is a somewhat remarkable position for a would-be neutral science. It is related to a profound ambiguity about the subject matter of economics. According to one tradition it is a science of human behaviour in relation to the material things of life, and therefore sheds light on the factors determining the growth of income and wealth. A different tradition sees it as the science or logic of choice (which of the two is itself controversial). According to the latter tradition, there is no such thing as economic ends. Economics is concerned with the allocation of resources, energy and time among alternatives, and the view of the economist as a philistine concerned to multiply material riches is itself a vulgar misconception.

There are usually deep-seated reasons why subjects do not fit neatly into logical pigeon-holes and the matter will not be resolved by proclaiming dogmatically that one or other concept is the right one. There is an inevitable strain between the two approaches, but they have co-existed (often within the same individual) for nearly a century and neither is likely to give way completely to the other. It is simplest, however, to start with the older view – which also corresponds to the layman's image – that economics is concerned with behaviour in relation to material things, particularly where money can be brought into the picture.

The economist has so far had very little to say on many of the most important determinants of output and living standards, in particular on science and technology and attitudes towards change and innovation. Technological matters are the concern of other specialists, and essays by economists on national attitudes and other psychological intangibles carry no more weight than those of anyone else. The main subject on which they can even aspire to a professional competence is the functioning of markets, and, in particular, the way in which supply and demand relate to prices and incomes. As we have already seen, the price mechanism, even when used for paternalist objectives, is a relatively *liberal means.*

In most individual markets price is the most important variable about which the economist can pronounce. Variations in the level of incomes may be important, but in any particular case, there is little that can be done about them. Whether an economist is investigating the steel industry or the structure of fares, there is little he can do about the incomes of those operating in the market; his contribution is likely to be mainly on pricing policy and the disaggregation of costs and receipts from different activities.

It is only when it comes to the attempted management of demand and output in the economy as a whole that an 'economics without price' has been evolved. Keynesian fiscal policy, of the type practised for most of the postwar period, has attempted to control output entirely via real incomes; indeed, the associated forecasts and policy recommendations have been in 'real terms' and have largely abstracted from any influence of either absolute or relative prices. It is therefore not surprising that economists of the 'national income forecasting' school are less wedded to liberal economic attitudes than their colleagues (but also less keen on detailed intervention, as they pin so much faith on global management). Even in their case, however, the role of price is forcibly brought home via the effect of the exchange rate on the external balance; and the competence of economists again lies in their analysis of front or backdoor exchange rate changes –

which are of course a special kind of price. It does not lie in exhortations to export more, or in whipping up enthusiasm inside industrial committees such as the 'Little Neddies'.

Another kind of economics which minimises markets or prices arises from growth models which make the proportion of the national income invested (especially in manufacturing industry) the key to growth and from this go on to suggest that the forcible reduction of the share of consumption in the national income (aided perhaps by overseas aid) is the key to prosperity. This structure of ideas still has some influence in advanced industrial countries; but it always had too many weaknesses to become the main strand of economic thinking there. Differences in investment ratios were found to be inadequate to account for observed differences in growth rates; in any case, the investment differences seemed at least as likely to be a consequence as a cause of growth. Moreover, the idea of the capital market and the rate of interest as having some relevance to choice between present and future satisfactions never entirely lost hold; and the various distortions in the market allegedly keeping investment too low have been offset in recent thinking by the emphasis on environmental spill-over which might make it undesirably high. It is mainly in connection with developing countries and the Third World that economic explanations which play down prices and markets have really captured mainstream thinking.[56]

Indeed, economics, conceived as the study of behaviour affecting material wealth, has remarkably little to say on the effects of different political and economic systems and ideologies. There have been fast growing economies in both the capitalist and the Communist world; and even among Western countries there has been almost no systematic relation between growth rates and degrees of intervention. It may be possible by forced draft methods, involving very undemocratic socialism, to increase a country's statistical growth rate, but the benefit of such methods to real living standards lies always somewhere in the future. No country relying on them has yet been seen to give its citizens a higher level of material prosperity than that prevailing in the U.S. or North West Europe, even when judged by conventional indices.

The obstinate question arises, however, how we should

know if and when this overtaking has happened, and here is where the other concept of economics as the logic or science of choice inescapably obtrudes. Talk of material wealth or money incomes 'at constant prices' cannot hide the fact that that is no unique way of measuring the changes in a bundle of hundreds of different sets of commodities and services, the composition of which is constantly changing. Money values can be used to add apples and pears only because, in a market system, relative prices are supposed to give some idea of individual preferences and choices. It is theoretically possible to reject consumer sovereignty and use some other basis of valuation; but in that case an alternative set of criteria has to be provided.

Individuals and Nations

Despite some lip service to other concepts, such as the social welfare function, the logic of choice as worked out by economists has been the logic of individual choice. Basic to this logic are the following propositions: (a) when means are limited, a given benefit should be achieved at the lowest cost; (b) if different alternatives cost the same, the one yielding most satisfaction should be chosen; and (c) scarcity of means of one sort or another, if only time, always limit the total of satisfaction to be obtained. The important point about these seeming platitudes is that both the costs and the benefits involved are entirely subjective. Professor Robert Mundell has even written of a composer of piano music maximising 'the effect of a sequence of notes always subject to the budget constraint that the notes he inscribes are on the piano and that the sequence of notes is within the physical capacity of a pianist'.[57]

This last example brings out some worries about the economist's concept of rational choice and optimisation. It can be a language for describing almost all human action, a set of predictive statements about how human beings will act, or a recommendation to act in certain ways. The early utilitarians were robust enough to take the third approach; later generations of economists have hesitated to confront head-on the seemingly irrational in human affairs. But if talk of minimising costs and maximising benefits is mainly a language, then very many apparently irrational actions appear rational after all. Professor Harry Johnson has, for example, argued that although the policies of economic nationalism adopted by new nations cause material loss, they also convey psychical satisfaction on individuals in their countries by 'gratifying the taste for nationalism'. He goes so far as to write that 'the psychic enjoyment that the mass of the population derives from the collective consumption aspects of nationalism suffices to compensate them for the loss of material income imposed on them by nationalist economic policies, so that nationalistic policies arrive at a quite acceptable result from the standpoint of maximising satisfaction'.[58]

Whether or not these remarks are tongue-in-cheek, they do suggest that the pure logic of choice could justify the most apparently absurd behaviour. Costly wars involving much human suffering and little tangible reward can be rationalised by saying that the psychic satisfaction from the thought of a certain disputed area being administered by people of one's own ethnic group outweighs all the miseries involved. Yet the making of this translation is not pointless. For it forces people who make it to be more self-conscious than they would otherwise be and ask: 'How much suffering is worth the gratification of my feelings of national pride? How much less take-home pay is worth my psychic satisfaction in Ruritanian ownership of Ruritanian resources?' It is a reasonable guess that self-consciousness about these issues would lead to policies of a less nationalistic blood-and-soil kind than simple reiteration of Horace's 'Dulce et decorum est pro patria mori'. The point is developed in Chapter 10. The economic theory of rational choice is based on 'methodological individualism'. The actions and goals of nations and governments are translated into the goals of the individuals who take the decision. The economic approach is, in this sense, reductionist, and here lies its essential affinity with both utilitarianism and liberalism.

If economics is to be a science with predictive value – even if it is to predict only in quantitative terms certain general results and not specific numbers – it must break out of this circle of tautologies. Costs and benefits have to be identified in such a way that they can be related to something observable, not necessarily monetary behaviour in a market; the pursuit of office and votes, and the cost in time and trouble of voting and the pursuit of information have been treated this way, most notably by Anthony Downs in *The Economic Theory of Democracy*. Having identified such costs and benefits, the exponents of the economic approach base their predictions on the assumption that men will act rationally in the face of them – as acting irrationally now has a meaning.

Opposed to this is what Brian Barry has called the sociological approach in his fascinating study, *Sociologists, Economists and Democracy*.[59] This approach was, in origin, largely a right-wing reaction to the French Revolution; it asserted that men were influenced largely by irrational forces and that there were distinct and relatively unalterable national characteristics. In our own day this has been followed by vociferous denials that man can be regarded as a calculating animal. They have images of themselves, their rights and duties which cause them to both fall below and rise above self-interest.

Instead of making either/or choices between the two approaches, we would do well to follow Barry in his judgement that the economic approach works better in some areas than others. It is at its best in the analysis of individual markets, although it applies in a clearer and more straightforward fashion to some markets than in others. It gives us some insight into macroeconomic phenomena such as inflation, unemployment and growth, although the sociological point of view is also relevant here. The economic approach has had least to say on the causes (as distinct from the logic) of wars, revolutions, racial tension and other such major issues – although it may make some contribution even here. The trouble is that although sociologists in principle ought to step into the vacuum, they have not been very forthcoming in refutable propositions deduced from a set of axioms alternative to those of the economists.

Even if successful predictions can be made by making inferences from the behaviour of the rational individual, it does not follow that his action will necessarily lead to desirable results. All that the economist can show is that on the basis of certain values and under certain environmental conditions such a result *may* be produced. A sociological approach in which myth, images and stereotypes predominate does not even raise the question of the consequences of following rational self-interest. Moreover, an economist whose predictive success is so dependent on inferences made from rational individual behaviour would be less than human if he did not tend to side with such an individual against those who wished to subordinate their behaviour to 'higher' or other values.

Those economists whose reputation depends on the behaviour of growth models closely linked with a politically determined rate of capital formulation, or who are primarily experts in handling specialist statistics, have vested interests of a very different type. But the main tradition and practice of Western economic theory is still involved – to the regret of some economists – in a view of society centred around the individual rather than groups or metaphysical entities.

The Real Difficulties

The real difficulties of economic liberalism lie, not with the economic, but with the liberal part of the concept. Liberalism, in the sense used in this essay, is an individualist ethic. It puts the emphasis on allowing individuals to follow to the maximum feasible extent their separately chosen ends. It is opposed by the desire, which has often been very powerful, for people to merge their own identities into something greater than themselves – whether a country, a regiment, a workers' movement, a tradition of honour, or the abnegation of self in the service of God, to name only a very few of the 'ideals' to which people have often gladly submitted themselves and their personal demands or impulses. As we have just seen in a different context all these activities can be reconciled with liberal beliefs by manipulating definitions. Brünnhilde can be said to be following a desire for self-immolation; a Jesuit who follows the teachings of Ignatius Loyola can be regarded as freely choosing to become 'as a corpse which has neither intelligence nor will'. There is a standing temptation for liberalism, like other ideologies, to avoid uncomfortable facts by taking refuge in tautologous formulations. But these simply evade the fact that the liberal mood is not one for all seasons or types of men; and when people are in the state described, it is absurd even to bring up the question of any liberalism, let alone the economic variety.

As K. R. Minogue has pointed out in that provoking but provocative study *The Liberal Mind*,[60] death is the worst possible evil to the liberal, because it brings to an end all desires, choice or action. 'On liberal premises it is irrational to die for one's country, unless perhaps the self-sacrifice is interpreted as an attempt to minimise the extinction of similarly desiring selves.' But there are moods in which heroism is justified not through some such rational backdoor, but because human life is regarded as serving some superior cause – the nation, the race or the creed.

There are many other difficulties too. In a society in which people are free to choose their own ends and values to the maximum feasible extent, there will be, in Minogue's words, 'many sources of status – money, birth, place of education, intellectual celebrity, popularity and so on.' Many people would undoubtedly prefer a single status system in which 'everyone can be conveniently assessed at a moment's notice.'[61] Much of the psychological desire for an 'incomes policy' comes from this urge. The difficulty, as well as the undesirability of attempting to go back to a status system in the present age has already been argued (pp. 117–20). But the desire exists and Minogue is right to deny that we can have variety without suffering, although wrong to pour scorn on the utilitarian desire to improve the trade-offs.

He goes, however, much too far in regarding liberalism as 'a solemn check on everything that is spontaneous, wild, enthusiastic, uncaring, or disinterested'. This is to equate liberalism with the spirit of Polonius rather than that of the Ninth Symphony. If Minogue wants to call the rationalistic (rather than rational) approach of Polonius liberalism, there is no point in arguing about labels, especially as historically there have been those who valued political and economic freedom purely as a means to some such grey goal; and they have successors who would seek to increase satisfaction by curbing desires, whether through religious asceticism or a ban on advertising. But the market economy has also been defended by a whole line of writers as an instrument for enabling people to follow varied and diverse goals of their own choosing, however wayward and irrational these may seem to others, with a minimum of collision.

Interestingly enough, of the two strands in economic liberalism identified earlier – the more conservative one with its emphasis on rules and conventions and the importance of the undesigned in human affairs, and the radical one which attempts to assess the specific consequences of each proposed action or policy without hindrance from traditional dogma – it is the former, more conservative one which allows greater scope for spontaneous and unorthodox initiatives. What has been called general utilitarianism fits much more easily with individual spontaneity than the 'particularist' brand. This is the grain of truth for 'the reverence for the traditional' which I found so uncongenial on first reading the *Constitution of Liberty*.

Such irritation has not wholly disappeared; for an emphasis on individual freedom must often lead to a desire to change convention and established practices. But if anarchy is ruled out, the only alternative to rules, conventions and tradition is the examination by authority of the specifics of every action which is outside the narrow category of the purely 'self-regarding'; and this is bound to give an enormous emphasis to the conventional wisdom of the age. The ideal would be to have a liberal set of traditions, conventions, and presumptions, which actually value non-conformity, innovation and eccentricity. Where such traditions do not exist, they cannot be invented overnight. The most one can hope to do is to develop the more liberal elements in our own tradition, and to downgrade the illiberal ones of the Eton and the Brigade of Guards type.

The fundamental difficulty for liberals of all hues is the fact of death, which brings to an end all the choices and actions to which they attach so much importance. The difficulty is very much less for other value systems which place the emphasis on the sinking of individual desires into something nobler or baser – whether the class war or the spirit of the universe – which are believed to continue beyond the life of any particular person. For such reasons some liberals have been tempted to shift the emphasis from the individual to

the family. Yet this is no more than a compromise. There is
an obvious, genetic and non-mystical reason why people
should be able to identify with the welfare and freedom of
their children and descendants. Yet each member of a family
is an individual personality with thoughts, feelings and goals
of his or her own; and a country with considerable freedom
for family units inside which the head of the household wields
despotic powers, such as Republican Rome or Victorian
England, is far from being a free society.

Conclusions

No philosopher's stone has been unearthed in this essay. If
there were one simple slogan for limiting the role of coercion
of human affairs, and for minimising the power of man over
his fellow men, it would have long ago been found and its
application to economic policy already known. All that has
been formulated have been a few broad presumptions: that
the aim of policy should be to satisfy the wants that people
happen to have rather than that they ought to have; that our
best chance of securing this is through what I have called the
'corrected market economy'; that the corrections and interventions should as far as possible take the form of general
rules with the minimum of administrative discretion; and
that we should consciously aim to limit the domain of the
politicians and of decisions made by 'society'. This last presumption is the most difficult of all to state precisely, but,
perhaps at the present time, the most important. Even these
rough guidelines are not worth much to those who have not
thought through their justification, or their application to
particular areas.

The danger that any broad doctrine, such as the interpretation of the market economy presented above, will either be
ignored as too complex, or misunderstood and vulgarised in
political application, is great and obvious. So much so that it
is tempting to conclude that the attempt to found policy on
principle is likely to do more harm than good and that we are
better off with the minimum of doctrinal baggage. Political
and economic principles, however simple they appear, are
normally a complex mixture of value judgements and em-

pirical generalisations. Nothing is finer to behold than a government acting on the right principles (i.e. the ones with which one happens to agree). Nothing is worse than a government persisting in mistaken policies out of an obstinate adherence to bad, or misunderstood, or misapplied, principles. An ideal U.S. administration in the 1960s would have had an approach to foreign policy which would have avoided the Vietnam imbroglio in the first place. But as a second best, a pragmatic or even cynical administration, prepared to disengage when it was running into difficulties was infinitely preferable to one that was prepared to press on in Vietnam regardless of the cost, for the sake of some misguided articles of faith.

The probability that people in high public office will have the time or temperament to reflect on the fundamental principles of policy and their application is a low one. The few leaders who have been strongly committed to general positions of any kind in the face of the temptations and distractions tend for that very reason towards the hair-shirt view of life: the sacrifice of the individual to the glory of the nation, a belief in dying for freedom which puts more emphasis on the dying than on the freedom, a preference for doing things the hard way as if this were itself a virtue, or an interpretation of the market economy that puts the emphasis on the disciplinary and cold shower aspects rather than the permissive and pro-consumer ones.

Nevertheless, the so-called pragmatic approach of taking decisions on their individual merits or 'on the facts' is a logical impossibility. Specific judgements cannot be made in a vacuum but implicitly involve both broad empirical judgements of the efforts of different types of situations and policies, and value judgements about the desirability of different types of outcome. Paradoxically, it is just because the principles of evaluation of the political empiricist are likely to be vague, muddled and inconsistent that his decisions are most unlikely to be related in any predictable way to any particular set of facts. The judgements of those who believe in treating each issue on its merits are likely to reflect the fashions of the moment, the influence of pressure groups, the clamour of the media, or the whims of the individuals concerned.

The best way of breaking through these difficulties is to regard political and economic philosophies, not as being aimed at the conversion of some great leader, but at influencing the climate of opinion in which decisions are taken, studies made, and advice evolved. It is conventional to believe that the trend of the times is away from a market economy based on 'the rule of law' and a limited political sphere. The most frequent argument is the inevitability of large units allegedly enforced by technological advance. This generalisation is drawn from a very limited number of industries and ignores many tendencies the other way arising from the proliferation of service activities of all kinds and the technological developments – even in the computer field itself – which may open up whole new areas to the smaller firm or establishment. Above all, the generalisation in question vastly underrates the amount of long run competition that does take place even between large units, especially if they are operating in an international market.

The real threats arise first of all from populist agitation for the government or society to enforce a view on every question and to determine the deserts of every man. Secondly, they arise from the undoubted fact that many people can gain, at least in the short term, by forming interest groups which circumvent the competitive process by restrictive practices or by political or industrial action. Once some people have gone in for group politics of this kind, others would be well advised to follow in self-defence. Indeed, the pattern of output and remuneration may resemble more closely that of a competitive economy if militant activity by some groups is matched by equal militancy by others and if monopolistic activities of sellers are matched by those of buyers. Galbraith's earlier notion of 'countervailing power' is a much more useful one than some of his more popular recent concepts. Unfortunately, one of the main troubles with a balance produced by self-cancelling interest groups is that it can have explosive inflationary potentialities (to be discussed in the next chapter).

A sensible economic liberal will not refuse to compromise. The test of his judgement is to pick the compromise that is second or third best, rather than fourth or fifth best, from the point of view of his beliefs. But before one can begin to compromise one has to have some idea of where one would like to go if the circumstances permit. In the case of interest group politics just discussed, it is worth remarking that interest group deals do much less harm if they are concerned with fixing remuneration than if they are supported by restrictions of entry into the groups concerned.

There may be times when the liberal has to decide where the greatest danger lies. Does it lie in a network of deals among men who run organisations or in populist attempts to enforce arbitrary concepts of social justice? Normally, the liberal will want to insist on the rule of law and oppose discretionary use of state power. But circumstances can be envisaged in which covert understandings between the political, business, trade union and civil service establishments – in the National Economic Development Council or anywhere else – may be the only way of heading off populist agitation, and preserving some areas of life from political interference. Faced with the tyranny of would-be perfect justice, it is well known that the liberal sides with the conservative. He need not apologise for this; but he knows that this alliance is temporary, uneasy and full of strain, and if he is wise, he will refrain from sounding the alarm bells too frequently.

But even in more normal circumstances, the liberal will not achieve anything except in alliances of convenience on specific issues at specific times. He must not hesitate to make use of the middle class dislike of high taxation where this can help achieve a genuine enlargement in personal choice. Equally he must not hesitate to ally himself with the popular dislike of 'Big Business', or traditionalist dislike of technology, to fight off the New Industrial State. It is only by such shifting alliances – and indeed, often in very doubtful company – that liberalism, whether economic or not, has ever made any headway.

The greatest ally of the liberal is the practical failure of attempts to shape society by centralised political means. Although men have a natural inclination to conform and follow fashions and leaders, they have an equally strong and contradictory tendency to find ways round authority and to devise new ideas and projects which neither the conservatives nor the collectivists expected in their ordered vision. There will always be a new product for which no controlled price exists, a new type of skill which society has not decided how to value. Even the highly dirigiste late Roman Empire and the feudal world of fixed status had all kinds of activities going on, which did not fit the established codes, and which historians have difficulty in fitting into a generalised model. After several centuries in which freedom and independence have been part of the official culture, it will be that much more difficult to suppress them; and in contrast to most conservatives and even many liberals I have taken the view that the so-called 'permissive society' is, despite the hypocrisies of some of its advocates, an extension and a strengthening of the liberal tradition.

Of course, to talk about alliances between people of different outlooks is far too mechanistic. Most people, even among the highly educated, react to specific events with very little firm commitment to generalised political philosophies. A liberal would be wise to accept as the first rule of a successful political process 'Don't force a specification of goals or ends' because agreement on specific policies can often be secured among people with divergent ends.[62] Freedom of speech and worship came about (to the extent that it did), not because people believed this approach deserved a trial, but because they found in mutual tolerance the best chance of being able to express their own belief without having their heads chopped off when their opponents were in the saddle. It is in supporting their own claims that the vegetarians, the Communists (in a capitalist society) or the Seventh Day Adventists became supporters of 'free speech'; and what has started out as a means is in time accepted as an end.

Similarly, if enough people find themselves on the liberal side in particular instances, they may find themselves becoming liberals. If they do, they will not have abolished the problems of the human condition – time, decay, pain, ugliness or death – or brought into existence love, friendship, beauty or exhilaration. These are not matters for political or economic systems. Such systems can make life worse than it need be; and the prevention of avoidable harm is the first priority. At the very best political arrangements can slightly improve the conditions under which human beings face their problems and opportunities. Medical and scientific progress can contribute more; but in the end much will always depend on the accidents of genetic endowment and the pleasant or unpleasant, lucky or unlucky encounters with other human beings from infancy onwards. This is the fundamental liberal message and, for that reason, it will never be very popular but will always be there in the background undermining alike the pretences of the hierarchal conservative state and the ordered collectivist society.

Appendix I: The Non-Liberal Case for Capitalism

Some form of capitalist market economy is supported by many businessmen and politicians who are clearly not liberal in the sense of this essay. If asked for their reason they might well say that it promotes efficiency. It is quite irrational to seek to maximise *engineering efficiency* under almost any political or economic system. If the heat–energy conversion ratio of a machine can be raised from 49 to 50 per cent by multiplying the cost tenfold, it would be extremely wasteful to do this except under the most freakish conditions of labour supply and final product demand.

Economic efficiency is, however, a subjective criterion. A businessman asked to produce x units of a particular commodity will search around the available production methods and any new ones he can discover until there is no further change he can find which will reduce costs any further. He is 'maximising his efficiency' from the point of view of his own self interest. (The exact efficiency conditions have long been given in books on economic principles, but were rediscovered in more complex mathematical form under such titles as 'operational research'.)

But why should minimum costs for a firm be a sign of efficiency from any wider point of view? The price an employer offers for every marginal unit of labour, raw material and other inputs he buys has to be high enough to cover what that unit could produce in its next best employment, before he can succeed in bidding it away. The price paid by the employer therefore represents the alternatives forgone by society to produce an extra unit of the commodity in question.

But how are these alternatives valued? Let us suppose that the final addition to the labour force has come from a cheese factory and the producer we are discussing manufactures ice-cream. There is no objective way of valuing ice-cream in relation to cheese. It is efficient to pay enough to attract an extra worker from the cheese to the ice-cream factory if the person or body judging efficiency accepts consumers' relative valuation of marginal units of the two commodities. If he does not, and values cheese more highly, it might be inefficient to move this man to the ice-cream factory, even though the shift was the most profitable course of action open to the two manufacturers and the man himself.

Productive efficiency can, however, be given a meaning under paternalist value judgements. Suppose that the Government decided that the social value of cheese was much greater than the free market price. It would then subsidise the production of cheese, at so much per unit. The cheese manufacturer would then be able to offer higher wages; and it might not then pay the ice-cream manufacturer to bid away any more labour. Thus, entirely different quantities of output, and perhaps different methods of production, might become more efficient on the basis of a change in the methods of valuation of the two commodities. Alternatively, the Government might ban ice-cream production as an undesirable product. This is tantamount to a nil valuation of ice-cream; and in the changed labour market it might then pay the cheese manufacturer to take on more men and expand his output still further.

The notion of efficiency only has a meaning in connection with some pre-announced basis of valuation. If the Government distrusts the consumer's judgement and announces neither a tax, nor a subsidy, nor a purchasing price of its own, but simply talks vaguely about the evils of ice cream, then the profit motive will not lead to an efficient allocation of resources even from the Government's own point of view.

It should *en passant* be noted that many of the most widely used criteria for assessing the worth of different kinds of output cannot derive from any value judgements held by sane men. One can justify consumer valuation on liberal value judgements; one can justify a zero price on drugs and a subsidy for milk from a paternalist desire to promote health. But there is no system of ethics which puts a special valuation on the balance of payments, or saving foreign exchange or promoting exports to preserve some arbitrary rate of exchange. Only those besotted with two or three decades of official half-truths could suppose otherwise. At most, on certain narrow, short-term nationalist assumptions, the U.K. can turn the terms of trade in its favour by exporting more, and importing less, than at a free trade exchange rate. This might justify limited import subsidies (or export taxes) if one is confident about the outcome of the ensuing trade war. It cannot conceivably support the view that exports or import-saving produce some special sort of value incommensurable with home output, and have to be promoted quite irrespective of return.

If we clear away these fallacies, the underlying logic of many Conservative supporters of the market economy (and of some others in the nonconformist tradition), who clearly do not accept an anti-paternalist or permissive society, is that the Government should seek to influence the direction of national effort by a whole series of taxes, subsidies and bans; and, on the basis of these corrected valuations, market forces could then be allowed to encourage productive efficiency of those things which it is good for us to have.

The liberal can, however, comfort himself with the knowledge that it is extremely difficult to put capitalism into a straitjacket of this kind. There is always an incentive to look for close substitutes for the banned or heavily taxed product, or to invent entirely new goods and services not envisaged in the rule book of the moral censors. Moreover, differences of view among the establishment will frequently prevent very comprehensive systems of paternalist valuation on the lines suggested in the previous paragraph. The example of the Nazi war economy, cited earlier, is very much an exception and not the rule. The history of capitalism has been one of gradual collapse of the restraining walls of authority and convention, with the profit motive always one jump ahead of the Lord Chancellor and the Archbishops. The process could even be beginning in Japan where, until recently, capitalism worked within a very highly authoritarian and dirigiste general framework.

Appendix II: 'Forcing People to be Free'

The object of the following illustration is to shed light on the uneasy relation between liberalism and utilitarianism which has been the major underlying problem of this essay. A liberal cannot divorce himself from utilitarianism; for if one attaches great value to individual preferences and choices, policy should be concerned to satisfy people's expressed wants as far as possible. On the other hand, a liberal can never go the whole hog and wish to satisfy wants which relate to the suppression of other people's activities.

Imagine a small community where incomes are initially equal. (The reader may define this equality in any way he likes – the aim is to rule out distributional problems.) A distinguished pianist arrives for a recital. Market research shows that, at the prices initially fixed, the demand for seats will be five times the supply. Should the price be raised to bring demand and supply into line? There is a vote among ticket applicants, which goes 99 per cent against the price mechanism solution. Should the concert promoter, who has been given a free hand to organise the occasion, but who happens to be a liberal, accept the majority verdict or enforce the price mechanism? To simplify the argument further, assume that all ticket applications arrive on the same day by post, and that the only alternative to the price mechanism is some lottery-type selection process, such as using a pin.

Let us assume that the 1 per cent minority consists of keen music lovers. (This need not be the case. Some of them could have supported a pricing solution on grounds of principle.) If their success on their ticket application is representative of the general average, four out of five of them will be extremely disappointed at not receiving tickets for the concert. In other words 0.8 per cent of the community of ticket applicants will be intensely disappointed. (This very fact will lower the real value of their equal money earnings compared with the 99 per cent who are less keen and the 0.2 per cent of the keen and successful applicants.)

The pure democrat will of course say, 'Use the pin'. The old-fashioned utilitarian will try to compare the present dissatisfaction of the 0.8 per cent with the dissatisfaction of the 99 per cent if the price mechanism were used. The modern 'welfare economist', who is a utilitarian of a different hue, will want to avoid interpersonal comparisons of satisfaction. Let us make things easy for him by assuming that the 1 per cent minority who favoured the price mechanism are, before the lottery is held, willingly given payments by the other 99 per cent of such a size that they feel adequately compensated for their low chance of obtaining a seat. The modern utilitarian would now reject higher prices; for the 99 per cent still feel better off without them, while the 1 per cent are now just as well off.

One out of five of all applicants now have tickets. (This has incidentally introduced a chance inequality into the community of just the kind that causes indignation when it arises from inheritance under capitalism.) The utilitarian economist may now suggest that private sales and purchases of tickets be permitted, as both buyer and seller are better off if this happens. This idea is put to the vote, but so great is the objection to the price mechanism that it too is rejected by 99 per cent; and the 1 per cent of dissenters can be compensated as in the previous case. The utilitarian economist then retires, puzzling over the peculiar welfare function of the community, but conceding that dealings in tickets should not take place. For the ban on dealings in tickets combined with the payments to the 1 per cent has brought about a 'Pareto improvement'. The 1 per cent are no worse off because of the compensation and the 99 per cent are better off, because they prefer to pay out the compensation money than see a second-hand market develop in tickets.

An objection may be lodged against the initial solution of charging higher prices on the grounds of the inconvenience and discomfort of choice. The 99 per cent majority may inherently dislike the introspective effort of working out how much money they are prepared to part with to hear a celebrated pianist and prefer a low conventional price and a lottery. But this objection cannot apply to the second price mechanism method of a free market in sold tickets. For those who dislike the effort of choice need not deal in the market and can accept the result of the lottery.

Misunderstandings of the price mechanism apart, the objection of the 99 per cent to the rationing of the tickets by price by the second method must, in the last analysis, reflect a desire not merely for equality but for uniformity of behaviour, which they will probably describe as 'a sense of belonging to the community'. Their overwhelming desire is that everyone who contemplates going to the recital at all should have an equal one-in-five chance of a seat. The thought of some people indulging their tastes by purchasing a 100 per cent chance, and others indulging their different tastes by retiring from the market, causes resentment and dissatisfaction.

A liberal is, as already explained, only a constrained utilitarian. He ignores dissatisfactions arising from the mere thought of how other people are behaving. This follows from his belief in maximising freedom of action provided it does not interfere with that of other people – as it would certainly not do in the case of a free market in seats. The liberal concert director would therefore use one or other form of the price mechanism without holding a vote on the idea at all.[63]

This example is far from trivial. It brings out, shorn of irrelevancies, the hard core case of those who insist that the state should invariably provide education as well as finance it, and of those who would do everything to discourage a private medical sector. It may also explain the psychology of waiting lists for certain high quality expensive cars and the curious national liking for queues which would otherwise appear as a negative commodity or pure 'disutility'.

2 Jobs, Prices and Trade Unions

> Money, when increasing, gives encouragement to industry, during the interval between the increase of money and the rise of the prices ...
>
> David Hume, 'Of the Balance of Trade'

Few subjects can have been the subject of more analysis, commentary and recommendation than the movement of total output, employment, prices and wages – especially in relation to the British economy. Yet there are two reasons why a summary chapter on these interrelated topics cannot be avoided in any restatement of the case for economic liberalism. The first is that the biggest single reason for distrust of *any form* of market economy is the belief that it cannot prevent an unacceptably high, and perhaps explosive rate of inflation – or can only do so at the cost of a politically and morally intolerable level of unemployment. Secondly, and this is connected with the first point, the consensus, which economists seemed to have reached following the publication in 1936 of Keynes's *General Theory* on the analysis and cure of unemployment in an advanced industrial economy, has crumbled in recent years.

It would be most convenient to my general case if I were able to endorse the orthodox Keynesian view that unemployment can nearly always be reduced by a sufficient injection of purchasing power. For an assurance that total employment can be kept up in this way offers us much the best chance of persuading people to accept the disturbances brought by market forces to particular industries, areas and occupations. Indeed, it would then be tempting to argue for a policy of running the economy at a high 'pressure of demand', even if this involved some inflation and exchange depreciation in order to minimise specific state intervention in particular industries of a make-work kind. This is what one might term the 'liberal expansionist' position, from which my book *The Treasury under the Tories*, published in 1964, was written; and too many commentators – whether or not they endorse the liberal half of that goal – continue to write as if this kind of demand management were still possible.

Unfortunately, the assumptions behind this position were questionable even in the 1960s, and have since become quite implausible; and it is no service to economic liberalism, or any other cause, to erect it on an edifice of wishful thinking. The first of the sections that follow will give my assessment of the influence of demand management upon unemployment, the second will discuss union monopoly power and the third will discuss the attitude an economic liberal should adopt to the endless proliferation of schemes for 'doing something about' incomes. But any one expecting me to propose a new once-for-all cure of my own will be disappointed. If such a mechanistic cure existed it would by now have emerged from the millions of words written on these subjects.

Demand and Unemployment

The modern tendency to formulate economic theories in a form where they can be tested by economic techniques is undoubtedly a step forward. For too long economics and the other social sciences had an excessive bias towards armchair reflection. The impulse to collect numerical data and formulate hypotheses which can be tested with all available mathematical and electronic techniques is therefore to be welcomed, provided it does not lead to an uncritical acceptance of every piece of work with the right fashionable trappings.

Unfortunately, there are signs that this is happening. How many times do we read supposedly factual newspaper stories beginning, 'A computer study has shown ...' or 'A rigorous mathematical study had demolished the belief that ...'? A slightly less crude form of this approach is too often prevalent among professional economists themselves.

Claims made for such studies in recent years include the demonstration that incomes policy reduced the increases in prices by 1 per cent per annum, that it had no effect at all and that it actually made inflation worse. We have been told that the level of national income at current prices is linked very closely to the supply of money, and that no relation between the two can be demonstrated.

At the beginning of the 1970s a number of highly qualified economists and 'economically literate' politicians endorsed a much discussed econometric model that 'demonstrated' that with adult unemployment of only 2.1 per cent (seasonally corrected), weekly wage rates would rise by only 3 per cent per annum – all without any kind of interference with normal collective bargaining. This is a rate of increase lower than anything experienced since early 1967; in subsequent years a much higher rate of unemployment did not suffice to prevent wages from rising several times as fast. Yet attempts to demonstrate the implausibility of the model, by references to what was actually happening to wages and prices, were dismissed as journalistic, or literary, or on the grounds that 'This may not be perfect, but it is the only serious piece of work we have so far.'[1]

There are, in real life, a large number of economic magnitudes all reacting on each other, and the relationships between them are themselves changing over time. A great deal depends on how these magnitudes (and, in particular, their rates of change) are measured, the exact way in which suggested relationships are stated, the periods chosen and the tests used. Subjects such as the relationship of the home market to exports, or of unemployment and wages, do not become less controversial because the controversies become more difficult to understand, or because hardware has been used for doing the sums.

All this is very far from being a Luddite plea to abandon econometric techniques. It is a plea for a less breathless and credulous assessment of their results. It is unwise to change one's economic philosophy with dizzying rapidity with each purported new finding. One can go quite a long way with certain long established elementary generalisations, and inferences from them. We shall, of course, feel more confident if they can survive modern statistical testing. But, before taking on board the results of such tests – and, in particular, before accepting numerical values for particular relationships – it is worth waiting until a number of studies employing different techniques point in the same direction and have survived professional criticism.

Any attempt to set out summarily a few fundamental notions on unemployment, monetary and fiscal policy must involve a large element of personal judgement. What follows is based on a combination of observations of policies and performance over many years and an attempt to distil what has emerged from academic investigation and debate. Perhaps only a financial journalist would have the effrontery to undertake such a task. Those whose appetite for arguments about demand management is limited and want to get down to the red meat of unions and incomes control will lose little by going straight on to the section on union monopoly power beginning on p. 179.

A convenient starting point is unemployment in an underdeveloped economy, especially one with a dense and rapidly increasing population. No intellectual puzzle is set by the existence of a large amount of open or concealed unemployment in such a country. There is simply not enough of the capital equipment, entrepreneurial activity and managerial and other skills which would have to exist alongside the pool of unemployed if it is to be put to worthwhile work. There may be some very low wage at which it would pay to offer jobs to all the unemployed, even with existing organisation, capital and techniques; but if that wage is below subsistence or what the jobless can obtain from living with their families and tribes, or on relief, the existence of such a theoretical equilibrium wage is of no practical relevance.

In a modern industrial market economy, by contrast, one would expect the stock of capital equipment to be adjusted to the size of the available labour force, and there to be sufficient resources of enterprise and management to adapt both the organisation of business and its physical capital to market requirements. One would also expect the members of the labour force to make some effort to acquire the skills that happened to be marketable, although employers would also have some incentive to take advantage of the relative cheapness of unskilled labourers. (Numerical or algebraic models can be constructed in which technical progress would have such a labour-saving, capital-using bias that it would be cheaper to use robots than pay a subsistence wage; but I am not attempting a complete taxonomy, and it is highly improbable that this is the present state of affairs.)

Now, even if a modern market economy were functioning extremely well, there would be no reason to expect zero unemployment. There is always transitional unemployment while people who have left one job search around among available job opportunities. Of a total of 923,000 unemployed in Great Britain in December 1971, some 315,000 had been out of work for less than two months and a further 60,000 were temporarily stopped or school leavers (the figures are not seasonally adjusted). A certain number of people who are virtually unemployable appear in the official statistics even when there are many unfilled vacancies; at a minimum estimate, these form 150,000 of the long term unemployed. There are also some 'false' unemployed, those who either work surreptitiously or are not genuinely seeking employment. The number in this latter category has been estimated by Mr John Wood for this period at about 100,000.[2] While these influences lead to a statistical inflation of the number of unemployed, there are other factors giving the official figures a downward bias. It is well known that a U.S. type sample census, in which people are asked if they would like a job, yields higher figures than the British method of basing statistics on unemployment pay. A British type system is itself sensitive to the degree of pressure imposed on unemployed workers to accept available jobs, while a U.S. type system is sensitive to the exact form in which the questions are posed.

Unemployment, however measured, will vary according to the efficiency of labour exchanges and other employment agencies. It will depend on the pace of change in the skills demanded, the availability of retraining facilities, and the willingness of redundant workers to use them – or to accept lower paid unskilled jobs. The unemployment percentage is also notoriously affected by any geographical imbalance between areas where work is available and those where the un-

employed live. One can argue whether workers who are
unwilling to move should count as involuntarily unemployed;
but, because of the spillover costs in congested areas not paid
for by the individual employer or employee, it may be
positively undesirable to encourage all the unemployed
workers to move to where the jobs are rather than *vice versa*.
Trade union wage bargaining and minimum wage laws can
also increase unemployment; and if institutional rigidities or
union pressure prevent relative wages from falling in other
industries to absorb the surplus labour, the national unemployment average will be that much higher. Opposition to
adult retraining by unions, or to new entry into occupations,
can have similar effects.

It is not necessarily true that the lower the statistical unemployment rate the better. The Redundancy Payments Act
and earnings-related unemployment benefits, which came
into operation in December 1965 and October 1966 respectively, caused an increase in recorded unemployment, as the
cost to the worker of spending time searching for a suitable
new job (or for that matter of 'taking a break') was reduced.
These measures were desirable both on humanitarian
grounds and because it is inefficient for an unemployed
worker to be forced by financial pressure into the first available job rather than search for something that really suits his
abilities and tastes. But the result of these measures by the
time they had worked themselves into the system by the end
of 1968 was, according to one study, to add slightly more than
two-fifths to the unemployment percentage than would otherwise have been predicted from a given level of unfilled vacancies. This means that a level of adult unemployed of 2 per cent
– or somewhat under 500,000 – would have corresponded to
well over 2.8 per cent, or 650,000–700,000 by the early
1970s.[3] The estimated correction is a high one, which admittedly takes into account other structural factors, apart from
social security legislation, which may have affected the relationship between unemployment and vacancies since the
middle 1960s. A more usual correction to make figures between earlier and later periods comparable is to take a straight
$\frac{1}{2}$ per cent off the figures for the early 1970s.

So far the discussion has centred on the 'real' forces affecting unemployment. While they are mostly familiar – and, with the possible exception of union influences, uncontroversial – it is only in the last few years that mainstream economists have begun to stress that they set a floor to the extent that unemployment can be reduced by expansionist monetary or fiscal policies. Ill-conceived financial policies can keep unemployment needlessly above this rate, but they cannot force it permanently below it, *and this is so even if we are prepared to pay a sacrifice in faster inflation to achieve fuller employment.* The relevant unemployment rate has been called by various writers the 'natural', 'warranted' or 'normal rate' of unemployment. The labels are all misleading because the percentage in question reflects use of monopoly power which would be too defeatist to label 'natural'. My own term would be simply the 'minimum' or, more pedantically, the 'minimum sustainable', unemployment level.

If the minimum sustainable level of unemployment is regarded as too high and the authorities try to bring it down further by budget deficits or increasing the money supply, trouble can be confidently expected. Let us, to take purely illustrative figures, assume that the minimum unemployment percentage, according to U.K. definitions of the early 1970s, is $3\frac{1}{2}$ per cent, but that the Government tries, by 'boosting demand' in the Budget and through the banking system, to get this percentage down to $2\frac{1}{2}$ per cent. The initial effects of these measures – assuming no perverse effects on confidence or other mishaps – should be to boost output and employment on orthodox Keynesian lines. Eventually, however, the greater demand for labour will lead to an acceleration in the rise of wages. In these more buoyant demand conditions unions will be more aggressive in their claims and employers will be more ready to concede them, or even offer higher wages themselves to retain labour.

The frequent assertion that the stage of the labour market has no effect on the rate of increase of wages borders on the fantastic. The original 'Phillips curve' made no allowance for changing price expectations and assumed that an x per cent rate of unemployment would be associated with the same rate of unemployment, whether workers were expecting a o, 3 or 33 per cent rate of increase of prices. That it should have collapsed by the end of the 1960s in the face of the increase in the rate of inflation was only to be expected. The real surprise is that it continued to perform so well as long as it did. If the relationship between unemployment (or, preferably unfilled vacancies) and wage increases is to be represented even approximately by a Phillips curve, it will have to be a family of curves corresponding to different rates of expected inflation.

To return to our original story, let us assume that the Government does succeed in getting unemployment down to $2\frac{1}{2}$ per cent. During the expansionary period, some people previously regarded as unemployable will be given jobs, people not even registered as unemployed will enter the labour forces, more overtime will be on offer, there will be less short time, and all the other effects stressed by the high demand school will be in operation. But, with the labour market now much lighter, hourly earnings will increase faster than before and this will in turn lead to higher prices. So long as 'money illusion' reigns and workers and their representatives take no notice of faster inflation the story need go no further. Lower unemployment will have been purchased at the expense of more rapid inflation; and one could argue the pros and cons of the change.

This is, however, only the first stage. As soon as money illusion begins to go and workers begin to think in real terms, they start insisting on still higher wages to make up for the faster rise in the cost of living. But once they obtain them, prices will rise still faster, which will in turn increase the rate of wage-push and give rise to an ever-accelerating inflation. Thus the long run trade-off is not between unemployment and inflation, but between unemployment and accelerating inflation.

Nothing that has been said above in any way implies that inflation always tends to accelerate. What I have called the 'minimum unemployment percentage' is that consistent with any constant rate of inflation. (In the above hypothetical example, the $3\frac{1}{2}$ per cent unemployment rate might well coexist with a steady 7 per cent rate of inflation.) It is only if unemployment is pushed below this minimum level that inflation will tend to accelerate.

In this example, the authorities are faced with a painful dilemma. They may try to keep unemployment at $2\frac{1}{2}$ per cent by ever greater monetary injections. In that case, they face accelerating inflation and an eventual collapse of the national monetary unit as a basis for business calculations[4] – and with it the end to any benefit to employment from their expansionary policies – not to mention the probable political and social repercussions. If the Government wishes merely to reduce the rate of inflation to wherever it was when unemployment was $3\frac{1}{2}$ per cent, unemployment may have to shoot well above $3\frac{1}{2}$ per cent, and the process may take many years. This is because of the great difficulty of reducing inflationary expectations once they have become embedded in the system. Should the Government be prepared to settle for a new and higher, but steady rate of inflation, it will still have to allow unemployment to creep back to $3\frac{1}{2}$ per cent; and even then it will take some time for the rate of inflation to settle down. No wonder that in such a situation Ministers will be tempted to break out of the dilemma by direct intervention in the labour and goods markets – with what success and at which price remains to be discussed.

The above view is sometimes known as the *theory of adaptive expectations*, because price expectations are adjusted to past experience. In order to explain clearly the basic long run forces which prevent the authorities from being able to maintain whatever pressure of demand and unemployment percentage they desire, an excessively schematic and mechanistic picture has had to be painted. I have not attempted here an account of the pathology of business or electoral cycles which are heavily influenced by time lags. Unemployment may, for example, be above its minimum level, but wages and prices may still be reacting to the demand pressure of months or even years ago. If one had a rough idea of the minimum feasible unemployment level, it would then be safe to reflate demand and unemployment up to that level without further aggravating inflation.

Moreover, although the demand for labour and the rate of cost-determined price increases have a major influence on wage inflation, they are far from being the only influence. Indeed, the basic assertion of the 'adaptive expectations' hypothesis is that workers are interested in the real value of their take-home pay. If real incomes have been squeezed in the recent past, wage demands will be more aggressive than would otherwise have been expected in the same economic climate. Here is probably one of the main explanations of the 1969–70 explosion. This came at the end of a five year period in which real personal disposable income had risen by a third of its long run average – and in the last year and a half of the period it had virtually ceased to rise at all.

The need for such a brake on living standards came partly, but not entirely, from the need to make a large shift from the home market to exports and import-saving in a short space of time. The legacy of such episodes is a more rapid rate of inflation, which governments will find difficult to subdue except by running the economy for a considerable period at *above* the minimum unemployment level.

In more fortunate circumstances, the domestic trade-offs can be made to look deceptively optimistic owing to the operation of time lags. An attempt to push down the rate of unemployment below its minimum may take some years before it produces an accelerating inflation; and the intervening period could be actually beneficial to price stability. If, for example, a Government is starting out with an unemployment percentage above the minimum and is trying to reduce it to below the minimum, there are likely to be very large budgetary handouts. These can be used to cut both direct and indirect taxation, and thereby to reduce both actual and (hopefully) expected inflation, as well as to increase the take-home pay associated with any given money wage income. As the tax reductions are financed from the Budget deficit, there need be no corresponding cut in the provision of government services. Moreover, because of the exceptional rise of output per man which may accompany the early stages of a boom, employers may be able to absorb some wage increases while still increasing profits. Thus, for a time, a virtuous circle may be at work, with price restraint and tax cuts engendering a de-escalation of wage settlements, which in turn put a brake on further price increases, the whole process being oiled by exceptionally fast productivity increases. This is the germ of truth in the 'at a stroke' theory.

The trouble with such a process – even if it can get going – is that by its nature it is temporary. The tax cuts, above-average productivity gains, increase in overtime opportunities, and so on, are all side-effects of *increasing* the proportion of productive capacity and available manpower employed. Once unemployment is down to the Government's target level, all these bonuses come to an end; there are unlikely to be further tax cuts financed by Government borrowing, and productivity growth will settle down to its normal rate. Thus, the forces making for reduced price inflation will have spent themselves. Meanwhile, with the higher demand for labour, wage increases will be gathering momentum, starting off a renewed price acceleration, and Hayek's tiger will be off on its run.[5]

This view of the inflationary process cannot be confuted by showing that wages and salaries account for only about half of the cost of total expenditure on home produced goods and imports. Most other costs tend to move in line with labour costs over a sufficiently long term. If employers seek to maintain gross profit margins, this element too will rise with wages. Import costs will also increase in line with home costs, either because other countries are undergoing similar inflationary experience or because, if they are not, we will probably have to devalue. It is only if there is a favourable movement in the equilibrium terms of trade, due, say, to a decline in primary prices relative to manufactured goods, that we can gain a dampening effect from imports; and even this is likely to be small. (A 6 per cent reduction in import prices will reduce the cost of final output by 1 per cent, and reductions on this scale are likely to be rare events.) Taxes on expenditure will – apart from exceptional periods of demand stimulus – also tend to rise in line with money incomes; and items such as interest rates and property rents are also likely to be influenced in an irregular and jerky way by the general trend of money incomes and prices.

Strictly interpreted, the minimum unemployment hypothesis implies that the Phillips curve is in the long run a vertical line. Expansionist demand management policies thus have a permanent effect only on the level of prices and not on output and employment. But, as David Laidler has pointed out, even if inflation is never perfectly anticipated (or over-anticipated), and there is some slight long run gain to employment from expansionist demand management, the policy dilemma remains largely the same. The important contention is that the long run Phillips curve is much steeper than the short term one (with the rate of increase of money wages measured on the vertical axis). If this is so, the greater part of the effects of a demand boost which takes unemployment much below the 'minimum' is temporary, and the authorities then have to choose between allowing unemployment to rise again and an accelerating rate of inflation.

A further elaboration, which embodies one of the basic earlier Keynesian insights, is that the effects of a departure from the minimum unemployment point or zone are not symmetrical. The Keynes of the 1920s already realised that the economic system was highly resistant to downward changes in the general level of wages; and it was on this basis – without departing from neoclassical monetary theory – that he opposed the 1925 return to the Gold Standard at the pre-1914 parity. To this we must add the further observation that the system is also highly resistant to downward changes in the rate of increase of money wages. If unemployment is reduced for any length of time below the minimum level, then – once the money illusion has burst – the economy will be landed with a much faster underlying rate of inflation which will not be easy to subdue. On the other hand, a comparable *increase* in the unemployment level may have only a modest retarding effect on the rate of inflation; and the economy may have to be run at a very high rate of unemployment for a very long time if inflation is to be reduced by that particular route. Fortunately it is not one that election timetables allow.

Because of this inertia of wages and prices, *sudden and severe attempts to halt the expansion of monetary demand will lead to stagnation of output and unemployment, while the beneficial effects on prices will come through slowly and very much later.* This is the origin of 'inflationary recessions'. The case for *flexible exchanges (for deficit countries) arises basically from the difficulty of making large and rapid downward changes in domestic costs and prices or in their rate of increase*; and this is why attempts to secure an underlying payments deficit by deflation *alone* will lead to otherwise unnecessary unemployment and stagnation.

The basic difficulty about convincing people of the validity of the minimum unemployment hypothesis is that money illusion can remain for an astonishingly long time during a period of moderate and relatively steady inflation, such as that which prevailed up to the middle 1960s. Until then wage bargains, interest rates, equity yields, salary arrangements, and similar phenomena were not adapted to the facts of inflation. Adaptation when it does at last come may be sudden; and for a time people may actually overreact on the basis of excessively pessimistic inflationary expectations, which then prove self-justifying. It is for reasons of this kind that econometric verification of the adaptive expectations hypothesis is so difficult. But it is hard to suppose that there can be much money illusion left now. The more that people learn to live with inflation by indexing pensions, wages, contracts, leases and other arrangements, the less the scope for others to gain at their expense during periods of rising prices; and the less favourable is likely to be even the temporary trade-off between unemployment and inflation, and the more likely that higher monetary demand will lead to higher prices rather than more employment.

The notion of a minimum unemployment level, zone or band, presented here is not the most elegant or easily applicable of concepts. It exists only in the long run – because at any one time we are always overshooting or undershooting it; yet its position can shift quite quickly depending not only on structural changes, but on a whole variety of chance factors, including the personalities of union leaders, currents of shop floor and management psychology, and the attitudes and skills of particular governments. It is like looking for a black cat in a dark room but one which is really there and likely to give one a nasty scratch.

The notion is thus tricky, but meaningful. Even the most extreme believers in the Treasury's ability to control 'real demand' have always conceded that there was some effective floor to the unemployment level they could achieve – whether 1, $1\frac{1}{2}$, or 2 per cent – without either being halted by physical bottlenecks, or the system becoming explosive (even if the Government were willing to let the exchange rate go). The implication of what I have been saying is that these very low postwar rates of unemployment were, like the high interwar rates, an aberration due *inter alia* to the persistence of money illusion.

The hypothesis presented here would be falsified if we were able to get back to target figures in the postwar range (adding perhaps $\frac{1}{2}$–1 per cent for the social security changes already discussed), solely by the use of fiscal and monetary policy. Unfortunately, the upward climb in unemployment rates in each successive recession in so many countries in combination with faster rates of inflation, reinforces the view that the relationship between unemployment and inflation is not a stable one, but sensitive to price expectations. The existence of these phenomena in so many different countries seems to rule out an explanation solely in terms of the train of events following from the 1967 devaluation. This was no more than an aggravating factor in the British case, just as the legacy of excess demand in the U.S. in the early stages of the Vietnam War was an aggravating factor on a world scale.

Despite the lack of any precise knowledge of the minimum unemployment rate, a recognition of its existence is of background help to the policymaker. It suggests, for instance, that if the rate of increase of monetary earnings is declining – even though still high – employment can be helped by a demand stimulus, although at some cost to the Government's anti-inflationary objectives. If, on the other hand, *the rate of increase of money earnings is still increasing, a demand stimulus will risk an explosive inflation without any more than at most a temporary benefit to employment.* In all cases, the question that must be asked is whether the recent behaviour of earnings reflects current labour market conditions, or is really the lagged effect of earlier and different conditions; and, if the latter, an allowance must be made for the lags by some mixture of econometrics and common sense. *But, if allowing for lags, a demand stimulus is seen to involve a serious risk of an acceleration in the rise of money earnings, it is a sign that unemployment is above the minimum sustainable level; and, if the latter is considered excessive, it must be tackled by some means other than overall fiscal or monetary policy.*

I conclude this brief survey of current macroeconomic controversies by noting that, at no point, has it been necessary to discuss the dispute between the apostles of fiscal and monetary policy. Both are means for managing demand or controlling the flow of money expenditure. The basic questions raised by the work of Friedman and the monetarists associated with him turn on (a) whether it would be better to place less reliance on discretionary short term policy and more on long term guidelines in both the fiscal and the monetary field (a question alluded to in the previous chapter), and (b) the contention that demand management by whatever means, cannot by itself achieve a predetermined target rate of unemployment or any other 'real' variable.*

Union Monopoly Power

The preceding involved, but oversimplified, excursion into the complexities of demand management has been intended to set the stage for the basic question: what do we do if the minimum sustainable rate of unemployment is too high to be tolerable – if it represents, not a misleading statistic, but the coexistence of unsatisfied wants and a large number of workers unable to find jobs at the going rates? There is a strong possibility that this situation has begun to recur in the U.K. and some other advanced industrial countries.

Any number of reasons could account in principle for high minimum unemployment rates. According to 'the economics

---

* Any attempt to cite all the writings relevant to these issues would involve a massive bibliography covering many areas of economics. Readers who want to explore a little further views related to, but not necessarily identical with, those put forward in the text, may wish to look at: Milton Friedman, 'The Role of Monetary Policy', reprinted in *The Optimum Quantity of Money* (Aldane Publishing Co., 1969); David Laidler, 'The Phillips Curve, Expectations and Incomes Policy', in Johnson (ed.), *The Current Inflation* (Macmillan, 1971); Edmund Phelps (ed.), *Micro-economics, Foundations of Employment and Inflation Theory* (Macmillan, 1970); J. E. Meade, *The Controlled Economy* (Allen & Unwin, 1971); Metcalf and Richardson, 'The Nature and Measurement of Unemployment in the U.K.', *Three Banks Review*, March 1972. My own more extended treatment of the subject can be found in the last two chapters of *Steering the Economy* (Penguin, 1971).

of Keynes' (as distinct from 'Keynesian economics'),[7] the price that gets stuck at too high a level to secure full utilisation of resources is the long term rate of interest. This, Keynes believed, tended to be above the rate of return on new investment to be expected in a fully employed economy because of psychological or instutional reasons or because of mistaken central bank policy (Keynes varied in the emphasis he gave to these different factors). As a judgement of the interwar period, Keynes may have been right; and he could be right again. But it is difficult to argue that the rate of interest, which after allowing for inflation has often been negative, has been the price that has been too high in the bulk of the postwar period. Overwhelmingly the most important reason for excessively high minimum unemployment rates in countries such as the U.K. in the last few years is to be found in the maladjustment of a different price – that of labour; or to put it more plainly, the use by unions of their monopoly power.

Excessively high long term rates of interest were, according to the economics of Keynes, a chronic long term problem. But in a depression another problem appeared: expectations about the yield of new investment were excessively pessimistic. This pessimism might not accord with fundamental long term factors, but would prove self-justifying so long as businessmen acted upon it. In this case, public investment projects or boosts to public or private consumption via a Budget deficit, would be desirable as temporary pump-priming operations to help break the vicious cycle of entrepreneurial expectations.

This second kind of malaise diagnosed by Keynes has not necessarily vanished. In an inflationary recession perverse entrepreneurial expectations and union monopoly power can reinforce each other as causes of unemployment. Indeed the exertion of union monopoly power by means of wage push and a subsequent profit squeeze can, as explained below, help to trigger off pessimistic expectations about the return from new investment, which may be partially justified, but will be certainly overdone as a result of the initial shock. Unfortunately, the difficulty of applying the remedies advocated by Keynes are much greater in this kind of recession, because, apart from the normal timing difficulties, there is the danger of triggering off an inflationary explosion.

It will, however, make for ease of exposition if we put aside these complexities for a moment and examine the effects of union monopoly at the level of individual industry or plant. Just as a price ring or cartel among employers can raise unit prices at the expense of a lower sales volume, a trade union can obtain a higher wage per head in its industry at the expense of a lower volume of employment – in other words, by pushing some workers out of jobs. The effects are the same whether the action is overtly aggressive or is a defensive measure to preserve the relative position of a group of workers whose relative position is threatened by industrial change – the popular justification for the coalminers' successful strike of early 1972.

Movements of relative wages have a function to perform in enabling people to adjust to change. If money wages in a declining industry rise less than elsewhere – and that is all that is in question in the postwar setting – there are two principal effects. First, a brake is exerted on the speed of decline via the effects on the final price of the product (and there may also be some further benefit to employment in that industry through a less capital intensive bias in its own modernisation programme). Secondly, the shift in relativities encourages a voluntary and gradual shift of workers to other industries, mainly through a fall in recruitment and the drifting away of younger workers.

If this shift in relativities is frustrated by union monopoly power – still more if it is reversed – the exit of workers from the declining industry is much larger and quicker, and has a much less voluntary character. The result of this is that there are more workers competing for jobs in other sectors.

It is important to be clear in what sense trade unions affect labour markets by exercising monopoly selling power. Union leaders frequently argue that, if there is to be a 'free-for-all', they are part of the 'all' and should grab what they can. The fallacy of this argument lies in the contrast between what John Nelson-Jones has called the 'individual pursuit of self-interest' and its 'collective pursuit'.[8] The former is compatible with the successful functioning of a market economy; the latter is a form of cheating. Mr Nelson-Jones rightly infers that the theoretical answer would be for workers not to bargain collectively; but he dismisses the idea as 'patently unrealistic', believing that ordinary people will never accept that 'what is desirable in individuals is undesirable in groups'.

It is always dangerous to predict what people may or may not eventually accept, especially as for so long very little attempt was made to explain what was involved. After all, governments do not hesitate to prevent employers indulging in the 'collective pursuit of self interest' by anti-monopoly policy; and the popular belief that wealthy employers have a bargaining advantage over unorganised workers is a deep-seated myth. Employers, however wealthy, do not have the power to screw down the wages of workers so long as they are competing among one another and there is a brisk demand for labour.

There are, of course, local pockets where a 'monopsonistic' employer may have an excessive influence. One of the few genuine cases of inferior bargaining positions is that of school-children. They are unable to escape harsh treatment, petty rules or uncongenial conditions by shopping around between schools. This is so (a) because of the restriction of choice in the state sector, and (b) because any available choice may in any case be made by parents. For these reasons efforts to organise genuine schoolchildren's unions (as distinct from attempts by revolutionaries to exploit children's grievances) deserve more support from liberals than many other trade union activities of which it is more respectable to approve.

Over the bulk of the economy, unions, if they succeed in increasing real wages at all, do so at the expense of other employees or of the general level of employment. Up to the end of the 1960s, at least, empirical U.S. studies suggested that most, if not all, the gains of union labour in the U.S.A. were at the expense of non-unionised workers and not at the expense of the earnings of capital. British figures suggest that, in this country, unions did succeed in raising the share of real wages relative to profits, even after allowing for cyclical influences – but at the expense of a lower level of employment, output, investment and growth.

It is often wrongly supposed that the influence of union monopoly power is related to the prevalence of national bargaining. A shift to plant bargaining *can* be helpful both to employment and efficiency if it prevents nationally agreed increases being *automatically* superimposed on whatever emerges from local wage drift and plant bargains. This benefit can, however, be frustrated, if union militants in individual plants force up wages and prevent the employer from offering employment at lower rates to would-be outside recruits. The cry among private employers that power has been transferred to the shop floor, and that agreements with national union representatives are useless, suggests that monopoly power can be very effective at plant level. Of course, like other monopoly power, it is not unlimited. A sufficient degree of induced unemployment, resulting from any sudden and obvious increase in the use of monopoly pressure, may exert a moderating influence even on shop floor unionists. Moreover, a plant monopoly power cannot be exercised beyond the point at which the employer would shut up shop altogether or shift elsewhere. This, in turn, depends partly on the degree of militancy in alternative locations in other districts, regions and countries.

The use of union monopoly power at the level of the individual industry or plant *need not* either raise general unemployment or set in motion a cumulative or explosive inflationary process, but it is, in fact, highly likely to do so. A large increase in redundancies, caused by union wage push in some industries, is likely, in any case, to place a great strain on the organisational and adaptive powers of the sectors expected to receive the discharged workers. If, on top of this either union activity or institutional rigidities prevent a sufficient fall in *relative* wages in these other sectors, a substantial increase in national unemployment is inevitable, which may well reach politically unacceptable levels. This, in turn, is likely to induce the authorities to attempt to keep up employment by pumping money into the economy, which can only be successful at the cost of an accelerating inflation. This is the 'micro' route by which Hayek derives his leaping tiger.

The above view of the relationship between wages and employment is sometimes disputed on the grounds of the supposed imperviousness of the labour market to the influence of supply and demand. The main evidence cited is a persistence of differences in earnings between workers of comparable skill in the same locality. Now, even if it were true that *workers* were indifferent to wage differentials in their job movements, wage differences and changes would still affect employment, provided that *employers* took them into account. A rise in wages in a particular industry is bound to affect employment, both through its effects on the final demand for the product and on the degree to which labour-saving methods are sought; an employer would have to be indifferent to costs, and risk being put out of business by his competitors, if he took no notice of changes in the price of labour in the production techniques he chose to use. Minimum wages, enforced by legislation, have an effect in pricing people out of jobs similar to union monopoly pressure. They are among the main reasons for high unemployment among black teenagers and unskilled white teenagers in the U.S.A.

But, of course, wage differentials *do* affect the supply as well as the demand side of the labour market. No theorist of any sense has ever denied the existence of human inertia, ignorance or attachment to traditional places of work, quite apart from the non-pecuniary advantages stressed by Adam Smith. The view that earnings differentials – except when maintained by monopolies – will vanish belongs to the excessively static view of competition criticised in the previous chapter. The most detailed plant-level investigation so far made, by a team of economists in the Glasgow empirical tradition, in work undertaken for the Department of Employment, suggests that low wage plants suffer from higher quit rates or labour wastage than high wage ones. Low wage plants can maintain their labour force, but it is of a fickle and volatile kind; and it is by more rapid transit through these low wage plants that the worker responds to labour market pressures.[9]

High wage plants are able to maintain stricter hiring standards; but the level of wages they pay is often above what is necessary to obtain the required quality of labour; nor are such high wage policies always associated with recruitment drives. The simplest explanation is that where firms are potentially able to earn above the going rate of return, owing to superior efficiency, good luck in their particular markets or some combination of the two, management has enough discretionary power to share the excess profits between shareholders and its own workers. It should be noted that those who lose from such policies are not merely the firm's shareholders, but potential employees for whom entry into the favoured firm has to be rationed. These factors complicate the workings of labour markets; but they do not make them in the least impervious to supply and demand.

Let us now abstract from the specifics of particular industries and glance at the consequences of union monopoly power at a 'macro' level. It is best to start by looking at a cost push, where the combined result of all union pressure is to generate a degree of increase in money wages far above the average increase in output per man. Even if we were prepared to accept a rapid, but steady, inflation as a price worth paying for full employment, accelerating inflation would be impossible to sustain for reasons already mentioned. Sufficient monetary and fiscal restraint would have to be used, in the absence of direct controls, at least to stabilise the rate of growth of money wages. There are three possibilities. The most optimistic is that after a temporary increase in unemployment, the system would settle down with a stable rate of inflation and a tolerable approximation to full employment. The most pessimistic is that the appetite and monopoly of union leaders for wage increases – whether through assertive ambition or simply because of incompatible ideas about relativities – would be such that monetary and fiscal policy would be unable to prevent wage increases from accelerating. If the authorities succeeded in stabilising the growth of total money incomes, it would be at the cost of continuously rising unemployment, with nominal national income growing at a steady rate, but shared among fewer and fewer workers. This, if allowed to go on, would lead to the collapse of the system and its probable replacement by something a good deal nastier.

The most likely result of trying to stabilise the rate of inflation by monetary and fiscal policy is intermediate between the two extremes. That is, it would be possible to stabilise the growth of money incomes, but at the expense of an intolerably high level of unemployment – which would be higher still if the Government were actually trying to reduce the rate of wage and price increases. This is yet another way of saying that the effect of union monopoly power is to increase the minimum sustainable rate of unemployment; and governments will oscillate between periods of permitting accelerating inflation and periods of high unemployment, and eventually be drawn to intervene directly in the wage-fixing process.

Why, it may be asked, were we able to combine a roughly stable 3 per cent rate of inflation with full employment during the first two postwar decades? One can either argue that union leaders refrained from exercising their full monopoly power, or that they or others were fooled for a long time by money illusion and accepted wage increases without applying a full inflationary discount. The two factors were of course interconnected. The postwar compromise lasted as long as it did partly because various groups such as those living on fixed incomes, white collar workers, professional groups and the lower paid, either failed to organise or (as in the case of holders of fixed interest paper) allowed themselves to be deceived. Once these other groups began to realise what was happening and organised in self-defence, the situation became explosive. The incompatibility of 'free' trade union bargaining with full employment and any non-explosive behaviour of the price level, far from being a *laissez-faire* doctrine, has been stressed for many years by socialist economists such as Lord Balogh.[10] It is also one of Beckerman's conclusions in his study of the lesson of the 1964–70 Labour Government.[11]

So far the 'macro' part of the argument has been expressed in terms of money wage increases, with the real consequences left deliberately in the background. The mechanism by which union monopoly power affects unemployment has been described in terms of monetary and fiscal policies, undertaken to prevent an inflationary explosion, which in turn lead to high unemployment. The neo-classical economists believed, however, that there was a quite *direct* link between *real wages* and employment even for the economy as a whole. If higher real wages were demanded, fewer people would be employed.

Keynes in the *General Theory* accepted entirely the idea of a functional relationship between real wages and employment, but argued that general cuts in *money* wages were an unsuitable or impossible way of achieving this, and the result could be better achieved indirectly by other routes.

Between the 1930s, when these arguments took place, and the late 1960s, the influence of real wages in determining aggregate employment (as distinct from employment in particular industries) appeared to diminish in importance. This was partly because direct costs are constant for many firms over a large range of potential output, and the marginal productivity of labour does not fall as output and employment increases. Indeed, given accounting conventions with regard to the spreading of overheads, some employers can even increase wages in the expansionary phases of the cycle, add to employment, and keep prices more stable than they can in the restrictive phases. Between one cycle and another, the practice of recovering wage increases which are out of line with productivity by increased mark-ups prevented too dramatic a gain in the share of labour at the expense of capital.

If, however, the mark-ups become insufficient and the trade unions do succeed, over a period of years, in increasing real wages at the expense of profits, investment is likely to become more labour-saving than it would otherwise be. Capital accumulation creates job opportunities, while labour saving innovations destroy them. In a smoothly progressing economy, there is a balance between the two. There is enough capital accumulation to employ the labour force at the going real wage rate, which will be rising through the time with technical progress and growing real output.

If the stock of capital tends to rise faster than the available labour supply, real wages will be driven up and capital investment will take a more labour-saving form. This is as it should be. But if real wages are pushed up simply by union monopoly power in the absence of a specially rapid growth of capital, new investment will still be given a labour-saving bias, even though there is no labour shortage to justify such a bias. If this goes on for some years, there may simply not be enough capital of a type adapted to consumer demand to employ the labour force – even if it became suddenly and miraculously possible to boost demand without any danger of an inflationary explosion. The U.K. would then have arrived at a situation reminiscent of that of many underdeveloped countries, where not even the most extreme Keynesians believe that unemployment can be cured by demand expansion alone. The fall in the share of company trading profits net of stock appreciation, as a share of final output, from a range of 10–12 per cent in the decade up to 1964 to 7 per cent in 1970 does not suggest that we are dealing with a flight of theoretical fancy; and figures of net profits properly adjusted for inflation might reveal an even more dramatic drop. A simple price index correction (which does not allow for depreciation and stock replacement) suggests that real profits fell by a quarter between 1965 and 1970.

This influence of real wages on employment is a long term effect. There can, at times, be a much more immediate connection. During a long period of steady and gradual inflation, employers become used to passing on wage increases in the knowledge that their competitors will do the same. But when there is a sudden acceleration in the rate of wage inflation, as at the end of the 1960s and the early 1970s, this confidence falls off; for with the established pattern broken, no one can be sure exactly what will happen to his competitors' labour costs, let alone how they will react; and human inertia will also make an industrialist much less happy about passing on a 15 per cent wage increase, which has hit him out of the blue, than a 6–8 per cent wage increase which he has been paying with minor variations for decades. Thus, even without an exchange rate constraint, the initial result of a sudden wage explosion is likely to be a rise in the share of wages and a severe profit squeeze, leading in turn to a 'shakeout' of labour and a reluctance to invest in the new capacity. Thus, a wage explosion telescopes within a short period a desirable attack on overmanning which would otherwise be spread over a longer period and therefore be easier to absorb.

There has been far too much equivocation and self-deception by economists in the debate on the relation between inflationary wage demands and unemployment. The Conservative Ministers who spoke in the early 1970s of trade unions pricing workers out of jobs were *right*, however inadequate their explanation of the process; while those who tried to deny this, whether in political polemics or by the use of short-run pseudo-Keynesian models were *wrong*. This is, to my mind, as certain as any cause-and-effect relation in this subject can ever hope to be.

It is time for frankness about the social and economic effects of trade unions. The belief dies hard that any progressive and enlightened person should either have instinctive sympathy with union wage demands, or at least refrain from giving comfort to their opponents. Even Conservatives who wish to show that they belong to the up-to-date wing of the Party, go out of their way to avoid 'union-bashing'; the controversial 1971 Industrial Relations Act was itself designed, in the minds of at least some of its authors, to strengthen 'responsible trade unionism'. The idea that trade union bargaining may itself be an anachronism as a method of determining wages, or that it has outlived its usefulness, is regarded as too radical to utter in public (although prominent politicians of all parties say so in private). Because anti-union arguments may have sometimes been associated with the type of person who believes in hanging or flogging and regrets the passing of gun diplomacy, this does not make them wrong. To ask 'In whose company will I be?' may be an inescapable shorthand method of approaching questions one has not the time or interest to investigate for oneself; but it can be extremely dangerous as a standard procedure. It would be a moderate assessment to describe the trade unions as agencies for increasing the degree of unemployment and for reducing the real living standards of some of the weakest and most unfortunate sections of the population in a period of rapid but uncertain inflation.

Choosing Among Evils

Enough has been said here – and has happened in the real world – to show that a 'hands off' policy in relation to trade union monopoly power is neither a desirable nor a likely policy. The economic liberal who maintains that all would be well with a stable growth of the money supply and a floating exchange rate (both of which remain in my view desirable) has confused what may be necessary conditions for achieving his ideals with sufficient conditions, which they are certainly not. He should not escape the less congenial task of deciding which kind of labour market policies would be least harmful to his ultimate beliefs.

Whether such measures are called 'incomes policy' or not is largely a verbal quibble. The main objection to the term 'incomes policy' is that it diverts attention from the source of the trouble in union monopoly power, particularly when it masquerades as 'prices and incomes policy'. Moreover, in so far as various governments are criticised for 'not having an incomes policy', it points the finger in the wrong direction. As a matter of usage, many (although not all) of the proponents of 'incomes policy' have in mind more illiberal policies than those who choose some other name for the interventions that they desire.

These semantic issues are a secondary matter. The important distinctions to an economic liberal are in the probable effects of different policies, irrespective of their labels. The best solution would be to treat collective bargaining as a restrictive practice, to be permitted only under certain exceptional conditions, such as the existence of monopsonistic power, or very high local unemployment rates, that give employers a genuine bargaining advantage. These could be 'gateways' under which collective bargaining would be allowed, like the 'gateways' in the Restrictive Practices Act, under which trade associations can apply to be allowed to continue price rings.

Unfortunately, an attempt to outlaw collective wage-fixing is not only unlikely to be tried, but, if it were, the law might prove unenforceable without a greater basis of consent than the suggestion would at present command. One must, therefore, also discuss second best approaches. But it is well to bear in mind what the first best suggestion would be, should the opportunity to move towards it arise. Suggestions should not be suppressed because they appear extreme or politically unrealistic. So did, at one time, most of the current conventional wisdom.

An exhaustive classification of plans for influencing wage

determination will not be provided here, but only a few notes on various schemes, that have been, are being, or are likely to be, attempted. By no means all the ideas are mutually exclusive, and some could operate at the same time. The nearest to the abolition of collective bargaining and restoring competitive market forces among those considered even remotely feasible, would be to give a central body reserve powers over all *negotiated* wage settlements. Employers short of labour would still be free to offer what they liked above the negotiated minimum to attract workers; but the government or some other central body would have control over the industry-wide rates to which these market premia would be added. This would be worth trying, but there are two snags. One is that union monopoly power at plant level could still generate explosive inflationary forces (and the drift of power to plant level would, of course, be accelerated). The second is that unless the central body were to impose a permanent nil norm (which it should do but would not), we would be back with the familiar problems of norms and criteria.

The type of official intervention that would interfere least with market forces would be one that did not worry about differentials, but periodically wiped out a given percentage of all wages and salaries. Strictly speaking, the reduction would have to be in the totals and not in the percentage increases. This, if it were possible, would eliminate the forces making for cost-push inflation, while retaining the market (adjusted in the ways explained in the previous chapter) as an instrument of allocation. It is something of this kind that many professional economists and Treasury officials have semi-consciously in mind when they speak of 'incomes policy'.[12]

The trouble with this approach is that knowledge of this paring-off process would affect the wage bargainers themselves. Behind the anti-employer façade, wage negotiations are primarily battles *between different groups of workers* over relativities; and the result at the end of the bargaining year is not one for which the losers would willingly have settled. The knowledge that the total wage bill was to be axed by a uniform percentage would be likely to lead to much bigger claims and more bitter and prolonged industrial strife;

and the state or employer would afterwards have the herculean task of reclaiming back earnings. Alternatively, the percentage reduction would have to be applied instantly and would depend on a highly complex formula, which would tend to produce ever greater reductions as time went on with all the incendiary risks of such a situation.

Nevertheless, one proposal, sometimes made in association with the paring-off idea, is worth considering. This is an attempt, whether voluntary or statutory, to synchronise pay settlements so that they come into force on the same day of the year. This could not easily apply to industrial plants where local negotiations are going on all the time. But it might work in some industries, particularly in the public sector. This device could not remove the explosive forces generated by incompatible views on differentials, but it might moderate highly inflationary settlements which were entered into simply as an insurance against others doing better. If, for example, the railwaymen, postmen and electricians were satisfied with their existing differentials, a simple known advance date for the payment of the new rates would provide some guarantee against their being outflanked by each other.

The suggestions so far mentioned might slightly alleviate the unemployment–inflation problem, but little confidence can be placed in their being sufficient to do the whole job. Another approach, which does not preclude anything so far suggested, is to concentrate on resisting inflationary wage claims in the public sector. The semi-monopoly position of public enterprises, and their access to the Treasury as a banker of last resort, can aggravate wage-push inflation. These special factors enable public enterprises to take an inflationary lead which may then be followed by the private sector. The Government can certainly assist matters by neither 'leaning on' public enterprises to bring industrial peace, nor providing a bottomless purse to finance the ensuing deficits. It can even attempt to move into reverse and use the public sector as the spearhead in an attempt to produce 'de-escalation' or at least 'non-escalation' in private industry. Apart from standing up to public sector strikes, the Government can also help by making only sparing use of official conciliation services and by diplomatic attempts to strengthen the resolve of private employers.

There is a great deal more to be said for such policies than it was fashionable to admit when they were inaugurated by the Heath Government in the early 1970s. But even if 'standing firm' in the public sector were ever to achieve its immediate objects, its long term success would depend on the private sector following the lead given. Otherwise the public sector would, in the end, have to raise wages in line with the private sector if it were to retain its employees and avoid becoming completely demoralised. Moreover, the 'standing firm' policy is extremely vulnerable to the demonstration effect of the occasional spectacular defeat, such as that of the miners' strike in 1972, which any non-omniscient government is bound occasionally to suffer through tactical errors and which can undo overnight many months of patient effort.

Above all, the transformation of every dispute in state-owned industries and services into a political confrontation between the Government and the trade union movement is an example of just that kind of overextension of the sphere of the political which was condemned in the last chapter. If every public sector wage claim is a test of overall Government policy, it becomes very difficult to give much weight to the special circumstances of the particular industry. This problem would be easier if there were (as may have happened by the time these words are in print) a limited revival of something like the old Prices and Incomes Board for the public sector – provided that this Board did not attempt a pseudo-scientific evaluation of different jobs, but worked on the clues it could obtain from the supply and demand situation in the industry concerned and the movement of comparable earnings in the private sector.

Although this part of the discussion has been conducted for ease of exposition in terms of moderating the rate of wage-push inflation, readers of the earlier parts of the chapter will realise that what is at stake is the reduction of the minimum sustainable level of unemployment consistent with non-explosive inflation. Short of treating collective bargaining as a restrictive practice, the best hope for achieving it is a reduction of the monopoly power of the unions on the ground.

The Industrial Relations Act may make a peripheral contribution by reducing the blacklisting of non-affected employers, or by bringing in the 'silent majority' of union members against the militants. But we should not pin too much hope on what is basically a reform of union law rather than an anti-monopoly measure.

One of the most interesting proposals here has been made by a left-wing economic liberal, Professor James Meade.[13] This is that the Government should lay down a norm, which would not be binding on either side of industry. If unions staged a strike for a claim above the norm various penalties would apply, e.g. supplementary benefits would become the liability of the union or the subsequent debt of the individual worker, accumulated rights of redundancy benefits would be lost, and the union would be liable to a tax on strike benefits. A tribunal would determine whether the sanctions should apply.

Unless there were hosts of recognised exceptional cases, almost any strike would be for something in excess of the probable norm. The Meade proposals amount, on analysis, either to the reintroduction of a complex policy for determining merits of individual claims, or to a series of penalties or withdrawals of privileges when union members engage in organised strikes. The latter types of measure should be examined separately on their own merits. Supplementary benefit to strikers' families should, as a matter of course, be loans to be recovered via subsequent income tax deductions. If this were done it would be impossible to make mud-slinging allegations about 'starving people back to work', but the taxpayer would not finance strikers. Nor is it any more reasonable that the income tax machinery should continue to pay out refunds to strikers immediately, while taxpayers who have left a job for other reasons have to wait much longer. Loss of accumulated redundancy benefits might, on the other hand, be unfair to people pushed unwillingly by their fellow workers into a strike. A tax on strike benefits, however, has much to be said for it, although it would be inflammatory in union circles and it might not be worth jeopardising the rest of the Meade proposals by including them in the total package.

A great many other proposals for intervention in incomes settlement are really suggestions for machinery, either for deciding what particular incomes should be, or for attempting to enforce these decisions. This applies to a whole range of suggestions ranging from the presence of a 'public interest' representative at all major negotiations, to a C.B.I.–T.U.C. compact, a Prices and Incomes Board 'with teeth', or a 'tax on excessive wage increases'. All these proposals assume that there should be an attempt to regulate the process of wage determination and not simply to alter the environment in which they take place. The tax proposal, for example, is simply a piece of machinery for penalising wage increases above a permissible level, which would have to be determined by the whole elaborate apparatus of norms, criteria and exceptions, with all their well known problems, distortions, inequities and opportunities for avoidance.

Nevertheless, because of the difficulties of other approaches, direct intervention in wage-fixing has been tried in most Western countries and is likely to be tried again at some stage in this country – perhaps before the reader has seen these words. Although the existence of rampant union monopoly power gives the economic liberal no reason to favour *laissez-faire* in this field, he should also be aware that the heart of any regulation of incomes is the problem of differentials; and the real danger of intervention is that some central body will try to determine how much one is worth in some quasi-moral sense compared to another. (The pitfalls of this were explained on pp. 103–9.) The liberal should not deceive himself by saying that such intervention is bound to fail.

It is true that econometric investigations of recent incomes policy have been controversial and inconclusive, and suggest that effects in most countries have been at best modest. But this may reflect partly a lack of ruthlessness on the part of social democracies in carrying them out. It is also true that history is littered with unsuccessful attempts to control wages and/or prices. The Roman Emperor Diocletian issued edicts in A.D. 301–2 fixing maximum wages and prices, enforced under threat of execution, but this did not prevent a galloping inflation.[14] The Statute of Artificers of 1563, which provided for the regulation of maximum wages by J.P.s, was no more successful in stemming the Elizabethan inflation. The Roman inflation sprang in fact from currency debasement to pay the Imperial Army, the Elizabethan variety from the influx of precious metals from the New World; and no incomes control can offset an excessive increase in the money supply or in government borrowing financed by the banking system.

One cannot, however, rule out some degree of 'success' for incomes intervention combined with a sufficient control of monetary demand. A determined government can, in all probability, control the growth of 'nominal' (i.e. money) income and output by monetary and fiscal policy. The role of intervention in the labour market would then be to ensure that the growth of national income took the form of increases in real output and employment, and was not wasted in inflationary increases in wages and prices and rising unemployment. To put the matter in yet another way: the role of incomes policy is to try to see that a limit on the growth of the money supply and on the Budget deficit, which is sufficient to prevent either a runaway or an undesirably high rate of inflation, is accompanied by a tolerable level of employment. Most of the economists who have explained how wage drift, variations in hours of work, upgrading of workers and many other devices of human ingenuity could defeat incomes control,[15] are implicitly referring to a situation of excess demand in the labour market where, even if unions did not exist, employers would bid for labour and push up earnings at an inflationary, and probably increasing, rate. Direct intervention in incomes is only feasible once this sort of excess demand has been eliminated.

Given that such intervention is likely to be attempted, the relevant question is: how does one minimise its harmful potential and maximise any possible benefits? One of the most important distinctions to draw is between emergency policies, such as a temporary freeze or ceiling on permissible wage and price increases, and policies designed for permanent operation.

The various short term wages or wage–price freezes have had greater apparent effects, while the more profound long term policies, which were supposed to follow them, have run into the sand. This was demonstrated by the Cripps, Lloyd and Wilson freezes in the U.K.; and Nixon's mistake in 1971 was to have made his freeze as short as three months and to put too much weight on the follow-up. A freeze or ceiling has the important additional advantage that it does not attempt to impose supposedly superior criteria on the wage and price differentials determined by the market, but accepts present differentials and postpones any further adjustment for up to say a year. Clearly, a long term freeze would ossify the economy, but as a short term shock measure to be used on rare occasions, not too easily predictable in advance, it has its place in the economic policy armoury.

The main case to be made for a freeze or ceiling is that it will reduce the expected rate of inflation and thus the level of wage increases associated in the short run with any degree of slack in the labour market. If the level of unemployment is at, or above, its minimum sustainable rate, then a temporary freeze or ceiling can reduce the amount and duration of any excess unemployment required to reduce the rate of inflation. If the level of unemployment, at the time of the freeze or later, is below the minimum level, then inflation will eventually start gathering momentum again. But even then time will have been bought. If a freeze or ceiling can reduce the expected rate of inflation from 10 to 3 per cent – admittedly an extremely favourable assumption – it will take some years for the pace of inflation to creep back to 10 per cent and the old problem to re-emerge. Time is worth buying with a problem as intractable as the inflation–unemployment one. The real trouble is that the more frequently a freeze or ceiling is repeated, the less will be the effect on expectations, and the shorter the amount of time it will buy.

The logic of threshold agreements is in some respects similar. If the rise in real incomes that the unions are insisting upon is out of line with the productivity trend, threshold agreements will not help. They can help, however, in specific situations when, for some reason, trade unionists are projecting an unnecessarily high rate of inflation into the future. The classic example was the autumn of 1969 when they were projecting the effects of the recent substantial devaluation, and the indirect tax increases imposed to back it up, into the future. By doing so, their fears became self-justifying. In more normal circumstances, threshold agreement can be of some use as an insurance premium, when unions are exerting their monopoly power not aggressively, but out of fear of what others engaged in the inflationary race will do. The key question is whether the amount of moderation that can be purchased by threshold agreements will do more to dampen price increases than the threshold compensation itself will to increase it. The situation will clearly vary from time to time according to the state of the cycle, union moods and other influences.

Thresholds or any form of 'cost of living indexing' have the disadvantage that they create a severe obstacle to a reduction in the normal rate of growth of real incomes which may be forced on a country by a variety of circumstances, such as a fall in the overseas market for its products, a major devaluation, a misfortune such as an overseas war, or a mistake in demand management. If threshold agreements are not then suspended, the country could face an inflationary explosion of post-World War I continental dimensions. The conclusion is that threshold agreements may be useful in certain industries, especially in the public sector, where it is both possible to keep a watch on their terms and the desire for insurance is high; but they must always be revocable in an emergency.

Permanent policies of intervention in wage-fixing have been deliberately left to the end of this chapter. The hope of the economic liberal must be that a combination of labour market policies and *ad hoc* expedients of the kind so far discussed can prevent inflation from becoming explosive at a tolerable level of unemployment. He is afraid that an incomes policy will be deliberately used to enforce a pattern of relativities based on a revival of the mediaeval myth that there is a 'just price' for goods and services, which would enable a group of wise men to say how much a milkman is worth relative to a doctor, or what is a fair price for a loaf of bread. This unfortunately is what most people probably have in mind when they talk of a prices and incomes policy. Yet even Lord Balogh vigorously repudiates the pseudo-scientific claims of job evaluation and admits that would-be scientific attempts to measure the worth of a man's work 'are subjective and politically coloured'.[16] Job evaluation is possible within a particular firm or even industry because of the existence of an outside market to evaluate the basic skills attributed to particular posts. If there is no such market, or it is ignored, there is no way of comparing the value of a carpenter's job with that of a lathe operator, or determining how many points to give skill, as against responsibility, irksomeness and all the other attributes in which jobs vary from each other.

Unfortunately, governments that hanker after an incomes policy are strongly tempted to go in for this wrong sort. Even if they stick to generalised restraint on the incomes side they are under a very strong pressure to attempt to buy union support – almost always unsuccessfully – by a whole series of actions, ranging from price controls in the private sector, pressure on nationalised industries to keep prices artificially low, to dividend control and penal taxes on profits and high incomes, or travel restrictions, which not only tend to ossify the structure of industry and bolster inefficiency, but if pushed too far are inimical to a free society.

Whatever may have to be said for public relations purposes, it is as well to say that, except in the case of short-term freezes or ceilings, intervention is needed primarily for wages and not prices and profits. This is often concealed by Whitehall for tactical purposes, and anti-profit gestures are made for the sake of union goodwill. Union leaders are not so easily deceived; and it might be better to state frankly that profits are a different type of animal from wages. There is abundant statistical evidence, cited above, that there has been, taking one year with another, no profit-push inflation in the U.K. or in most other Western countries, and that, apart from the effects of changing import prices and indirect taxes, the main statistically identified influence on the general price level is the movement of wages in relation to productivity.

If some guarantee is really required that wage restraint will not lead to an increase in the share of profits in the national income, the way to provide it is by adjusting the level of company taxation in the Budget. Such guarantees were indeed given in Budget speeches and other Government statements in the Maudling–Brown era; but they were either not understood or disregarded. If they are to be revived again, some allowance would have to be made for the marked falls in the share profits in the decade up to 1970, which needs to be reversed if investment is not to be severely hit and employment is to be maintained at satisfactory levels.

The most difficult choice for an economic liberal is whether it would be worse to have income relativities influenced by some sort of C.B.I.–T.U.C. compact (with or without government involvement) or to have a statutory policy. The exercise of economic power by producer groups insulated from both market and political disciplines is obnoxious in a free society. But the one redeeming feature of arrangements of this kind, is that, so long as they lack statutory sanction, they are likely to have many gaps. There will always be some workers and entrepreneurs who do not 'play the game' and charge the market rate for their services. These chinks in the system will provide some opportunity for innovation and personal initiative which may not be there in a government-enforced system. Moreover, given the existence of union monopoly power, it would be a lesser evil for the rival union monopolies to work out a deal on relativities than to impose a high rate of unemployment or an explosive inflation on the public as a by-product of their power struggles.

Where the liberal should draw the line is at any attempt to convey quasi-governmental power on the C.B.I. or T.U.C., whether by legislation or by Ministerial arm-twisting directed against those who do not comply. If government power is to be permanently involved, statutory control exercised through known rules is the only approach compatible with the 'rule of law'. Whether the government delegates the determination of individual cases to a separate board or boards is a secondary matter. The important point is that the criteria should be as clear as possible and the outcome of particular cases reasonably predictable.

If we do have to face centralised determination of, or official influence on, wages and other incomes, it is important for the liberal not just to withdraw in disgust. His fallback position should be to insist that the relative scarcity of different types of workers should be among the factors taken into account by any wage-fixing authority. There is no need for this to be the only principle; traditional ideas of relativities will inevitably temper the speed with which relativities adjust to supply and demand; and fads, fashions and headline pressures will unavoidably play a part in determining the case law. But some recognition of the importance of scarcity or surplus of the type of labour concerned is necessary if we are not to be forced into a painful choice between poor economic performance (which would make social tensions worse) and ultimate direction of labour on the lines analysed in the last chapter. An open admission of the role of supply and demand could also play a part in creating the public consensus on differentials, the lack of which is both undermining the market system and preventing any alternative from operating. An emphasis on market conditions as *one* of the criteria to be used in determining relative incomes would bring home to people that something less was being attempted than an evaluation of relative moral worth and, that if pop singers continued to be paid more than headmasters, this would be a by-product of satisfying consumer choice with no deeper judgement implied.

3 The Economics of the Alternative Society

Hör auf zu beben
Bereite dich zu leben

Cease from trembling
Prepare thyself to live.

From lines added by Mahler to
Klopstock's 'Resurrection Ode'
and used in his Second Symphony

There is little that is new in the indictment by the present
generation of radicals and revolutionaries of technology and
the 'consumer society'. The Bible abounds in admonitions
against the vain pursuit of riches. The 19th century Tories
derided the commercialism of their Whig and Liberal opponents; prophets such as Carlyle and Ruskin, as well as socialists of the Tawney school, thundered against the acquisitive
society; and T. S. Eliot, writing as a Christian conservative
was deeply disturbed by the value of a 'mechanised, com-
mercialised, urbanised way of life'.[1]

Orthodox Labour thinkers, such as Mr Crosland, are
understandably sceptical of the new fashion;[2] but it has undoubtedly affected the mood of a great many respectable
'progressives' well outside the New Left; and the increase of
consumer spending has come to be regarded as an establishment, conservative goal to be scorned by the enlightened.

In the form now fashionable among progressive egalitarians, the anti-materialist attitude contains a great many
contradictions. As Assar Lindbeck has pointed out in his
sympathetic but critical study, *The Political Economy of the
New Left*,[3] 'If additional consumption is so unimportant,

why is *equality* in income and consumption so important?' There is also a fundamental incompatibility between the attack on the consumer society and the almost automatic support among most of the New and Old Left for trade union union wage claims.

These contradictions reflect, however, the inconsistencies (to put it no worse) of individuals or groups. It is possible to imagine a genuine change of values which would cause people to place much less emphasis on the acquisition of additional material goods and services. This essay is not concerned to argue whether such a change would be good or bad, but to examine some of the economic consequences of such a change, and, in particular, whether it need involve the suppression of market forces and private property either by some form of command economy or, at the other extreme, a more anarchic form of behaviour.

Altruism

It is possible that the revulsion against the pursuit of ever greater material wealth, at present characteristic of a few radical students (and also some upper and middle class traditionalists), is a portent of wider change. It is always worth examining the implication of developments at present visible only on a small scale and still very untypical of the bulk of the population. Let us then suppose that there were a widespread weakening of the desire towards additional personal consumption. What would be the consequences?

Such a shift in outlook could come about in various ways. It is convenient to start off by assuming that it is part of a new ethical outlook, rather than a mere change of tastes. Both are of course involved in the movement towards the 'alternative society'; but the analysis of an ethical revulsion against selfishness is, in fact, less complicated than that of a shift of preferences from consumer goods towards other things. To make any progress at all, it is necessary to proceed in stages.

What, then, follows from the belief that the search for maximum individual self-gratification is wrong, and from the desire to see a new order, based on altruism rather than institutionalised selfishness? General altruism is a concept capable of several interpretations. The most extreme form is the advocacy of complete unselfishness and total dedication to the welfare of others. This would be internally inconsistent if adopted as a general rule. The paradox of total unselfishness is that it is only possible to be selfless because some people are concerned with their own selfish desires or needs. If everybody were only concerned with the welfare of others, there would be nothing for altruists to do. A second, slightly less extreme form would be to love one's neighbour as much as – but not more than – oneself. A practitioner of such an ethic, carried to its logical conclusion, would devote his efforts to improving the welfare of the human race, or his fellow countrymen, and would be prepared to forego, for their benefit, any excess of his income above the general run. A third sort of altruistic ethic would allow some modest material objectives, by definition less than the maximum obtainable, but forego any available excess for the sake of others.

Altruism and benevolence, if they are to be any other than individual eccentricities, presuppose a certain measure of self-regard; and novelists and psychologists have always known that those who despise themselves cannot love other people. Thus, we can confine our attention to the second and third varieties – an unwillingness to obtain for oneself more than either the generally available average, or some specified minimum, while there are others who are worse off. Various qualifications and permutations of these codes can be envisaged. An ethical inhibition against maximising one's own standard of living, present when the poorest are suffering from malnutrition may, without any fundamental change of outlook, disappear if poverty comes to mean possessing only one car.

This essay is not concerned with those who are only prepared to make such penal sacrifices if others do so as well. My concern here is with the logical consequence of altruism as an individual ethic. An almost insuperable, initial difficulty is deciding what is the correct reference group. Is an altruist to forego personal riches to raise the standard of living of his fellow countrymen or of the entire human race?

It is difficult to find any convincing argument for limiting altruism to the frontiers of the nation-state – except for a pathological nationalist who has intense feelings of brotherhood for his fellow countrymen, but regards everyone else as a member of a different species. There seems no more reason for restricting benevolent and unselfish behaviour to the inhabitants of the U.K. than to the inhabitants of Greater London or, the enlarged E.E.C. or members of one's own profession. The conclusion would seem to be that the consistent altruist should want the benefit of any limitation on his own living standard devoted to the poorest inhabitants of the poorest countries.

An altruist who felt that 'development aid' did more harm than good could subscribe to purely charitable relief organisations. Apart from worrying about the forms in which this help should be given, or its long-term effect, the altruist may despair at the smallness of the impact of his efforts, and those of like-minded people, if spread thinly over thousands of millions; and he may prefer to make a discernible impact on living standards nearer home, which he is also in a better position to assess for himself. But once he does this, he is conceding that he does not attach equal value to every human being; and he can have no tenable objection to the liberal–individualist ethic which attaches most weight to one's family and friends, somewhat lesser weight to professional colleagues or others with shared interests and outlook, and so in ever widening circles until the boundaries of the whole human race are reached. (The implications of such a realistic weighting are discussed in the essay on *Morality and Foreign Policy*, on pp. 337–40.)

But however the altruist solves these conundrums, one general observation can be made. This is that there is little reason for him to refrain from maximising his own income. The difference between himself and other citizens, if he is logical, should be in what he does with his gains. Indeed, if anything, he should work beyond the point at which the self-centred citizen decides that the extra reward is not worth the effort, in order to increase the surplus he has available for charitable purposes. A society dominated by dedicated and consistent altruists would, therefore, be a pretty puritanical one, which is one of the reasons why I do not find the prospect attractive. Indeed, there have been resemblances to it among the frugal, hard-working devout rising middle classes during several eras of economic advance. The main difference is that the wealth that was foregone in personal enjoyment was devoted only in small measure to improving the lot of other human beings, but was largely devoted to the 'higher' purposes of religion or further capital accumulation.

The important point, however, is that there is no reason why an altruist should not, with the limits to be mentioned below, play to win. The presumption in favour of buying in the cheapest market and selling in the dearest, and gaining the best return on his talents, applies at least as much to him as to his self-oriented colleagues. A businessman does not serve his fellows, least of all the poorest of them, by selling a product at a minimal profit well below that which the market will bear.

If he were to do so, the most likely result would be a mis-allocation of scarce resources, which is likely to make the community worse off; and there is no presumption that the poor will escape the effects. Even the apparent direct transfer from his own pocket to others by holding his prices down will be misdirected, as a large part of the gain will inevitably flow to those who are, by altruistic lights, undeserving of his largesse. He would be better advised to behave in a normal commercial manner and use the larger sum then at his disposal for redistribution according to his own philan-thropic principles.

The above advice, is of course, only an approximation to the truth, due to the imperfections of economic policy. Al-though it would be best if the state were to lay down rules of the games and adjust its taxes and subsidies so that the pur-suit of self-interest also promoted the general prosperity, we know that a market economy will never, in practice, be managed with ideal wisdom. Firms are not always made to pay for the overspill costs that their waste products or their heavy trucks impose on the community. Workers displaced by technological or other change may not be reabsorbed into other jobs – whether because of mistaken official financial policies, or the monopolistic activities of trade unions. Undesirable changes in the distribution of income, caused, say, by a rise in basic food prices, are best corrected via the tax and social security system; but we cannot always rely on the correction being made.

Thus, the playing of the market game must always be tempered by common sense; and this applies not merely to the declared altruist, but also to the ordinary humane citizen. The absence of a law making me pay full compensation for all the foul products my factory pours into a river, does not give me a moral licence to go on polluting regardless (although I may be under financial pressures to do so). There is no general politico-economic outlook that can excuse inflicting specific harm on others, especially identifiable individual human beings in a weaker position than oneself, without attempt at redress. The takeover king who shows the faithful servant of the old firm the door, without asking what is to become of him, is not a good Manchester liberal but a callous malefactor.

These qualifications do not destroy the general presumption against subordinating the profit motive to some supposedly higher ideal. A businessman, however altruistic, should be very careful before reducing his rate of return for some abstract goal, such as 'lower prices', 'an incomes policy', 'the export drive', or 'the need to invest'. He is not professionally qualified to calculate the remoter consequences of supposedly patriotic deviation from the pursuit of his own interest. Nor, in all probability, are those who provide these exhortations. Moreover, even when it comes to avoiding specific harm to known individuals, an altruistic or humanitarian employer would be better advised to concentrate on such matters as the early spotting of redundancies and making personal efforts to retrain and find other jobs for those displaced, rather than attempt to maintain an inflated work force, or to 'buy British' when the foreign product gives better value. Of course, painful dilemmas cannot always be avoided in this way; but the sensible humanitarian will try to minimise them by intelligent planning of *his own* activities rather than by taking pride in the smallness of his profits.

A Change of Tastes

An altruist of the kind described may be very fond of consumer goods and simply think it wrong to have more of them than his less fortunate neighbours. It is, however, useful to extend the analysis from altruism to a more general rejection of the striving for ever increasing amounts of goods and services as a false goal.

It is possible that the existence of a minority of people, who had already undergone such a change in tastes and preferred idleness or social security benefit to the extra material gain available from work, may have had something to do with the much higher unemployment figures in the early 1970s than in previous cyclical peaks. But, in default of worthwhile evidence, I should be surprised if this is more than a part of the explanation. In any case, whatever may have been the motivation of the unemployed, there is not the slightest reason to suppose that the saturation of consumer wants is the reason for the difficulties that have occurred in recent years in maintaining 'effective demand' at levels which have previously been customary. The anti-consumption values under discussion are still shared by a minority. Most people could still find plenty on which to spend extra income.

Tastes and behaviour are not, however, immutable; and it is worth asking whether a revulsion from any further increase in material consumption – feelings which are at present confined to minority groups – would be compatible with a competitive market economy. However strong the historical contention between the rise of capitalism (or earlier mercantile systems) and materialistic preoccupations, need this connection hold good in the future? This question is best investigated by treating the revulsion from the pursuit of ever more goods and services as a pure change of taste in a society that has already reached an advanced level of technology and is capable of producing a Gross National Product that is, by historical standards, high.

It is, however, necessary to distinguish between two forms of aversion towards the consumer society. There is the purist assertion that additional consumption of any kind is of negligible or negative importance. There is also the lesser contention that it is only additions to private consumption that have a zero or negative utility, but that additional output in the public services – whether health, education, or the use of resources to improve the physical environment – is abundantly justified. As Lindbeck points out, Galbraith in *The Affluent Society* simultaneously embraced both versions of the over-consumption doctrine without distinguishing between them (or noting their incompatibility).

This essay is concerned with a swing of taste against consumption of the first and purer form. The second 'pro-public, anti-private consumption' form of the doctrine would still require a concentration on economic growth and efficiency, but the extra resources would be spent by the state and there would be little increase in post-tax real income. It would therefore represent a much less fundamental change.

The simplest case to envisage is that the majority of the population become satisfied with a lower level of material award, in the form of either private or collective consumption, than they could obtain from the earnings of a working week of the present customary length. The higher the general level of hourly real wages (in other words, the more successful 'the system' has been in the past), the more such people there are likely to be; and the less heroic, or ascetic, they will need to be to sustain such an attitude. Let us at this stage assume that they can fill extra leisure hours to their own satisfaction.

A competitive system based on market forces is surely likely to prove most satisfactory to such non-consumers. For a profit-making businessman is not interested in the private values of his workers. If they wish to work fewer hours for less money, or only one week in four, that is their affair. If irregular and unpredictable working habits impose difficulties in keeping up a smooth flow of production, the rate for the job will be *pro rata* less than for workers willing to work in a more regular way. Indeed, as soon as it becomes apparent that there is a pool of potential workers available, who will be easier to recruit or require to be paid less provided that they can work in amounts, and/or at times, of their own choosing, it will pay businessmen to find methods of adapting their methods to such preferences; and those who do adapt in this way will be able to undercut those who insist too rigidly on traditional working practices.*

The difficulties in the way of the 'alternative' culture come from the monopolistic and anti-capitalist element of our society. This would be readily admitted in the case of restrictive practices by businessmen who agree not to undercut each other with irregular labour. But the greatest obstacles arise from union monopolies, who insist on fixing wages and conditions by collective agreements, which do not easily permit variations to suit minority preferences. It would not take long for the shop stewards to 'call everyone out' if an employer were to be found taking on individual workers at below the regular rate in return for an unusual and costly pattern of working hours or a toleration of absenteeism. (The systems now being introduced experimentally are presumably not very costly – they may even be beneficial – for company efficiency.) The point would be blindingly obvious were it not for the traditional association between being on the left and pro-union sympathies. It is no coincidence that the occupations suggested in that excellent publication *Alternative London*,[4] which range from interviewing for market surveys and selling charter flights, to minicab driving, 'busking', window cleaning and working in bistros, are the least unionised of activities. Nevertheless, if the preference for leisure, or irregular work, over take-home pay became sufficiently widespread, even union negotiators would be forced to give it such attention.

An interesting corroboration of this line of argument is the degree of toleration of those who 'opt out' in different countries. It is greatest in countries with vestigial attachment to competitive capitalism such as the U.S. and the U.K.; it is least in the centrally planned Communist societies, and in countries with a tradition of state-regulated capitalism and a dislike of market forces, such as France, the position is midway between the two.

* Since this was drafted, timing systems to enable companies to offer flexible work hours or 'flextime' have been marketed commercially. One of the pioneers was Messerschmidt in Germany; and after *The Financial Times* described the introduction of such a system into Pilkington Laboratories (18 April 1972), it was 'bombarded' with enquiries.

If the distaste for accumulation of goods and services came to be predominant, competition would, of course, change its nature. There might still be a good deal of investment and entrepreneurial action, if consumer desires, although modest, were subject to frequent alterations of taste; the 'gear' that is fashionable might be subject to frequent change, or trips to old coal mines might alternate with visits to Kabul or painting one's home in a novel manner as ways of spending leisure.

The need for such continuing investment would reduce social welfare as conventionally defined by economists. For people would have to sacrifice some leisure, or work a little less irregularly or make do with fewer goods and services, to leave aside a margin for this investment. But it could well be argued that it is only such changes of tastes and fashion that would prevent the envisaged society from becoming utterly stagnant. (The alternative view that the bulk of its members would be fruitfully occupied in spiritual contemplation or in personal relations strains credibility a little too far.) It is a defect of the treatment of changes of tastes by writers on welfare economics that these are seen only as wasteful reductions in the standard of living.

Purely for the sake of analysis, let us, nevertheless, assume that consumer requirements are not merely modest but static, and that there is no population growth. *Provided that the transition from the present pattern to this situation is sufficiently gradual*, there is no reason to predict general bankruptcies, the collapse of capitalism, or that it would be impossible for any other reason to give effect to the new pattern of static tastes and desires.

As the growth of consumer demand declines during the transitional period, we should expect that net investment would eventually drop to zero. The rate of return on capital and the real rate of interest would fall off. The situation would be similar to what Keynes had in mind when he spoke of the euthanasia of the *rentier*. Owing to the fall in the rate of return, the share of interest and profit in the national income could be expected to fall drastically over time. Whatever profits there were would largely be distributed, as there would be no scope for reinvestment. Where, however, as in small businesses, profits were a substitute for managerial salaries, market forces would keep them in existence.

The stock of fixed interest securities (including deadweight national debt) would not yield any more real income (unless prices fell); but their capital value and the wealth of their owners would rise severalfold as interest rates dropped, and this would tend to counteract the other forces reducing the inequality of wealth. The owners of these securities could work even less than the rest of the community – assuming that they, too, did not desire more material goods. But the effect on the welfare of everyone else would, in these circumstances, be trivial. If 90 per cent of the population worked ten hours a week and 10 per cent with fixed interest securities now had to work an average of only one hour, the loss to the 90 per cent from the existence of this private wealth would be one hour more work per week than would be otherwise necessary. Should even this be regarded as unacceptable, the wealth effect on fixed interest owners could be counteracted by means of a moderate annual capital levy.

Mention of Keynes is very appropriate in this context. For the kind of situation here discussed is one in which there could well be involuntary unemployment, in the sense that, in the absence of appropriate policies, effective demand for goods and services might not be sufficient to employ people even for the limited number of hours for which they were prepared to work. Involuntary unemployment, if it occurred, could be cured in this situation by some combination of monetary expansion and budget deficits.

Nor is there anything that need be incomprehensible to the layman in these remedies. All one has to do is to imagine everyone in our ten hour a week 'non-consuming' society receiving a cash sum through the post. Either he would spend slightly more or (if the static wants hypothesis is taken literally) he would want to work less, or some combination of the two would occur. The demand for labour would rise and the supply would fall off, until there was eventually no more involuntary unemployment.

It is worth listing the advantages of maintaining a monetary economy based on the market even in our hypothetical society where consumer wants are very modest in relation to potential output, and have ceased to grow. Obviously a capitalist or mixed economy would, in such circumstances, be a very different animal from anything we now know. The capital goods sector would be very much smaller, as it would be concerned only with replacement and not with expansion or modernisation. Entrepreneurial or technological ability would command a smaller market price; and parts of business, and perhaps government, would become a routine. The society would, in some ways, resemble the mercantile economy that existed before the Industrial Revolution or the more stagnant economies of the West such as Spain or Ireland until a couple of decades ago – with the all-important difference that there would be no involuntary poverty or unemployment to disfigure it.

It is important to note that, in this type of economy, consumer wants would be static but not satiated. There could be no satiation of wants while labour still had a 'marginal disutility' – in other words, while people still regarded work as something which they would rather not do, or would rather do less of, were it not for the need to earn a living. For if wants were literally satiated, but the last hour of work still carried a disutility, it would pay people to reduce their hours of work and their earnings until goods reacquired some utility at the margin. The assumption of static wants implies that people would seek to enjoy the benefits of technological progress entirely in the form of reduced hours of work and not at all in increased take-home pay.

The retention of money payments in this static economy would allow people to choose their own combination of goods and services, which would not be possible if consumption were organised collectively; and, above all, people would be able to retain choice of their own employment. Production would be organised as efficiently as possible – which, in this situation, means that given wants could be supplied with the minimum of work hours. For, if a more efficient method were anywhere available, profits would ensue for a temporary period to anyone who utilised them – although these would eventually be eroded by competition and the system return to its static state.

Above all, no one would be forced to conform to a single life style. People who did not share the prevailing anti-consumption, anti-work ethos could 'opt into' the consumer society without disturbing their neighbours; and there could still be luxury hotels or ocean cruises for those who wanted them and were prepared to work to obtain them. At the other extreme, those who were prepared to sacrifice even more monetary income than the majority – in return for, say, a five hour week or highly irregular work – could do so. Indeed, it will have struck the economist reader that the traditional theoretical arguments that competitive markets (subject to certain well known exceptions and necessary corrective devices) produce a 'social optimum' come into their own in the static condition we have been describing – although the result will not look much like capitalism as we know it.

The New Left would probably claim that a less consumption-orientated society could not hope to come into existence, because capitalism would smother it. A great deal of the case boils down, on examination, to the grossly inflated view of the powers of advertising, discussed in the Prologue. Clearly the business community has a vested interest in maintaining at least some economic growth, but its political power to distort choice in this direction almost invariably springs from *interventionist* economic policies designed to prop up unprofitable enterprises in the name of technology, nationalism or a *simpliste* interpretation of full employment; and a bias in favour of intervention is one of the unfortunate heritages bequeathed by the Old Left to the New. Unfortunately, the extensive and indefensible rigging of the market by political authorities to favour particular interest groups, is not the only reason why the opponents of the consumer society feel that the dice are loaded against them. Indeed, if anything, their bias is in favour of such intervention as a matter of principle. Their real difficulty may be that most people do not as yet share their tastes; and toleration of people with different tastes is not always the hallmark of those who talk most about 'liberation' and 'freedom'.

A Work Scarce Economy

So far it has been assumed that as a result of a combination of advancing technology and declining appetite for further consumer goods, most people will want to work for a very much smaller number of hours than at present. This is certainly one possible inference from the decline of the work-oriented puritan ethos.

But another development is also possible. This is that people will not be satisfied with more idleness or what are now termed 'leisure pursuits', but will find their main enjoyment in activities at present regarded as work. Labour would then become, as Marx put it, 'not only a means of life, but life's prime want'.[5] This may be because of the delight in creativity for which Marx was hoping or for the status reasons mentioned by modern writers, such as Charles Carter, who emphasise that 'it is degrading to have no work'.[6]

Neither the 18th century aristocrat nor the 19th century gentleman of means found lack of work degrading; and in this, as in so much else, there is an analogy between the attitude of the traditional leisured classes and some of the young radicals of today. But we must take, on board at least, the possibility that these will remain minority attitudes, and that for one reason or another many people will wish to have an occupation of the type now associated with earning a living.

Hitherto, we have assumed that in the non-consumer society of tomorrow, as well as in today's world, the last bit of extra work contributed by most people is something that, other things being equal, they would prefer not to do. It is only contributed because the loss of goods and services through lower earnings would be a still greater evil. Even in the ten-hour week society with static wants considered above, it was assumed that if a sudden technological discovery enabled them to buy the same goods and services with only nine hours' work, most people would be glad to make the exchange.

Now let us imagine a society where most people either enjoy their work very much, or at least regard every hour spent on it as a lesser evil to an equivalent hour of 'leisure'. The jargon term 'marginal disutility of labour', mentioned above, is a useful one for the subjective sacrifice involved under present conditions in any net addition to the amount of work a person does. It is normally assumed that, so far as modern standardised procedures allow, people will work up to the point where the extra earnings from an additional amount of labour are equal to the marginal disutility of labour. To work beyond that point would mean an extra sacrifice greater than the value the person concerned puts on the extra earnings involved. One can assume that trade union negotiators, both nationally and at shop floor, transmit, in however imperfect a form, some sort of average view of the length of a working week at which this point is reached.

There is no reason why the first few hours of work a week should not have a positive utility for many people even in our present society. The more hours a person works, the lower this utility will normally be; but, so long as it is positive, he will wish to extend his working week, as he is also being paid in goods and servces which he values. Thus, each additional hour of work increases his welfare. It is only when the descending marginal utility curve enters the negative region that there is something to balance against the additional earnings, which are themselves declining in utility as their quantity increases.

In our imaginary society of the future the marginal utility curve for work would have a similar shape, except that we would be sure that it would start at a positive quantity. The problem concerns what to assume about the marginal utility of the goods and services that money income would buy. We could, for the sake of symmetry, assume that this becomes negative as extra goods were regarded as harmful nuisance. But this is an artificial and unnecessary assumption. We need only assume that, at that point in the working week where the marginal utility of work has become zero, the marginal utility of goods and services is also zero. So in this society equilibrium would be reached at a length of working week where the marginal utility of both goods and work balanced out at zero, instead of at equal and opposite signs as at present.

The above comparison can be illustrated by the following very simple table.

TABLE 3

	Marginal utility in equilibrium of:	
	Goods and Services	*Work*
Present Society	+	—
'Work Scarce' Society	o	o

At present people exchange work, which (at the margin at least) they would rather not do, for goods of which they would like to have more. In the new society, work would be desired for its own sake and goods would be plentiful. At present, people work up to the point where the declining but positive marginal utility of goods is balanced by the increasing marginal *disutility* of extra work. In the envisaged society they would work up to the point where the marginal *utility* of their work was zero and where the marginal utility of goods was also zero. In either society the point of balance for any group of workers determines the length of their working week. As we shall see, the 'work-scarce' economy is probably not a feasible proposition; but some interesting results can be obtained by entertaining the hypothesis for a while and following out its implications.

There could still be a market economy in this brave new world, but it would be almost the mirror image of the present one. Wages would be zero and goods would be 'free'. Work would then be the desirable commodity. The labour market would be brought into equilibrium by competition in offers of different kinds of work. Just as at present a fur coat has a price in terms of so many mini-skirts or restaurant meals sacrificed to buy it, in this new world one kind of work would have a price in terms of other kinds of work. There might well, for example, be an oversupply of people wanting to provide meals-on-wheels relative to potential dustmen or hospital cleaners. Business activity would then involve the pricing of one type of work in terms of another, so that one hour of providing meals-on-wheels would exchange for several hours of refuse disposal.

The market in labour would, however, differ in important ways from the present market in consumables. One can buy consumption services in two forms. There can be a single act of consumption, such as purchasing a meal or a coach trip. If a person desires the same form of consumption again, he must make fresh payment. Alternatively he can purchase the right to a continuous flow of services over a time, either by purchasing physical assets such as land that will themselves provide a flow of services, or indirectly by purchasing assets which will yield a money income which can be used to finance such a flow of consumption. The existence of intermediate cases, such as consumer durables, which can be analysed either way according to convenience, does not affect the principle of the distinction.

In our present society the emphasis is on individual acts of consumption rather than on the purchase of long-term or permanent rights to consume in the form of property. Indeed, large numbers of people, not all poor, can and do go through life without any property worth mentioning. Where work is scarce, the emphasis would have to be the other way round. While an individual might purchase, say, a week's work as a labourer, or as a restaurant worker, there is a question about how he would pay for it. It would in the first place be in terms of money. But he could only obtain money by selling something; and in our hypothetical world the only thing that would be of value would be the offer of scarce work – in which he would have to have a property right.

The question arises how the property rights to different kinds of work would be allocated in the first place. It would presumably be by firms, local authorities, nationalised concerns and voluntary bodies who at present provide employment. Once ambulance workers become prepared to work for 'nothing', the authorities would have to select drivers on grounds of ability, length of previous service or on the principle of first come, first served.

This would, no doubt, be very arbitrary and would look more like a physical allocation than a pricing system. But eventually there would be a market in rights to do an hour's work of different kinds. The price of one hour's cleaning work might be low in terms of opportunities for providing meals-on-wheels. The right to do one hour a week of the latter might exchange for the right to do, say, twenty hours at a laundry. Equilibrium would be established when it no longer paid anyone at the margin to exchange one kind of work for another; and a new class of entrepreneur would spring up who would, for example, offer those with the right to do ambulance work the opportunity to work longer hours in laundries.

If prices were sufficiently flexible, full employment and consumer sovereignty would be maintained, in the sense that everybody would be able to do some work, although not as much as he liked; and would be able to choose between short hours at the more popular activity and longer hours at the less popular ones. This is the exact parallel to the existence of the opportunity to earn a living under the present system, although not to earn as much as one would like, and the choice between larger quantities of cheaper goods and smaller quantities of expensive ones. Businessmen would be rewarded for their middleman activities by the work they did. Successful entrepreneurs would work much longer hours than the average person; and this would be resented as outrageously unfair by egalitarians. The advantages and disadvantages of the market economy would be remarkably similar to what they are in the present society in which shortages are of goods rather than of work.

There are, of course, some snags about the analogy between work at present and goods in a future society. While an individual is capable of producing a continuing stream of work throughout his active life, and a whole community can do so as long as the population endures, goods and services are not quite like that. Perishables or services, which cannot be stocked, are extreme examples of the general proposition that the stock of commodities will decline over time – both through consumption and natural deterioration – if they are not replenished. This leads one to suspect that the work-scarce, goods-plentiful society is not a stable one; and that eventually the stock of goods would run down until they became scarce enough for some of them to recapture a positive marginal utility.

There is another reason too for doubting the feasibility of a situation where goods in general have a zero or negative marginal utility. In the simple model above, it was assumed that goods required only labour for their production. It is reasonable to regard capital equipment as labour at one remove. But the production of commodities also requires land. Even if man-made substitutes were available for all the 'original and indestructible properties of the soil', the production and enjoyment of all goods and services requires space. At least two factors of production will always be required: labour and land. Although astronomical increases in output per unit of labour can be envisaged, land-saving innovations are unlikely to be on anything like the same scale – especially if one bears in mind that the product mix demanded by a rapidly advancing society is land-intensive: homes, gardens, roads, airspace, beaches, mountains, and so on. The population increase compounds what in any case would be a growing demand for space. The demand for space-intensive products is equally characteristic of the culture of the alternative society: open space for pop group rallies, solitude for certain types of 'trips', wildernesses for hermits and gurus, and countryside for rural communes.

It is thus, in fact, extremely unlikely that either because of a widespread desire for work to kill boredom, or a cultural shift away from materialism, that *all* commodities will cease to be scarce. There are always likely to be some scarce goods and services: scarce in the sense that some people would like to have more of them than are available, irrespective of the distribution of income and wealth in the country.

A more Realistic Model

Nevertheless, the analysis of a work-scarce, goods-surplus society has been well worthwhile. For one can readily imagine a mixed situation in which some goods are no longer scarce and some types of work are. Some goods are even now so cheap that people of average income can afford to be indifferent to how much they spend on them. There are already all kinds of work – known as hobbies – which people will pay to do. (Standing for Parliament would thus count for some as a hobby.) While for the most part people pay in money (i.e. forgone goods) for their hobbies, this is not entirely so. People pay for one type of hobby in terms of foregone opportunities for pursuing another. Members of the establishment pay for

sitting on the marginal committee by not being able to sit
on yet another on which they place a slightly lower valuation;
and they would forego a great many hours on minor advisory
groups for the sake of much fewer hours on a really pres-
tigious Royal Commission. We are already moving towards
a situation in which many kinds of work have a positive
utility; to the extent that market prices prevail, they will
have a cost not merely in commodities foregone, but in terms
of other kinds of pleasurable work.

On the goods side, a growing number of commodities can
be expected to enter a category, which for want of a better
label, I shall call 'non-economic'. My definition of a non-
economic commodity is one for which the demand is no
longer responsive to *relative* prices. In other words, the person or group of people under consideration, will not shift to
substitutes, and will buy the same amount whatever happens
to its price *relative to other prices*. Of course, if the price of
any commodity rises, this will itself reduce the real value of
any given income. To allow for this factor, we should assume
that real incomes are constant and that a compensating financial sum is paid in such cases to make them so. This is not,
of course, a policy proposal, but simply a way of defining
'other things being equal'.* (We are thus defining a non-
economic good as one for which the pure substitution elasticity of demand is zero.) The smaller the proportion of income going on a particular commodity, the less important is
this definitional complication.

It should be noted that a non-economic good is not the
same as the usual definition of a 'free' good. The latter is a
commodity that is not in scarce supply – each member of the
community can have as much of it as he likes without anyone else having to sacrifice any other desired commodity. An
example would be fresh air in an uncontaminated rural area.
This would have a zero cost in foregone alternatives. Bread
might come into the category of a non-economic good, if
demand were invariant to price. But it would not be a free
good, as farming, milling and baking would take up scarce
resources, which could be used to produce alternative goods

* This is indeed Milton Friedman's interpretation of the ordinary demand
curve. See *Essays in Positive Economics* (Chicago, 1953).

which the community has now to do without.

My definition of a non-economic good is, however, very close to the usual definition of a 'necessity'; I suspect, however, that there are few necessities, the demand for which is literally unresponsive to relative prices. It is a reasonable guess – although no more than that – that as a community grows wealthier, more and more goods enter the truly non-economic category. There is, of course, always the question of: non-scarce for whom? A starving man with a few pence in his pocket will take into account relative prices very carefully before he decides what to buy. Indifference to price for a growing number of commodities is only a reasonable guess even for the future, if it is assumed that a minimum level of personal income is maintained by state action, and that this minimum itself increases in line with general prosperity.

The opponents of the price mechanism and the monetary economy have a strong case in relation to such non-economic goods, and *only in relation to them*. For if the quantity sold has no relation to price, then the function of prices in helping to allocate consumers' expenditure in line with their preferences disappears. So equally does the function of prices and profitability in allocating production between alternative activities. The whole business of taking money, with all the distributional, clerical and policing problems is thus a costly waste; and the state might as well purchase, in a block order, the quantities required by the public at a price just sufficient to make it worth the while of the supplying firms, and allow people to take as much as they like 'for free' in any convenient way. In this manner, the role of money and prices can be reduced in all those areas of our lives where they are not worth the bother, while retaining them in all the remaining areas in which they are still a vital instrument for combining freedom with prosperity.

Certain traps have to be avoided if this proposal is not to do more harm than good. First, the identification of non-economic commodities is not nearly as obvious as it may seem. For example, domestic consumer demand for salt may be invariant to price, but not industrial demand. It would be very difficult to have free salt for housewives and restaurants only, while a general supply of free salt could lead to an irrational choice of production process in the chemical and other industries.

Secondly, and even more important, it is essential that a state distribution system for 'free' products should not be given any sort of monopoly whatever. For example if bread were free, there might still be all sorts of varieties, not supplied by the state authorities, for which people would still be willing to pay. In addition, the number, location, or opening hours of distribution outlets for free bread may not suit some people. *The only way to ascertain whether there are needs or desires left unsatisfied by the state scheme is to allow people to make a profit by trying to do better. Without this safeguard, the above proposal will only bring comfort to the enemies of personal choice and the friends of enforced uniformity.*

The *assumption* of a minimum income rising with the general level of prosperity was made above simply to help with a matter of definition. But I should now like to make it a definite proposal. What I have in mind is *not* statutory minimum wages, which have caused involuntary unemployment wherever they have been introduced, but social security payments to guarantee a certain cash flow related to family size. These would have to be well below the average or median wage if they were not to be ruled out on 'incentive' grounds. But in an affluent society this could still provide a standard of living far above subsistence. This proposal cuts out the whole argument about 'scroungers and shirkers' by giving up the vain attempt to hunt them down. The potential shirker would be told in effect: 'The community is now rich enough to give you two choices: You can "opt out" if you wish and you will receive an allowance, which will be far from princely and well below the normal wage, but will allow you to live, and will also rise as the nation becomes richer; or you can work and go after much larger material prizes.' (I do not need to be told that such a concept would at present be unpopular with the electorate.)

The feasibility of the scheme depends partly on the empirical question of the size of the loss (arising out of the disincentive effect of a 100 per cent marginal rate of tax) from providing guaranteed subsistence to that portion of the population who have skills of relatively low market value, or who are the most work shy.

At the beginning of 1970 George Polanyi and three co-authors published a scheme for a Minimum Income Guarantee that would make up to the Supplementary Benefit Level all incomes at present below.[7] Of the 3 million householders that were expected to benefit, some $2\frac{1}{4}$ million were headed by retired people. The disincentive to extra effort from the 100 per cent marginal rate would thus have applied to some $\frac{3}{4}$ million people – mostly workers with large families whose earnings were below the Supplementary Benefits minimum.

The real problem, of course, was whether the unconditional guarantee of such a minimum as a 'right' would be prohibitively costly in terms of the number of people stopping work altogether and settling for this minimum. Policy here has been too long dominated by the spectre of Speenhamland, the late 18th century system under which magistrates made up to minimum levels the wages of farm labourers. This led to large-scale resort to public assistance in preference to work. The reaction of Parliament was the notorious Poor Law of 1834, which confined relief to people entering 'indoor institutions' on very rigorous conditions.

The counter-argument of Polanyi is that such effects were to be expected at a time when the normal wage was no higher than the subsistence minimum. In 1970, probably no more than 2–3 per cent of the full-time occupied population had incomes below the suggested guarantee. The majority of workers would take a large cut of income if they chose to live on State benefit.

Thus, with present attitudes towards material goods, the cost of a modest income guarantee would be small; and only a limited number of people might take advantage of it. A combination of changing attitudes and the effects of increasing prosperity in raising the level of the guarantee would lead to more people taking advantage of it in the future. But then the very same factors would reduce the burden that the provision of this minimum was felt to impose on those who preferred to work for a living.

In the Polanyi scheme, the minimum income guarantee would be given in the form of a reverse income tax. Poor

people who worked would thus not receive the full guaranteed minimum, but only the amount by which their actual
earnings fell short of this minimum. While the scheme was at
this stage, snooping and inspection would be necessary to
check on undeclared earnings.

I would hope, however, that this would be only an intermediate stage and that eventually we would be prosperous
enough to pay out the guaranteed minimum as a 'social dividend' irrespective of income from other sources. When that
happened the whole invigilatory aspect of social security
could come to an end – both the feelings of humiliation at
the receiving end and the feelings of being duped on the part
of the working taxpayer.

An attempt has been made in the last few pages to outline
a compromise between a market economy and the beliefs of
the alternative society, which combines the best elements of
both and is not just splitting the difference. The aspirations
of those who wish to opt out of a work-oriented monetary
economy are respected and acknowledged by the option of a
modest but rising minimum payment, irrespective of effort.
In addition a limited but growing number of standard goods
and services will be provided without cash payment. This
latter aspect will free even the more conventional of us from
petty and irritating financial transactions, where there is a
real utility loss in attempting too virtuously to maximise
utility. Thus, the market economy can hopefully be gradually
divorced from the puritan ethic.

But in return for these changes, the apostles of the alternative society must be prepared to tolerate the activities of the
remainder of the community who have aspirations for things
which are still scarce – whether fur coats, Georgian houses, or
visits to baroque churches – and who wish to continue to take
part in a monetary economy. Paradoxically, the faster the
general advance of prosperity, the earlier these choices between different life styles will become a reality; and anti-
growth propaganda only serves to prolong our present
materialist and envious ethic.

There is a great deal to argue about in the above proposals
on figures and details. But if the New Left reject the offered

compromise, which will allow them to practise the values that they preach, and insist on transforming the whole of society in their image then they are at least as tyrannical opponents of free expression as the Greek colonels and the other dictators against whom they demonstrate. This charge is valid whether the proportion who do not accept their values is 99, 49, 9 or 0.009 per cent of the population. Freedom is not a matter of counting heads. Orthodox opinion may legitimately query my suggestions on grounds of *present* cost; but if it rules out minimum incomes for the work shy, or zero prices for non-economic goods, on grounds of principle irrespective of the level of affluence, then it, too, is motivated by just that moralistic resentment of other people's well-being, which it is so fond of decrying in the egalitarians. A liberal should attack a zero value to the pain arising from intolerance of others' enjoyment, from whatever side of the political spectrum this intolerance comes.

Postscript on Communes

One expression of the dislike of commercial society is the renewed vogue for communes – which so far from being daring innovations are among the oldest kinds of human groupings.

The characteristics of a pure commune may be regarded as the absence of individual income or property and the consequent absence of money inside the organisation, and the willingness of members to work as agreed by collective decision with no relation between work performed and individual living standards – the collective decisions including how to spend the communal income and distribute goods among members. By adopting this extreme definition one is distinguishing a commune very sharply from a mere co-operative and perhaps highlighting the leading ideas behind the concept.

Now there is no reason why communes cannot exist – as kibbutzim do in Israel – within a normal commercial society, buying in the cheapest market and selling in the dearest, while ordering their own internal affairs on non-commercial principles. If all productive enterprises were organised by communes, the economy might not be as responsive to opportunities as it would be with a more directly capitalist form of ownership; but, if the percentage of communal production corresponded to the percentage of the population with a taste for communal living, there would be no cause for complaint. It would be part of the data with which the market would have to cope; and if consumer demand has by then become fairly static in both quality and quantity, this lack of responsiveness will not matter all that much.*

How an individual commune should organise its affairs is its own business. The main concern of a liberal is with the availability of outward transport from it. Nevertheless, there are certain points that suggest themselves about the way in which a commune might rationally organise its affairs.

The members of the commune are, we may assume, prepared to work an equal number of labour units. These may be measured in hours; but an hour of regular or strenuous work may be regarded as equivalent to more than an hour of irregular or less taxing work. We can either dodge the problem of how the exact equivalence is determined, or regard it as being based on labour market data from outside the commune. Members will, of course, have different abilities; and some products that the commune could make will bring in more revenue than others. It therefore pays the commune to arrange its working activities so that it cannot gain any more revenue – or achieve the same revenue with a smaller amount of labour – by shifting a marginal labour unit from one activity to another. This means that the least productive

* It could, in fact, be even more difficult to preserve full employment by demand management policies in an economy of communes than at present. In a capitalist economy, an increase in total money expenditure should lead, at least for a time, to increased output and employment, even if it also brings in its wake some increase in the price level. In an economy of communes the effect will be entirely felt in the price level. For it will pay the partners of a commune to increase their selling price to maximise the value of net returns per head and not to dilute the gain by enlarging its size. Such considerations also suggest that price fluctuations could be greater in a communal than in a capitalist economy. Full employment policies would have to be long term structural ones designed to encourage the setting up of more communes if unemployment develops. (These problems are discussed in J. E. Meade, 'The Theory of Labour-Managed Firms and of Profit Sharing', *Economic Journal*, March 1972 Supplement.)

additional unit of labour must yield the same in all occupations.

This arrangement is not necessarily, however, the happiest one for the individual members of which the commune is composed. For people may not enjoy most doing the job that makes the greatest contribution to the revenue of the group; and some of them might even be prepared to make sacrifices in other aspects of their personal living standards to do something more congenial. One is tempted to suggest that money payments should be reintroduced, but the suggestion will not be followed up, as it is out of keeping with the beliefs that brought the people into the communes in the first place.

Short of that, there are other expedients which could still increase individual satisfaction. One method would be to allow people to choose their own jobs initially. The commune administration would then see that there were, say, too many library attendants and not enough bricklayers compared with the optimum distribution, and so on. It could then offer people fewer hours of work if they were to switch to the less favoured jobs, but demand more hours at the attractive jobs. It might be able to juggle with the ratio of required hours of different kinds, until there were a voluntary movement of workers towards the required pattern. Thus, a labour market would have been established in hours of work, instead of money wages.

Such juggling might not, however, be possible if the degree of aversion to certain types of work were too great and no reduction in hours required could produce a sufficient supply of manhours in these activities. In that case another way of establishing a labour market in hours of work might be tried. Workers would be assigned work by the commune administration in relation to their aptitudes, but be allowed to trade jobs with other people. Someone assigned a bricklaying job which he disliked might do 20 hours' work in the library in return for which four library attendants would do 5 hours of bricklaying each. Once a labour market with proper prices was established, there would be no need for this neat divisibility; it could turn out that 5 hours' bricklaying was equivalent to 27 hours in the library. The administration would have to make sure that the hours of work being traded were of a standardised degree of efficiency for each occupation. Despite this complication, a voluntary exchange of this sort would be an improvement on either assigning jobs with no choice, or making everyone do a little of everything.

The standard objection to the suggested 'labour market' is that it would reintroduce 'inequality', as some people would work for longer hours than others. The objection presupposes, however, that there is equality in the first place, despite the fact that some people will have been assigned jobs which they detest and others jobs which they quite enjoy doing. Even if everyone did a little of everything (with great detriment to total wealth) the situation would be subjectively one of extreme inequality. For a pattern composed of a small amount of all activities from lavatory cleaning to fishing, typing and writing pamphlets, would suit some people and be hell for others.

Moreover, the inequality of working hours in our imaginary commune would have none of the features to which egalitarians object in our present society. Everyone would start off from the same basis. There would be no inherited unearned income, or differences in ability to pay for education; and shares would be reshuffled in each generation entirely in accordance with relative tastes.

Nevertheless, if unequal working hours were ideologically objectionable, then the commune would have to choose between what might be a very severe loss of prosperity if people were allowed a complete free choice of jobs and strict regimentation if they were not. There is, in any society, a complex three way trade-off between freedom, prosperity and equality, but which is specially noticeable in a commune. Real-life collectives work by some unformulated compromise between free choice and direction of occupation for their members, with perhaps some unofficial barter between jobs as well.

We must now go one stage further and ask what the position would be if an overwhelming majority of the population wished to live in a communal way. Would it be a good idea to abolish money altogether and run the country as one big commune? The reader will not expect me to welcome this idea, but the interesting question is 'Why'?

Even if consumer desires were modest in relation to potential output, this does not mean that people would be indifferent to what they received. In an economy of individual communes, each of modest size, it might be feasible for a purchasing committee to take note of what members like, see which stocks are most depleted, and order accordingly. But how would individual desires be registered in a commune the size of the whole nation? One might imagine moneyless shops, which acquired fresh goods and services according to the stock position and the individual orders it received. But what mechanism would ensure that the working population organised itself to supply what was required? By a heroic stretch of the imagination one might envisage people looking up in a registry which goods were in short supply, which in surplus, and which occupations were in most demand, and shifting jobs accordingly. But let us suppose that dustcarts, and drawing boards, sewage workers and factory managers were all in excess demand. Who would determine which people should leave the jobs where their services are surplus, to become sewage workers or managers or whatever the case may be? We come up against the problem of allocating manpower, which already exists in the individual communes but on a gigantic scale, and without the possibility of tackling it by the informal compromises that can often be made in a face-to-face society.

It is almost certain that money, money prices and money incomes would creep back again in a disguised form, say as computerised indices of the strength of particular demands and the relative attractions of different occupations. The three-way trade-off between preserving the communal principle, preserving free choice of occupation, and prosperity or efficiency, would appear in a particularly harsh form. It is difficult to escape the conclusion that, even in a society where the desire for communal living was widespread, it would be much better to preserve a monetary economy with free market relations between individual communes, which should be left to develop their internal relationships in their own way.

Part Two

Applications

4 Conservatism and the Market Economy*

(Of Tories) ... There are few men of knowledge or learning ... who would not be ashamed to be thought of that party; and in almost all companies, the name of Old Whig is mentioned as an incontestable appellation of honour and dignity.

David Hume, 'Of the Parties of Great Britain'

According to the majority of political commentators, the Conservative Government elected in 1970 differed not only from its Labour predecessors, but also from previous Conservative governments, in its emphasis on market forces, free competition and non-intervention by the state. These tendencies were described with some bitterness as 'an end to the consensus', the 'burial of the Middle Way' or the 'funeral of Butskellism'. The only ray of hope arose from the reflection that governments usually became less ideological and more pragmatic as their term of office continued. Even the minority

---

* An earlier version of this essay entitled *Government and the Market Economy*, was originally published as a 'Hobart Paperback' by the Institute of Economic Affairs in 1971. This study was written during the first year of office of the Heath Conservative Government, elected in 1970. Many of the topics dealt with in the original version have been introduced as examples into the earlier essays of this book. The substantially revised study which appears here is therefore a good deal shorter than the original. But the emphasis on the first year of Conservative office remains. For there is a particular interest in examining governments in their initial phase, when ideals or illusions are still fresh, and when tiredness, muddling along, 'the Whitehall point of view' and electoral calculations are not yet the mainsprings of action. Moreover, to the extent that the Heath Government shifted away from its initial emphasis on market principles, this may well have been due to a misapprehension of their nature already apparent in its early months of office.

of commentators who favoured a move to a market economy did not, for the most part, make it seem any more attractive. They regarded it as extremely unpleasant, but good for the nation, and sounded rather like apologists for corporal punishment or compulsory cold showers.

We should hardly expect a party with the label 'Conservative', even with a capital 'C', to have identical priorities to those of an economic liberal, even with a small 'l'. Although anti-Conservative polemicists talk disparagingly about the 'market', the vast majority of active Conservatives rarely use the term. They will occasionally talk about 'competition', although it is far from being favoured among all sections of the party; but they will hardly ever talk about 'the price mechanism'. The terms most frequently used in such circles are 'less government', 'disengagement', 'lower taxes', 'less government spending'; they are often coupled with calls for patriotism, authority and discipline, and for people to 'wake up to their responsibilities' (and by the latter Conservatives do not just mean enlightened self-interest).

Some articulate Conservatives in the higher reaches of the party have, it is true, at times adopted some of the market philosophy. But even among them there is a subtle shift of emphasis from the kind of ideas with which many economic liberals would be at home. No one to my knowledge has been able to formulate a theme linking together the key features of the tough-minded, business-oriented, stand-on-your-own-two-feet brand of Conservatism which initially characterised the Heath Government. Such a theme to be worthwhile would have to be more than a slogan (friendly or hostile) or mnemonic, but would enable one to predict future policies and applications. The tough-minded Conservative may find a good deal of common ground with the economic liberal in opposing left- and right-wing paternalism, and both should take advantage of this overlap; but their mainsprings of action and their approach to crucial policy details will be different.

Both may take, for example, a similar attitude to unprofitable industries and bankrupt firms, and some critics will leave it there. But attitudes of mind make a difference; and one that emphasises the welfare and freedom of consumers (which all of us are) is different from that which emphasises the discomfort of the unprofitable and the bankrupt as almost desirable in itself. The case against protection or subsidies is not the need to 'wake people up to their responsibilities'. The 'liberal' argument against such protective devices is that they force the rest of the population to purchase goods from a particular source, or to make sacrifices in their living standards, for the sake of the privileged producer group. Moreover, as people change their place of work, even the gains to protected groups from this assistance will diminish over time and they may well in the end be worse off. Financial assistance to those making the re-adjustment is therefore preferable to 'make-work' policies.

Political Choice

In many countries it is indeed an open question whether the right- or left-wing party is closer to the philosophy of the market economy. It is arguable that the German Christian Democrats, especially since Dr Ludwig Erhard's departure, have demonstrated, for example in their opposition to changes in the German mark and their determined stand for farm protection, that they are further removed from it than the Social Democrats. The latter have had no hesitation in championing the 'social market economy'. In their Godesberger Programme of 1959 they formally dropped the goal of a centrally directed economy and announced that the party 'supports the free market, where real competition is always present'. Indeed German governments were in some ways more energetic in promoting the market economy after 1966 when the Social Democrats began to participate and Professor Schiller was able to hold office as Economics Minister for six years before he parted company from his party.

It is unfortunately impossible to say the same for the British Labour Party. Even Gaitskellite Labour leaders are separated from economic liberals by their penchant for 'specific egalitarianism' (discussed on pp. 140–4). While the economic liberal prefers to provide cash and personal help to the less well off, even moderate Fabians are heavily committed to state-provided health and education embracing as much as possible of the total population, subsidised council houses,

rent controls, earnings-related state pensions for the majority
of the population, and so on. There are, however, genuine
difficulties about applying market principles fully to all these
services and benefits; and differences of opinion here need
not prevent Labour from applying market principles to the
other 75–85 per cent of the economy outside the welfare
services.*

The real stumbling block which prevents a fruitful alliance
between Labour and economic liberals is the Labour Party's
anti-profit and price mechanism approach to ordinary trade
and industry, and the associated desire to 'save' firms or jobs
threatened by economic change. But attitudes can also
change; and, looking further ahead, Labour would do well to
ponder whether it might not make more headway by becoming the party of the consumer, even if this means standing up
to trade union as well as business interests. As things stand,
however, the economic liberal cannot be identified with
either main party (nor even with the Liberals). The economic
liberal, like the liberal in other fields, must make use of whatever overlap happens to exist between his ideas and those of
any party or group able to influence events.

'Lame Ducks'

If forced to hazard a guess about the Heath Government's
domestic economic policies, when it had still been in office for
less than half the length of a normal Parliament, one might
say that the success for which it will deserve to be remembered
will be tax reform, the bringing forward of a scheme for
reverse (or negative) income tax and – despite all the populist
agitation against it – the overhaul of housing policy. The
battle against union monopoly power was, at the very least,
courageous, whatever its ultimate success proves to have
been.

---

* The main welfare items are social security payments, which at the
beginning of this decade absorbed just over 10 per cent of the Gross National
Product, rent which (with rates) absorbed $7\frac{1}{2}$ per cent, and health and
education, which together absorbed just over 10 per cent. (A small amount
of double counting is involved in adding these items, some of which are
expenditure and others transfer payments.) Although social security payments are financed collectively, they consist of cash benefits, which can be
freely spent at the discretion of the recipients.

The area in which this Government got off to a particularly bad start was industrial policy. This may seem paradoxical in view of the identification of its most influential members with business efficiency. In part the troubles it got into here were the result of bad luck. The inflationary recession which it inherited, and which no group of economic forecasters adequately foresaw, was the worst possible environment in which to launch a policy of less intervention – this was the other side of the coin to the good luck which enabled the Government to make such a strikingly rapid start on its tax reform proposals. In part, however, its industrial policy difficulties were the result of an inadequately thought out initial philosophy.

The vacillations and contradictions of industrial policy were symbolised by the expression 'lame ducks'. It was originally used to refer to the Government's dislike, when it came to office, of spending public money on propping up loss-making industries and firms and of intervening generally in the conduct of industrial affairs. Within two years the symbolism had been reversed and 'propping up lame ducks' became the label for what the Cabinet's industrial team was mainly engaged in doing.

In fact, the 'anti-lame duck' approach did not guide Government policy even in its earliest days, except in a very partial and one-sided way. But before citing specific instances it would be better to state the criteria, which in a humane, but market-oriented, economy ought to govern *specific industrial intervention.* By this expression I mean government action by financial support, special contracts, legal prohibition or privileges, or other methods *affecting specific industries or firms,* to influence what should be produced and by whom. Defined in this way it excludes all measures to improve the climate in which the market operates, as well as all other *general* measures, such as regional policy or investment aids, which have an across-the-board effect over a wide variety of industries and firms. The arguments for and against such 'specific' intervention should not be confused with the argument over public *ownership.* Some of the biggest subsidies and privileges are provided for privately owned concerns – Concorde and the old Rolls-Royce company being examples –

while nationalised concerns can be, and have at times been, under strong pressure to earn a commercial return on their assets.

There are two main motives for specific industrial intervention, although they often become confused in practice. One is the 'cushioning' motive, the other the desire to take action of a 'positive, dynamic' variety. Mr Harold Lever, the former Labour Financial Secretary to the Treasury and Paymaster-General has written of the first sort:

> We must make more systematic our basically sound concept of state help motivated by social considerations, for example, in declining industries where we act to soften the cruelties and waste of unimpeded market forces. With the coalmines we have a notable example of this which rebounds greatly to the credit of the Labour government, an achievement only possible because it was able to harness the patriotism and discipline of the miners. [This was written before the 1972 miners' strike.] But in shipbuilding it is still not clear whether we are seeking to shape it to a viable size, protecting against intolerable unemployment in the process, or trying to recreate it in all its old glory. When we intervene to avoid social hardship, we must use our resources for this purpose and not yield to an understandable reflex that everybody ought to stay in the same job in the same industry for ever.[1]

The best kind of cushioning machinery is temporary assistance to enable workers in declining industries to find jobs elsewhere. Wage-related unemployment pay and redundancy compensation were important innovations of the mid-1960s, which enabled the market economy to work more efficiently. Re-training of adult workers is of equal importance. It is also worth remembering that among the most stubborn obstacles to mobility are artificially low rents, with the consequent scarcity of rented accommodation.

Apart from government measures to aid mobility there may occasionally be a social case for more specific action. Mr Lever has called for intelligible guidelines and principles to govern such intervention. The alternative, as he put it in an earlier passage, is '*ad hoc* interventions whose nature and extent are determined by the belly reactions or contacts of Ministers'. Such guidelines have, indeed, already been evolved by the architects of the post-war German 'social market economy'. The most important is that 'each intervention should be temporary and degressive'. (One German writer with the national genius for personifying abstractions, has spoken of 'measures which are in a position to render themselves superfluous'.) Among such measures preference should, according to the German neo-liberals, be given to those which have no major adverse side-effects, which achieve their aim in the shortest time and which stimulate productivity.

Positive intervention

The second kind of specific intervention, the 'positive, dynamic kind', designed not to cushion the victims of the market but to secure an improvement in performance, should be viewed with the utmost scepticism. It is easy to think of theoretical justifications for intervention: private savers or investors may not look far enough ahead, or they may discount too heavily the interests of future generations; some large-scale projects may require more capital than the City is accustomed to raising for a single project; there may be 'spillover' benefits which the promoters of the project cannot recover in the market-price of the final product; and the list could be extended.

One trouble with this case is that it is usually based on a comparison of the market, with all its shortcomings in practice, and some ideal intervention by an omniscient government equally free from the influence of pressure groups and from the temptation to pursue prestige projects unjustified by their true return.

Another difficulty about positive industrial intervention is that governments hardly ever base it on known rules laid down in advance, and it would be very difficult in practice to do so. Nevertheless, a framework of known and predictable rules is an essential part of a free society; and once punishments and rewards are meted out according to the arbitrary whims of particular politicians or officials, we are on a slippery slope. The benefits of discretionary action may occasionally be so large as to outweigh this general objection; but the onus of proof must be on those who propose it.

Specific industrial intervention, so far from promoting more efficiency in serving people's needs than the unaided market could do, tends, in the real world, to be a mixture of measures designed to protect industrial and occupational interest groups from change for as long as possible, and of prestige ventures unjustified by any sober cost-benefit calculation. Mr Lever, who believes that intervention to support high technology industry is in principle justified has, in the article quoted, the following to say about its practice.

One of the consequences of over-concentration on high technology is the neglect of lower technology such as house-building systems, iron and steel casting and the like. Rolls-Royce has a lesson here too. A wide range of its high quality production has been starved and jeopardised by one high technology contract. We must not repeat this kind of error on a national scale. It is worth noting that, between Concorde and the RB-211 alone, the nation could well expend £1,000 million of its resources in the areas of its highest skill with little or nothing to show for them. We must topple the uncritical worship of the false gods of size and science. We must abandon irrelevant notions of national prestige and fallacious and unquantified balance-of-payments arguments which too often are jostled together in a ragbag of arguments to support intervention.

The extent of 'specific intervention' cannot be measured merely by the cost to the Exchequer; a small interest rate subsidy or guarantee, a state contract, or some back-door protection against imports can make all the difference to activities which appear in the statistics as private expenditure. Nevertheless, a break-down of the public expenditure figures does provide at least a starting point. Table 4 details the main items of over £5 million of 'assistance to private industry, etc.' shown in the Labour Government's Memorandum on the 1970–1 Estimates.[2] A few items financed from the National Loans Fund are excluded from the official estimates, but they do not add much to the total or change the impression made. The more comprehensive but less detailed Public Expenditure White Paper shows that the aerospace industry figures even more prominently, with total annual expenditure of £112 million (including the Ministry of Aviation Supply's own activities).

The inescapable conclusion is that, if one leaves out of account expenditure to promote investment or local employment, the overwhelming bulk of government subvention to private business is designed either – as in agriculture or shipbuilding – to protect a domestic industry from foreign competition, or – as in aerospace – to bolster up high technology products which could not otherwise pay their way. (The agricultural element will decline in future years, but this will simply be because the burden of protection will be transferred from the Exchequer to the housewife who will have to pay higher prices under the levy system to support farmers both in Britain and in Continental Europe.)

TABLE 4: *Assistance to Private Industry, etc., in the U.K. Estimates for 1970–1*

	£m	£m
Investment grants	554	
Regional employment premium	105	
Other expenditure to promote local employment	62	
Export promotion	7	
TOTAL OF MAIN 'GENERAL' ITEMS		737
Agriculture, fisheries and farming	315	
Development and production of Concorde	66	
Other civil aviation assistance	19	
Assistance to shipbuilding	17	
Loans to the aluminium industry	13	
Hotel and other tourist loans	11	
Assistance to I.R.C.	10	
TOTAL OF MAIN 'SPECIFIC' ITEMS		451
Corporation Tax, transitional relief		25
Total of minor items		35
GRAND TOTAL		1,248

There was nothing cushioning, temporary or degressive about the types of expenditure involved. Individual projects might come to an end; but the prevailing philosophy would have soon brought others in their place. The 'excessive commitment' to the aircraft industry was severely criticised in the Brookings Report on the U.K.[3] As for the interventions of the Industrial Reorganisation Corporation (which involved much smaller sums of public money), it would be silly to write them *all* off as misjudgements. But one can echo the Brookings comment that the I.R.C. embodied the theory of 'finding the most efficient firm and merging the [others] into it'. Insufficient thought had been given to the possibility that (a) the efficient firm may not remain so after absorbing the others, (b) its management was mortal, and (c) increased efficiency, if achieved at all, might be at the cost of more monopoly. The I.R.C. had, according to Brookings, rushed to create industrial giants 'with an enthusiasm worthy of the buccaneers of the 19th century American capitalism'.[4]

The curious belief of a section of the British Labour Party that state-aided and -protected capitalism was preferable to the competitive variety was one reason for the fashion for state involvement in the 1960s. Another arose from a misreading of post-war experience in France, Italy and Japan, which owed a good deal to mixed public-private ventures. The real reason that these ventures were necessary was that the countries concerned lacked effective capital markets; and state financial institutions helped to fill the gap. Whatever else is wrong with the British economy, it is not the lack of a capital market, weakened though that was by the discrimination against distributed profits up to 1958 and again in 1965–72.

One could not help noticing that, not long after Mr Wilson 'took over' the Department of Economic Affairs, the electricity industry was asked to put up more coal-burning power stations than it considered efficient. There was a similar rush to push money into make-work projects, in areas where the political pressure was strong, after the Conservative change of front in the winter of 1971–2. The politics of the 'pork barrel' are to be found in every country; but one could be more tolerant of them if they were not presented as radical devices for securing faster growth.

Political expediency apart, the provision of public finance on better than market terms has often been urged as a backdoor method of subsidising exports or import substitutes. Indeed, this is what much of the economic case for specific industrial intervention amounted to in the 1960s. It comes out in the aluminium and shipbuilding items in the table, as well as in many of the I.R.C.'s ventures. It was one of the main supporting arguments both for Concorde and the RB-211 contract. In its Wilsonian heyday selective intervention was an attempt to achieve in a roundabout and clumsy way what could have been achieved much more simply, quickly and effectively by the price mechanism in the form of exchange rate changes. This indeed is what happened in the end, although the alteration of the parity was jerky, reluctant and delayed, and not at first supported by adequate restraint of domestic demand. In its Conservative form 'selective intervention' was mainly aimed at 'providing employment' for those thrown out of work by industrial change, regional imbalance, union monopoly power or mistakes in official financial policy; but whether these problems can be cured by tackling symptoms is very much open to doubt.

Rolls-Royce and Concorde

The issue of industrial intervention has been confused by two red herrings: bankruptcies and public ownership. Bankruptcies are not an evil to be avoided at all costs. The plant and employees of a bankrupt concern do not disappear with the company's name; and it is better both for the nation – and ultimately for the workers themselves – that their services should be put to use where they can earn a higher return. On the other hand, there are some undesirable side-effects of a large bankruptcy, for example, on the position of supplying firms; and bankruptcies are not an end in themselves. The important point is that any state cushioning should be of a temporary and diminishing kind, and not lead to the preservation of uneconomic projects for prestige or make-work reasons. It was for this reason that the original Labour support for the RB-211 engine (undertaken in the sacred name of exports), the Conservative Government's original offer of

£42 million to Rolls-Royce, and its later willingness to spend £130 million (increased within a year to nearly £200 million and no doubt mounting still), were equally questionable.

An economic liberal need neither attack the Government for having taken over the Rolls-Royce rump nor congratulate it ironically on its conversion to nationalisation. He should be much more interested in whether non-paying 'high technology' projects will continue to be state-financed. Such finance can be provided just as easily through subventions to 'private' enterprise as through the losses of nationalised concerns. Indeed, the latter often attract more adverse criticism.

The supposed 'social' argument for bolstering such projects implicitly assumes that jobs lost in one sector of the economy can never be replaced in another. Provided that employment is maintained by fiscal and monetary means, it would be much better to assist the workers directly until they find new jobs. If, however, it is unsafe to boost demand because of the dangers of an inflationary explosion by these means, it is unsafe to do so by specific items of public expenditure. Even if the unemployment problem is conceived of in purely regional or local terms, the answer lies in an increased level of *general* regional incentives rather than by trying to keep particular projects artificially alive. (Having failed to think this through, Conservative Ministers were in the end panicked in 1972 into trying both approaches in belt-and-braces fashion.) The propping up approach either embodies the 'lump of labour' fallacy or assumes that 'full employment' means the same employment.

The most flagrant example of the Government rejecting the market economy from its earliest days was its continued support of Concorde. The case against supporting this aircraft is often presented entirely on anti-noise and environmental grounds, and the case for it in terms of technical progress. It is often forgotten that there is no case for the aircraft even in ordinary profit-and-loss terms. This follows from the huge involvement of the British and French Governments in its finance for little or no return. The airlines themselves do not believe that enough passengers are willing to pay the very high fares which would enable supersonic aircraft to cover their costs and earn a normal return; if they did there would be no need for such a heavy taxpayers' subsidy.

A sub-group of the U.S. Joint Economic Committee reported that there was little prospect of the U.S. Administration earning a reasonable rate of return on its investment in supersonic aircraft, and that it was entirely possible that none of the investment would be recovered. Similar calculations have been made for the U.K. The estimated total cost of developing the Concorde up to production stage was £150–170 million in 1962. By 1964 the cost was estimated at £280 million. The following winter the Labour Government abandoned its attempts to cancel the aircraft, allegedly because it might have had to pay £100 million in compensation to the French Government. By 1966, the cost estimate had risen to £500 million. By December 1970, it was put at £885 million at current prices.

Taking an extremely conservative estimate of further escalation and adding about £100 million for jigging and tooling, Mr C. B. Edwards of the University of East Anglia has estimated a total pre-production cost of £1,000 million, of which some £500 million was still to be spent during 1971–3. (At the time of writing this looks very much of a minimum estimate.) Mr Edwards makes an optimistic assumption of a production profit of £2 million per aircraft, including spares, and an even more optimistic assumption of sales of 200 aircraft in 1973–80. On the assumption that the Conservative Government's commitment to Concorde was finally made by the winter of 1970–71, ignoring everything invested before on the principle of letting bygones be bygones, and charging interest of only 8 per cent per annum on the remaining £500 million, a loss was estimated of £444 million to the two Governments, or £200 million to the U.K. alone.[5] Even if one makes the assumption that foreign exchange is worth, say, 10 to 20 per cent more than the conversion at the official exchange rate, the loss remains. A Treasury Under Secretary, Mr F. R. Barratt, confirmed to a Commons Trade and Industry Sub-Committee in 1971 that there was no prospect of recovering in full Concorde's research and development costs, and that, if the project were proceeded with, there would be 'a substantial loss'.

The project was then a prize candidate for the chopper,

according to the dictum of the then Secretary of State for Trade and Industry, Mr Davies, that 'we cannot as a country afford to spend money on things that are not worth having'. There is reason to suppose that Whitehall's own estimates also point in the direction of a negative return on funds expended, even after writing off everything spent up to 1970. Indeed, it looks as if British and French airlines may have to be subsidised to buy this already subsidised aircraft; and there may be even a third subsidy to bring down the level of supersonic fares.

It is characteristic of such aerospace projects that, when account is taken of the 'external', 'social', or 'spillover' effects, which do not appear in the commercial balance sheet, and which are so often cited by the interventionists, the case against them is even stronger. The technological 'spin-off' seems extremely small in relation to the cost of Concorde. The Council on Technological Fallout of the U.S. President's *Ad Hoc Review Committee on the Supersonic Transport Programme*,[6] reported that its magnitude 'is very difficult to assess, but appears to be small'. It added: 'We believe technological fallout to be of relatively minor importance in this programme.' In the U.K. the 1965 Plowden Report on the British aircraft industry concluded that technological fallout could 'not be advanced as a major justification for support to ensure that the industry survives or is maintained at any particular level.'[7] On the other side are to be placed the losses from noise and pollution around airports, the effects of the supersonic bang on shipping and on so-called 'sparsely populated areas', and other adverse environmental side-effects, no more speculative than the supposed technological spin-off. As for the supposed effects on employment, if £1,000 were paid as compensation or adjustment assistance to each Concorde worker, the cost would have been £25 million, much less than that of going on with the project.

Thus, so far from being an exception to whatever general presumption there may be in favour of market forces, the exceptional factors in the case of Concorde were the other way round: the social loss was greater than the money calculations indicated. The psychological impact of Concorde (and to a lesser extent Rolls-Royce) on younger people in the academic world, the Civil Service, Whitehall, and even in the

City, who might otherwise have been prepared to give the 'market forces' approach a hearing, can hardly be overestimated. Nor was the strong support for Concorde of those in the business community who saw it as part of 'putting Britain on the technological map' a helpful factor. In fact it illustrates how wide the gap may be between a 'pro-business philosophy' and a market economy, but the association of the two, even in the minds of the politically educated, is very hard to break.*

Anti-Consumer Policies

Subsidies for Concorde and the abolition of free school milk are flagrant inconsistencies for any kind of economic liberal, irrespective of how crudely or subtly he interprets the principles of the market economy. (They may not be contradictions for exponents of conservative or other philosophies. This is briefly discussed in Chapter 1, pp. 159–62.) But there were other acts of policy, which may have superficially appeared in keeping with a 'market forces' approach, but in fact showed a failure to appreciate the concept adequately.

The most glaring example of measures which Ministers wrongly supposed to increase the role of market forces but in fact did the opposite, were the changes in agricultural policy in the Conservative programme – undertaken quite irrespective of E.E.C. membership. But there were also more subtle misjudgements in the field of what Adam Smith called 'indiscriminate benefit'. These are the benefits which are available to people as a 'free ride', whether or not they pay for them. They arise from the practical impossibility of charging for such services in such a way that the benefits are confined to those who pay the price. This is a classic area where economic liberals have always seen a case for state finance. The standard

* The violent attack delivered by Senator Barry Goldwater on the opponents of *state investment* in a supersonic aircraft (who, he believes, are involved in a desperate attempt to channel ever more funds into 'social welfare programmes') shows how far removed the extreme political right, even when it proclaims a supposedly old-fashioned private enterprise *credo*, can be from the market economy and confirms the error of identifying the two positions. (Article in *The New York Times*, 16 December 1970, reported in the *Financial Times*, 17 December.)

examples are in the provision of information on scientific or market research, the fruits of which can be fully or partially enjoyed by those who have not paid for them and in which the private sector will – if left to itself – be inclined to under-invest.

Some of the 'cuts' made by the Heath Government in its initial phase were in this category. Examples included the abolition of the Consumer Council, the end of the grant to the British Productivity Council and the decision not to go ahead with a proposed Design Council. A few of the economies in scientific research expenditure may also have been in this category.

The activities of all such bodies should indeed have been carefully examined. The 'indiscriminate benefit' argument is not an incantation which removes the need to make out a case for all of them. It is notoriously difficult to eliminate any type of expenditure of any body once it has been well established and accepted in Whitehall. One cannot, however, suppress a fear that some valuable expenditure, which did not involve specific or discretionary industrial intervention, may have been lost for the saving of much smaller sums than are involved in any single aerospace project.

The case in which these fears were most clearly justified was the abolition of the Consumer Council – an example of a 'tough-minded' action directly inimical to the successful working of a market economy. It is almost a truism that the better informed consumers are, the more the search for profits in a free market will lead to socially satisfactory results. Yet, for a tiny saving of expenditure, estimated at £240,000 per annum, or about one three-hundredth of annual British expenditure on Concorde, Ministers were prepared to remove a prop to the market system itself. This example is interesting for the light it sheds on the difference between simple disengage-ment-cum-axe-wielding and promoting an effective market economy. The latter does not establish itself automatically, but requires the very careful fostering of an environment in which competition will flourish and yield socially desirable results.

The Government eventually came to realise its error in abolishing the Consumer Council. In a characteristic 180°

reversal of policy it proposed, in 1972, a much more cumbersome apparatus of a Director-General of Fair Trading, aided by a large advisory committee. The project seemed at least as much designed to play to the anti-business gallery as to deal effectively with the real problems.

The Regions

Thus, even before the Government's official change of mind on industrial intervention brought on by the high unemployment figures of the winter of 1971–2, its espousal of market forces appeared selective, and perversely so. It seemed keenest on them when it came to Health Service charges or school meals or milk (all areas where the paternalist case is most difficult to destroy completely), but impervious to profitability considerations when interests with which it sympathised were threatened. Thus, it was not well placed to deal with the pressures in favour of Upper Clyde from those on the left with an opposite set of prejudices.

The diffused effect of such intellectual inconsistencies on the climate of opinion – and on those who provided Ministers with their briefs – was much larger than generally realised. But the factor that did most to reverse the earlier brave intentions about 'lame ducks', and to bring back selective intervention well outside the aerospace industries, was alarm over regional unemployment.

Here again the Government's difficulties were increased by the initial appraisal which the Conservatives made in Opposition and the first few months of Government. Indeed, nothing better illustrates the underlying detestation of many of the 1970 breed of Conservatives of policies working through the prices mechanism and impersonal market forces than their attitudes to the regions. This was evident even before the election with the commitment to phase out the Regional Employment Premium.

This is not the place to discuss the optimum scale of regional incentives; but an economic liberal can support the provision of some such incentives with a good conscience. No sensible person would commit himself to an attempt to freeze for all time the existing geographical distribution of industry and population. An extreme regional policy would have led to an attempt to preserve the ancient centres of the woollen industry in the Cotswolds and East Anglia and to prevent the Industrial Revolution from taking place in the Midlands and North. Yet there would be heavy costs in going to the other extreme and abandoning all attempts at regional policy. The most obvious is, of course, local unemployment. If this were the only argument, a policy to assist labour mobility, combined with compensation for the victims of change, might be preferable to regional incentives. But, in the absence of such a policy (which would be very difficult without a free market in rented accommodation), regional incentives are a lesser evil than the social evils and economic wastes of large pockets of local unemployment.

Another cost, which the private industrialist does not take into account, is the new 'social' capital – schools, roads and so on – required in the areas to which workers move. The argument is often overdone since much of the existing social capital in areas such as the North or Scotland was obsolescent and had to be replaced in any case if industries were to be attracted. Perhaps the most important unpriced cost that the concentration of new development in places such as the London area or in the West Midlands imposes is in the form of congestion – from discomfort on the roads to the loss of countryside – which the industrialist does not take into account in his calculations. (He takes into account the congestion that he will have to face himself, but not the extra costs his entry will impose on others.) The market economist might well favour a congestion tax, which would, however, present difficulties while cost inflation is a major problem. In the absence of such a tax there is a special need to tilt the balance positively in favour of the less fortunate regions.

The liberal economist has his own trade-off to calculate. If he wants to contain inflation by controlling the general level of demand, and if he wants to take a fairly tough attitude to 'lame duck' projects, he should, in return, support measures to prevent the concentration of unemployment in regional black spots. For it is these black spots which create most of the political and emotional steam both for inflationary demand management and for make-work industrial policies.

The Regional Employment Premium introduced by the Labour Government in September 1967 was essentially an attempt to reduce regional disparities by means of the price mechanism. A fixed wage subsidy was given to increase the attraction of employing labour in the high unemployment areas. It relied on market forces and involved no discretionary administrative judgements by governmental officials. Indeed the R.E.P. was equivalent either to a slower growth of regional money wages (of the kind that might have been expected under market pressures in the absence of trade union or other frictions) or to a regional devaluation, but combined in either case with a cash transfer from the rest of the country.

The main defects were the absence of a premium for service employment (outside certain tourist areas) and the *per capita* instead of payroll basis of payment, which both discriminated against skilled labour and led to the erosion of the value of incentives as money incomes rose. These could have been corrected by converting it into a general payroll subsidy (or as a second best employers' National Insurance contributions could have been remitted in these areas). Such changes would have strengthened the basic principle, but the resulting measure would have looked so different administratively that the Conservatives could still have claimed to have replaced R.E.P. by something better.

But not only did the Government turn down this face-saving approach which would have genuinely improved the measure.* As an unintended by-product of the switch in the form of national investment incentives, it also initially reduced the value of the differential value of these incentives to the high unemployment regions. It was therefore hardly surprising that there was a switch in industrial and regional policy in the spring of 1972 in which heads rolled – mostly the wrong ones.

As Peter Jay remarked at the time, 'the White Paper of March 1972,[8] might as well have sprung direct from Mr

---

* R.E.P. was not due to be phased out until the end of 1974. But even if there is a subsequent reprieve for R.E.P. or some substitute measure, the damage to expectations by the announcement of its phasing out has already been done.

Wedgwood Benn in his Mintech heyday.'⁹ An Industrial
Development Executive was set up to provide 'selective' and
'flexible' assistance, over and above the announced incentives.
The words 'selective' and 'flexible' here essentially mean on
a discriminatory basis without any announced principles or
guidelines. Such 'selective assistance' was also to be made
available on I.R.C. lines outside the aided regions too. To
complete the I.R.C. analogy, the Minister was to be advised
by an 'Industrial Development Board' of prominent persons
in industry, banking, accounting and finance'.

So far as the announced incentives were concerned, the
new policy managed to graft on to itself all the errors of the
old. These took the form of the restoration of investment
grants, which could hardly fail to give a capital-intensive bias
to new projects in areas of labour surplus. Fantastic to relate,
for all the Conservative mockery of Labour's obsession with
manufacturing industries, these new incentives were by the
spring of 1972 still not available for the service trades. Thus,
two of the main features stressed by most economists who
favour a market economy – general rules rather than discretionary intervention and the intelligent use of the price
mechanism – were cast aside.

Of course, not everything in the White Paper was wholly
bad. Packages assembled from a trawl around Whitehall
departments rarely are. The increased training facilities and
grants to assist mobility could be welcomed; and, in view of
the size of the problem even inferior regional incentives were
probably better than none whatever. It goes without saying
that in the new atmosphere a rescue operation was launched
to enable all the divisions of the bankrupt Upper Clyde to
remain in business. As in the case of the aid previously provided by Mr Benn, the hope was expressed that the yards
would eventually become commercially profitable on their
own. Several other less publicised organisations, such as the
Post Office Giro, previously under threat of the death sentence, were also quietly reprieved.

In the new environment of 'Conservative socialism', the
Bank of England began 'round table discussions' with institutional investors and the C.B.I. on ways of using their influence to 'improve the direction and management of public

companies'. Earlier decisions to limit the support for the
British computer industry were reversed and, indeed, support
was extended to microcircuitry in general to help meet Far
Eastern competition. The Wilsonian idea of the state acquiring an equity when it put money into the corporate 'begging
bowl' was again under consideration – this time in the form
of convertible debentures. The reference to begging bowls is,
however, somewhat unfair, as in some cases the Government
was pushing concerns to remain in the vanguard of technological development that would themselves have preferred a
less exposed position.

But even these seemingly drastic departures had been foreshadowed by the new Conservative Government in its earliest
months of office when it attempted to rescue Rolls-Royce in
the autumn of 1970 before the bankruptcy of the company. It
tried initially to raise money for the company by a personal
appeal from the Governor of the Bank of England to City
institutions. People were expected to act against their commercial judgement, not in accordance with any laws, but at
the personal behest of Ministers or their representatives –
as always on such occasions, on patriotic grounds. The execu-
tive-mindedness of a good deal of Conservative thinking
points in the opposite direction from the kind of market
economy that is based on known rules applicable to all, and
savours too much of the corporate industrial state.

There was a striking parallel in all this to the 'Great Socialist Revival' during the Nixon Administration of which Galbraith has written,[10] citing in evidence the attempts to put
Federal funds into Penn Central, the Government support
for Lockheed, the heavily subsidised supersonic transport aircraft, and the proposal for a billion dollars official guarantee
for a fund to protect investors from losses against Wall Street
failures. Galbraith is right to point out that the thrust behind
this right-wing socialism comes from managers and investors
in the industries concerned. But as far as one can penetrate
the ambiguity, Galbraith seems to welcome these developments as part of a desirable recognition of the facts of life,
which he had never hoped to live to see; and he is quite
wrong to pour scorn on the U.S. radicals of the first two post-
war decades who – unlike their British counterparts – were

cool to the idea of government takeovers, as 'that would be to put the Pentagon, the C.I.A., the Department of Justice, J. Edgar Hoover and the rest', even 'more in charge'. This is exactly what it will do – with the exception of Hoover, who is now dead.

On any set of beliefs, the initial industrial policies of the Heath Government were a waste of the time and energy of able people. If 'discretionary industrial intervention' was to be the order of the day, what was the point of winding up the I.R.C. in a fit of pique and then re-establishing its activities under other names and organisations? Indeed the I.R.C. might have been marginally preferable to an economic liberal to the setup that was emerging in the early 1970s. At least the earlier body had to publish details of its market intervention together with their financial results. It was far from clear that the Conservatives' Industrial Development Executive would have even that degree of accountability.

The Bank of England, which became much more involved in questions of industrial and corporate structure, is not indeed accountable to Parliament in any realistic sense at all. It can remain highly secretive, and, in operations of this kind, is effectively accountable to no one. Moreover, it is extremely unwise to give the central bank, which is primarily responsible for monetary policy, a watchdog brief over industry and commerce generally. For this means the Bank is expected to exert the prestige and influence, acquired in the City as a result of its monetary role, in an attempt to suggest to companies and financial institutions that they ought to conform with official desires. Such action is more objectionable than anything the I.R.C. did in its heyday. This is yet another illustration that the Government's readiness to axe machinery inherited from Labour was not identical with the promotion of a market economy.

The preference for selectivity and dislike of across-the-board measures has, in fact, been apparent for years among many Conservatives. (Indeed, Mr Macmillan had it as an inheritance from the 1930s, but was fortunately too involved in world affairs to do much about it.) This preference is sometimes defended on the grounds that across-the-board incentives benefit existing as well as new activities. This argument was applied for instance to the 1964–6 export rebate and to the 1967 devaluation. Such talk is deeply misguided. All market mechanisms, whether spontaneous or policy devices, work by showering incentives on those who need to be influenced as well as on those who are already being virtuous; and the ethics of discriminating against the latter are, to say the least, highly dubious.

Some Conservatives are, I think, confused by the paradox that 'selectivity' fits well with a market philosophy in the social services while non-discrimination fits better in the industrial field. The paradox is only apparent as the word 'selectivity' is being used in different ways. A selective social policy, discriminates among *people* by the non-discretionary general criteria of income, wealth and financial need. A selective industrial policy discriminates among products, industries, locations, or firms; and, unlike a selective social policy, it involves discretionary judgement by politicians or officials on what should be produced and who should be encouraged to produce it.

The Nationalised Industries

The retreat by the Conservatives from the application of commercial principle to the nationalised industries has already been described in Chapter 1 (pp. 80 *et seq.*). This proved much more important than the 'hiving off' of the peripheral activities of these industries which caused so much ruffling of feathers after the 1970 election. Examples of the latter under way or under discussion included the sale of Thomas Cook, the retail distribution of gas and electrical appliances by public boards, British Rail hotels and the hotel-booking service provided by the Coal Board computer.

There are two dangers arising from these ancillary activities which might justify 'hiving off'. One is their ability to under-cut private competitors because of privileged access to capital or ability to survive with less than commercial returns. An opposite and more frequent danger is that these peripheral activities might provide profits which can be used to subsidise their main activities. As *The Economist* remarked: 'It is important that any success of the Coal Board in searching for North Sea gas should not mean that more finance is made available for propping up hopelessly uneconomical coal mines in South Wales.'[11]

The argument against 'hiving off' state subsidiaries is that many large private concerns are also highly diversified, with the deliberate aim of cushioning the organisation against a run of bad business in any one product or market. The tax structure may encourage excessive diversification; but a good deal would occur in any case. The matter is arguable either way, and of only fringe importance. The peripheral activities of nationalised corporations have no monopoly privileges; they operate in highly competitive markets and for this reason are the last of the problems posed by public enterprise.

Some talk of 'hiving off' referred, not to the publicly-owned corporations, but to the Government's own activities. Examples included the Stationery Office and local employment exchanges. If the 'hiving off' is to a publicly-owned agency, neither denationalisation nor competition is at issue. The arguments here are largely administrative, the most attractive being that it might leave Ministers and senior civil servants freer to concentrate on policy questions. The biggest difficulty is to ensure that the new agencies remain subject to some form of ultimate political control – perhaps via parliamentary committees – without hampering their day-to-day managerial independence. The market economy would only come into the picture either if a service were contracted to *more than one* competing private enterprise (preferably operating in the same part of the country) or if several private firms made competitive bids for a particular agency's functions.

The economic liberal is interested in competition more than ownership. More fundamental than any of the ideas so far mentioned would be reforms to subject state concerns to more competition in their main activities. Many of the nationalised industries have to compete for customer goodwill against formidable rivals; for example, the nationalised fuel industries against one another and against oil, and rail against road and air transport. But this is no argument against carrying the process further. It would be no justification for a monopoly in cream-cakes to say that the industry faces formidable competition from ice-cream and chocolates;

or for a monopoly in sound radio receivers to speak of the competition from television, record-players and tape-recorders.

It would be perfectly feasible to break up the coal, electricity and gas industries into more than one autonomous unit, even if they remained publicly owned. Few if any economies of scale would be lost in the process. It would be possible to have a number of autonomous regional electricity authorities, which would both distribute and generate, and be linked to the jointly-owned national grid. An urgently required action is the complete separation of the mail and telephone services. One is the main competitor of the other; and there is no justification for a single corporation having a monopoly of both.

The introduction of some private equity capital into nationalised corporations was popular in Conservative circles in the initial period of the Heath Government. It was labelled the 'BP-type' solution and was being strongly urged for the steel industry. Such a course would involve nationalised concerns borrowing directly from the market without Treasury guarantee and perhaps on equity as well as fixed interest terms. The simple announcement of the ending of the guarantee would not be enough. It would have to be seen in practice that the state was no more and no less likely to meet their losses than those of private undertakings. It might be marginally desirable in putting these concerns on a more comparable footing to their private rivals, but it is out of the question, so long as the state concerns are used as pace-setters in price restraint and their financial objectives set aside.

There are many ways of extending the degree of competition. One approach is import liberalisation. The *permanent* freeing of coal imports and the removal of the fuel-oil duty would be more important than most of the 'hiving off' schemes discussed above. The most important reform, however, would be a review of the nationalisation and other statutes preventing private concerns from competing with public corporations. The 1971 postal strike raised the question whether the Post Office (once shorn of its telephone responsibilities) should have a monopoly over the public mails.[12] The provisions preventing any commercial concern from gen-

erating electricity, making gas or mining coal for outside sale
are also difficult to defend.

A further example is the monopoly position of the public
transport undertakings. There is a strong case, for instance,
for allowing so-called 'pirate' buses to compete with London
Transport and similar corporations. There is no reason to
confine these services to a few rural or out-of-the-way subur-
ban routes, where it does not pay London Transport to
operate. Genuine competition is provided only when rival
services operate in the same areas. (If a change of policy of
this kind were contemplated it would be necessary to re-
examine the control exercised by the Traffic Commissioners
– and in London the G.L.C. – over fares. Another difficulty is
the absence of effective road charges on private vehicles, but
this is at most an argument against unrestricted bus services
in city centres. It applies much less to other routes.)

The one Government policy that fostered private competition with public corporations was that of establishing commercial radio to break the B.B.C.'s monopoly over the
medium. One should not be deterred here by the superstition
that there is something philistine or uncivilised in 'pop' provided by commercial radios, compared with the same kind of
noise put out by a public corporation. If the B.B.C. is concerned with quality, its main job is to attend to the standard
of its own programmes and not to throttle competition.

Technological changes are in prospect which should eventually make possible a much more extensive introduction of
competition into both television and radio. There may in
future no longer be any physical need to limit broadcasting
to a small number of channels. Instead there could be an
indefinite number of services, among which consumers could
select and pay for directly. The distinction between publishing and broadcasting would then largely disappear, with a
consequent extension of cultural diversity and freedom. But
there are so many institutional interests involved in present
restrictions, and such passionate feelings exist about what
other people should be prevented from watching, that a
strong rearguard action is likely to prevent any new technological opportunities from being fully utilised.[13]

The transfer of certain air routes to the 'second force' of

private operators seemed superficially like a similar move in the competitive direction. Certainly Labour fury was aroused. But to the economic liberal this party squabble was largely irrelevant. He would like to see, not a transfer of routes from one monopoly group to another, but state and private concerns competing on the same route. He does not see why routes should be allocated by the Government at all, except when there is a clear danger of congestion. Otherwise he would allow free entry to any airline that can meet safety requirements.

Limitations on the entry of private airlines, or their frequency of operation, to protect state airlines are the enemy of competition. Even more so is the fixing of standard fares. If there really are insuperable technical reasons why only one airline can be allowed a given internal route – or if there is traffic for only one carrier – the franchise should at least be auctioned or sold at a market price. A government which did this would be making some use of market principles and introducing some diversity into our transport without any suspicion of handing over monopoly profits to its political friends.

On domestic routes the British Government has considerable room for manoeuvre. Internationally, it is restricted by the price ring operated by the International Air Transport Association and by governmental restrictions on landing rights. It should, however, be an object or policy to renegotiate the I.A.T.A. rules to allow more flexible pricing. Not least of the disadvantages of the present system is that the absence of price competition has directed rival airlines into ever more advanced engines and aircraft. This distortion deprives the passengers of the choice between cheapness and more advanced technology, and encourages projects such as the Concorde or the RB-211 which turn out to be such burdens on the taxpayer.

Apart from trying, wherever possible, to reduce their monopoly privileges, the Government should press the nationalised concerns to make more use of the price mechanism. Its absence is particularly noticeable in transport. For example, before cancelling any bus or train services, transport authorities should be strongly encouraged to experiment with much higher fares and more refined pricing for varying qualities of service. (The doubling or trebling of fares should have been tried by London Transport before it asked to suspend the rural branch of the Central Line between Epping and Ongar. However unpopular, this could not be worse than ending the service altogether.) Experiment should also be made with all-night tubes (interrupted only by minimum servicing breaks) and buses at specially high fares, which would enable the authorities to pay sufficiently lucrative night rates to attract the staff required. Trial policies of this kind would do more for the general welfare than any amount of 'hiving off' of British Transport travel agencies and hotels.

Competition Policy

For a variety of reasons, including the pressure of the E.E.C. legislation on the Parliamentary timetable, as well as doctrinal hesitations, there was little direct action to promote competition either in the public or private sector in the first couple of years after the 1970 election; and the Fair Trading Bill did not appear until the end of 1972. Until then the general impression given was that the existing legislation was being somewhat more loosely administered and that some proposed mergers, which would have been referred to the Monopolies Commission by the previous Government, were given on-the-spot clearance. The new measure may lead to more effective investigation and enforcement, but the criteria for what is or what is not permissible could well turn out to be just as vague, and subject to the fashion of the moment as the law it is designed to replace.

There was, however, one area where the authorities acted promptly after the 1970 election. This was the abolition of the clearing banks' cartel, which had hitherto fixed deposit rates and minimum rates on advances. At the same time, the official 'ceiling' on overdrafts was abolished. If pushed through with vigour, the new proposals could transform both commercial banking and the operation of monetary policy. The aim is to shift from physical controls to overall regulation of the money supply and the allocation of credit by means of the price mechanism. As part of the new deal, the Bank of

England abandoned automatic support purchases of gilt-edged securities of over one year's maturity.

The move to a more competitive system cannot, however, quite be taken for granted. The time to cheer will be after the Bank of England has weathered the first period of restrictive monetary policies under the new system without falling back on directives, 'advice' or ceilings. One does not know what weight would be given in such circumstances to the words in the official announcement about the possible need to protect savings banks and building societies from bank competition. All one can say is that there is at least a chance of really radical change in the monetary sphere which did not exist before.

The argument that the ending of the bank cartel might, in some circumstances, mean higher rates for borrowers as well as lenders should have negative appeal to anyone with the slightest sympathy for a market economy. The traditional system meant that bank lending was regulated by overdraft rationing by managers instead of by charging borrowers the market price for money. In other words, clearing bankers had to be part-time government officials, deciding which activities were in the 'national interest' and which were not. Inevitably the smaller up-and-coming or unconventional firm felt the restrictions with particular force; and frustrated demand was channelled to the secondary market where interest rates were much higher than they would have been if the price mechanism had operated over the whole market.

It is not customary to mention taxi cabs on the same page as banks, but they are both consumer services; and a different, if apparently minor, reform which could increase the welfare of many would be to end the monopoly position and regulated prices of the traditional taxi cabs. This would among other things promote the development of privately operated mini-buses offering a cab service whose fares would be shared *pro rata* among all the passengers. This form of transport would be better suited to the present level of affluence (and the campaign against drinking and driving) than either normal fixed-route public transport or the ordinary taxi.

One argument against the liberalisation of the cab trade is the resulting increase in the number of vehicles – in the absence of road charges. It is based on the entirely unproven assumption that extra cab traffic would be at the expense of public transport, whereas it is at least as likely to be at the expense of car journeys; and a cab, which is conveying passengers a large part of the day, is more economic in use of road space than a private car. The other arguments about exploiting customers' ignorance or possible disputes, are not convincing. It could be laid down that a taxi-driver could choose any fare scale he liked provided he displayed it prominently – or there could, as in Copenhagen, be two types of cabs plying for hire; a closely regulated 'official' service offering certain guarantees to the traveller, and a freer service operating in competition. Unfortunately, the Stamp Committee, which included two distinguished economists, dismissed such ideas for more flexibility with too little examination in 1970 and its report was accepted by the Government.[14]

Taxes and tariffs

The opportunities for further direct action against restrictive practices are, in fact, more in services than in industry, where new anti-monopoly measures can make only a very marginal contribution to promoting competition. Something might be achieved by the elimination of the tax discrimination against distributed profits and trimming of high tax rates on investment incomes, which together formed up to 1972 a strong incentive to new acquisitions by existing firms that brought capital gains for their shareholders.

Even more important would be the slashing of tariffs and backdoor protection devices (such as the preference for British tenders by the Electricity Generating Boards and other public authorities). E.E.C. membership need not have been an obstacle to the immediate unilateral reduction of all British tariffs which are above the Common External Tariff or the unilateral reduction of tariffs towards the E.E.C. ahead of the agreed schedule.

Unfortunately, British policy was moving, if anything, in the opposite direction. With domestic unemployment becoming critical, not only did Ministers abandon any freer trading ideas they might have had, but began to join in the general international protectionist drift. Quotas on Commonwealth textiles were retained for 1972 in addition to the tariffs which were designed to replace them, and Mr John Davies, then Secretary of State for Trade and Industry, was off to Japan to complain about the bilateral Anglo-Japanese trade on an 'imports bad, exports good' ticket. It is only fair to point out that Mr John Davies, did once 'think aloud' about cuts in car tariffs after a particularly inflationary settlement in the motor industry and was howled down for his pains. A contributory factor to many of the policy misjudgements discussed in the preceding pages was the climate of opinion in the media and elsewhere. The Government was usually attacked for the wrong reasons on the wrong issues; and however critical one was of Government policies, they were usually rather better than those being urged by all the many voices urging it to 'move to the centre'.

Both trade and competition policy are, of course, going to be increasingly determined by the evolution of the enlarged E.E.C. rather than by internal British developments. The E.E.C. is discussed in a separate chapter. Membership can lead either towards or away from a liberal market economy. The Community will impose upon us a highly protective agricultural system which will involve a transfer of real resources away from this country; but it will probably increase the effective degree of competition in British industry. Of the two leading economic liberals of the 19th century, John Bright would almost certainly have campaigned vigorously against E.E.C. entry as a 'dear food' policy; Richard Cobden, one feels, would have agonised a good deal more about the issue. The real worry is, however, whether the U.K. representatives will really work to make the economic side of the Community a common *market*, geared to serving consumers, or whether they will co-operate with 'conservative socialists' who desire a producers' association geared to a taxpayer-financed 'high technology', and seeking to preserve loss-making situations from outside competition.

Inflation and Unemployment

It requires no great diagnostic skill to show that the interventionist and protectionist trends in British policy in the early 1970s were connected with the domestic unemployment crisis – although I have tried to show that there were other elements deriving from the beliefs with which the Conservatives returned to office. Nevertheless, high unemployment put the interventionists on top and decided the argument in their favour on many borderline issues. If unemployment should begin to decline, the market-orientated school would have a better chance of a hearing. Even the most ivory tower economic liberal does not fight for more Japanese imports when unemployment is above a million and rising – as it was up to the spring of 1972.

The Government's struggles with the inflationary recession have not figured more prominently in the preceding pages, partly because the underlying problems have been discussed in Chapter 2, and partly because the battle is still raging while these words are being written. Mr Heath's efforts to combat the union wage-push which was pricing people out of jobs, deserved wholehearted support, whatever one might think of some of his other policies.

If there was a criticism to be made it was that he might, nevertheless, fail and be forced to follow President Nixon's example of August 1971, and impose wage and price controls as he did in November 1972. The effectiveness of the British Government's confrontation policy suffered from the fact that its pre-election thinking on the subject of the unions had been largely in industrial relations terms and had failed to evolve an economic policy to deal with the monopoly problem they posed. The result was that the Government had to rely on day-to-day expedients and a general philosophy of firmness without the benefit of a coherent strategy. This meant inadequate contingency planning at the political level, so that there was a danger that if controls had to be used in the end, they might have to be of an unnecessarily harmful variety.

The Exchange Rate

There was one vitally important area where the Heath Government did move nearer to price mechanism solutions after its first year in office, and that was the exchange rate. This enters into every single commercial transaction containing overseas payments, directly or indirectly. It is the link between British overseas costs and prices; and, if it is at the wrong level, the market mechanism will not give the right signals, and the profit motive will fail as a pointer. Adherence to a wrong rate – or even the fear of the rate becoming overvalued in future – would lead remorselessly to fresh acts of state intervention in one field after another in the sacred name of export promotion or import savings. We would be back with pseudo-patriotic exhortation to exporters, disguised export subsidies, pressure on companies to accept unprofitable overseas contracts, the extension of export credit on giveaway terms, state-financed 'export' projects and all the rest. An undervalued rate also creates plenty of problems as the Germans and Japanese discovered.

The point of principle involved is whether the exchange rate is to be adjusted whenever necessary, and by whatever means, as a normal instrument of policy; or if the Government is to treat it as a prestige symbol to be changed only in the very last resort after everything else had failed. *Mr Barber was the first British Chancellor to declare – in his 1972 Budget Speech – that domestic policy would no longer be distorted to maintain an unrealistic parity.* It is a mark of the limited influence of rationality in human affairs that it should count as an historic statement.

The reservations therefore moved from principle to technique. It is one thing to make such a statement when sterling is strong, and another to make the right change in the parity at the right time. Although the Government now accepted the role of the price mechanism in balancing overseas payments, it remained resolutely opposed to free markets for currencies. (The distinction between the two concepts is discussed on pp. 66–7.) When forced to float the pound temporarily by the Nixon measure of 1971, it imposed a great number of restrictions and intervened heavily – which did not prevent it, along with other European Governments, having to accept in the end an appreciation against the dollar of a size it was trying to avoid. By supporting, and participating in the E.E.C. plan for narrower margins (even before Common Market membership), it was needlessly reducing its own room for manoeuvre. The combination of narrow margins with Mr Barber's pro-flexibility declaration meant a risk of very great speculative pressure once the pound came under any sort of serious suspicion.

The private hope of the Treasury and Bank was that they would be able to devalue, if this proved necessary, earlier instead of later than expected. While not impossible, this would involve a difficult feat of both market and diplomatic management. There was thus a possibility that, faced with serious pressure, the Chancellor might have to float the pound again temporarily as he did in 1972. This was an unconvenanted bonus, which – thanks entirely to the speculators – allowed the Government to depreciate the sterling exchange rate in advance of E.E.C. entry without any of the internal or external embarrassments that might otherwise have impeded it. Unfortunately, the commitment to European monetary union and the opposition of the Government to floating rates as a system meant that, despite Mr Barber's brave declaration quoted above, there was still a danger that at some future date the U.K. might be stuck with a wrongly valued exchange rate which it would be difficult to change.

The Social Services

Cuts in public expenditure featured prominently in the initial year of the Heath Government. They were, as we have seen, quickly reversed in the industrial sphere. There were also signs of greater reluctance by Conservatives in Whitehall, and in local authorities, to provide grants for urban commuter passenger transport. This reluctance was overborne by the general price restraint policy, but it still affected the structure (as distinct from average level) of passenger fares; and the issue could become acute again.

Reductions in such grants to finance tax cuts will only give the individual more say in the allocation of resources if the relative prices he pays for rail, and for private and public road transport, reflect the true costs of these alternatives. It is well known that a rail commuter, considering whether to bring his car into town, does not have to pay anything like the full extra costs his car imposes on the community (whether measured in extra congestion or the increase in road expenditure required to relieve it). The optimum solution might well be a system of road pricing, varying with location, time of day, etc., and perhaps levied by a metering device. But in the absence of such pricing, grants to commuter rail services may be a good second best and superior to nothing at all. This is yet another example of why cuts in public expenditure* cannot be regarded as synonymous with the pursuit of an effective market economy.

The most controversial items in these cuts were, of course, the increased Health Service and school meal charges, the ending of free school milk and the reform of housing finance. Apart from the last-named these were hardly worth the fuss they caused. It was unfortunate that to many people they became symbolic of a market economy, as they were undertaken in a sphere where the paternalist case is least easy to refute. The difficulty arises from the fact that the family is not identical with the breadwinner. Even if tax and social service charges are so arranged that the poorer families do not lose out, free school meals or milk are consumed directly by the child, while a tax reduction or cash grant may be pocketed by the father.

One of the main criticisms of these small gestures in the charging field is that they spoiled the market for more fundamental changes which would be less open to the above objections. The economic liberal would question whether health and education should forever be treated as public goods; and he would be inclined to ask whether the private provision of such services should not be encouraged by a method such as the voucher system. It is certainly less undesirable that parents should make decisions on behalf of their children than that public officials should do so. A liberal should always prefer literal paternalism to the state variety. But parental choice should certainly not be unfettered. The scheme for educational vouchers, equivalent to the average cost of a state school place[15] and cashable against school fees, does impose considerable restrictions on parental choice. The parent is not left free to decide how much he can spend on education, but

---

* The subject is discussed more fully in my essay 'Cuts in Government Spending and the Tax Illusion' in Robson (ed.), *Taxation Policy* (Penguin, 1972).

is forced to spend at least the specified average on his own child. Indeed, the voucher scheme provides a more positive stimulus to increased expenditure on education than either the present system or the alternative market-type scheme of charging fees in state schools.

Vouchers of this kind would count as public expenditure under the Treasury definition; and there would thus be no reduction of public expenditure as measured by the usual statistics, although there would be an extension of parental choice. Support for experiments with vouchers in no way involves a desire to strengthen the traditional type of public school; on the contrary, it rests on a belief that an extension of the private market for education is much the most effective way of securing a wider variety of types of school; and it is no accident that so many educational experiments have been pioneered in the private sector.

Health is a much more difficult subject for liberal reform than education, because it is desirable to combine greater freedom of choice with redistribution of a very special kind – not in favour of any particular social or economic class, but in favour of those who are ill; and redistribution should be in direct relation to the amount of medical treatment required. Do we believe that someone who has been struck by a severe illness, which is costly to treat, should be financially ruined, or see his family ruined, and perhaps even not obtain treatment, either because he failed to insure, or because the insurance does not cover the full cost of the treatment? My own answer is 'No', and it is a valid criticism of U.S. society that such cases occur.

But it is a fundamental fallacy to suppose that this value-judgement can only be met by state provision of medical services. The main requirement is a compulsory insurance scheme, with the state ready to step in to meet the cost of exceptionally expensive treatment in excess of what can be reimbursed from the standard policy. The rival plans that the U.S. Congress has discussed provide for compulsory insurance rather than a Federal Health Service. Another alternative is the system common on the Continent whereby patients meet their medical bills and are then reimbursed up to a large percentage.

We are not, however, starting at the beginning, but already have an established N.H.S. An economic liberal, while wanting to preserve the redistribution of income in favour of the sick, would also want to remove the deterrents to the private provision of services. These arise from the fact that, while the N.H.S. is still largely 'free', the full market rate is charged on private treatment. One useful step would be to provide tax concessions for those taking out medical insurance policies. (If these took the form of a 'tax credit' or voucher of, say 50 per cent of such expenditure, the value of the benefit would be the same for an individual in a low as in a high tax bracket; anyone paying less tax than the credit was worth, or not paying tax, should be able to claim cash.)

The biggest difficulty about redistribution towards the sick is that there is no objective criterion of the amount of medical treatment needed. There is a large discretionary margin, which is likely to increase. As more drugs and alternative methods of treatment are developed people in the same general state of health will have different views about the time and trouble worth devoting to purchases from chemists, visits to doctors and similar expenses. Prescription and other N.H.S. charges can be justified as a rough and ready attempt to meet this problem. The supply of drugs and appliances at far below cost preserves the redistribution towards the sick; but the charges do encourage people to take costs into account in choosing between medical and other forms of expenditure. I doubt, however, if such charges can be pushed very much higher (adjustments for inflation apart) without placing an undesirable burden on those with the bad luck to be ill; and compulsory insurance covering medical expenditure above a certain minimum would be socially more desirable than a National Health Service with very heavy charges for those using it.

The one really radical measure aimed at reducing the growth of expenditure, among the 1970 spending cuts, was the new housing policy. The reduction in public expenditure was not, in fact, expected to be all that large. But the measures were comprehensive, and new policies involving the replacement of indiscriminate subsidies on council housing by rent rebates related to income were introduced. These rebates will

– and this is a revolutionary step – be available to private as well as council tenants.

The housing problem is mainly due to decades of rent control and subsidised council building. Such measures not merely enlarge demand; they also diminish almost to vanishing point the supply of new non-luxury accommodation designed for letting. They will always lead to a permanent housing shortage unless the public authorities are prepared to supply to the full all the extra demand created by their policies. This would involve an expensive and open-ended commitment which no government of any party has seen fit to fulfil.

In the absence of such fulfilment the control-and-subsidy approach has led to predictable and proliferating evils. A council house becomes a valuable privilege, not to be given up lightly. But the privilege is conferred, not on those in most need of an income subsidy, but on sitting tenants and those who have stayed in an area for enough years to come to the top of a waiting list. Council rents for comparable accommodation, traditionally varied in an arbitrary way, according to the age distribution of a local authority's housing stock and its rate subsidy policy. Rents paid by tenants were thus related neither to the value or quality of their accommodation nor to their capacity to pay. Not surprisingly, as the 1968 Family Expenditure Survey disclosed, a far higher proportion of poor families rented private rather than council accommodation. Yet these tenants received no public subsidy.

The new policy will not restore a free market in accommodation; but it should reduce, for most tenants, the difference between their own and market rents. Within the public sector it will do this by raising the level of council rents before rebate, and within the private sector by shifting more tenancies from the old system of controlled tenancies to the more flexible 'regulated' system of fair rents inaugurated in 1965. The formula for determining a 'fair rent' is an absurd one based on removing the scarcity element from the value of a property (which would make it zero!). In practice, the 'fair rents' average in most areas is about 20 per cent below market values, according to the Francis Committee. The Committee also found that 'controlled rents', of which there were still

1.4 million, were usually 'far below' the level of regulated 'fair rents', of which there were 1.2 million at the end of 1969.[16] Thus, with respect to both council houses and rent-controlled private tenancies, the new measures should reduce, although not eliminate, the attachment to existing accommodation as if it were a feudal right. They should thereby ease the difficulties in the way of geographical mobility, which is desirable on grounds of personal liberty as well as economic growth. The attachment of subsidies to families rather than properties should also have this effect, as well as concentrate help where it is most needed.

Instead of attacking the reform of public housing finance on the *simpliste* grounds that it raised rents, left-wing critics of the Government policy would have done better to have concentrated on two demands. One was that any sums 'saved' should be allocated to cash benefits or to tax reliefs strictly confined to the lowest end of the income scale. The other was for a parallel pruning of subsidies to owner occupiers.

Tax relief on mortgage interest payments are a subsidy to home owners, so long as other interest payments are subject to tax, as they still partially were even after the 1972 Budget. The abolition in the early 1960s of Schedule 'A' (tax on the income in kind from home ownership) was again a subsidy. For a rich man it can be a very large subsidy indeed, as one can see if one asks how the tax position of the owner of an expensive house would suffer if he moved into a cheaper house or rented accommodation, and used the proceeds for ordinary investment.

Left-wing critics did, of course, make these points, but not by way of proposals for *supplementing* the Conservative housing policies. There has, indeed, been far too little analysis of whether there really is a case for pushing more resources into either owned or rented houses than people would be inclined to devote if left to spend their income in their own way. Public discussion on this – as on every topic involving tax or expenditure, be it pensions, S.E.T. or dustmen's wages – suffers from a compartmentalised treatment which does not face up to the truth that more spent on one desirable object must mean less on something else. To be strictly fair, one should add a caveat that so long as the average rent-payer

receives a public subsidy, there is a case for some limited help
to home ownership to prevent the choice between the two
forms of occupation from being distorted. But the hidden subsidies to home owners could easily overtake in value the help
afforded to tenants, if this has not already happened.

The Conservative approach to the social services was not,
of course, entirely a matter of cuts and rationalisation. Apart
from the increase in physical expenditures on direct state
outlays on health and education, there was a notable innovation in the shape of the Family Income Supplement (F.I.S.).
This was the first step ever taken in this country towards
raising to a minimum level the incomes of families with a
full-time breadwinner.

There were, nevertheless, two serious criticisms, recognised
by the Government itself, of the pattern of charges and benefits that was emerging from the Conservative measures of the
early 1970s. The first was the very human point that a poor
person had to be very clever and alert to gain everything to
which he was entitled. The family whose income required
supplementation had to pick up a little from exemption from
medical charges, a little from free school meals and welfare
milk, something from rent subsidies and something from the
new Family Income Supplement (of which the take-up was
small), as well as other reliefs from local authorities.

Secondly, the separate operation of a whole series of
different means tests, overlapping with the lower reaches of
the income tax, led to arbitrary and sometimes extremely
high marginal rates of tax for the poorest workers, even in
excess of 100 per cent. This was described by Mr Barber in
his 1972 Budget Speech as the 'poverty surtax'. The one
satisfactory way to tackle both these evils would be to mop
up most of the specific subsidies, grants and rebates and unify
these payments with taxes, by means of a simple system of
income tax, direct or indirect.

Mr Barber recommended a scheme which goes a long way
towards such a negative income tax, worked out by his personal tax adviser, Arthur Cockfield; and it emerged from the
work the latter was doing on the simplification of P.A.Y.E.
The basic idea was beautifully simple. For the 90 per cent of
the population to whom the scheme would apply, the present

tax allowances – single, married and child – would be abolished altogether. They would be replaced by a tax credit, set off against tax liability. Where the credit exeeded the liability the result would be a negative income tax. For the ordinary taxpayer, the present 450 P.A.Y.E. codes would be replaced by a simple assessment based on income and a standard offset.

The tax credit scheme would replace family allowances and the greater part of the F.I.S. scheme, and it would reduce the number of people needing to draw 'supplementary benefits'. Mr Barber did not suggest that it should ultimately replace most rent rebates or 'free' N.H.S. supplies and school meals for the poor. But if it is to meet the two criticisms just raised of the trend of Conservative social policy, it should, in time, be enlarged in this way. There might also be a case for paying out some or all of the tax credit to the mother, as family allowances are at present.

The present task is to get it off the ground; it cannot come into effect until well into the 1970s. It is not too much to say that whether the Heath Government is finally remembered for good or ill on the social service front will largely depend on the outcome of the Tax Credit scheme, or any alternative form of negative income tax that may be produced by the investigating committee.

Of course no form of negative income tax is a panacea which will enable us to avoid choosing how much to transfer to the less well off – and at what cost in incentives. But a good scheme should make for clearer understanding; and more honest debate on the desired pattern of income transfers. In all cash benefit schemes there is a trade-off at any given level of generosity between the amount of help given to the poorest and the alleviation of 'poverty surtax'. The Cockfield scheme leans in the latter direction, with an implied marginal tax rate of 30 per cent throughout. This means that if it is to do as much, or more, for the poorest as the schemes it replaces, it will have to be expensive, as a lot of the benefit will spill over to the not-so-poor. The Minimum Income Guarantee scheme by contrast (described on pp. 223–5) goes for the maximum selectivity and help to the poorest at the expense of accepting heavy disincentive effects among that section of the population.

Whatever scheme is adopted, we shall always need a discretionary body, or bodies, to pay out additional sums for people not covered by the rules, to give practical advice and help, keep in contact with the education and health authorities, arrange home helps and so on. There is nothing in the single standard cash benefit approach that condemns one to a cold, inhuman view of the social services by which the less fortunate are given a few pounds and left to their own devices. But if poorer people are always given benefits in kind, they will never gain the experience that enables them to make their own choices.

A Final Word

The economic and social policies of the Heath Government were a mixture of good and bad, with more of both than is normal in left-wing, let alone right-wing governments. Neither the good nor the bad policies could be explained by a single-minded devotion to market mechanisms which simply did not exist even in its earliest years of office.

But explanation is one thing and assessment another. This essay should have shown that a battle to preserve every official body, every subsidy, every control and every tax was not the only or the most promising stand from which to criticise the Heath or any other government. A sensible and humane interpretation of market principles (and I make no apology for the subjective adjectives) provides a much better basis for the appraisal of policy.

5 Some Common Market Heresies*

> ... Not only as a man, but as a British subject, I pray for the flourishing commerce of Germany, Spain, Italy, and even France itself. I am at least certain that Great Britain, and all those nations, would flourish more, did their sovereigns and ministers adopt such enlarged and benevolent sentiments towards each other.
>
> David Hume, 'Of the Jealousy of Trade'

The difficulty with the Common Market debate is that while it is littered with spurious and doubtful arguments, people are terribly reluctant to state the real reasons for their attitudes towards entry. Because of the inhumanities committed in the name of racialism, the expression of any form of preference for particular ethnic, linguistic or geographical groups has become taboo in polite society. But the existence of this taboo does not make these preferences go away.

It is apparent that a great deal of the British opposition to entry into the E.E.C. came from a dislike of the idea of closer association with Continental Europeans. On the positive side it may have expressed an English nationalism or – in more respectable circles – a preference for the English-speaking people over Continental Europeans. Such attitudes emerged very strongly from a *New Society* survey into attitudes to various nationalities (16 June 1966). It is not disgraceful to prefer Americans or Australians or Africans to Frenchmen, Germans or Italians. But it was a little unconvincing when

* An updated and expanded version of an article which originally appeared in the *Journal of Common Market Studies*, June 1970.

people who were strongly motivated by such preferences spoke entirely in terms of food prices or the balance of payments. There is surely nothing that many of the anti-Common Marketeers would have regretted more than the complete demise of the Common Agricultural Policy.

The motivation of the pro-Common Marketeers is more complicated. In some cases it consists of a positive attraction towards our Continental neighbours which may, but need not be, accompanied by political or cultural anti-Americanism. This motivation is a totally different matter from political federalism, which is a second source of support. But the pro-Europeans and the federalists together would not have been able to convert the country's political establishment. A vital third element has been the fashionable belief among many business figures that British industry needs a 'mass market' which is more likely to be achieved by their joining the E.E.C. than in any other way. Here genuine motivation and the professed arguments come closer together than among any other group of supporters. But it is still legitimate to point out that it reflects the home market psychology which has been at the root of so many British economic ills. A fourth motive, and perhaps the most important, has been the desire of our political leaders to play a prominent international role. (A discussion of the historical and institutional roots of this desire, which has cut across all sorts of other political differences, would be a fascinating matter.) Events since the war have shown a rapidly diminishing scope for the old kind of internationalism – one need only recall the fate of British attempts to organise summit meetings, the weakening with each successive Prime Minister and President of any British claim to a special influence over U.S. policy, U.K. military withdrawals, the fading of illusions about the Commonwealth, and a whole series of individual fiascos from Suez to Rhodesia by way of Anguilla.

How exactly the E.E.C. can serve as a substitute is rarely stated explicitly. There seems to be a hope either that an enlarged Community will itself provide a mini-international stage, or a hope that Britain may, via the leadership of a united Europe, again be able to exercise a world role. It should not be forgotten that Britain has a large experienced and high-status diplomatic service, which is in danger of becoming underemployed. The suggested alternative role of export salesmen is unlikely to be the right substitute outlet for their particular blend of abilities and aspirations.

The Unknowns

There is nothing dishonourable in any of the motives so far mentioned, on either side. Indeed, it would be healthier if they were more frequently stated. But let us suppose that our main concern is with the welfare of the inhabitants either of Western Europe as a whole, or of that part of it which is now called the United Kingdom. There are a vast number of relevant questions on which we are almost totally ignorant. We have no idea of the ideal size of a unified economic area. Who can really say whether southern Italy gained or lost from the unification of the country, or whether economic and social tensions would have been smaller or greater in the present territory of the U.S.A. if the South had succeeded in breaking away?

The final expression of economic union in a non-gold standard world, is a common currency. But the theory of optimum currency areas has run into the sand. A number of considerations have been put forward, but no way has been found of putting numbers to them in actual situations. Nor do we know whether the embellishment and strengthening of a customs union is likely to lead to political fusion or whether, on the contrary, common political institutions are the key to full economic union. There have been several post-war political federations in the ex-colonial world, imposed from above, which have broken up, and it is too early to say how much economic unity is likely to remain among the fragments. The German Zollverein, which was established in 1834 preceded political unification by 30–40 years; but unification was achieved (as it was in Italy) by military means. We do not know whether political union would otherwise have developed organically from the Zollverein, nor even the extent to which the Zollverein smoothed Bismarck's path.

We can indeed believe that a world political authority

with a monopoly of nuclear arms and ultimate control over all forms of military force, would be desirable – indeed, it is the greatest blessing that could be conferred upon mankind. But short of world federation, would a West European federation increase or diminish the dangers we face? (The effect on Eastern Europe would of course have to figure in any discussion of this question.) And will the emergence of regional federations, adding to the number of super- or semi-superpowers, be more likely to hasten or to retard the ultimate world goal?

A flourishing common civilisation is certainly possible without political unity, as both classical Greece and Renaissance Italy demonstrated. (In the case of Greece unification was followed by cultural decline.) The great disadvantages of political disunity in both these cases were internecine warfare and vulnerability to external conquest. Machiavelli, after all, called for Italian unity to drive out the barbarian hordes. A war between the countries of Western Europe is not very high on the list of present dangers; and it is not immediately clear whether in a nuclear age a West European political union would increase or diminish the chances of remaining neither red nor dead.

As these questions are probably unanswerable in our present state of knowledge, the best I can hope to do is to approach a few of them indirectly. This involves a few brief remarks on certain unfortunate features of British post-war external policy which are necessary to put the European debate into perspective. I shall then go on to compare the assumptions behind the E.E.C. with a few other international economic organisations, and finally, add a few words about the U.K.'s own economic interests, and the economics of British membership. My main purpose is to suggest that the 'anti-Europeans' and the supporters of the present Community philosophy have between them been allowed to get away with too much. There is a third approach which has just as much claim to the label 'European' as that of the Commission in Brussels, but is very different in some respects.

Mention has already been made of the desire to play a leading role on some supposed world stage, which has characterised British policy for so long. This approach, together with a preoccupation with prestige and dignity at the expense of bread-and-butter issues, led to a whole series of errors in British post-war policy.

Irrespective of where they stood in the E.E.C. debate, most people would now agree that the refusal of governments of both parties to take part in the European movement in the early 1950s, when we could have helped to write the club rules, was an error for which we will continue to pay for many years. It is more controversial but valid to point to the crippling of the British economy in the post-Korean rearmament drive of 1950–53, from which many of our subsequent weaknesses sprang.

It is less often remembered that the Labour Government of 1964 began its career by arranging a personal briefing on the proposed import surcharge for American leaders. European capitals were informed by diplomatic cables over the weekend when only duty officers were present. U.S. officials themselves suggested that the Germans and Dutch be informed, but too late – one of the most expensive mistakes the Government made. During all the negotiations on international liquidity and in the various financial crises of the 1960s, it was an occasion for remark if the British representatives differed from the American. (Interestingly enough the Bank of England was less wholeheartedly Atlanticist than the Treasury.) General de Gaulle's statements about Britain's transatlantic allegiance were not quite as far off the mark as it was customary to believe.

Another example of our determination to keep up the pretence of Great Power Status was the insistence on a so-called independent nuclear deterrent. This was one, although only one, reason for the overinvestment in expensive aerospace and atomic energy projects, so heavily condemned by the Brookings Report.

At a different level there was the failure out of pride to fund the sterling balances after the war, and the long-continued refusal to contemplate any changes in the international role of sterling. The Basle arrangements of 1968 could have been made many years before had the will been there. Part of the same psychology was the attempt over so many years to preserve the pound at an overvalued exchange rate. Apart from internal political motives, the expensive battle to save the $2.80 rate was also tied up with the belief that if the pound 'went' the dollar would go too, and that this would embarrass Britain's relations with the U.S. and unleash a world economic calamity.

The best-known example of our over-committed overseas role was, of course, the pile-up of expensive commitments in the Near, Middle and Far East. This urge to be involved everywhere has some distasteful features. The British Foreign Secretary felt he had to endorse American policy in Vietnam, while the 'Labour Left' in taking the opposite line shared the same belief in the immense importance of British attitudes in a conflict where we were not involved. It occurred to no one that the Government might refrain from public pronouncements on them. This itch to intervene and take sides unnecessarily was seen at its most repellent in the Nigerian conflict, where death and suffering may have been prolonged because of a departmental commitment to Federation in London.

There is no one neat formula which will cover all these cases. Sometimes it has been the desire for a special relationship with the U.S.A., sometimes the post-imperial hangover, sometimes vanity and prestige mongering, and often a mixture of different ingredients. There is no guarantee that close political or economic links with Western Europe will weaken these urges. Indeed it is easy to think of people who were both committed Common Marketeers and fervent believers in East of Suez. Nevertheless, I would venture the hope – I certainly cannot prove it – that closer association with Western Europe will *on balance* weaken the temptation to indulge in the wrong sort of overseas and prestige activities. The drive to join the E.E.C. is itself an example of the British internationalist tradition. A pro-European view on my part involves the judgement that European entanglements are likely to prove some barrier to more harmful entanglements further afield. It also involves the judgement that a Swedish or Swiss position for the U.K. is, even if possible or desirable, not a political runner. Nothing can, however be taken for granted. If ever the West European countries form a sort of political community, the battle between the Cobdenites and the Palmerstonians will have to be fought afresh on a Continental scale.

One of the most appealing single arguments is that if we were a member of some form of European Community, the British Government's own powers over its citizens would be diminished. Measures such as travel restrictions might become more difficult; and there would be freedom to move house and take employment over a far wider area than at present – both important gains for personal liberty. But again we should be cautious in view of the ability of the French Government to get away with travel restrictions in periods of 'crisis'.

The possibilities of a common European foreign policy should be cautiously stated, if we are not to fall into interventionist traps. It is probably still utopian to hope for some co-ordination to avoid the financing and arming of rival sides in areas such as the Middle East or Nigeria. Yet I have no doubt that this is an infinitely more worthy eventual aim than the payment of customs duties to the Brussels Commission. A joint European attitude on Vietnam might not have been terribly effective, but a degree less ludicrous than statements in the British House of Commons.

Rumours of a U.S. withdrawal from Europe should be taken with more than a pinch of salt – the removal of the U.S. nuclear guarantee is extremely unlikely. There is still probably more reason to fear an excessive than an inadequate U.S. response to a Russian move. Yet there clearly are defence problems which it would pay European countries to discuss together; and there is a case for a strictly conventional European defence force on a modest scale.

The Community's Philosophy

Membership of a European group of the kind I have been discussing would mean that consultations with Bonn, Paris, or Rome would take the place of the instinctive reaching for the hot line to Washington when a monetary or foreign policy problem arises. It also involves the removal of barriers to prevent movement and trade on our small Continent. But it is very different in flavour from the Common Market Commission and the more enthusiastic Eurocrats, who emphasise three other features – *harmonisation, integration* and the *institutional approach.*

The best example of the effects of making any kind of integration an end in itself is the Common Agricultural Policy. The one principle on which the Commission is immovable is that there must be a common price for each commodity, a common method of dealing with imported supplies and a common set of rules for treating domestic farmers. At first glance this looks like the agricultural equivalent of the industrial customs union, where free trade within E.E.C. establishes a common price for comparable products in any one centre – apart from the operation of goodwill, brand loyalty or imperfect information. These similarities are deceptive. For the outstanding difference – which puts the two systems leagues apart – is that the common industrial prices are set by market forces, while the agricultural ones are set by official decree. To enforce this there have to be variable levies at the frontier instead of a common external tariff. But once the point of self-sufficiency is reached, even this is not enough, and the Brussels authorities have to buy up supplies, store them or dump them in third countries. The next stage will almost certainly be the imposition of national production quotas.

The E.E.C. countries were not ready for a genuine free market in agriculture when the Rome Treaty was signed and are not so today. But the C.A.P. has done more than recognise this fact. It has *increased* the degree of farm protection over and above which would have been likely if individual markets had not been 'integrated'. If the E.E.C. did not exist, a German Government might still want to give heavy support to domestic farmers. But it would still pay Germany to meet her residual import requirements in the cheapest world market. Enjoying self-sufficiency in a greater number of products, a French Government would be more concerned to shut out imports. But in view of the lower costs of French farmers, the level of internal support prices would be lower than in Germany. The E.E.C. bargain thus combines an import and financing policy suited to French needs with a price level suited to the high cost German farmers.

With hindsight it would have been better to have kept agriculture out of the Common Market until more progress had been made in moving farmers to other jobs (a movement which the C.A.P. has so far only retarded). This judgement would not, however, appeal to those who prefer integrated policies to good ones. If production quotas are now imposed, we will have reached the paradoxical position that in order to save a certain institutional apparatus, the high priests of European unity will themselves have brought back discrimination on national lines. (Should this happen, the economic damage and the nationalist element will be reduced if all quotas can be bought and sold in the market.)

Federalist sentiment was not the only reason for the stress on harmonisation. When the Brussels Treaty was negotiated in the 1950s and the Commission established, post-war Europe had little experience of countries with different levels of wages, social services and tax systems trading freely and to mutual advantage. France had not yet had the devaluation and internal financial reforms of 1958–59; and it was not appreciated that co-ordination could take place through the price mechanism, as well as through meetings of Ministers and officials. Failure to realise this was one reason for the devotion of so much time and effort to the harmonisation of turnover tax systems and the efforts still going on to harmonise social security, industrial training and a hundred and one other activities.

The outstanding example of perverse would-be harmonisation has been the unsuccessful campaign of the Brussels Commission against exchange rate changes. Whether or not it will ultimately be desirable to have a common currency from Iceland to Sicily – or for the whole Western world – I do not pretend to know. A self-confident Federal government might rationally decide to allow separate currency areas between which exchange rates could vary. What is certain is that any attempt to freeze the pattern of European currency parities before the conditions for a unified currency area exist would be disastrous, not least to the functioning of the Common Market itself.

Movements of prices and competitive conditions in member countries have often been closer to those of third countries than to fellow E.E.C. members. Germany had had to revalue three times in the twelve years up to 1971 and France had to devalue twice. Thus both the mark and the franc were nearer to the dollar in their movements than either was to each other. If the parity changes in these two currencies had been prevented, Germany would have had to tolerate excessive inflation and France excessive unemployment – or alternatively impose all sorts of open and hidden controls on trade and payments.

The Common Market Commission sees in these very difficulties an opportunity to play a role in fiscal and monetary policy – where so far it has had almost no influence – by calling for more co-ordination of member-policies. There is the obvious objection that in attempting to freeze exchange rates before successful co-ordination has actually taken place, the Commission has put the cart before the horse. But there is a more subtle point too. Even if member governments show a dove-like willingness to co-operate, there may be no feasible pattern of internal financial policies in member countries which would secure an acceptable behaviour of unemployment and price levels. In the past few years a degree of financial toughness in France, sufficient to have preserved external equilibrium without parity changes, would have involved an unacceptable degree of unemployment; and in Germany it would have involved unacceptable inflation. A grand European co-ordinator would have had to face the fact that the more he helped the Germans to avoid inflation, the worse French unemployment would be, and the more he helped the French to avoid unnecessary unemployment the worse German inflation would be.* It will take many years before reactions of employers and unions, and general public psychology, become similar enough throughout Europe for a single currency area to be on the cards. Meanwhile, by opening up trade, the Common Market has increased the sensitivity of each member country's balance of payments to small differences in costs, prices, delivery dates and other

* The two countries have differing 'propensities to inflate'. In the terminology of Chapter 2, the expected rate of inflation, which cannot be reduced without an abnormal increase in unemployment, has tended to be higher in France.

aspects of competitive performance, without providing an adjustment mechanism – apart from substantial parity jumps. The drawing rights available will do nothing to bring about payments adjustment, but will simply finance deficits for a while; and one knows from U.K. experience that this can be a dubious blessing. The same applies to plans for pooling reserves.

There is no economic reason why floating parities should be incompatible even with the Common Agricultural Policy. The translation of Unit of Account prices (effectively dollars) into fluctuating national units is a simple computer job. As Graham Hallett has shown,[1] the tensions arise not from exchange rate movements as such, but from divergent movements in the productivity gap between agriculture and industry in different countries. Imagine that productivity in German industry and agriculture rise at the same pace. Then, if wages rose less than in other countries or productivity more, appreciation of the mark might still have been necessary. But the fall in agricultural prices, measured in D-marks would have been compensated for by a favourable movement in German farm costs relative to those of other countries. The trouble occurs when German industrial productivity rises more quickly than agricultural productivity in a way that is not parallelled in other Community members. In this situation, an exchange rate which secures overall equilibrium, and can be borne by German industry, will harm German farmers. An exchange rate that keeps the farmers happy will, however, result in a chronic German surplus. The dilemma reflects 'real' rather than monetary divergencies and would emerge sooner or later whatever the currency regime.

So far the Commission has managed by playing on various national hopes and fears to create a climate of opinion in the Community adverse to fully floating rates. But the same emphatically does not apply to compromise forms of flexibility, involving small discretionary changes in parities. The effects of such a system on the Common Agricultural Policy will be no different in kind, and smaller in degree, than those arising from normal revaluations or devaluations. Indeed, nothing could have been more disruptive than the

large premia and discounts which prevailed in forward
markets when the mark and franc rates were distrusted, and
which enabled German merchants to buy French grain for
future delivery at far below the price which German farmers
were receiving.

The basic mistake made by the Commission's sympathisers
is a too-simple identification of the *results* of a far-reaching
economic union with the *means* of achieving them. If the
Community were being formed today, unified exchange rates
would be seen as the end product of many years of evolution,
rather than something to be superimposed at an early stage.
More generally if the Community had to be renegotiated
from scratch, it would surely take the form of an industrial
free trade area or customs union with some *ad hoc* bargains
on agriculture to make the arrangement palatable to agricultural countries. On the other hand, there would be
stronger mechanisms for co-operation in defence, foreign
policy and financial diplomacy.

The Commission

Meanwhile let us not forget one simple piece of political
sociology. This is that the Common Market Commission will
inevitably push proposals, and 'solutions' to problems, which
increase its own role. This is perfectly natural and proper.
Its behaviour here is no different from a Whitehall department or I.C.I. Indeed, one has considerable professional respect for both the Commission and the French negotiators.
These are the two parties who have known what they wanted
and gone out to get it. One wishes one could say the same of
the British Government or of the other Seven Community
members. But meanwhile let us recognise the Commission for
the interested group that it is. Idealistic support for it is entirely misplaced.

It is worth glancing for a second at the work of one or two
less glamorous organisations: G.A.T.T., I.M.F., the Bank for
International Settlements and O.E.C.D.'s Working Party
Three. These have been successful experiments in *international government* in two ways. They have persuaded
countries to take into account the interests of the wider

Western community; and, where unilateral moves, such as devaluations, have occurred, there have been consultations and co-operative efforts to minimise disruption. Moreover, while claiming no sovereign powers, the staff of these bodies has built up a marginal, but at times decisive, role over and above individual national governments. One could indeed argue that they are now dealing with more important problems and exercising more influence even inside Europe than the Community institutions. It would be wrong to suppose that tariffs no longer matter; but, as a result of successive rounds of G.A.T.T. negotiations, they are down to a level where businessmen feel, perhaps rightly, that non-tariff barriers such as customs procedures, hidden discrimination, diverse technical standards or the purchasing policies of public bodies, are more important. The Community has so far not had much success in dealing with non-tariff barriers; and it is by no means obvious that it will make more progress with them than G.A.T.T. or O.E.C.D.

U.K. Entry

It is agreed against this broader background that we should examine the effect on the U.K. of the negotiated entry terms. In doing so, we should not go by a crude balance of payments or price index calculation. The standard of living should not be confused with the cost of living; and a major historical decision should not depend on the accident of the pattern of international exchange rates and money costs that happens to prevail at any one time.

Much the most important element in the true cost of membership is agriculture. This is so both in the narrow sense of a measurably adverse impact on the British economy, and in the broader sense that the E.E.C.'s agricultural policy is the most wasteful of all its operations. The biggest measurable aspect is the British contribution to the Community budget, by far the greater part of which is devoted to farm support.

The costs of membership consist of two main items: the rise in the price of imported foodstuffs and the direct British contribution to the Community budget by means of transfers

of levies and Customs duties (plus a variable fraction of the
V.A.T. yield), to Brussels. We will start with the direct
British budgetary contribution.

We are here on moderately firm ground. For the British,
contribution in 1973, the first full year of membership, has
been fixed at 8.64 per cent. The estimate of British officials,
that the E.E.C. budget will then have risen by 10 per cent
from its present level to reach about £1,400 million, may or
may not be fulfilled. But at least this gives a rough idea of the
magnitudes involved. On this basis, the U.K. gross contribution would be £120 million and the net U.K. payment, allowing for receipts, would be about £100 million.

In the course of the 1970s we will be gradually transferring
an increasing proportion – ultimately reaching 90 per cent –
of both our agricultural levies and our customs receipts,
directly to the E.E.C. The Community will also be able to
exact a contribution of not more than the yield of a 1 per
cent Value Added Tax on member countries. By 1980, the
fully automatic system will be in operation. The working
assumption (not disclosed in the 1971 White Paper) is that
the British gross contribution might then reach 25 per cent
of the total, and that gross U.K. payments will be around
£400 million; and, on present Community policies, about
£100 million might be received in return. 1980 is distant
and much will depend both on the agricultural situation in
the Community and on its farm policies, in which Britain, as
a member, will have a say. It is recognised by all concerned
that no one country will accept an unfairly large total burden;
and the size of the total budget, the pattern of payments from
it or the methods of financing it, could be changed to prevent
this happening. Nevertheless, it will be the first year in
which the full costs of the C.A.P. will be paid without any
transition or tapering off; and any exposition of the burden
must, therefore, focus upon it.

Secondly, we come to the food imports. The eventual
annual addition to the food import bill forecast by the 1971
White Paper is £50 million – a small and innocent sounding sum, well within the margin of error of any calculation.
Yet this needs to be broken down into two components – a
£190 million *increase* in the *price* of a given quantity

of food, and a £140 million *decrease* in the volume of food imported.

To pay for the extra £190 million in higher prices we shall have to export more for nothing in return. By contrast, the saving in import volume is much less important. For to replace imports by home-grown food involves a diversion of capital and labour from other activities. Indeed, there is a positive cost in inefficiency if more resources are pushed into home agriculture as a result of the E.E.C. There will also be a loss of consumer welfare as the result of the shift to a less preferred pattern of consumption (compared with what people would choose to eat at relative prices prevailing on world markets). The most commonly quoted example is a predicted shift from beef to pig meat.

Marcus Miller has attempted to convert from the crude balance of payments arithmetic of the White Paper to the more significant costs in terms of real income.[2] This involves taking into account the terms of trade loss from the parity charges required to make the payments across the exchanges. He comes to the conclusion that the 1971 White Paper implied an eventual real income cost of £500–600 million per annum. This *excludes* the loss in efficiency resulting from greater protection for British agriculture and the loss in consumer welfare resulting from the forced shift to less preferred foodstuffs.

If one compares these eventual costs with a possible G.N.P. total of £50,000 million (expressed in constant 1969 prices – the same base year as in the 1971 White Paper), the eventual cost amounts to 1 per cent of the G.N.P. Let us adjust it upwards to $1\frac{1}{2}$ per cent to take account of these other sources of inefficiency and of the existence of more pessimistic estimates. From 1973 to 1980, we should be having to subtract from the normal annual growth rate of 3–4 per cent about 0.2 per cent per annum.

Agricultural Reform

Before going on to discuss the benefits to weigh against these costs, it is worth adding a word on the chances of the Community moving towards a more sensible agricultural system.

One of the few blessings of the rapid rate of world inflation is that it has reduced the effective degree of agricultural protection in the E.E.C. Community farm prices have risen less than would be required to maintain the real value of the farm guarantees. Of course, the farmers will fight back. But there may be a chance of channelling the extra aid into re-settlement assistance, or specific aid to categories such as hill farmers, instead of indulging in wasteful all-round increases in prices. The political balance between farmers and the rest is likely to change radically. Even among the original Six, the proportion of the working population in agriculture looks like falling from a quarter in 1958 to no more than a tenth in 1980. We should welcome – instead of being embarrassed by – the American pressure on the E.E.C. to modify the protectionist impact of the C.A.P.

The Benefits

What does Britain have to gain in return for the costs? The strongest reasons for joining the Community are to be found in the intangible and unquantifiable politico-economic arguments with which I began, and not in any of the fashionable industrial arguments. It is difficult to attach a precise meaning to all the talk of a mass market mysteriously appearing out of nowhere. The C.B.I. has calculated that the removal of the tariff barrier around the Six will just about compensate for the loss of Commonwealth Preferences.

The more sophisticated pro-E.E.C. arguments assume that membership will provide some form of competitive jolt. From this point of view the abolition of the (somewhat higher) British tariffs towards the E.E.C. will be just as important as the elimination of E.E.C. tariffs towards the U.K. The main argument is that both the rewards of success and the penalties for failure will be greater than they are at present in a more competitive market.

There is, in addition, the controversial view that because of 'dynamic economies of scale' the growth of output per head in any one sector depends on the growth of total output in that sector, and that on a national scale growth will be faster if it is export led. If there is something in these theories, the increased specialisation brought about by membership could provide a boost to the growth rate.

It may be asked why import liberalisation and G.A.T.T. tariff cuts have not provided the same kind of stimulus that may be expected from the E.E.C. Part of the answer is that they have. There was an acceleration in the British growth rate between the mid 1950s and the mid 1960s. Since then demand has had to be held back, first because of an over-valued exchange rate and more recently because of domestic inflation; and this has, in turn, depressed investment.

It is also possible that businessmen would respond more to membership of the E.E.C. than they would to an arithmetically equivalent widening of their market resulting from tariff or exchange rate changes. They may do so because they regard the E.E.C. tariff cuts as irrevocable, because they think that they are less likely to be hampered by non-tariff barriers within an enlarged Community, or simply because they are influenced by headlines and speeches about 'a home market of 300 million'.

The Insurance Premium Aspect

As so often is the case, some of the most important arguments are negative. After the Nixon measures of 1971 – involving a surcharge and other even more undesirable restrictions which were totally unnecessary once the gold window was closed – the risk of a lurch towards protectionism in the U.S. which other countries would then be tempted to copy, is very real. We can no longer take for granted the post-war liberal trading world. Membership of a customs union embracing, for practical purposes, the whole of Western Europe and linked by trading agreements with most of the developing countries provides very important safeguards for British trade.

The argument is a subtle one. For some of the American protectionist pressures are in reaction to slights from the E.E.C., both real and imagined. An enlargement of the E.E.C. will – given present Community policy – increase the area in which the Americans complain of discrimination. On the other hand, it will increase the chances of the E.E.C. adopting a more outward-looking policy, as French commentators seem to have conceded. Moreover, even if an enlargement of the E.E.C. does increase the risk of American protectionism, there would have been that risk even without the enlargement.

The insurance premium argument points not to the presence of desirable effects but to the mitigation of some otherwise extremely undesirable changes in the international economic environment. Some economists have alleged that this is the only good argument ever put up for joining the E.E.C., and I would concede that the others are vague and debatable. But a good argument cannot be destroyed by qualifying it with the adverb 'only'.

The Real Dangers

A zero or negative weight should be attached to the conventional wisdom about advanced technological industries, such as aerospace or computers, in which Europe 'needs to unite' if it is to compete with the U.S. Whenever he hears of 'advanced technology', the European taxpayer ought to be on his guard, as it is normally a pretext for making him subsidise high prestige industries which do not pay commercially and which, as in the case of the Concorde, may have hideous social and economic side-effects, which do not appear in the books of departments or companies involved. The fact is that, owing to their large defence overheads, the Americans do have a comparative advantage in certain high technology products; and it is entirely rational to purchase these products from the U.S. or make them under licence, rather than develop them on this side of the Atlantic.

The real disadvantages of the Community are not the ones conventionally voiced. They relate rather to the form of state-subsidised capitalism favoured by many in the Brussels Commission and their supporters.[3] This originates from a desire to seek not the best solutions to problems, but those which will increase the role of the Community institutions. The archetypal example is the suggestion that Britain's agricultural payments should be balanced by a huge expansion of the Community budget in areas such as 'advanced technology' and 'regional policy'. The height of such fashionable wisdom is that Britain should prop up ailing Continental farmers in return for Continental support for British industrial lame ducks.

But it would be quite unnecessarily defeatist to assume that this concept of the Community must prevail. There are other visions of the future of Europe. The repeated failure of the Commission to prevent the floating of the German Mark is one sign of this. The battle between those who desire a producer-dominated, *dirigeste* Community and those who would prefer one sensitive to the consumer and to market forces is entirely open; and the dividing line cuts across nationalities and across political parties.

Assessment

To sum up, membership of the E.E.C. involves, on the view presented here, annual payments rising gradually to about 1–2 per cent of the national income. These are not small sums even though they will be approached gradually in annual steps of a couple of decimal points of a per cent. In return for this entrance fee we obtain (a) a substantial chance of an eventual boost to the growth rate comparable to the cost; (b) a modest chance of a much more impressive boost; and (c) an insurance against a world-wide retreat into protectionism. For the same money we also gain some insurance against possible political dangers and a gamble on certain political benefits.

6 An Excess of Pragmatism (Monopoly Policy)*

> The government ... must act by general and equal laws, that are previously known to all the members, and to all their subjects.
>
> David Hume, 'Of the Origin of Government'

Objectives

The title of this working group. 'The Objectives of Economic Policy' is a temptation first to jot down the familiar list: growth, price stability, full employment and balance of payments equilibrium and then guess how much monopoly policy contributes to each, and how it could be altered to contribute more. But to do so would be wrong. Monopoly policy has a very important effect on two other objectives: the development of a free society and the rule of law. Nor can these other aspects be banished to some imaginary conference of political philosophers taking place somewhere else. The effects of policy on freedom and the rule of law are sometimes only evident after a careful economic analysis; and if the economic student neglects them, he cannot rely on anyone else to take them up in his place.

One vital aspect of a free society is freedom of choice. The concept embraces Sir Isaiah Berlin's 'negative freedom' – the absence of coercion. But it extends a little wider. If a laundry closes down in a small town, leaving me a smaller range of choice as either a consumer or a laundry worker, it would be stretching the meaning of words to say that I am coerced; but my freedom of choice has certainly been narrowed.

* This paper was first published in the Department of Trade and Industry report *International Conference on Monopolies, Mergers and Restrictive Practices*, H.M.S.O., 1971. This contained the proceedings of a conference held in 1969.

In the laundry case an ideal index of my real income would show a reduction, even though my earnings and the general price level are unchanged. But the possibility of this kind of phenomenon being taken into account in any foreseeable national income calculation is so remote, that for policy purposes we should regard freedom of choice as an objective in its own right rather than as an aspect of any narrowly economic goal. If we do this, we are able to consider other aspects of a free society, such as the concentration of power in the hands of individuals and groups, which could hardly be brought into even a theoretical real income calculation without distortion.

The concept of 'the rule of law' that I am using here has been outlined by Hayek in the following words: 'It is because the law-giver does not know the particular cases to which his rules will apply, and it is because the judge who applies them has no choice in drawing the conclusions that follow from the existing body of rules and particularly facts of the case, that it can be said that laws and not men rule.'[1] Conformity with abstract and impersonal law should not be the only criterion of policy; but it should be one and given some weight in our discussion.

The slaughter of restrictive practices

There are two main classes of problem in 'monopoly' policy: restrictive arrangements between otherwise independent firms; and the size of economic units.

The British economy has moved in radically different directions in these two areas. It has become much more competitive, in the sense that there are fewer price rings and cartel-like agreements, but it has also become more monopolistic, in the sense that a handful of firms – sometimes only one – hold a dominant position in far more industries today than a few years ago.

In his chapter in the *Brookings Report on the UK*, Professor Caves speaks of 'revolutionary changes' in British attitudes to restrictive practices. Before the Second World War some 30 per cent of factory employment was estimated to have been in trades covered by price rings and other restrictive practices. In his 1967 Report, the Registrar of Restrictive Practices was able to declare that 'the mass of price fixing agreements has been dismantled and there is no backlog of important agreements awaiting their turn to be referred to the court'. The use of information agreements as a possible loophole has been made more difficult by the 1968 Act, giving the Board of Trade power to call for their registration. This was in great contrast to the position less than ten years before when over 2,000 agreements to fix prices, restrict entry or share markets, were registered under the 1956 Act.

Resale price maintenance was a later victim, but it has been crumbling since the 1964 Act. A few years before it was believed to cover about a third of consumer goods sold to British householders. The Monopolies Commission has condemned the fixed scale of fees to estate agents, and other professional practices are still being investigated by the Commission.

Action against restrictive practices scores high marks for all objectives of policy. It releases resources previously tied down in inefficient operations, gives the consumer a choice between different combinations of price and service, breaks down barriers to entry, and makes it easier for distributors to offer a wider range of products. This branch of policy also scores highly from a 'rule of law' point of view. Certain classes of agreements are treated as prima facie against the public interest, and exceptions must be justified along established gateways to the Restrictive Practices Court rather than to a Government department. Of course, the Court does in practice have to make an economic judgement, sometimes of a peculiar kind. But the area of predictability is much greater than in the case of monopolies or mergers, and the scope for free-ranging Ministerial judgement, or behind-the-scenes dealing, very much less.

It is interesting that even this branch of policy was originally on a discretionary and 'pragmatic' basis. Under the first Monopolies and Restrictive Practices Act of 1948, the Monopolies Commission was required to examine each agreement referred to it, on a case-by-case basis with no prior presumptions of any kind. But the same kind of case and the same kind of argument occurred so frequently that the desirability for a more general approach became obvious. The seal was set by a Report of the Commission on Collective Discrimination which, by a majority, declared practices such as collective boycotts, exclusive dealing and aggregated rebates against the public interest.

Recent legislation would undoubtedly have been much less effective in a different industrial climate. The majority of registered restrictive practices and resale price maintenance agreements were abandoned without a fight. Had each agreement been defended in court, the backlog of cases would have lasted many years (and until the 1968 amending Act the Registrar lacked effective sanctions to secure registration). Continued full employment and good order books undoubtedly made firms more willing to abandon defensive arrangements born of the Depression years. It was just because the business climate was less 'competitive' in one sense of that much abused term that it could become more competitive in another.

The effects of competition

How effective the slaughter of restrictive practices has been in promoting productivity or holding back prices is not easy to ascertain. There is some circumstantial evidence on the prices front. For year after year in the second half of the 1960s, the rise in prices in relation to wages was less than had been expected by official and unofficial economic forecasters. Indeed, it was because prices at factor cost rose so little that the Treasury had to step in so frequently to 'mop up' purchasing power by raising indirect taxes.

This lag in prices below forecasts reflects both a falling secular share of profits in the national income at least before tax and allowances and some spurt in productivity. The N.E.D. Office estimates that pre-tax trading profits net of capital consumption rose by an average of 1.9 per cent p.a. between 1960 and 1967. During this period weekly wage earnings rose by over $5\frac{1}{2}$ per cent. In 1968, when devaluation was expected to give pre-tax trading profits a sharp boost, they rose, after allowing for stock appreciation, by only 2.7 per cent.

Despite all the international league tables, British productivity has been accelerating for over a decade. Allowing as best one can for cyclical influences and other disturbances, real G.N.P. per person employed was rising at about 1½ per cent p.a. in the early 1950s, just over 2 per cent in 1955–62, and by 1966 had probably accelerated to about 3 per cent. The underlying movement since then is particularly difficult to determine, but it has probably risen to about 3–3½ per cent. By historical British standards this is a remarkable performance.

Clearly many factors must have been at work. There are, however, grounds for giving competition policies some of the credit. In the course of the 1960s, the British home market actually became more protected. The Dillon Round tariff cuts of 1961 were rather small, perhaps 7 per cent for most industrial countries. After they had taken place, the effective level of protection in Britain was increased by the import surcharge of 1964–6, which was followed by the 1967 devaluation – and the imposition of Import Deposits in 1968. These dwarfed the first instalment of the Kennedy Round Tariffs Act introduced in July 1968.

The secular decline in the rate of return on capital, and the share of pre-tax profits in the national income, was probably due to a number of factors: overall demand management; the differential effect of prices and incomes policy on prices; overseas competition (despite the protective barriers); and perhaps a decline in the marginal productivity of capital. Policies on restrictive practices can certainly find a place within this catalogue. One would expect a search for lower-cost, labour-saving methods in such a situation; but the low level of aggregate investment could pose a threat for the future. The way to deal with it is not to back-pedal on restrictive practices, or allow excess demand to be created, but to alter those elements of economic policy which artificially depress the share of profits.

The growth of concentration

A large share of credit for the improvement in productivity should also go to the takeover bids of the period. This thought might make a good transition to the more topical half of monopoly policy: mergers and size. Yet one must be careful. For a takeover bid need not lead to a merger to have a healthy economic effect. On the contrary the healthiest kind of takeover bid is probably one that is successfully shaken off at the cost of an internal revolution in the courted firm. One might argue that the healthiest event in post-war British company history was I.C.I.'s unsuccessful bid for Courtaulds in the early 1960s, which failed, but led to a change towards a much more profit-conscious management on the part of Courtaulds. The battle was severely condemned as a bad advertisement for capitalism by leader-writers and M.P.s of different political persuasions; and this should have given a clue that something desirable was taking place. A comprehensive study of firms which have successfully escaped the takeover bidders would make a useful piece of research.

Unfortunately, however, this has not been the typical situation; and in the majority of practical cases there is no escaping the vexed question of how one assesses the gains which are claimed for larger units and weighs them against the possible costs.

There has been a rapid increase in the degree of concentration since the end of the war. Research into the share of the fifty largest units in total gross profits in manufacturing and distribution suggests, according to Professor Caves, a rise from 1908 until 1938, a fall between 1938 and 1950 and a rapid rise in the 1950s. The trend of the 1950s is shown even more clearly by another measure: industries in which the three largest firms controlled more than 50 per cent of net output. These accounted for 12.7 per cent of British manufacturing in 1951 and 21.7 per cent in 1958.

The movement accelerated in the 1960s. This is demonstrated by a Monopolies Commission survey of quoted manufacturing companies with net assets of more than £0.5m at the beginning of 1961. The twenty-eight largest companies in this survey held 39 per cent of total net assets in 1961, but by 1968 their share had risen to 50 per cent. The total population of companies, defined in the above way, fell from 1,312 in 1961 to 908 in 1968.

Clearly not all the increase in the degree of concentration

has been due to takeovers and mergers. Existing large companies have increased their share of the market and some smaller concerns have gone out of business. But the merger movement has been the biggest as well as most dramatic influence in recent years. The book value of the net assets acquired by quoted companies in the eight years covered by the Monopolies Commission survey was £2,750m, no less than one-fifth of the total. Figures for individual recent years are even more startling. Net assets transferred by mergers were 1½ per cent of the total in 1966, 3¾ per cent in 1967 and 6½ per cent of the total in 1968.

It would be absurd to project this series into the future, as it would show the whole of manufacturing industry under one big firm before very long. Even so, recent trends show an increase in the degree of concentration which would have been found highly alarming by the Founding Fathers of the U.S. Anti-Trust Acts.

A further reason for concentrating attention on mergers is that it is much easier to prevent the birth of an industrial giant than to break it up once it has been formed. The simple presumption against higher concentration found in U.S. law will not do in the U.K., or in most other European countries, for well-known reasons. In economies which are so much smaller than the American, a high degree of concentration will arise with firms of much smaller absolute size. In addition output per head on this side of the Atlantic has not yet reached a level where economic losses can be completely disregarded in any comparison with the wider social benefits of competition and diversity. There is no escape from some form of cost benefit approach.

Criteria for mergers

The economic analysis of mergers has been outlined in a recent paper by Professor Beesley in terms of the trade-off between the cost-reducing and price-increasing effects.[2] If the reduction in costs per unit exceeds the increase in profit margins arising from increased market power, then the merger should be allowed, *provided that there are no alternative ways of gaining the benefits.* If the price per unit is likely to rise, there will be still a gain in potential national income but consumers as a whole will be worse off; and a judgement will be required on the likely duration of the monopoly situation, as well as of the uses to which the merged concern will put its profits.

This sort of analysis normally leads to the conclusion that, while horizontal or vertical mergers need to be carefully watched, conglomerates present little danger and should be allowed. Such a conclusion reveals the dangers of too narrow a preoccupation with individual industries and firms. If one takes into account the range of choices available to citizens in a wider sense, the degree of concentration in the whole economy begins to matter. An individual's freedom of choice in his working life is intimately connected with the number of potential employers among whom he can choose. Moreover, the heads of the top few dozen companies have a great deal of influence of a less tangible kind. They exercise considerable powers of patronage; they can set fashions in subjects ranging from architecture to economic policy. They can make certain political views respectable among influential opinion, as well as finance their propagation. The list of such activities is open-ended; and provided the firms which exercise such influence are sufficiently numerous and diverse in outlook, society is likely to be freer as a result of this rivalry. Professor Milton Friedman has a perfectly legitimate point when he describes how some of the victims of the McCarthyite persecution found refuge in the private sector.

But if one reduces the number of such top managements sufficiently, and allows them to approximate to a common type, what was an influence for diversity becomes an influence for uniformity. The point of greatest danger is in fact the utopia of the 'indicative planner' when all the industrialists who matter can meet in one room, together with Ministers and officials, and arrive at a common view. Whether this is seen as monopoly capitalism dominating the Government on the Marxist model, or as free enterprise selling its birthright, the result is equally alarming.

It may be a price which small cohesive countries such as Sweden or Switzerland have to pay for political and economic independence. But for countries like the U.K., where the public school cum trade-union tradition of the 'done thing' is already great enough it would be a total disaster. There is still sufficient diversity in the British economy for the threat to be a distant one; but it is a reason for not allowing the reduction in the number of decision-making units revealed in the Monopolies Commission Report to go on indefinitely.

The ideal criteria for judging the potential anti-competitive effects on large units cannot be set out in any simple way. The old formulae of market shares, or the elasticity of demand facing the merged concerns, have well known deficiencies. Freedom of entry is often more relevant than static market shares. The existence of a certain number of conglomerates on the look-out for fields with above average rates of return can actually promote new entry in monopolised industries. The threat to freedom arises if there are too few very big conglomerates taking up too large a part of total activity. A distinction has also to be drawn among 'conglomerates' between the large diversified organisation with a single top management, and the holding company which leaves its subordinate managements as separate entities and is only interested in the financial return on the assets invested. Thus the balance to be struck is an extremely delicate one.

If we are interested in freedom of choice, a takeover by an overseas concern may often be preferable to a domestic merger. The introduction of a different approach to business life, and of a firm less likely to play according to the local rules, gives an increased range of choice to both the customer and potential employer. On the narrower economic front, numerous studies have shown the return on capital output per head and level of exports of U.S. subsidiaries to be on average higher than those of native British companies.

It would be foolish to deny that there can be problems of conflict of jurisdiction. The governments of both the host country and of the parent may have rival claims over subsidiaries. It would also be desirable to have more international European companies, which would add an element of variety to the business scene, and would put a brake on the spread of a uniform American-type culture throughout the Continent. In the meanwhile, the same wider social considerations, which should cause one to welcome a substantial overseas stake in local industry should make one reluctant to see U.S. predominance in too many industries, on the Canadian model. For as the proportion of U.S. ownership goes beyond a certain critical range it becomes an influence for uniformity, instead of diversity, and a restriction of the range of choice.

It has often been stated that firms which might seem monopolistic on a national scale are not so when viewed as part of the international market. Even the new giant, G.E.C.-English Electric has sales well below those of General Electric of America and is of approximately the same size as Philips of Holland, or Siemens of Germany. The possibility of combining effective competition with larger units is one of the better economic arguments for British membership of the E.E.C.

Efficiency and intervention

The whole discussion on balancing the gains of larger units against the loss of competition presupposes that larger scale would provide efficiency in a country like Britain. The argument for this proposition is roundabout and devious, but is not necessarily false.

It is difficult to find any direct correlation between size and efficiency. A study by Professor Bain in the 1950s quoted by Caves found that if the average U.S. plant was taken as 100, U.K. plant size in the median industry was seventy-eight. This is hardy a convincing explanation for comparative productivity, when we note that the corresponding figure for France was thirty-nine, for Canada twenty-eight and for Sweden thirteen. A study by G. F. Ray of the National Institute found no observable tendency for German export performance to be particularly superior to British in industries where German advantage in plant size was particularly marked.

Professor Caves suggests, however, that small scale interacted with high product differentiation and low capital intensity to produce a comparatively low level of productivity. A P.E.P. survey has also shown a strong correlation among *firms* between size and both export volume and export expansion, although the relationship levelled off once the level of 1,000 employees was reached. This suggests that some further concentration may help to improve the terms of trade at which we can stay in payments equilibrium.

The Monopolies Commission has had since 1965 to vet the efficiency arguments advanced for mergers in order to balance them against the dangers of increased monopoly power. The new development is that the Commission is sometimes required to express a view on the efficiency aspects, even where it sees no serious threat to competition. It recommended in 1969 a ban on Rank's bid for De La Rue because it believed that the 'efficiency and trading volume' of the latter would be adversely affected, and not for any reason of monopoly policy.

There are two dangers in bodies such as the Commission setting themselves up as judges of efficiency: the economic risk and the threat to the rule of law. The Monopolies Commission found that the proposed Unilever–Allied Breweries merger would do no harm to efficiency and might do a little good, while the Rank–De La Rue merger would have reduced efficiency. These conclusions do not follow at all clearly from the data in the Commission's reports. Someone looking at the latter might easily have predicted that the verdict would be the other way round. The Commission's view must have been based on subjective impressions not fully documented. The threat of departures of senior executives in a contested bid was the Commission's only important explicit argument – thereby establishing an extremely dubious precedent.

Three main arguments have been used by the Monopolies Commission for disputing the market's judgement on the merits of a bid or a takeover, which have nothing to do with monopoly policy:

(1) In a contested bid the Commission may have more information than shareholders in either company.

(2) Shareholders may pay too much attention to short as distinct from long term prospects in their market judgements.

(3) Bids may be made for mysterious 'financial' or 'fiscal' reasons, unconnected with either efficiency or the exploitation of monopoly power.

The first argument at most suggests that the Commission should publish the information it has gained to improve the judgement of shareholders. (One should distrust unsupported judgements of the Commission made on the basis of information too secret to reveal.)

The second argument is more serious. I have no wish to argue that the rate of time discount thrown up by stock market prices provides a social optimum. Many economic theorists would argue that it discounts distant gains too heavily. My point is that if the Board of Trade or Monopolies Commission wish to introduce a different rate of discount, this should be announced and explained; and similar principles should be applied to different situations.

At this point, the economic arguments link up with the 'rule of law' ones. The real danger of present official policy is not that the market is sometimes over-ridden; but that the fate of companies should depend neither on the market, nor on known rules of public policy, but on the unpredictable reactions of a shifting group of individuals invested with public powers. This is not a mere abstract fear of Austrian or Chicago economic metaphysicians. It is a serious matter when the fate of a company depends neither on the decisions of its management, nor on market prices, nor on known rules of public policy, but on the accident of whether Mr X happens to be sitting on the appropriate Monopolies Commission or I.R.C. panel.

The danger becomes even greater when judgements about desirable industrial structure are laid down not even by the Monopolies Commission, but by Ministers of the Crown. An example was the President of the Board of Trade's temporary 'ban' in the late 1960s on any merger among the 'Big Five' of the Lancashire textile industry or against any overseas take-over of the firms. Despite this ban he made clear that he had no objection to Courtaulds' plans for diversifying further into fibres. The President's move did not derive from any known principles concerning excessive concentrations. The ban on any overseas takeover does nothing to preserve competition in the industry and may even hinder it. The 'standstill' was in fact a highly political intervention in a power struggle involving *inter alia* I.C.I., Courtaulds, Viyella and English Calico in which the Board of Trade came down against Courtaulds on one issue, but in its favour on others; and on the whole

Courtaulds – unlike Viyella or I.C.I. – probably had reason to be satisfied with the outcome as things stood in June 1969.

The supposed 'fiscal' or 'financial' motive for takeover, unconnected with efficiency, requires further elaboration than the vague references in official pronouncements. Increases in the private return on assets, unconnected with their more efficient utilisation, must surely reflect anomalies of company or tax law, such as the allowance of debenture interest but not dividends against tax. Even if it is impossible to deal with such situations by general changes in the law, it should at least be possible to set out in advance the types of financial manipulation which the Board of Trade regards as relevant to merger considerations.

The case for general rules

There is no reason to derive public policy from only one value. The goal of a government of laws rather than of men is one of several desirable aims between which compromise has to be struck.

It was easy to sympathise with Mr Crosland's reluctance to emulate the guidelines of the U.S. Department of Justice. These suggest that mergers of specified size – for example if the two firms each have 4 per cent of the market or more – will be automatically challenged in a 'highly concentrated' situation where the four principal firms already have more than 75 per cent of the market. Such guidelines would indeed be unsuitable to the British economy. But because guidelines are difficult to formulate, it does not mean that the attempt should be abandoned. The so-called pragmatic approach is no cause for pride or self-congratulation. The judgement of those who believe in treating each issue on its merits is likely in practice to reflect the fashion or political pressures of the moment.

The balance has moved much too far away from publicly known and predictable rules to the discretionary judgement of public officials. If this argument is accepted, imperfect publicly known rules may be better than no rules at all. Simply to stimulate discussion, it might be worth making the following suggestions for a more generalised approach.

(1) Separate accounting information should be provided for the original units of mergers above a specified size along the lines recommended by the Monopolies Commission. The accumulation of case histories should gradually improve the market's ability to judge merger proposals.

(2) When the Commission wishes to override the market on questions of efficiency (as distinct from monopoly), it should be required to publish a reasoned, numerate argument. Where the market is condemned for taking too short a view, there should be an illustrative calculation of the rate of discount of the future implied in shareholders' evaluation. The alternative 'social' rate of discount preferred by the Commission should be disclosed and its implications explained.

(3) Where a merger brings the degree of European concentration up to a specific level, there should be automatically a U.K.–E.E.C. review of the tariff structure. The onus should be on the parties concerned to demonstrate why all the relevant tariffs should not be reduced.

(4) When a merger would bring the danger of concentration in an industry up to a specified high level – say two leading concerns with over 65 per cent of the market or three with over 80 per cent of the U.K. market – the onus should be on the management concerned to demonstrate in a published document that reductions in costs or improvements in service would counter-balance the monopoly risk. Otherwise the merger should be automatically referred to the Commission.

(5) For conglomerate mergers, there should be three bands of asset sizes. New conglomerates with assets above, say, £250m, should be presumed against the public interest for reasons discussed earlier, unless the management can provide very good reasons why an exception should be made. In an intermediate area – say £100–£250m – a reference to the Commission should be automatic, while in the lowest band conglomerate mergers should be left to run their course. The figures mentioned are purely illustrative; the methods of valuation of assets would have

to be specified; and there may be a case for alternative criteria in terms of turnover.

These suggestions are a rough first shot, put down in the hope that they will be replaced by better ones in the course of discussion. Their weaknesses are ground for amendment or replacement, not for a retreat into a spurious pragmatism.

Part Three

Policies, Nations and Individuals

7 Uplift in Economics

All plans of government, which suppose great reformation in the manners of mankind, are plainly imaginary.

David Hume, 'Idea of a Perfect Commonwealth'

Too many Englishmen are never happy until they have converted a technical or political question into a moral one – by which they mean finding someone to blame, even if it is only the public at large. This escape into moralising is the device most frequently used to avoid facing difficult issues about which the experts are bound to disagree; and nowhere is this pseudo-moral approach more rampant than in the economic sphere.

The temptations are certainly great. On the one hand, the policy issues are technical, and the technicalities seem particularly uninviting. On the other hand, the country's economic difficulties have – or appear to have – a connection with the daily activities of all the working population, whether in the boardrooms, factory or sales offices, in a way which could not be asserted of defence or foreign policy.

These two contrasting characteristics combine to produce a most congenial climate for the pseudo-moral approach. Such an approach pervades *The Times*'s letter columns, political speeches, TV current affairs programmes, and it has even infected the pronouncements of professional economists. Its effect is to take economic policy out of politics and into the arena of the preacher, nursemaid and infant-school teacher.

* Reprinted from *The Spectator*, 1 July 1966.

In approaching their subject in this way, television producers or leader writers are doing no more than follow in the path of twenty years of exhortation from housemaster Chancellors on the theme that it is 'up to all of us' to win the House Colours. To take a sample from the last budget speech, which could have come from any post-war Chancellor: 'The battle for success will be won or lost in the factories, workshops and boardrooms of this country.... The Government pin their faith to the willingness and understanding of the British people to make the policy of productivity, prices and incomes succeed and so secure our triple objective.' In other words it is supposed to be not the Chancellor's job to manage the economy but that of the general public; and, as a result, every budget speech becomes a sermon.

Not all cases of the pseudo-moral approach are as easy to spot as good old-fashioned ministerial exhortation. A different species of pseudo-moralising emerged in the reaction to the Selective Employment Tax. The tax was designed as a means of raising revenue, spreading the tax burden more evenly, increasing productivity, and promoting the country's export capacity. It is arguable that the tax was badly designed for the purpose. But much of the public discussion has evaded the real argument. Both critics and supporters have assumed that taxes are a moral instrument designed to reward righteous activities and punish wicked ones. Indeed, the initial reception of the tax by Conservative and Labour backbenchers was in some ways extraordinarily similar. Each group wanted to penalise particular activities of which it disapproved; and there was even a great deal of overlap about what these activities were. The main disagreement was that the opponents of the tax were more incensed by the rebate to printers of dirty books and makers of gambling machines, while the supporters found sufficient compensation in the taxation of gambling clubs or West End hairdressers.

Apart from a few economists nobody seemed interested in *removing distortions* from the tax system, so that people could make up their own minds what to buy on the basis of prices that reflect relative costs. On the contrary, one has had the extraordinary spectacle of right-wing critics asserting that the tax is not selective enough and leading a hue and cry to make it more selective, in the company of the most committed left-wing interventionists.

Nowhere is the belief that we should sit in collective judgement on the virtues and vices of different ways of earning a living more apparent than in incomes policy. The real purpose of an incomes policy is to keep down the price tags in the shops without resort to large scale unemployment.

To persuade the unions to do a deal, this basic anti-inflationary ingredient has had to be tied up in a wider package, including a number of logically unrelated 'social justice' measures, such as a capital-gains tax and better social security benefits. The separate aim of adjusting discrepancies between different groups of workers in favour of the lower-paid, has been grafted on to the economists' idea of incomes policy, in the hope of making the latter more palatable. There would be no objection* to a bargain of this kind, if only there were some sign of it being honoured.

Presentation of incomes policy in these terms does however have the unfortunate side-effect of increasing the popular passion for asking unanswerable questions such as: How much is a nurse worth? Should the doctors have been given such a large rise? Are the seamen paid enough? Even if they are not, should they have gone on strike? Given the chance to moralise in this way, most people will have little time to spare for the less emotive arithmetical truisms which incomes policy is really about.

A pattern of relative earnings based on market forces has much to be said against it. But at least it does not attempt to pass a judgement on the moral worth of different groups of human beings. Supposedly 'social' evaluations of the relative worth of different people's occupations at best reflect the market values of a generation or two back. At worst they favour the groups which happen to hit the newspaper head-lines or make some sort of appeal to people's unconscious guilt feelings.

There is one other bad habit in the popular approach to economic controversies, which does not necessarily involve the pseudo-moral approval, but in practice often runs in

---

* I would now say 'less objection' in view of the arguments of Chapters 1 and 2.

tandem with it. This is to suppose that economic issues are about what goes on in factories, workshops and export sales offices rather than about government policy. While it is taken for granted that defence policy is something for the Defence Secretary or the Cabinet or their professional advisers to decide and carry out, no such assumption is made about economic policy. This is regarded not as a matter for the Chancellor or the Bank of England, or even the pressure groups that act on them, but for ordinary people in their daily jobs. Clearly there is no harm in an investigation of, say British salesmanship, backed by specific examples. But such a treatment easily slides back into the pseudo-moral approach of sitting back and discussing 'Whose fault?' instead of asking what public policy can do to change (or live with) the attitudes described.

The common element in the different varieties of pseudo-moral approach is the tendency to downgrade technical assessment and political choice alike, and put in their place the passing of judgement on our fellow citizens. Ultimately, of course, economic policy does involve moral issues. For it is a branch of politics; political decisions have effects on human beings, and it is sophistry or worse to draw an iron curtain between decisions taken in private and public life and exclude the word 'moral' from the latter. The objection of the moral approach to economics is that it is 'moral' only in quotation marks, and that the morality it expresses reflects an intolerance of a free society, an unwillingness to let individuals make their own choices about what to buy, how long to work, and how to behave themselves in their leisure.

An alternative approach might start with the premise that courses of public self-improvement should have a very low priority in government activities. The Government's main economic task is to promote the greatest possible prosperity on the basis of people's behaviour as it actually is, rather than as ministers think it ought to be. Its first job in this connection is to maintain the internal and external balance of the economy – and this is a technical job which certainly cannot be done by the public at large, and which no recent British government has yet succeeded in getting right. The old-fashioned liberal economist believed that the best way to run the economy was to interfere as little as possible. The old-fashioned socialist planner favoured a great deal of government intervention and regulation. Neither supposed that preaching virtue could make a large contribution to the running of the economy. But then neither school was brought up on admass economics designed to evade all issues.

8 Is Economic Growth a Mistake?*

Shower upon him every blessing, drown him in a sea of happiness, give him economic prosperity, such that he should have nothing to do but sleep, eat cakes, and busy himself with the continuation of his species, and even then out of sheer ingratitude, sheer spite, man would play you some nasty trick. He would even risk his cakes and would deliberately desire the most fatal rubbish, the utmost economic absurdity, simply to introduce into all this positive good sense his fatal fantastic element.

Dostoevski

To imagine, that the gratifying of any sense, or the indulging of any delicacy in meat, drink, or apparel, is of itself a vice, can never enter into a head that is not disordered by the frenzies of enthusiasm. I have indeed heard of a monk abroad, who, because the windows of his cell opened upon a noble prospect, made a covenant with his eyes never to turn that way, or receive so sensual a gratification.

David Hume, 'Of Refinement in the Arts'

Is Britain really in such a bad way economically? It is astonishingly difficult to give an honest answer to the question. It depends so much on the level at which it is asked. When talking to someone who is interested in how well the Government is managing the economy, a cold douche of pessimism is required, especially if the person asking the question believes the official propaganda about redeployment and 'toughness'.

But if, however, the question is asked at a deeper level by

* Reprinted from *The Financial Times*, 5 June 1967.

someone – say a poet, or an art historian – who wants to know whether there is anything fundamentally wrong with the British economy, and whether this is a symptom of a more deep-seated national malaise, then a very different answer is needed. An L.S.E. economist, E. J. Mishan, does well to remind us* that most of our economic problems are pseudo-problems, or more accurately, self-created problems. We have created a balance of payments problem by simultaneously keeping the exchange rate pegged and refusing to control imports. We have created our internal problems by a Canute-like refusal to face the fact that price stability is inconsistent with very high post-war levels of employment, and that a choice must be made. There is very little justification for the present mood of national guilt, which magnifies our problems of economic management but does less than nothing to solve them.

There is, however, an interesting difference between Mishan and most of the other economists who have called for import controls or exchange rate changes. While most of the latter have done so in the name of faster growth, Mishan advocates them for precisely opposite reasons – as a way of ridding ourselves from our present obsession with growth, efficiency, modernisation and of opting for a less abrasive human environment.

The paradox is not as great as it seems. For both Mishan and the more intelligent of the 'growthmen' would agree that we do not *need* to accept everything that is 'new', 'modern' and 'dynamic'. As Mishan remarks, the word 'need' should not be invoked in framing economic objectives. It is up to us to balance the gains against the losses. We can safely disregard the politicians and other public figures who proclaim that we have no real choice, that we must either move forward or backwards, that we must 'face the 20th century' or go bankrupt. In fact we do not stand at any cross-roads or parting of the ways, and we have, if we disregard self-imposed political restraints, a very wide choice of policy ends.

How then are we to use our freedom of choice? Should it be to secure faster growth, or is, as Mishan argues, the continued pursuit of economic growth detrimental to wel-

* E. J. Mishan, *The Costs of Economic Growth* (Staples Press, 1967).

fare? Mishan certainly makes a powerful case against an urban civilisation where 'lorries, motor cycles and taxis belching fumes, filth, stench, snarling engines and unabated visual disturbance have compounded to make movement though the city an ordeal for the pedestrian, at the same time as the mutual strangulation of traffic makes it a purgatory for motorists.'

But is this an argument against economic growth, properly understood? By far the best part of Mishan's book, Part II, is not really an attack on growth at all but a popular exposition of Welfare Economics and an ingenious application of it to present day problems. Welfare Economics is not, as its title might suggest, about the Social Services, but about those benefits and damages inflicted on other members of society in the process of producing or using certain goods which do not enter into market costs and prices. Despite the light relief provided by the intrusion of the author's more extreme prejudices, despite even the attack on financial journalists whose aptitudes are 'not difficult to pick up', the book deserves to be widely read.

Among Mishan's most interesting suggestions is that privacy, quiet and clean air should be recognised as an *amenity right*, which no firm or public authority should be allowed to violate without compensation. One of the illustrations he uses, that of a new airport to which local inhabitants object, has more topical relevance than even the author would have imagined. He points out that a more rational decision could be made if the airport authorities had to compensate the local inhabitants and such compensation payments entered into the calculations of those taking the decision.

In developing his policy ideas, two Mishans are in evidence. There is the strident opponent of the 20th century who would like to ban all cars and airlines, and the liberal economist who puts forward the more tolerant alternative of *separate facilities* for people of different tastes. Just as there are smoking and non-smoking carriages, there could be residential areas where no motor traffic – or only public transport – is allowed, and a selection of mountain and coastal resorts deliberately deprived of airline services and motorised traffic. After all, no 'enthusiastic pace-maker' need feel deprived if some areas are set aside for those with old-fashioned tastes.

Mishan has many other worthwhile ideas (mixed in with the intolerant ones) for making life more bearable, such as adapting the Underground to carry freight at night and restricting shop-deliveries to between 3 and 7 a.m. (or better still by a levy on deliveries later in the day).

But what has all this got to do with economic growth? Mishan would presumably argue that the recognition of amenity rights, so that people had to assess a wider range of costs in their profit and loss calculations might reduce an index of physical output. But it is surely an error to identify economic growth, sensibly understood, with any increase in the production index, however brought about. If people choose to take increased wealth in the form of more leisure rather than more goods, this is their affair. Gross Domestic Product per hour worked would be a better index than the crude output figures. If it were possible to legislate for Mr Mishan's suggested amenity rights, the published figures would be still further improved as an index of the type of growth that is worth having. But the fact that even then growth would be difficult to measure sensibly does not mean that it is a bad thing. One very attractive way of taking out the fruits of faster growth would be to make the working environment itself less abrasive, even at the cost of some sacrifice in production. But to be able to do this without making unacceptable inroads into real wages we will require *more rapid* growth in our productive potential. Paradoxically, one of the best arguments for more rapid growth is that we could then more easily afford to be inefficient.

There is, admittedly, more to the argument than Mr Mishan's attribution of stupidity and insensitivity to those whose use of language is different from his own. Unlike Mr Mishan, I would guess that a 4 per cent growth rate, even as conventionally measured, would bring more opportunities for constructing a decent environment than if growth is only 2 per cent; and I would require strong evidence that this slow growth was due to a voluntary cut in hours, or some unmeasurable gain in amenities, to throw over this presumption.

One of Mr Mishan's own main policy aims is, quite rightly, to secure more resources for the replanning of our towns and

cities. Is this more likely to happen if the growth of our productive potential is slow or fast? There is absolutely no reason
to suppose that a poor growth performance is helping to make
Britain a more congenial or human place. The Prime Minister's measures of July 1966 which held back growth were not
intended to save our Cathedral cities.

9 A Balance of Payments ABC

It is easy to observe, that all calculations concerning the balance of trade are founded on very uncertain facts and suppositions.

David Hume, 'Of the Balance of Trade'

The balance of payments need never again be the nation's main economic problem. The principal limitations on our standard of living and on the aims we can achieve are the efficiency with which we use our resources, and the extent to which they grow. To improve our performance in this respect should be the principal aim of economic policy. The gaining of exports, or the saving of foreign exchange, should never be an independent objective of policy to be pursued irrespective of the effects on efficiency or personal liberty. To suppose otherwise is to confuse means with ends. One can do no better on this point than to quote Para. 23 of the excellent 1970 C.B.I. report *Britain in the World*:

> To resist changes in parities, deficit countries have, of necessity, introduced restrictions on imports, exports and capital movements. These restrictions, which can be of a fiscal, exchange control or other administrative nature, represent some of the costs of maintaining the present system, since all restrictions on trade and capital movements impede the exercise of sound business judgement in the management and development of industry, thereby reducing the efficiency of the economy.

A word should be said on the operational meaning of a

* Extracted from an introduction to a report by a private study group.

payments deficit. Under the present system the authorities are committed to selling foreign exchange for sterling in the market to prevent the rate going below the official lower limit, and to buy foreign exchange to prevent the rate from going above the upper limit. Such support operations, when the pound is under downward pressure, are, of course, a drain on our reserves; and they cannot go very far without borrowing from the I.M.F. or other central banks. They are the actual manifestation of a payments crisis in terms of specific operations.

All that is definitely known is the amount of foreign exchange gained, lost or borrowed by the authorities; and more emphasis should be put on the C.S.O. presentation in terms of 'total currency flow'. Balance of payments statistics are simply attempts to estimate the source of these flows. The conventional definitions of the balance of payments cover only a fraction of the total flow. The inflow of funds to London in 1969, for example, was twice the estimated 'basic' payments surplus. Movements of short term balances or 'leads and lags' in commercial payments may, at any one time, heavily outweigh the changes in the trade and long term capital accounts.

These considerations show the importance of confidence and of not doing anything to upset it needlessly. The publication of a monthly 'trade gap' or 'surplus' which excludes 'invisibles' is one example of self-inflicted damage. The remedy is not to suppress the monthly figures, but to redefine them to incorporate the tentative estimate of invisibles already given in the notes to the Board of Trade Press notice, but not included in the main calculation. The impression given by official statements, often inadvertently, that the balance of payments is mainly a matter of physical exports and imports, is also unfortunate. The distinction between visibles and invisibles, like the related one between goods and services, has no intrinsic economic interest, but arises from the fact that the transactions are recorded differently.

While bad handling of the 'confidence factor' has, in the past, aggravated our difficulties, better handling of it will not necessarily be sufficient to prevent future problems. The long term direction of causation in the payments table is

TABLE 5: *Total Currency Flow, 1969*

£ million (rounded)

1. CURRENT BALANCE		+365
Investment and other Capital Flows		
2. Official long-term capital	−95	
3. Private investment in U.K.	+710	
4. Private investment abroad	−595	
5. Total of current balance and capital items = 'Basic balance'	(+385)	
6. Net Euro-dollar borrowing for overseas investment	+70	
7. Currency balances held by U.K. investors (increase−)	−75	
8. Total U.K. export credit (net)	−280	
9. Total U.K. import credit (net) (including finance of import deposits)	+280	
10. Balances (gross) of sterling area countries	+280	
11. Other short-term balances	−105	
12. TOTAL INVESTMENT AND OTHER CAPITAL FLOWS		+190
13. BALANCING ITEM		+185
14. TOTAL CURRENCY FLOW (i.e. 'total of official financing')		+740

(Source: *Economic Trends*, March 1970)

from the upper to the lower items. If the current balance is inadequate, the total financial flow will sooner or later turn adverse. The resulting crisis will be all the more severe if the gap has been temporarily covered by attracting to London 'hot' money, which has a habit of leaving just when it is most needed.

The vague term 'adequate' has been deliberately used to describe the required level of the current balance. Once debt repayments to the I.M.F. have been completed, the average current surplus will have to be approximately large enough to finance net 'long term' overseas investment, plus net export credit, minus the annual allocation of S.D.R.s and minus the average inflow of currency balances to London. Post-war experience suggests that we would be rash to count on any large net inflow of short term balances even if these were desirable. This tentative appraisal cannot be summed up in a precise calculation; and the required current surplus will have to be found by experience. A very rough guess, on the assumption that I.M.F. repayments have been completed, and excluding E.E.C. implications, would be that a current surplus of around £250m will be needed in an average year.

Having said this, a brief explanation is necessary of why the balance of payments need not be Britain's Number One Problem. An inadequate current balance of payments may arise from one of the following situations:

(1) A level of home spending which is excessive in relation to available resources. In that case the payments deficit is just a symptom of excess demand; and piecemeal measures such as import controls, or overseas investment restrictions, will fail because the suppressed expenditure will appear in another form.

(2) If excess demand were removed, however, and the current account still inadequate taking one year with another, this would be a sign that with the prevailing levels of international costs, prices and exchange rates and world trade, it did not pay businessmen to replace home demand with exports or import-saving activity on the scale required. This second situation is known in I.M.F. jargon as a 'fundamental disequilibrium'.

A balance of payments problem is thus a symptom either of lax demand management or of inappropriate ratios of home to overseas *money* costs and prices. Whether tackled by operating on home costs or exchange rates, what is wrong in such a case is essentially a set of numerical ratios. Developments entirely unrelated to our own efficiency, such as a wage explosion on the Continent, or a German revaluation, can transform a deficit into surplus or vice versa.

The balance of payments problem is thus in a very different category from, say, the limitation on growth imposed by a low level of productivity increase, which cannot be tackled by altering numbers on pieces of paper, as it reflects the basic efficiency with which we use our resources.

Commercial policy is an aspect of making the most efficient use of resources. It follows, from the above analysis, that a distinction should be drawn between commercial policy and balance of payments policy proper. Even if we had a world currency, or complete control over our money costs, or freely floating rates, it would still be necessary to assess the effects on our real income of, for example, different tariff levels or alternative arrangements for agricultural imports. Commercial policy is best decided on the basis of the arrangements which will maximise real incomes through its effect on the terms of trade and on resource growth, on the assumption that overseas payments are in any case in balance. Any attempt to use commercial policy to compensate for excess home demand or wrongly valued exchange rates will lead to distortion and damage.

10 Morality and Foreign Policy*

> A nation is nothing but a collection of individuals.
> David Hume, 'Of National Characters'

When we are faced with a political decision, whether it is the determination of the Bank Rate or the recognition of Communist China, factual knowledge by itself will not tell us how to act. When we have amassed the maximum of technical information about the probable consequences and implications of alternative courses of action, we still have to choose between them. We may make our choice on the basis of the results we desire to bring about, or in relation to some general principle to which we adhere (the two are not necessarily incompatible), or in some other way. But whatever procedure we adopt, no amount of empirical investigation or logical analysis can free us from having to make the value judgement involved in deciding how to act.

It is sometimes asserted that political actions in general, or foreign policy in particular, cannot be judged from a moral standpoint. This is a big departure from common usage, as we would normally suppose, at the very least, that any human act done deliberately, not under duress, and with effects on others (this last requirement may not always be necessary) can logically be judged from a moral standpoint. But even if we decide to use the word 'moral' in such a way that some or all foreign policy decisions either can be, or necessarily are,

---

* This essay, hitherto unpublished, was written in the aftermath of the Suez crisis of 1956. Some brief subsequent reflections are to be found in the Note to the Reader at the beginning of this book. If I were writing now, the treatment would in some ways be different, but on the main themes I am unrepentant. Indeed some readers may notice a relationship between the approach to foreign policy in this essay and that to economic policy in Chapter 1.

non-moral in character, this neither frees us from the need to choose nor tells us what choices to make; and nothing follows – one way or the other – from this linguistic choice with regard to issues such as the role of war or the desirability of adhering to U.N. principles.

Nevertheless, statements of the type 'Moral considerations are out of place in foreign policy' are made and in times of stress, such as the Suez crisis, they can become a subject of fierce controversy. People do mean something by remarks of this kind, though there are probably more meanings than speakers, and an examination of two or three possible meanings may be a useful way of introducing some general observations on the conduct of foreign policy.

The assertion 'Moral considerations are out of place in foreign policy' is sometimes meant as a well-justified attack on a certain approach – or rather family of approaches – to international affairs, an approach that is 'moral' only in quotation marks and is better termed moralistic. This approach is easier to indicate than to define.

In its extreme form it involves the view that the political colour of a government may be a sufficient reason for not holding negotiations which would otherwise have been held, and from which one's own side might have benefited; in the present world situation, according to this view bargains based on mutual self-interest should not be made with the Russians or the Chinese because of our disapproval of dealings with totalitarian regimes. And even less extreme exponents of the moralistic approach (who would, of course, resent the label) would regard it as a normal part of the professional duties of a Foreign Secretary to pass judgements on the desirability of the governments and political systems of other countries.

It would be wrong to give the impression that the moralistic approach is confined to right-wing Republicans. Ideological opposition to diplomatic dealings with tyrannies is deeply rooted in a section of the British Left and was evident in the case of Czarist Russia as well as Falangist Spain. Contemporary instances of the moralistic approach are the lectures read out to Western statesmen on their duties and obligations by 'neutralist' conferences in Cairo and Bandung.

The case against the moralistic approach has frequently

been made out, and will only be outlined here. What needs to be stressed is that this case does not – or need not – depend on the belief that, in some mysterious sense, foreign policy is a self-contained activity in which our normal ideas of correct behaviour towards other human beings can be ignored. Nor need it rest on any desire to weaken the rules and restraints which governments may aspire to observe in their international dealings.

The first argument for rejecting the moralistic approach is an empirical one. Although this approach may sometimes be rooted in a sincere desire to make the world a pleasanter place, its practical effect has usually been to increase violence and tension. Perhaps the main reason for this is that it tends to deprive diplomacy of its normal function of attempting to ease disputes without recourse to war and of negotiating a settlement when war has broken out. For once a dispute is seen, not as a conflict of interests, but as a struggle between good and evil, then bargaining with the other side is at best an odious expedient, at worst a betrayal of all that is sacred. And a war, once it has broken out, will be pursued until the enemy's system of government has been destroyed. This process was at work in the 17th century at the time of the Wars of Religion; in the 20th century its most disastrous fruits have included the 'War Guilt' clauses of the Versailles Treaty, the doctrine of 'unconditional surrender' and the U.S. refusal to have diplomatic relations with Communist China.

A second argument, which is specially important for those who believe that the above paragraph places too high a value on peace and order compared with other objectives, is that the principles most frequently proclaimed by the 'moralisers' are arrogant and presumptious. The assumption that people in one part of the world are in a position to pronounce on what form of government is suitable to other people in very different circumstances – or to lecture to them on how to behave – is, to say the least, unwise. But, even if we think we know what is best for the inhabitants of other countries, the attempt to impose this knowledge is intolerant. In Mr Kennan's words: 'Let us by all means, conduct ourselves at all times in such a way as to satisfy our own ideas of morality.

But let us do this as a matter of obligation to ourselves, and not as a matter of obligation to others.'[1] There is no reason to be tongue-tied about the excesses of Stalin or his successors, but it is not our job to prescribe to the Russians an alternative system of government.

It may sound a little more sophisticated to say that people living under dictatorial regimes should not be forced to adopt a constitutional democratic system, but should at least 'be free to make their own choice of system of government'. It is however often an unsatisfactory way out of the problem. For 'free to choose' is meaningless unless it is laid down how this choice is to be exercised and the usual suggestion is by means of elections or referenda. But unfortunately the habits of behaviour that make this kind of ballot box procedure more than a corrupt farce are the outcome of many years' evolution; they cannot be grafted on to countries that have only known the alternation of tyranny and anarchy. The Middle East is littered with the carcases of legislatures which have been the results of attempts to export the British or French constitution to that part of the world.

Eastern Europe is a special case, where there is clear evidence of opposition to Soviet-type Communism among a large majority of the population and where it would not be unduly moralistic to press for a closer approach to free elections in diplomatic bargaining with the Russians. But it would be moralistic to expect the Russians to agree to this from 'a change of heart' and without any concessions on our part.

A third argument against the moralistic approach is that it is usually put into practice with a hypocritical (although sometimes unconscious) inconsistency, which deprives it of any justification it might otherwise have had. If one is to base one's willingness to negotiate with other governments on judgements of their virtue, the first essential is that consistent standards be applied. Unfortunately, the exponent of ideological politics is usually as selective as he is severe in proclaiming his censure. Aggression becomes vicious when North Korean attacks South Korean but not when Guatamala is attacked by her neighbours. The rigging of elections is inexcusable when undertaken by the Communists in Eastern Europe, but bad form to refer to when carried out by the Government of Iraq. The death penalty for carrying arms indicates the new low to which tyranny has sunk in Hungary; in Cyprus it was just an unfortunate necessity.*

Quite separate from the attack on the moralistic approach, although too often confused with it, is another and very different meaning of the assertion 'Moral considerations are out of place in foreign policy'. This is that what is right and proper in the case of individuals and their dealings with each other is often not right and proper in the case of states, and vice versa. Indeed this is often said outright. It is a most dangerous assertion; and it is possible to oppose a moralistic outlook without in any way assenting to it.

Insistence on the irrelevance of beliefs about individual conduct to international affairs is, at the very most, an expression of one particular set of value judgements with which we are at liberty to disagree. It is particularly insidious, as it is often enunciated as if it were a fact of life which those experienced in international affairs have empirically established and we have therefore to accept; or still worse, it is presented as a conclusion which political thinkers are supposed to have established by *a priori* reasoning, or of which letter writers to certain newspapers have innate knowledge. There are perfectly sound reasons why a naturally humane person may decide on occasion to support a 'tough' foreign policy; he may, for example, believe that in the end less lives will be lost thereby. But it is probable that in many cases people are misled into supporting policies at variance with their own beliefs about right and wrong because they suppose that there is something 'in the nature of' politics or foreign affairs that makes these beliefs irrelevant.

---

* The consequences of this approach are illustrated in the following quotation from Prof. Butterfield: 'Many people will no doubt remember the tremendous shock which Hitler's invasion of Norway in 1940 gave to one's moral susceptibilities. A pupil of mine, who had been one of the most authentic of conscientious objectors, and had been exempted from military service, was so appalled by the attack that his whole attitude was shaken and he died not very much later in naval service. I have wondered sometimes what his reaction would have been if he had lived to know that Great Britain had had the prior intention of invading Norway – and this even irrespective of the desire to help Finland – and that Hitler, initially unwilling to undertake the adventure, had decided to forestall us.' [Herbert Butterfield, *Christianity, Diplomacy and War* (Epworth Press, 1954), p. 32.]

There are, of course, obvious differences between private and international affairs, which it is often important to stress. International affairs concern – though at one remove – large masses of people, rather than a limited number of identifiable individuals. For some purposes it may be helpful to regard relations between states as a special case of the interaction of organised groups, such as companies, churches and trade unions. Indeed, there are striking similarities between some aspects of power politics and the interactions of giant firms under *oligipoly* (i.e. rivalry among a small number of concerns in a single market). The business analogy has its deficiencies, but it is closer to the mark than the more frequent comparison of disputes between countries to quarrels among individuals. The treatment of nations and their foreign policies in anthropomorphic terms usually leads to confusion, as the issues involved often bear very little analogy to the disputes of private life.

None of these considerations should be allowed to blur the truism that a nation is composed of individuals* and that the 'national interest' is a short-hand way of referring to some of the interests of these individuals – that is to say, the national interest is a function of the interests of individuals.

Nations and national interests are convenient portmanteau terms with which we could not easily dispense (and which will be used liberally in the next section), but as complex entities we are more likely, if we are not careful, to talk of them in a confused and misleading way. When important 'national interests' are at stake, and patriotic emotion is running high, it would facilitate clear thinking to ask 'which interests?'; and, 'who suffers and who gains from an attempt to protect them?' The individuals whose interests are concerned in foreign policy decisions cannot always be named, as they can be in private life. Nonetheless, statements about nations which cannot be related to a series of parallel statements about individuals, not necessarily nameable, are nonsense, and dangerous nonsense.

Recognition of these rather obvious points in practice

---

* Some would include the dead and the unborn among the individuals; I accept this for the sake of completeness, despite the many objections that could be raised.

would have far-reaching implications. Take the question of 'armed conflict'. *If* one sincerely believes that it is wrong to kill other human beings except in literal self-defence, or in defence of one's family, then calling the killing a 'war' does not make it justifiable. Most people, who are not complete pacifists, would under pressure make some additional exceptions to the rule against killing. But even they may be misled into condoning killing and being killed through the uncritical use of cliches about 'national interest', 'duty to one's country' and 'military action'. Let us suppose that British troops have intervened on one side in a tribal conflict in South Eastern Arabia to safeguard certain oil interests. The action is likely to involve the death of British soldiers as well as of additional tribesmen. If someone is asked: 'Are you prepared to support the killing of a certain number of Arabs and send so many British citizens to their deaths to secure for the remaining individuals in Britain whatever benefits they may derive from more secure delivery of a portion of their oil supplies?' and the answer is 'Yes', there is no inconsistency in supporting the action. But if the answer is 'No', and the man has, nevertheless, been in favour of it, he has been inconsistent, and has been misled by the use of abstractions into the support of policies at variance with his own personal beliefs about right and proper human conduct.

It must be admitted that, even if people habitually spoke of foreign policy in individual terms, many extreme nationalist positions could still be logically upheld, although they would be expressed in terms of men's feelings towards other men of the same nationality and towards foreigners, and in terms of their feelings towards patches of soil, flags, buildings and other symbolic objects. But with the private value judgements at present common in Western countries, assessment in individual terms would bring a new perspective to many issues. Decisions involving loss of prestige – frontier adjustments, evacuation of colonies and the acceptance of arbitrary foreign nationalisations might well take a different turn if the financial costs and human sacrifices of a tough policy were weighed against its actual benefit to individual citizens, the swelling of patriotic breasts included among the benefits.

Acceptance of standard patriotic maxims, such as the duty

and honour of fighting for one's country may be – though not necessarily is – the result of a confused and uncritical use of 'country'. If someone believes that the benefits which may result from fighting to the individuals who remain alive are worth the loss of life, the possible grief of his family and the suspension of all the private plans which he and his friends have formed (and he has no scruples about going to war on the particular issue), then he is guilty of no confusion. And he is logically entitled, if he thinks they are important, to include feelings of pride in the extension or preservation of the influence of his government and in the valour of the soldiers of his own nationality among the benefits, for which it is so honourable to fight. But someone who accepts the need to fight for his country, but would not endorse the corresponding propositions about individuals is being inconsistent; and this inconsistency would be avoided, if the issue were not posed in terms of the misleading concepts of 'country', 'honour' and 'vital interests'.

It is quite probable that profound unconscious conflicts and projections are more potent influences behind wars than the perverse use of abstract language. But until we have worked out what would be involved in rational decisions about the employment of military measures and other forms of force, we have no standard by which we can assess the distortions brought about by unconscious conflict, and we have no target for which to aim in any attempt to reduce them or channel them into less harmful forms of expression.

Codes and Rules

Nothing that has been said so far is meant to imply that a Foreign Secretary should consider the interests of all the individuals in the world as of equal importance. It is perfectly reasonable and even desirable for him to make the advancement of the interests of his fellow-countrymen, within the framework of internationally accepted rules, the main objective of his policy, although not with such fanaticism that any interest is pushed regardless of the cost to individuals in other countries.

One of the most important reasons for holding this point

of view is a negative one; the alternative to the conscious and open pursuit of national interests turns out in practice to be not a genuinely disinterested and understanding attitude to all mankind, but the moralistic approach. The pursuit of limited and selfish objectives leads to a truce; a more lofty approach to a fight to the finish.

More positively, politicians and diplomats are representatives of people who normally place their own interests above the interests of foreigners. There is no need to discuss in this context the question of how far a democratically appointed Minister ought to take advantage of his power and skill to pursue policies, which would not be approved by the majority of the electorate if they were understood. It is clear as a matter of fact that if politicians attempt to move more than a certain distance away from the views of their fellow-nationals, they are likely to be repudiated. Moreover, there is nothing shameful or second-best in a body of individuals, whether a nation or a trade union, attempting to further certain interests which their members have in common. In periods of crisis, enormous harm is done by two opposite kinds of extremists: the so-called idealists, who, in the name of morality, ask the government to abandon any attempt to protect or to advance the interests of the inhabitants of this country, and the so-called realists who favour an international free-for-all uninhibited by the observance of any code of permissible conduct. (This last view is, incidentally, yet another meaning of the proposition 'Moral considerations have no place in foreign policy'.) I suggest as an alternative that good behaviour in international affairs consists not in abandoning the pursuit of national interest but in observing some generally accepted 'rules of the game' in this pursuit. The analogy with business behaviour is again useful here. Company directors are expected to seek high profits; their obligations are limited to what might be called 'fair dealing', a complex amalgam of law, custom and unwritten convention which rule out certain types of business behaviour.

The case for observing an international code rests partly on the disapproval which some of us have for certain instruments of policy, such as unprovoked aggression. But fortunately, it also rests on the belief that, just as it pays a company in the long run, although not in every instance, to observe the business code, so it normally pays a nation to observe the rules applicable to international relations. The dangers that arise if there are no recognised limitations on the type of policy which a country can pursue should need no emphasis today, when there is a risk that some state – especially a small country in an exposed area – might set off a world-wide conflict through miscalculation.

Part of the importance of an international code is simply that it increases the predictable element in the behaviour of states; and greater predictability helps to avert violent and ill-considered actions. It is worth noting in this connection that some of the rules of international good behaviour are, like the rules of the road, highly conventional in character; it does not matter exactly what the rule is, provided that it is kept. The convention confining territorial waters to a three-mile limit from the shore is a case in point.

The view is sometimes put forward that international rules are pious aspirations and that there is nothing to be gained from this country observing them, as other countries do not. This argument usually depends for its appeal on the identification of all international rules with the more ambitious aspirations of the U.N. Charter. The evolution of any code must be a long and painful process, but over at least a certain portion of the globe some distinctions between legitimate and illegitimate means of achieving objectives are beginning to emerge. The cynic looks at the struggle in Kashmir, but forgets that both India and Pakistan feel under some kind of obligation not to solve the problem by a simple invasion of the relevant territory. He draws attention to the Palestine conflict and the tensions within the Arab world, but forgets that some kind of sanction prevents the major Arab states from settling their differences by simple invasion – and despite the recent Sinai campaign the Palestine conflict has been kept within remarkably narrow bounds considering the bitterness of feeling on both sides.

No one will dispute that these sanctions have been deplorably weak and that they depend to a large extent for their effectiveness on the fear of Great Power intervention; but the argument of the cynic implies that what conventions there are should be thrown to the wind and that the Great Powers should give up trying to enforce them. The existence of an international code is one of the few obstacles to the complete subordination of the interests of weaker countries to those of the Great Powers. If any nation has a selfish interest in fostering it, it is the United Kingdom with its extreme vulnerability to political and economic breaches of faith.

Even in the field of Soviet–Western relations certain unwritten 'Cold War' rules have sprung up, although they are incomplete and badly defined. There are certain parts of the world, which, despite our protestations, we recognise as coming within the Soviet sphere of influence and others where the U.S.S.R. recognises that her interference will not be tolerated. (This was one of the reasons why the Western Powers did not interfere in Hungary and would have been badly advised to have tried.) These limitations on both sides depend mainly on the knowledge that their disregard may mean an atomic attack; but the point is that the rules, in so far as they exist, lay down how far each side can safely move and the unwritten conventions go far beyond the undertakings of the Atlantic and Warsaw Pacts.

The rules which we should do well to observe in international politics are related to U.N. principles and the pronouncements of international lawyers, but the relationship is not a direct or a literal one. For the principles and pronouncements are important in this connection only in so far as they provide an approximation to 'rules of the game' which governments endeavour to observe, although often with much backsliding in their actual conduct; or to rules for which force of example may secure a chance of such observance in future.

It is unfortunate that in their campaign against the British intervention in Egypt, Labour and Liberal spokesmen put so much weight on particular U.N. resolutions or on the probable pronouncement of international law if the issue were ever brought up at The Hague. Politicians excavate for propaganda purposes particular U.N. resolutions inconvenient to the other side, but no one expects that they will actually cause any country to reverse its policy, and it is no service to international standards of good behaviour to exaggerate the importance of numerical majorities in an Assembly based on the farcical principle of 'one country one vote'.*

The tentative rules which more enlightened statesmen aspire to observe are, in their nature, midway between legal and customary restraints. Laws and resolutions are too rigid a terminology by far to describe the tentative gropings towards an agreed standard of international behaviour. Perhaps it would be most appropriate to regard our aims in this field as the gradual evolution of certain notions about the 'done thing' and 'bad form' in international behaviour.

I have no wish to deny the possibility of exceptional cases, when it may be advisable to disregard the rules. There may be special circumstances where rigid observance is likely to lead to results of extreme undesirability in comparison with turning a blind eye. If we are convinced after long and careful study that a minor military act which is technically aggression would very much reduce the chances of atomic war, it would be perverse to refrain out of legalistic scruples. But this is not the type of move which should be undertaken when there is only a gambler's chance of success. *For in gauging the consequences of an individual breach of the international code we must – even from the most narrowly national standpoint – take into account not only its immediate consequences but also its long-term effects in disrupting the still fragile code of international good behaviour.*

A Weighting System

The recommendations advanced in the previous section go some way, I believe, towards providing usable criteria for foreign policy. But they leave aside some important questions: What do we do if we have qualms about a certain policy in a sphere where there are no 'rules of the game' that have gained general acceptance, or when we are wondering whether we ought not to impose restraints on our behaviour

---

* Although a rigid adherence to the letter of even the U.N. Charter may sometimes be unwise, there is a much stronger case for obeying U.N. *principles* than there is for automatic adherence to the interpretation of them provided by U.N. *resolutions*.

additional to those required by the rules? And conversely, just how desirable do the results of observing the rules have to be before we can contemplate breaking them? And undesirable to whom? And how much long-term weakening of the international code are we prepared to countenance in exchange for a short-term gain? Moreover, if the pursuit of the national interest is to be the main objective of foreign policy, what are to be the other objectives and what place is to be given to them when they conflict with the main one? In the first section it was suggested that the national interest was a function of individual interests. But what is the nature of the functional relationship? Which interests of which individuals are to count, and for how much?

The purpose of this section is to put forward a neo-utilitarian criterion which will not answer these questions but which, if accepted, will help the reader to answer them for himself. This criterion could well have been advanced earlier on, but it has been deliberately held back as the main part of my argument can be stated without it.

The criterion can most conveniently be presented in terms of an individual deciding between alternative courses of policy. To abstract from the question of whether a Foreign Secretary should be guided by his own value judgements or those of his countryman, I shall assume for formal purposes that he is voting in a referendum, or in a general election fought on foreign policy issues.

To make his decision he should, according to the suggested criterion, estimate as well as he can the probable consequences of the different alternatives to all the human beings concerned and make his choice on the basis of the effects he would most like to bring about. To do this he must fix his own subjective weights to determine the relative importance of different individuals and interests and the relative importance of short- and long-term consequences.

This criterion involves the value-judgement that it is the effects of an action which govern its desirability. It is therefore opposed to the doctrine that there are certain principles of absolute validity which should be followed irrespective of their effects. (There is however no reason why adherents of the latter view should not employ the neo-utilitarian criterion in all those cases which do not come within the scope of their basic principles.)

An immediate objection to this criterion will be that it would cause enormous confusion if everyone pressed for a foreign policy to suit his private fancy and that it would undermine that very predictability which it was earlier stated is so desirable in international affairs. This is an argument for deciding as much as possible on some rule-of-thumb basis, governed by the highest common factor of agreement and not bringing up private principles when they can be avoided; it is also an argument in favour of following the strategy of the second-best, when the answer with which the neo-utilitarian criterion provides a particular person is unlikely to be acceptable to many of his fellow citizens. But it is not an argument against the criterion as such.

A more serious criticism is that the criterion is an empty one, as it is in the determination of the weights that the whole problem lies. This emptiness is in part deliberate. I am suggesting that in deciding objectives, as distinct from tactics, a person should make up his own mind on the basis of his differing attitudes to the various other individuals in the world. This intensely subjective element will irritate many people. And there is something cold-blooded in attempting to give comparative weights to, say, the lives of British soldiers and foreign civilians, or to the lives of British soldiers and British civilian economic interests. But this is done by implication whenever the Governor of a dependency decides on the degree of harshness he should adopt in his 'emergency measures'. The weighting language is indeed an unattractive one and should be used sparingly; but when the actual decisions are being made, it is as well to use a language that brings out as explicitly as possible the value judgements involved in the various alternative policies.

It is easy to ridicule the weighting concept by asking questions such as 'How many Egyptian deaths would it be worth having to get the Canal and unseat Nasser? Would it be worth doing if 100 Egyptians were killed, but not if 101?' It would be absurd to pretend that we can talk about these weights with any exactness. But it is a fact of life, which it would be well to recognise, that many people who would be prepared to see a few hundred Egyptians killed to secure certain policy objectives would stop short of killing the whole population of the Nile Valley for them. To quote Professor Popper, 'The precision of a language depends just upon the fact that it takes care not to burden its terms with the task of being precise ... In physical measurements for instance, we always take care to consider the range in which there may be an error; and precision does not consist in trying to reduce this range to nothing, or in pretending that there is no such range, but rather in its explicit recognition.'

The main reason for putting forward this neo-utilitarian criterion is that it does justice to the great diversity in the extent of our feelings of obligations towards different categories of people. Most of us have strong feelings of obligation towards certain relations and close friends, and some feelings towards colleagues, members of the same class or cultural group, and people of our own race, nationality or creed. Different people would place these latter groups in different orders, but the majority would have stronger feelings towards them all than towards the human race in general.

Political conduct, designed to fit these successive circles of feelings of obligation, might appeal to some less exalted than an equal concern for all human beings; but surely it would be preferable to a narrow nationalism which arbitrarily rules out the small but existent sympathies that most people have for their fellow men of different nationalities? How far should we go in sacrificing the standard of living in this country to aid the underdeveloped areas? To what extent should we be inhibited from bolstering up (as distinct from merely dealing with) a pro-British regime that oppresses its own inhabitants? In such problems the use of the weighting concept would bring our foreign policy into line with our own personal outlook and values when not consciously talking politics, and do away with both the spurious altruism and the unnatural harshness which different groups of people are misled into adopting by the abstractions of political discourse.

Appendix on Neo-Pacifism

The object of this appendix is to state a particular point of view on the issue of pacificism which fits in with the general approach adopted in this paper, although it does not logically follow from it.

Pacifism, in its extreme form, is part of a complete renunciation of the use of force in human affairs. There is, however, another, and I believe more defensible, form of opposition to war, which might be called neo-pacifism. This holds that neither the defence of national interests, conventionally interpreted, nor even the defence of certain forms of government, is a sufficient ground for the murder and break-up of private lives involved in a major war. This neo-pacifist position has no connection with 'turning the other cheek' and does not necessarily imply that every military action has always been unjustified. It might support a small local war, if that were the only way to stop a more horrible conflict and it might even support a major war if the aim of the other side was, for example, racial extermination. The case for neo-pacifism is particularly strong, in the present East–West conflict. Here people may prefer Communist domination to fighting either because they believe that a Third World War would be even more unpleasant, or because they believe that, whichever side won, free institutions would nevertheless perish in the conflict. But the argument is a general one, which could have been put forward if the atomic bomb had never been invented.

For somebody holding such views, the best tactics would be to act *as if* he were in fact prepared in the last resort to preserve national interests and institutions. The orthodox argument, that unilateral disarmament would be *less* likely to prevent major wars than a policy of possessing sufficient military strength to deter a potential aggressor, is valid for the neo-pacifist. For an unarmed country without alliances is too strong a temptation for other powers and, sooner or later, one of them may start making demands. If the demands are granted for the sake of peace, this is likely to encourage fresh demands. A point will then be reached, where most citizens will be prepared to fight and push aside those leaders who prefer surrender to war. Thus, through a policy of weakness, the country lands itself unprepared into a war which might have been avoided. As a matter of prudence the neo-pacifist, knowing that he is likely to be in a minority, when the crucial test comes, should be the last to support an appeasement policy of the Munich type.

As put forward by a neo-pacifist, the policy of deterrence is undoubtedly one of bluff for if it came to the test and the deterrent failed, he would meet almost any demands rather than fight. This is not a crucial objection. The starting point of my argument is that many people do not share the neo-pacifist position and would fight rather than surrender; therefore the Soviet leaders would be well advised to assume that the West will defend itself with all available weapons.

But even if this were not the case and all the people likely to make the crucial decisions in the West were converted to neo-pacifism, it would still be worthwhile attempting a deterrent policy. For the Soviet leaders would still not know whether we were bluffing or not (especially if due self-restraint were to be observed in public discussion) and there would be a chance, if only a small one, of avoiding both Communism and a Third World War.

11 Wilson and the Left[*]

> He had been guilty of the offence, which of all
> offences is punished most severely; he had been
> overpraised; he had excited too warm an interest
> and the public, with its usual justice, chastised him
> for its own folly.
>
> Macaulay

There is an unsolved problem about Harold Wilson. Millions
of words have been written about him, in terms of both
extravagant praise and hysterical abuse. At times he has been
seen as a peacetime Churchill even by many members of the
City establishment – his finest hour there was in July 1966
when he pledged himself to the pound and defied the unions
to do their worst. But he has also been revered as a guide,
leader and friend by the heirs of Aneurin Bevan. Later, some
of these feelings of admiration changed to an equally exaggerated loathing; and many of those who were loudest to
shout his praises came to regard him as the great betrayer.

All this is difficult to reconcile with the actual flesh and
blood individual who is certainly not built on so grand a
scale, either of heroism or of villainy. Yet until the advent
of Enoch Powell, he seemed to exercise an unbroken fascination out of all proportion to his real influence on events; and
common antipathy to this individual has given rise to the
strangest of personal and political friendships.

Paul Foot goes some way to explaining the peculiar phenomena in a trenchant introduction on the new style of journalism and politics that crossed the Atlantic about the time of
the 1960 Kennedy campaign. The first essential of this tech-

---

* A review of Paul Foot's *The Politics of Harold Wilson* (Penguin, 1968)
first published in *Crossbow*, January-March 1969.

nique 'is the portrayal of the leading personalities in larger than life images'. The end product is a 'patchwork quilt of irrelevancy, sycophancy and personalisation'. Above all, this form of journalism is as devoid of scepticism as it is uninterested in ideas.

Harold Wilson played on this new mood to the full. As Paul Foot remarks, 'Hugh Gaitskell's answer to the charge that the Labour Party was out of date was to try to change its policies. Wilson's was to seek to change its image.' But an analysis of the fashionable and largely phoney 'new radicalism', conceived essentially in advertising terms, does not really explain why exactly Mr Wilson was so perfect an object for these techniques. Nor indeed were these techniques the whole story. There was something in the Prime Minister's television manner – quite apart from what was written in the newspapers and was spoken in the surrounding programmes – which stirred deep unconscious roots in millions of people. It is easy to say that he appeared as a father figure, and afterwards attracted the hatred of a father who has failed. But what exactly were his father attributes? After all, anyone can put a pipe in his mouth and many politicians have greying hair. A psychologist's report on the subject would be interesting, not so much for the light it might shed on the Prime Minister, but for what it might reveal of the depth psychology of the British public.

Paul Foot's own main interest however is in political biography rather than psychology. He has carried out on Harold Wilson, especially on his earlier career, the kind of research job normally performed by historians on long-dead figures. He has ploughed through endless newspaper cuttings and volumes of *Hansard*; he has interviewed friends of the young Harold Wilson, and he has consulted experts in the particular fields through which his anti-hero has passed. Paul Foot makes no secret of his own commitment to some – not very clearly defined – form of Socialist fundamentalism; and his Penguin is illustrated by a very funny drawing of a two-headed animal, one end of which deprecates appeals to the Dunkirk spirit, and the other end of which believes that 'the spirit of Dunkirk will carry us through to success'. These two very different facts have prevented some reviewers from realising that the book is largely a work of academic research; and one does not in the least have to share the author's political views to benefit from his investigations.

The impression that emerges is of an intelligent and decent – if not very glamorous – undergraduate Harold Wilson. He was influenced enough by what he had seen in his working class background of the defects of pre-war capitalism to want to devote his main efforts to the problems of unemployment, but dispassionate enough to join the Liberal Keynesian school of reform, as this seemed – and here he was perfectly correct – to be the best route to success. One can also see, that although he quickly got the drift of the Keynesian message, his own bent was for the detailed accumulation of facts and figures rather than for fundamental intellectual problems. Paul Foot has no difficulty in showing that in his early days as a young President of the Board of Trade, Mr Harold Wilson was thoroughly committed to private enterprise and to the profit motive, which he believed – again perfectly correctly – could be a powerful instrument for serving the nation's needs if harnessed under the right institutional framework.

Somewhere towards the end of the 1940s there seems to have been a change, and something more like the political animal we know today was born. Several factors may have contributed to this. There may have been Wilson's disappointment at being passed over for several senior jobs in the Cabinet. There is no doubt, too, that withdrawal of support for the Labour Government by the Federation of British Industries, as part of one of these sudden changes of fashion which sweep the various British establishments, had a permanently souring effect on him, and made him less scrupulous about appealing to the primitive jealousy which most people in Britain possess towards the capitalists and their doings.

A familiar note creeps in with the bickerings over the 1949 devaluation. Wilson's own position seems to have been equivocal from the start; and an all-too-familiar note of pettiness intrudes with the attempts to claim that he had been the Cabinet emissary to Cripps, when the latter was convalescing in Switzerland. In the ensuing Parliamentary debate the now familiar attacks on foreigners who had attacked sterling and the good name of Britain already made their appearance.

But it is really in the period between his resignation from the Cabinet with Bevan in 1951, and his assumption of the Party leadership in 1962, that Paul Foot's strictures seem most damaging. The author has little difficulty in showing that Wilson resigned over the practicability of the Korean Rearmament Programme rather than any of the wider foreign policy issues that influenced Bevan. Moreover, there is considerable evidence that he tried until the very end to find some face-saving compromise which would enable him to stay in the Government. Then there was a studied and successful attempt to play on the heartstrings of the 'Labour Left' – a perfectly valid expression to describe a group of identifiable individuals, however suspect as part of a spectrum concept. Having establish his 'left-wing' credentials, it was not long before Wilson was back as a leading figure in the Shadow Cabinet.

To my mind there are two particularly damaging quotations from this period. There is the boast that after a Labour Party Conference accepted German rearmament by the narrowest of margins 'I never spoke against German rearmament again'. This attitude – which would be shared by many in the Tory Party who generally value loyalty and unity above all else – reminds one more of the Soviet conception of democracy than of a society based on free discussion. Then there is Wilson's reported comment to John Junor, the editor of the *Sunday Express*, that Macmillan was a genius in holding up the banner of Suez for the Conservatives to follow, while leading the party away from it. 'That's what I would like to do with the Labour Party over nationalisation.' This kind of supposedly hard-boiled politics is always appealing in the short term. But it brings a bitter pay-off in the not so long run. Surely, one of the reasons for the bitter disillusionment now sweeping the Labour Party is that Wilson gave up the difficult and 'theological' task of redefining the Labour Party's aims which Gaitskell had begun; and the post-devaluation policies followed by the Labour Government have received a worse reception in both the Labour Party and the country than if there had been more straight talk from the beginning. In this sense, to place personal responsibility for the disappointment of the last few years on Harold Wilson is not 'frivolously to dabble in personalities' as Paul Foot concludes. This is as well, for if the author's conclusion were right, it would be difficult to see the justification for writing his book.

Paul Foot carries out a much needed demolition job on the undeservedly famous 'Science and Socialism' speech at the Scarborough Conference of 1963. As Mr Foot points out, 'nothing is as uncontroversial as fact'; I can remember my own astonishment that what had long been considered as a standard subject for sixth form essays for *those on the arts side* should have aroused such enormous national enthusiasm. Yet a newly elected Labour M.P., the son of one of the Red Clydesiders, said with great emotion that his whole conception of Socialism had changed as he listened to the speech. I can remember a normally hard-boiled Conservative Minister saying to me how he wished he had had the wit to make the speech first himself. As a matter of fact, its basic premises are open to serious dispute. For despite all the ballyhoo that has been written, the technological development of the last 20 or 30 years have probably made less difference to our daily lives than the invention of railways, electricity, and the internal combustion engine – not to say the universal provision of piped water.

From the time that Mr Wilson became Prime Minister in 1964, Paul Foot's narrative cannot hope to be as exhaustive or as definitive. For inevitably, Mr Wilson's personal activities become submerged in those of his Government, and his precise personal role at every stage will take some time to unravel. But in many cases Paul Foot seems to hit the nail on the head. My main complaint is that he does not make a clear enough distinction between the Prime Minister's much professed commitment to economic growth (of which he disapproves) and the errors and prejudices which have marred his pursuit of that goal. But we receive a very necessary reminder that Harold Wilson insistently used two bogeys against the Tories in the 1966 election: the Means Test State and inevitable deflation. He also insisted that a wage freeze 'was unthinkable'. Paul Foot remarks that the Prime Minister was 'not bluffing. He meant it.' All this, and his

volte face on Europe and on many other issues would be
entitled to more sympathetic study, if only Mr Wilson had
ever been ready to admit that he had changed his mind on
any matter.

Paul Foot makes an important personal contribution of
his own in the chapter on race, Rhodesia and South Africa,
which is worth reading on its merits, even by those who have
had their fill of the pros and cons of Harold Wilson. Mr Foot
provides a strong argument that the Tiger Constitution 'was
more reactionary and more acceptable to the racist Rhodes-
ians' white minority' than the Constitution imposed under
the Tories in 1961. He believes the only two possible ways of
bringing down the present Rhodesian regime would be military force or a showdown with South Africa. Those of us
who would hesitate to accept either of these courses should
at least recognise that any guarantees which might be given
by Mr Smith in any future settlement will not be worth the
paper they are written on and should refrain from hypocritical praise of the statesmanship of those involved.

Mr Foot makes another interesting personal contribution
in his analysis of Wilson's curious appeal to the 'Labour Left'.
The latter accepted policy after policy from Wilson which
they would never have taken from Gaitskell; and he could
only find one case, that of Mr Eric Heffer, who had refused
to take a job in the Government because he was unwilling
to defend policies of which he disapproved. The sentiment-
ality and servility of the Labour Left towards a leader whom,
despite all evidence to the contrary, they insisted on thinking
of as 'one of us', is particularly disheartening, as there were
a number of issues, including support of American policy in
Vietnam or attitudes towards the Greek dictatorship, on which
some people who would not even claim to be Socialists at all
would have liked the ex-Bevanites to have broken with the
Prime Minister. The Left supported Wilson over the pound,
some years after Tory journalists and independent economists
had already begun to demand devaluation, and the retreat
from East of Suez was brought about by a combination of
events and pressure from the ex-Gaitskellites, rather than by
anything accomplished by Wilson's natural supporters.

Limits should, however, be placed on one's strictures on

the subject of this book. Harold Wilson's real virtues have been the opposite of those he has proclaimed in his pseudo-Churchillian oratory. With Mr Wilson at No. 10, at least one feels that no trigger will be pressed which would bring suffering and destruction to thousands in the name of some principle. This is not something of which one can be as sure with the Gaitskell-Heath type of leadership. The latter is magnificent if it chooses to make a stand on something that is both right and humane, less magnificent if it fights in the last ditch over something that is cruelly mistaken. How much one should value a man of principle over a man of expediency will depend on one's view of the risks that the principle will be wrongly chosen or mistakenly applied. These are in my view quite high.

Although Wilson's decisions were taken too late and soft-pedalled, there was in the last resort no immovable obstacle once a sufficient body of respectable opinion had been converted and sufficient pressures built up around him. This happened with devaluation and East of Suez. It is happening to some extent over selectivity in the social services and will happen in future with personal tax incentives. One can indeed think of more inspiring forms of leadership; equally one can think of more disastrous kinds.

12 The Need for a Modern Cobden[*]

In all my travels ... three reflections constantly
occur to me: how much unnecessary solicitude and
alarm England devotes to the affairs of foreign
countries; with how little knowledge we enter upon
the task of regulating the concerns of other people;
and how much better we might employ our energies
in improving matters at home.

Richard Cobden to Mr Bright,
18 September 1847
from John Morley, *The Life of Richard Cobden*

Freedom and Reality is not the coherent outline of Mr
Powell's political beliefs for which we are still waiting. It
consists of sections of Mr Powell's speeches over the last few
years, lovingly extracted and rearranged by John Wood – an
imperfect substitute.

There are, nevertheless, a great many passages which are
infinitely nearer the mark than the conventional wisdom of
Mr Powell's colleagues. One can, for instance, only applaud
Mr Powell's forthright condemnation of the £50 travel allowance as the economic equivalent of the Berlin Wall and
wonder how deep is the real devotion to liberty of a nation
that can so meekly tolerate it. Mr Powell gives as good a one-
sentence summary of our payments troubles as can be found
anywhere when he says that if the price of a country's money
'is fixed at a point away from the true price (that is that at
which supply and demand balance) then, as with any other

* A review of *Freedom and Reality* by J. Enoch Powell, first published in
The Spectator, 25 April 1969.

thing sold at a fixed price, there will be either a surplus or a deficit'.

His former front bench colleagues could also benefit from his warning against expecting too many wonders from the reform of trade union law. Perhaps the most important of his domestic utterances are his frequent denunciations of government by ministerial request, and of businessmen who are too anxious to keep in the good books of authority. But it is the Bank of England, even more than Socialist politicians, who are most insistent on regulation by winks and nods, and one fears that most other prominent Conservatives would follow the establishment line and prefer 'voluntary methods' to unambiguous and legally binding directives.

Overseas, Mr Powell makes mincemeat of the notion of a British 'peace-keeping' role, and a British presence in the Mediterranean and Persian Gulf, which were, in fact, quite powerless to prevent local governments from turning the oil taps on and off, or converting their sterling balances whenever they wished. He justly remarks, 'Nations, competitors of ours, which depend equally or more on trade, have outstripped our performance without any military presence either in the areas from which their raw materials are derived or in those where their principal markets are situated.'

Where, then, is the snag? In the first place, Mr Powell seems to have read no economics. Imagine a man of good brain and an interest in philosophical problems, but completely out of touch with the writings of philosophers. One would then expect the occasional passage going to the heart of the problem, more sharply than many professionals, yet a great deal else that is oversimplified and dangerously open to attack.

But the matter goes much deeper. The case for the market mechanism and consumer choice, as normally presented, makes sense only as part of a wider set of beliefs which regards individuals as the best judges of their own interest. It is difficult to accept the sincerity of the professed free market beliefs from the kind of Tory who rails against the permissiveness of our age; even on the purely economic side, the supposedly *laissez-faire* beliefs of some extreme Tory activists are barely skin-deep.

There is no evidence for putting Mr Powell in this latter category. But his economic liberalism is allied uneasily with an attachment to the nation state as the absolute political value. Most economic liberals, on the other hand, while conceding that Englishmen would naturally have a greater feeling for other Englishmen than for Peruvians, regard the national interest as a function of the interests of the individuals who compose it, and are highly suspicious of supposedly superior collective entities. Indeed, once the supremacy of overriding national goals is admitted it is difficult to see what arguments there are against Mr Wilson, having been elected by a national majority, decreeing that an excessive consumption of candyfloss is against his conception of the British idea.

This brings one to the most notorious manifestation of Mr Powell's extreme nationalism: his speeches on race and immigration. They do not read any better in hard covers. The reaction of a liberal to these speeches could range between two extremes. He might point out, justifiably, that Mosley had some better ideas on economic policy than his conventional rivals and then resume his march with the army of the virtuous Powell-haters. At the other extreme, he could say that it is fortunate that Powell has acted as a catalyst for unpleasant feelings which might otherwise have found a more dangerous outlet.

One would need a crystal ball to say which of these attitudes will turn out more nearly correct. But certain results are already evident. Mr Powell has undoubtedly attracted to his banner the anti-blacks, hangers, floggers, censors and the martinets, who support him despite, rather than because of, many of his actual beliefs. The result is that many of the younger and more liberal Conservatives have become so preoccupied with fighting 'Powellism' that they believe – quite understandably – that they must rally round the official leadership, which is given a clear run on issues such as economic policy, overseas defence or Vietnam. The leadership itself interprets the strength of 'Powellism' as a signal to pay more attention to the traditional beliefs of Tory activists and is even more obdurate on those issues where Mr Powell speaks for enlightenment. The need for a modern Cobdenite movement which would combine a belief in both personal and economic freedom with non-intervention overseas has still to be met. It might attract much more general support than the conventional Tory or Labour politician would suppose.

13 Further Thoughts on Left and Right

> To determine the nature of these parties is perhaps one of the most difficult problems that can be met with.
>
> David Hume, 'Of the Parties of Great Britain'

Late in 1968, a book of mine was published entitled *Left or Right: The Bogus Dilemma*.[1] I am tempted to say that the book 'fell dead-born from the press', but this would not be quite accurate, as more people were willing to dispute what they thought it said than actually to read it.

The central argument was that classification of political positions according to a spectrum running from extreme left to extreme right 'obscures more than it illuminates'. At no point did I suggest that terms so deeply ingrained as 'left' and 'right' are, could, or should be, dropped; and there were certain uses of the terms, such as the 'Labour Left' which were extremely useful ways of identifying known groups of people. My main objection was to the use of left–right as a one-dimensional calibrating scale suitable for all purposes. This could be summed up by saying that the terms were overworked, and 'less use' should be made of them.

The object of the present essay is limited. It is to restate in summary form my thoughts on the concepts of left and right as modified by events, the writings of others, and my own subsequent reflections.

The problem of left and right is a special case of the general problem of the links between beliefs on different topics and issues. These linkages can be strong or weak. At one extreme, if there is no relation between views on, say, nationalisation, nuclear weapons, E.E.C. entry, the death penalty, the Royal Family and sexual permissiveness – or any other alternative selection of issues – then policy attitudes could be described as 'atomistic'. If, at the other extreme, there is a close relation between views on such separate issues, it is reasonable to talk of ideologies, belief systems or 'policy packages'.

It is important to note that the question can be posed in an empirical or a quasi-logical form. One can ask: 'Is it reasonable for those who are hostile to nationalisation to be in favour of the death penalty?' By this one is asking whether there is any wider set of value judgements or view of human affairs which would lead to similar opinions on such apparently disparate subjects. Alternatively, one can simply ask how strongly related attitudes to different issues are in fact. 'Do people who favour the death penalty tend to be anti-nationalisation?' We can also ask: 'Is the direction of such linkages the same among different groups or at different periods?'

My starting point should have been the observation on p. 87 of *Left or Right: The Bogus Dilemma*, that a vast number of different permutations have been observed in different societies. Among some ascetic religious sects, a belief in plain living has been linked with an abhorrence of technological progress, among other equally ascetic sects such progress has been highly prized. Some fiercely nationalistic groups have been strong believers in hierarchical class distinctions; others have been strongly egalitarian. *It is, moreover, always possible to invent an ideology which will link together the most surprising beliefs.*

As several reviewers pointed out, *Left or Right: The Bogus Dilemma* was strongly critical of mainstream Conservatives for combining relatively permissive attitudes in economic policy with an authoritarian approach to questions of personal conduct. How far was this a fair criticism? It would be perfectly possible for anyone with the requisite training to draw up an internally consistent belief system which would be compatible with an interventionist bias in economic affairs, an anti-permissive attitude to personal morality, and – for that matter – a 'hawklike' attitude to foreign policy. A very rough sketch of some elements of one possible Conservative economic philosophy can be found on pp. 159–62 of the present volume. The fact that most Conservatives have little taste for this kind of theorising is irrelevant to its possibility.

Where Conservatives are fairly open to attack is when they argue for free enterprise, or oppose certain types of state intervention, because of a professed belief in the overriding importance of individual liberty. So long as they refrain from using the rhetoric of personal freedom in defence of their economic attitudes, they are impregnable to the kind of attack mounted in *Left or Right: The Bogus Dilemma*; but once they do use this language there is a *prima facie* charge of hypocrisy or inconsistency to answer.

Whether I was right to become indignant about this phenomenon, I am now far from sure. For people do not enter politics with rigid and unchangeable value systems, but can, on the contrary, be influenced by their own slogans. The fact that many Conservatives choose to defend private enterprise and 'less government' by invoking individual freedom, makes them slightly more uneasy about their anti-permissive attitudes elsewhere than they would otherwise be; and within the economic field it makes them slightly more amenable to intervention designed to make the market reflect individual choice in relation to all relevant costs, and slightly less likely to adopt a purely pro-business view. The word 'slightly' is important. The main influences on attitudes are of a different kind; but so far as the words used do make a marginal difference, the libertarian is better off with the present situation than with one in which the Conservatives used economic arguments which more closely reflected their more authoritarian instincts and which were less obviously inconsistent with their behaviour in other fields.

On the empirical issue, the view put forward in *Left or Right: The Bogus Dilemma* that political belief systems, whether of a left–right or any other kind, were very weak among the mass electorate, has been abundantly confirmed by the most detailed examination yet made of British data, by Butler and Stokes in *Political Change in Britain*.[2] As these authors stress, most people 'have wholly atomistic responses to the issues of politics'.[3] Even on individual issues, there is little indication of firm opinions. Only 50 per cent of the sample were consistent in either support or opposing further nationalisation over three interviews in 1963–6. Evidence is cited to show that this was due 'to mere uncertainty of response and not to genuine attitude change'.[4] Voters simplify the problems of choice by shifting attention from policies to consequences – beliefs in the latter are formed by 'simple inferences from who is or was in power'.

In a correlation analysis *confined to those who held stable views between surveys,* the relationship between attitudes to different issues was found to be small. The correlation coefficient between views on nationalisation and on immigration was 0.06. (If there were a perfect correspondence between attitudes on the two issues, the coefficient would be 1.00; if there were no relation whatever the coefficient would be 0.) The correlations between nationalisation and the death penalty, and nationalisation and attitudes to nuclear weapons, were both below 0.20. (Most remarkably, Butler and Stokes found that even party activists failed to show stronger correlations in the expected directions on such issues.) The one impressive correlation (0.65) was between attitudes to nationalisation and trade union power. Otherwise the only correlations which arose above 0.30 were between nationalisation and attitudes to 'big business' (0.37) and between immigration and the death penalty (0.33). This, in conjunction with the voting data confirms that the operational meaning of left and right among the mass electorate is that Labour-voting electors are more inclined to favour the lower paid and the trade unions (whose interests they would like to harmonise at the expense of the rich), and Conservative voters are more hostile to the unions and more concerned with gains for the middle classes. This is the main policy content of differences between the two sets of voters, and even these linkages are very mild with numerous exceptions. The smallness of the observed relationships between views on different issues is more fundamental than the fact that only a minority of the electorate is sufficiently familiar with the terms 'left' and 'right' to know that Labour is supposed to be left of the Conservatives.

But one must be careful not to go too far. Anyone likely to be reading this will have met many people whose views on most issues are predictable from the moment they have opened their mouths on any one of them. Moreover, statistical psychologists have found significant, although moderate, correlations between views on different issues which enable them to locate 'opinion clusters'. There are probably several reasons for the difference in the findings of the political and psychological statisticians. To some extent, it reflects a difference of professional approach. While political researchers find inter-relations of 0.2 or 0.3 fairly small, psychologists regard a cluster of such relationships as evidence of some common influence. The psychologists also tend to apply their tests to more educated or politically interested groups than do the political students, who are interested in the mass electorate. Psychologists tend to ask about a much wider range of topics – including, for example, school uniforms, beatniks, modern art, suicide, student pranks, electronic music, conventional clothing, nudist camps, learning Latin and pyjama parties – than political researchers; and it is possible that there is more tendency for clusters of attitudes to be formed on these more 'human' issues than on the remoter topics on the political agenda. One wonders, however, whether the psychological testers take as much trouble to probe the meaningfulness and reliability of their responses as have political researchers such as Butler and Stokes and their U.S. forebears.

These questions cannot be pursued further here. Relatively too much political research is conducted among the mass electorate for whom politics is at most, in Schumpeter's words a 'sub-hobby', and much too little among the politically conscious minority. There is little doubt that groupings of attitudes do exist among the latter. The interesting questions are about their strength and nature.

The fact that the left–right classification omits a great deal that we need to know about political attitudes has long been known in a general sort of way. Its limitations should be obvious enough; but just to spell them out:

(1) Many issues cannot readily be classified in left–right terms.

(2) People can be, and are, on the left on some issues

and on the right on others; they can be extreme left on certain topics, and 'moderate left' or 'moderate right' on others, and so on. A general average of attitudes can therefore be very misleading.

(3) Even when considering individual subjects to which 'left' and 'right' are relevant, a simple scale measurement can be distorting. It puts, for example, in the same 'centre' position, someone who merely splits the difference between the extremes and another person with a different approach of his own.

The simplest way of bringing home the weakness of the conventional classification is that Hitler and Stalin are at opposite ends of a left–right spectrum, while men such as Lord Butler or Roy Jenkins would be in the middle. Yet, despite their somewhat different attitudes to private property, Hitler and Stalin had far more in common with each other than either had with any British middle-of-the-road politician.

The most widely known method of dealing with this paradox is Professor H. J. Eysenck's suggestion of measuring attitudes along two axes at right angles to each other.[6] One of these axes is entitled 'tendermindedness–toughmindedness', and the other 'radicalism–conservatism'. The latter is measured and used by Eysenck in a way that makes it virtually synonymous with left–right. Stalinist Communists then emerge as toughminded radicals and Fascists as toughminded conservatives. Gandhi and Tolstoy would be tenderminded radicals, while a quietist saint would be a tenderminded conservative. The Eysenck classification was originally derived from statistical investigations in W.E.A. classes, but later supplemented by surveys among other groups and countries.

The view I took in my own book in 1968 was that the Eysenck two-dimensional scale was (a) a great improvement on the single left–right scale, but (b) was nevertheless, itself open to objection. The most serious was to the way the tough–tenderminded axis was constructed. Few people, who have not studied the relevant questionnaires, would guess that opposition to birth control or belief in compulsory religious education counted as tenderminded, while support for

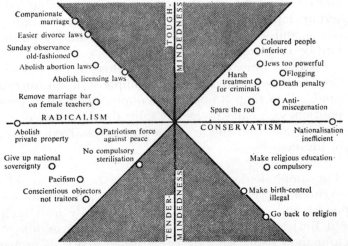

DIAGRAM 1 : *The Eysenck Classification: Distribution of attitudes with respect to toughmindedness and radicalism*

easier divorces or abortion, or for liberalising Sunday observance laws count as toughminded. There now seems a fairly wide agreement among psychologists that this dimension is, as presently constructed, misleading, as it is to some extent a measure of religious orthodoxy. Professor R. T. Green made the point vividly by asking: 'Was Torquemada (the first Inquisitor General of Spain) tenderminded?'

The basis of the dimensional approach to political attitudes is that attitudes to different issues – say, belligerency in foreign policy and severity on punishment of criminals – are ranked along separate scales. These are set at an angle corresponding to the relationship between them. In the example cited, one would expect some small angle of less than 90° between the lines. Those who believe in a belligerent foreign policy are also likely to have harsher views on the treatment of criminals (itself a psychologically revealing fact), but the correspondence between the two will be by no means perfect. A few foreign policy belligerents may have highly humane attitudes towards penal reform; and of the rest, some will be much more hard-line in their penal attitudes than others. Where there is no relationship at all between attitudes to different subjects, they are measured by lines at right angles to each other. Although only two dimensions can be shown on any plane diagram, any number of dimensions can be envisaged that seems useful for the purpose in hand.

A remarkable feature of Eysenck's own diagram is that no attitudes are shown anywhere near the tough–tenderminded axis, which is purely a hypothetical construct. If, however, the axes are rotated by 45°, we get two different dimensions running South-West to North-East and South-East to North-West. These have plenty of attitudes on or near them. The South-West–North-East axis is more like a genuine tough–tenderminded dimension, but to avoid confusion with Eysenck's terminology, I shall call it a 'dove–hawk' dimension. 'Hawks' tend to be racialist and punitive, while 'doves' are sympathetic to pacifism and conscientious objectors. The South-East–North-West axis is clearly a scale of social permissiveness. The abolition of licensing laws and easier divorce are at points successively further removed from the centre along the permissiveness axis, while opposition to birth control is at the other extreme.

This rotation of the axes runs, however, into a difficulty. As can be seen from the diagram, neither the dove–hawk axis, nor the social permissiveness axis is independent of the radical–conservative one. Hawklike attitudes are partially correlated with political conservatism, and socially permissive attitudes are correlated, although highly imperfectly, with political radicalism. Thus, if one rejects Eysenck's hypothetical construct involving a tenderminded Torquemada, one does not have dimensions that are independent of each other.

At this point I took a wrong turning. Worried by the above problem, and also uneasy that the radical–conservative dimension confused the class-related attitudes with the general disposition to challenge orthodoxy, I postulated a three dimensional classification of my own. These scales were:

(a) Egalitarianism versus elitism
(b) Radicalism versus orthodoxy
(c) Liberalism versus authoritarianism

(I regretfully dropped the dove–hawk classification as being too obviously correlated with, although not identical to, the liberal–authoritarian dimension.)

The least satisfactory of my three dimensions was undoubtedly the radical–orthodox one. It conflated the desire to get to the root of the matter rather than accept unconditionally conventional beliefs – which has been exhibited by some people of quite conservative beliefs, such as David Hume, or (to a lesser extent) the 3rd Marquis of Salisbury – with a bias in favour of change or even of an espousal of revolution for its own sake. While an egalitarian or a liberal can be identified with relatively definite views over quite long periods of history, a radical can be associated with almost anything, depending on the conventional wisdom against which he is reacting and the nature of his professed alternative. The concept I was trying to identify by the label radicalism in my book was really more a quality of mind – some combination of analytical intelligence, an eagerness to question conventional assumptions and a readiness to raise major issues of principle and not just to amass detail.

It is no accident that these were the qualities that characterised the otherwise diverse group of individuals such as Brown, Crossman, Jenkins and Crosland, who are believed to have queried the Labour Government's decision not to devalue in July 1966. Similar qualities were shared by those Conservatives, such as Maudling, Powell and Joseph, who did not rule out flexible rate changes *in principle* in the 1960s, when such a flexible attitude was not yet generally respectable. Such qualities of mind may be more important than political attitudes, and it is reasonable to assess a politician or Cabinet partly in terms of their presence or absence. (This does not imply that radicalism of this probing, sceptical kind is a good thing politically. Maudling and Jenkins achieved less in the way of lasting reform at the Treasury than some of their predecessors and successors who were less well-endowed with such qualities, but who made up for them in doggedness and application.)

The really basic criticism of my three axes is, however, that they are probably not independent of each other – in terms of the diagrammatic convention they are not quite at right angles. It would be surprising if there were not some moderate positive correlation between egalitarian, radical and liberal views, even in my special sense of these terms, and between elitist, orthodox and authoritarian views. Similar criticisms have been levelled against Eysenck's original two dimensions and at other proposed schemes. The search for a number of entirely independent dimensions now seems to me the wrong way of remedying the grotesque oversimplification of the simple left–right scale. What different attitudes and individuals, who are characterised as left or right, or 'extreme left', or 'extreme right' or 'trendy left' or 'hard-line right', have in common are, to adapt a metaphor of Wittgenstein's, 'family resemblances'. Each member of a family will have resemblances in one or other respect to some of the other members, although the qualities in which they resemble each other (whether build, features, colour of eyes, gait or temperament) and the degree of resemblance will vary widely, and it will be possible to find pairs of individuals between whom there is no resemblance whatever.[7]

I did, in fact, use this metaphor of family resemblance in trying to come to grips with the concept of radicalism, but failed to see that this was the clue to the treatment of left and right as well. A sufficient combination, for example, of any of the following beliefs will justify the label 'left-wing' in a broader sense than mere proneness to vote Labour: nationalisation, opposition to the death penalty, willingness to give up national sovereignty, active promotion of racial equality, opposition to compulsory Latin, sexual permissiveness, Church disestablishment, pyjama parties, unconventional clothes, unilateral disarmament, disapproval of strict obscenity laws or censorship, abhorrence of corporal punishment, legalised abortion, co-education, atheism, abolition of the licensing laws, support for price control, high taxes on the rich, more aid for developing countries, abolition of private schooling, more expenditure on the social services, relaxation of the immigration laws, republicanism, high taxes on 'inessential goods' – one can go on adding to this deliberately varied list indefinitely. Not all permutations of such beliefs will qualify for the epithet 'left-wing'; but a very large number of them will. Two people may hold entirely non-overlapping combinations of views, and have nothing in common with each other; yet both may qualify as left-wingers, and even as being 'left' to an equal degree.

This concept of family resemblances enables one to use the terms left and right when they seem appropriate, but it does not force one to overemphasise similarities between different left-wingers, nor to overemphasise differences between left-wingers and right-wingers. Where the most natural descriptive term for one kind of economic liberal (as opposed to other kinds of economic liberal) is 'right wing', as in the example on pp. 86–7, there need be no inhibition about using the term. It also enables one to take care of historical evolution, as certain family traits drop out and others become important. For example, a belief in accelerated technical progress was, up to the early 1960s, a left-wing characteristic, but has since become very much the opposite. It follows from these linguistic facts that, although there will be some relationship between left-wing attitudes today and those ten years ago, being 'on the left' or 'on the right' can come to mean utterly different things over the course of generations.

One is also then perfectly free to stress other kinds of family relationship terms when these seem more relevant than left or right. There are family resemblances characteristic of 'doves', of libertarians, of Atlanticists, humanists, puritans, internationalists, inflationists, and innumerable other classes of people. One should use the label that is most appropriate and evocative for the purpose in hand without worrying either about the fact that there will be considerable divergence within each camp, or about the degree of correlation between different systems of classification. Similarly, one can talk of the 'New Left', the 'Parliamentary Left', the 'libertarian left', the 'libertarian right', the 'radical right' or the 'authoritarian right', taking full advantage of all the penumbra of associations – themselves changing over time – thrown up by these terms.

Thus, the objection is not to the use of the left and right, but rather to their employment when other distinctions would be more useful. It is also an objection to a misconception of the way in which 'left' and 'right' actually function in modern political speech. The aim of a critique of linguistic usage should be to liberate us from a straitjacket, not to impose another in its place. We are left with the problem of sorting out the family relationships which actually exist in a particular country or group of countries (or, if we are madly ambitious, in the human race). As already mentioned, a different descriptive framework seems to suit politically inclined psychologists, interested in the rich varieties of human attitudes, from that which suits political scientists concerned with the narrower problem of voting in a two party system. The model that seems to suit many post-Eysenck political psychologists best is that of specific and general factors, of the kind found in the study of human abilities rather than that of dimensions at right angles to each other.

To take an illustration of Professor Richard Lynn's: there is likely to be strong, although far from perfect, correlation between support for 'saving the Argyll Regiment', military training at school and the retaining of a British nuclear deterrent. These are linked together in a 'narrow specific attitude' which Lynn calls 'strong army' but which a less sympathetic observer might call 'militarism'. (It does not matter if the examples are a little dated and if an up-to-date militarist might not be quite so keen on a school training corps – the principle should be clear enough.) There are also imperfect, but positive, correlations between militarism, opposition to coloured immigration and belief in white superiority, which constitute a broad specific attitude which Lynn calls 'patriotism' and for which others might find a less flattering title such as 'xenophobic aggression'. Other broad specific attitudes emerge, such as support for capitalism, élitism (as opposed to egalitarianism), support for organised religion, insistence on 'sexual morality' and an emphasis on law and order. Correlations between these broad, specific attitudes are weak, but positive, and contribute a general right-wing factor which Lynn labels 'conservatism'. There is a similar hierarchy of issues, and narrow and broad attitudes, leading up to the general factor of 'leftism'.

It is essential to emphasise how weak this general factor is. The structure of attitudes is quite consistent with a very large number of religious people being strongly anti-xenophobic, or with many pro-capitalists being sexually permissive. The

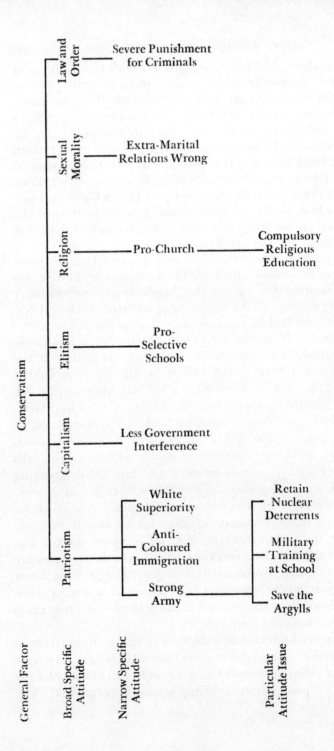

DIAGRAM 2: *The structure of Conservative political attitudes. Only a few of the narrow specific attitudes and particular issues are shown as illustrations.*

weakness of the general factor is shown by the fact that Labour voters, who are egalitarian rather than elitist in their beliefs, tend to adopt right-wing attitudes on law and order. All the general factor tells us, as I understand it, is that working class voters, who are particularly fierce on law and order, are *slightly* less likely to be egalitarian in their outlook and *slightly* more likely to be 'working class Tories'; while middle class voters who lay especial stress on law and order are likely to be a little more elitist than the bulk of their class and, even less likely to vote Labour.

The correlations between the different attitudes which make up the general factor are probably about 0.30 among the politically active. For comparison, the correlations between the sub-factors, such as memory, speed, verbal and mathematical ability which make up the general factor of intelligence are about 0.5. One should add, too, that given the vast number of pairs of low to moderate correlations in attitudes to different issues, which can be built upon, psychologists have a considerable amount of choice in the particular factors they choose to isolate.

Attitudes to change are no longer a good explanation of the unifying force behind the left- and right-wing general factors. This is not only because the 'Left' has spent so much of its energies in rearguard actions against changes proposed by right-wing governments or independent commentators. More fundamentally, a desire to slow down or halt technological change to preserve some natural balance, which was formerly a romantic Tory attitude, is now more a left- than a right-wing family trait.

Special problems arise in relation to the structure of attitudes among M.P.s which are different from both those of the mass public and the politically sophisticated minority outside the House of Commons. It was asserted in *Left or Right: The Bogus Dilemma*, on the basis of published studies, that there was a modest correlation of attitudes among M.P.s who belonged to a Tory Right, but there was no left–right spectrum which would enable one to predict the views of any other Conservative M.P. on one issue from his views on another. Views on the market economy in particular, were inexplicable in left–right terms – and here one does not even have to make an exception of the Tory Right, which embraces extreme paternalists and apostles of *laissez-faire*. Nothing has happened to modify this view. On the other hand, the left–right spectrum among Labour M.P.s, which appeared to be weakening in the 1960s, re-emerged strongly in the early 1970s, with the eruption of violent hostility between the 'Tribune Group' and the 'Jenkinsites', with a centre interested in keeping the peace. Even so, whether a Labour M.P. stood in the centre–right range of the Parliamentary Party depended far more on his views on the leadership and on the single issue of the E.E.C. than on any closely linked network of beliefs.

Even if the conventional left–right measuring rod is overused and misused, the question remains: 'What harm does it do in practice?' In the first place, it leads to a downgrading of issues which cannot be easily expressed in these terms – which for many practical purposes means issues other than those related to the views on the distribution of income or wealth. Questions relating to personal freedom are *par excellence* ones that cannot be easily reduced to these terms; and it is, therefore, natural for a writer who believes these to be important to feel particularly dissatisfied by excessive concentration on issues and political divisions expressible in left–right terms.

Overuse or misuse of left and right leads also to another sort of harm which is not related to any special preoccupation with the freedom issue. This is that it encourages a weakness of leadership in the mainstream of British politics. Because of the sheer unpleasantness of many of the attitudes associated with the extreme left and extreme right, it is natural for many politicians to want to keep their distance from both and to try not to stray too far from the centre. The mythology of a spectrum linking these extremes has, however, an unfortunate effect on how the centre is regarded. Policies in the area of overlap between the two Front Benches, or midway between them, receive an accolade that they do not necessarily deserve, and mainstream politicians tend to follow rather than initiate. A great many sensible policies are delayed or even killed because of guilt by association with the extremes. Trade union reform and selectivity in the social services were postponed for so long, partly because they were originally regarded as very right-wing ideas, like hanging and flogging. Conversely, mainstream politicians went on endorsing the policy of burning human beings alive, dignified by the name of the Vietnam War,[9] because opposition to it was associated with the Labour Left and its Clause 4 associations.

The spectrum concept also has a debilitating effect on those who do not regard themselves as in the centre. I would gladly reiterate the passage in *Left or Right: The Bogus Dilemma*, which states that 'So long as they keep off class or economic matters, M.P.s such as Michael Foot, as well as others on the literary and artistic left, speak for much of what is best in British life.'[10] But because of their tendency to think in terms of packages and stereotypes such M.P.s were prone to regard steel nationalisation and similar trivia as partial compensation for a British Labour Government's support of the U.S. in Vietnam. The way the Labour Left probably reasoned was that, however unhappy they were over foreign policy, at least they had steel nationalisation, and with some leader other than Harold Wilson they could not be sure of even getting that. Thus, those who should have spoken for the conscience of the nation were distracted by irrelevancies and acted as the Praetorian Guard for a Labour Prime Minister, whose three main interlinked pillars of policy were the Anglo-American special relationship, the sterling exchange rate and a British presence East of Suez.

What I did not emphasise enough was that stereotyped packages of ideas are an indispensable short cut which all of us use for issues which we have not had time to examine for ourselves. Anthony Downs explained ideologies in this way, as a means by which ordinary electors simplify the process of decision; but even politicians, civil servants or academics have not time to study every subject in depth, and asking 'From what stable does this particular proposal come?' may seem to them better than going by pure hunch. It is along such lines that one can explain the theoretical belief in the abolition of capitalism by many in the fringe theatre, who would soon have to cease their activities if their wish were granted. For on subjects outside their own professional knowledge they tend, inevitably, to take on trust the views of friends and supporters, who lay claim to more expertise, or simply to pick up beliefs that are fashionable in the circles among which they mix.

Since it is inevitable that people who think about politics at all seriously will think to some extent in terms of policy packages, the best one can hope for, is some revision of current ideas on 'what goes with what'. Indeed one of the basic aims of the present volume is to weaken a little the association between socially permissive beliefs and opposition to the values of the market place, and to contribute a little towards establishing an opposite linkage.

Much the most extensive and fair-minded criticism of these views has come from Wilfred Beckerman.[11] He argues that it is not surprising that the two parties differ mainly over the equality issue or – as I should prefer to call it – the division of the spoils. For it is a dislike of 'inequality at the top' that serves as a rallying cry for Labour supporters (there is much less agreement over 'less inequality at the bottom' which could make a far bigger contribution to welfare). Where I part company with Beckerman is his assertion that this is the only economic issue on which they *could* differ.

Beckerman rightly says that most of the supposed objectives of economic policy such as price stability, 'growth', or overseas balance are means to other ends. He himself recognises two ends: 'higher standards of living' and 'some desired degree of equality of income (and wealth) distribution'. Since the parties can hardly differ over higher living standards, this leaves only equality. This needs rephrasing. For, even were the Conservatives to accept '*some* degree of equality' as a goal, if there is any trade-off between the growth of living standards and equality (a possibility that Beckerman admits), the parties could differ on where along this trade-off they wish to be.

Moreover, there is surely a real debate on the desirable pace of technological advance and the increased production of material goods. The size of the adverse spillover from such advance, whether conceived in terms of the ecological balance of the planet, or simple 'neighbourhood' effects, is largely a matter of guesswork; and this lack of knowledge, together with different views on the rate of time discount to apply to the happiness of generations yet unborn, makes the issue much more a political than a technical one.

The major difference of opinion lies, however, in Beckerman's dismissal of the individual freedom as a major issue of political principle. He appears to regard it as a Conservative attempt 'to overcome a sort of moral inferiority complex' on equality. If this is really what causes Conservatives to talk about individual freedom (and this is not implausible), one should give three cheers for their inferiority complex. The truth, of course, is that freedom *is* a political issue, although one that cuts across party boundaries. Instead of seeking to downgrade it, Professor Beckerman would have done better to have strayed a little from the economic field to emphasise the libertarian achievements (with some cross-bench voting) of the two Labour Parliaments in 1964–70 in areas such as the reform of the laws on abortion and homosexuality. These have done more for individual freedom than all the attempts of Tory Governments to 'set the people free' in the economic field, which have floundered because of the Tory Party's distaste for the analytical thinking that would be involved (in addition to political courage) in making such economic aspirations a reality.

Professor Beckerman's other objections are based mainly on the misconception that I think it feasible for political parties to reflect a great variety of preference patterns among the electorate on many different topics. For this to be possible there would have to be many thousands if not millions of political parties. The party battle in the 19th century, to the extent that it was issue-related, did, however, centre more on the age-old tussle between freedom and order than does the contemporary argument, which is mainly over income distribution; and I did express a hankering for a return to a party division in which one side puts together, in Cobdenite fashion, freedom in all its aspects and non-intervention overseas.

This is not as utopian as it may sound. With the growth of affluence and the crumbling of status barriers, the pattern of partisan division could yet swing back from class-related issues to those concerned with freedom and authority. But, in expressing a hankering for such a turn of events, I was taking a great risk. For, if the authoritarian party happened to be in power for the greater part of the time, the outlook for freedom would be dim; and it may be that libertarians do better with a party division on present lines, with some members on both sides trying to promote different sorts of freedom. If I felt more convinced of the need and urgency for a party realignment in a book published in 1968, the reason is to be found in the events of the immediately preceding years. There were then a number of key issues which cut across party lines. These included the East of Suez presence, the maintenance of the sterling parity and sterling exchange rate, the 'special relationship' with the U.S., and E.E.C. entry.

Changes of front on all these issues were part of the difficult job of reconciling the political classes to the fact that the U.K. was one of several medium-sized European countries and no longer had a special (and onerous) world role, either financially, or as a privileged ally of the U.S. The emotional barriers to the required change were very great; but making them seemed so much more important, even for domestic living standards, than the normal arguments about dividing the cake or the minutiae of internal policy, that it would have been worth shaking up the established parties to accomplish them. The division that mattered in those years was between those who showed a radical cast of mind on such things and those who did not. Fortunately, the required changes were eventually brought about – mainly by events – and arguments even among the *cognoscenti* reverted to more bread-and-butter issues. One hopes that the overseas decisions of the late 1960s were irreversible, but it would be right to keep one's fingers crossed against any surprise act of international folly while these pages are in the press.

In looking ahead, it is probably best to hope, not so much for a party realignment, as for a franker recognition of the party struggle as one between 'ins' and 'outs' with the issue content confined to a minimum of class-related matters (which events have shown to be a less explosive basis of difference than ethnic or religious matters). If we went the whole hog towards recognising this state of affairs, a more relaxed attitude would become possible to intra-party differences or inter-party agreement on other issues; and no one would expect arguments on subjects such as the virtues of a market economy, or alternative foreign policies, to be mirrored in the party debate. The outcome of such arguments might, nevertheless, have some effect on the policies – probably in the end very similar – which the two party leaderships adopted.

Notes and References

NOTE TO THE READER

1. F. A. Hayek, 'Why I am not a Conservative', *The Constitution of Liberty* (Routledge, 1960), pp. 410–41.

PROLOGUE: CAPITALISM AND THE PERMISSIVE SOCIETY

1. Joseph Schumpeter, *Capitalism, Socialism and Democracy*, 4th edition (Alen & Unwin, 1954), Chapters 11–14.

2. F. A. Hayek, *Studies in Philosophy, Politics and Economics* (Routledge & Kegan Paul, 1967), Chapter 12.

3. *Journalists at Work* (Constable, 1971).

4. G. J. Stigler, *The Intellectual and the Market Place*, reprinted in *Price Theory* (Penguin Modern Economic Readings, 1971).

5. Assar Lindbeck, *The Political Economy of the New Left* (Harper & Row, 1971).

6. J. K. Galbraith, *The New Industrial State* (Penguin, 1969).

7. C. Carter, *Wealth* (Penguin, 1971), pp. 136 *et seq.*

8. For details of these and many other instances, see *Galbraith and the Planners*, by Professor Frank McFadzean, University of Strathclyde, 1968, and *Economic Fact and Fantasy*, by Professor G. C. Allen, I.E.A. Occasional Paper No. 14, 1969.

9. Lindbeck, *The Political Economy of the New Left*, p. 43.

10. Cited in Galbraith, *Economics, Peace and Laughter* (Deutsch, 1971), p. 72.

11. H. G. Johnson, *The Economic Approach to Social Questions* (Weidenfeld & Nicolson, 1968).

12. For one of many instances, see Galbraith, *The American Left and Some British Comparisons* (Fabian Tract 406, 1971).

13. E. G. Dolan, 'Alienation, Freedom and Economic Organisation', *Journal of Political Economy*, September 1971.

14. Hayek, *The Constitution of Liberty*, p. 119.

15. A. Peacock and A. Culyer, *Economic Aspects of Student Unrest*, I.E.A. Occasional Paper No. 26, 1969.

16. H. Johnson, 'The Economics of Student Protest', *New Society*, 7 Nov. 1968.

17. N. Saunders, *Alternative London* (published privately but available from W. H. Smith & Co. Ltd, 2nd edition, 1971).

18. M. Grant, *The Climax of Rome* (Weidenfeld & Nicolson, 1969), p. 150.

19. Ibid.

1 A RESTATEMENT OF ECONOMIC LIBERALISM

1. In *Two Concepts of Liberty*, reprinted with related essays and a new Introduction in *Four Essays on Liberty* (Oxford Paperbacks, 1969).

2. Hayek, *The Constitution of Liberty*.

3. Ibid., p. 41.

4. J. W. N. Watkins, 'Philosophy' in A. Seldon (ed.), *Agenda for a Free Society* (Hutchinson, 1961).

5. M. Friedman, *Capitalism and Freedom* (University of Chicago Press, 1962).

6. B. Barry, *Political Argument* (Routledge & Kegan Paul, 1965), pp. 38, 66, 94.

7. F. Machlup, 'Liberalism and the Choice of Freedoms' in Streissler (ed.), *Roads to Freedom* (Routledge & Kegan Paul, 1969).

8. J. W. N. Watkins, *Agenda for a Free Society*.

9. Hayek, *The Constitution of Liberty*, p. 16.

10. *Utilitarianism* (Everyman 1948 edition), p. 6.

11. E. J. Mishan, *Welfare Economics: An Assessment* (North Holland Publishing Co., 1969), Chapters I and III.

12. E. J. Mishan, *Cost Benefit Analysis* (Allen & Unwin, 1971), Chapter 45.

13. E. J. Mishan, *Welfare Economics*, pp. 29, 85.

14. J. Meade, *The Theory of Indicative Planning* (Manchester University Press, 1970).

15. Some comments can be found on British experience with indicative planning in my own *Steering the Economy*, 3rd Penguin edition, 1971, especially Chapters 4, 7 and 8.

16. Hayek, *Studies in Philosophy, Politics and Economics*, Chapter 17.

17. For a good account of these complications, see I. M. D. Little, *A Critique of Welfare Economics*, 2nd edition (Oxford, 1956).

18. This argument is developed in my book *The Price of Economic Freedom* (Macmillan, 1970), which also contains a bibliography citing some of the empirical studies.

19. Cited in Brittan, *The Price of Economic Freedom*, pp. 51–2.

20. On all this, see Mishan, *Cost-Benefit Analysis*.

21. Machlup, *Roads to Freedom*.

22. For elaboration of these points, see Mishan, *Cost-Benefit Analysis*, especially Chapters 18 and 19.

23. R. W. S. Pryke, *Public Enterprise in Practice* (MacGibbon and Kee, 1971).

24. G. and P. Polanyi, 'The Efficiency of Nationalised Industries' in the *Moorgate and Wall St. Review*, Spring 1972.

25. Patrick Hutber, 'Letter Box Lunacy' (*Sunday Telegraph*, 7 November 1971).

26. C. Foster, *Public Enterprise* (Fabian Research Series 300, 1972).

27. H. L. A. Hart, *The Concept of Law* (Oxford, 1961), Chapter VII.

28. J. W. N. Watkins in *Agenda for a Free Society*.

29. I have derived this suggestion from Professor John Rawls's essays 'Justice as Fairness' and 'Distributive Justice', reprinted respectively in Laslett & Runciman (eds) *Philosophy, Politics and Society*, 2nd series (Blackwell, 1962) and 3rd series (Blackwell, 1967). A full statement of Rawls's position is to be found in his book *A Theory of Justice* (Oxford, 1972). This appeared after my own manuscript was completed. The expression 'derived from' has been used because, while the conception of disinterestedness used in the text arose as a result of reading Rawls, this does not imply an acceptance of his complete system – or conversely that he would necessarily approve of my own. See also the note at the bottom of p. 134 in the main text.

30. Hayek, *The Constitution of Liberty*, p. 153.

31. Ibid., p. 158.

32. Essay XIV in *Essays: Moral, Political and Literary* (Oxford, 1963).

33. It is expounded further in my book *Steering the Economy* (Penguin, 1971), Chapters 10 and 11.

34. F. A. Hayek, *Road to Serfdom* (Routledge & Kegan Paul, 1944, reissued 1971).

35. Hayek, *The Constitution of Liberty*, pp. 88 *et seq*.

36. D. Jay, *Socialism and the New Society* (Longmans, 1962).

37. F. A. Hayek, *Kinds of Rationalism* in 'Studies in Philosophy, Politics and Economics' (Routledge & Kegan Paul, 1967).

38. A. Downs, *The Economic Theory of Democracy* (Harper & Row, 1957).

39. Schumpeter, *Capitalism, Socialism and Democracy*, p. 261.

40. See Gordon Tullock, 'Public Decisions as Public Goods', *Journal of Political Economy*, February 1972.

41. These phrases were coined by Professor Paul Samuelson in *Problems of the American Economy* (University of Athlone Press, 1962).

42. E. J. Mishan, *The Costs of Economic Growth* (Penguin, 1969).

43. 'A Case for a Select Committee on Economic Affairs', by P. Jay and S. Brittan, *Second Report from the Select Committee on Procedure*, House of Commons 123, 1969–70, Appendix 2.

44. D. Jay, *Socialism in the New Society*, p. 9.

45. A. B. Atkinson, 'On the Measurement of Inequality', *Journal of Economic Theory*, No. 2, 1970.

46. Hayek, *The Constitution of Liberty*, pp. 125–6.

47. The earlier discussion on p. 94 is relevant here. The relevant references are given in Note 29 above.

48. Friedman, *Capitalism and Freedom*, p. 4.

49. Lord Robbins, *Politics and Economics* (Macmillan, 1963), p. 85.

50. J. M. Keynes, *General Theory*, reprinted 1936 edition, p. 374.

51. See National Income Blue Books and J. R. Hicks, *The Social Framework*, 4th edition (Oxford, 1971).

52. J. Tobin, 'On Limiting the Domain of Inequality', *The Journal of Law and Economics*, October 1970.

53. This point is well brought out in H. B. Acton, *The Morals of Markets* (Longman, 1971), pp. 51–5.

54. Plato, *The Republic*, trans.: Cornford (Oxford, 1941), pp. 161–4.

55. B. Russell, *History of Western Philosophy* (Allen & Unwin, 1946), p. 125.

56. For reflections on this phenomenon, see P. T. Bauer, *Dissent on Development* (Weidenfeld & Nicolson, 1972), and H. G. Johnson (ed.), *Economic Nationalism in Old and New States* (Allen & Unwin, 1968).

57. R. Mundell, *Man and Economy* (McGraw-Hill, 1968).

58. Ibid., p. 9.

59. B. Barry, *Sociologists, Economists and Democracy* (Collier-Macmillan, 1970).

60. K. R. Minogue, *The Liberal Mind* (Methuen, 1963), p. 28.

61. Ibid., pp. 170–1, and p. 30.

62. Cited by Charles Schultze in *The Politics and Economics of Public Spending* (Brookings, 1968).

63. Prof. A. K. Sen is surely right in the discussion he inaugurated in the *Journal of Political Economy* in 1970 that liberalism may conflict with Pareto optimality, unless one or the other is defined in a specially restrictive way.

2 JOBS, PRICES AND TRADE UNIONS

1. The reference is, of course, to the Lipsey–Parkin article first published in the May 1970 issue of *Economica* and further defended by Parkin in the November 1970 issue. The reference has been deliberately relegated to a footnote, as the elaboration of models which turn out false is part of the process of scientific advance; the strictures are on the initially uncritical acceptance of it by so many, and on the channelling of so much of subsequent technical discussion into the statistical methods employed instead of into the model's degree of predictive success.

2. J. Wood, *How Much Unemployment?* (Institute of Economic Affairs, 1972).

3. Damodar Gujarati. 'The Behaviour of Unemployment and Unfilled Vacancies: Great Britain, 1958–71', *The Economic Journal*, March 1972.

4. One of the best expositions of the consequences of such a breakdown is to be found in Keynes's early *Tract of Monetary Reform*, 1923, reissued by Macmillan in 1971.

5. This metaphor is taken from a compilation of Hayek's writings entitled *A Tiger by the Tail*, published by the I.E.A. in 1972.

6. I have given a summary of this controversy in *Steering the Economy* (Penguin, 1971), pp. 156 *et seq.*

7. The expression 'economics of Keynes' is used to describe the interpretation put upon the doctrines held by the real life Keynes in the 1930s by Prof. Axel Leijonhufvud, as contrasted both with the national income models used in post-war economic forecasting and the 'neoclassical–Keynesian' synthesis appearing in many academic texts. Leijonhufvud's ideas can be found in *On Keynesian Economics and the Economics of Keynes* (Oxford, 1968). A briefer exposition will be found in his *Keynes and the Classics* (Institute of Economic Affairs, 1969); but the shorter work may be puzzling without the longer version by its side.

8. John Nelson-Jones, *The Wages of Fear* (Bow Publications, 1971).

9. Mackay *et al.*, *Labour Markets under Different Employment Conditions* (Allen & Unwin, 1971).

10. A notable restatement is *Labour and Inflation*, Fabian Tract No. 403.

11. W. Beckerman, *The Labour Government's Economic Record* (Duckworth, 1972).

12. A good survey of the most prevalent ideas for incomes intervention can be found in an article 'Incomes Policy and Inflation' by Frank Blackaby in the November 1972 issue of the *National Institute Review*.

13. J. Meade, *Wages and Prices in a Mixed Economy* (Institute of Economic Affairs, 1971).

14. See for instance Michael Grant, *The Climax of Rome* (Weidenfeld & Nicolson, 1968).

15. A good example is the article 'Why an Incomes Policy Would not Work' by David Metcalf and Ray Richardson, *The Financial Times*, 3 February 1971.

16. Lord Balogh, *Labour and Inflation*.

3 THE ECONOMICS OF THE ALTERNATIVE SOCIETY

1. T. S. Eliot, *The Idea of a Christian Society* (Faber, 1939), p. 62.

2. See for instance *A Social Democratic Britain*, Fabian Tract 404. 1971.

3. Lindbeck, *The Political Economy of the New Left*, p. 89.

4. See Note 17 to Prologue, above.

5. K. Marx, *Critique of the Gotha Programme*, 1875.

6. Carter, *Wealth*, p. 75.

7. *Policy for Poverty*, Institute of Economic Affairs.

4 CONSERVATISM AND THE MARKET ECONOMY

1. Harold Lever, 'Lame Ducks Home to Roost', *New Statesman*, 12 February 1971.

2. Cmnd 4331, 1970.

3. Brookings Report on the U.K., *Britain's Economic Prospects* (Allen & Unwin, 1968).

4. Ibid., Chapter 7, by Richard Caves, p. 321.

5. C. B. Edwards, *Concorde—A Case Study in Cost Benefit Analysis*, revised edition (University of East Anglia, 1970).

6. *Congressional Record*, 31 October 1969.

7. *Report of the Committee of Inquiry into the Aircraft Industry, 1964–5*, Cmnd 2853, H.M.S.O., 1965, para. 172.

8. *Industrial and Regional Development*, Cmnd 4942.

9. P. Jay, 'The Government's Waste Paper on Regional Policy', *The Times*, 21 March 1972 (earlier editions only).

10. J. K. Galbraith, *Economics, Peace and Laughter*, Deutsch, 1971.

11. 'Let Them Compete', *The Economist*, 5 December 1970.

12. An issue discussed in Ian Senior, *The Postal Service: Competition or Monopoly?*, I.E.A., Background Memorandum No. 3, 1970.

13. The economic implications of the new technological developments in broadcasting are discussed by Peter Jay in his contribution to the *Manchester University Extra-Mural Department Second Symposium on Broadcasting*, 23-25 November 1970.

14. *Report of the Departmental Committee on the London Taxicab Trade*, Cmnd 4483, October 1970.

15. Voucher systems are analysed in principle and discussed in alternative forms in a number of I.E.A. publications and studies, including Alan T. Peacock and Jack Wiseman, *Education for Democrats*, Hobart Paper 25, 2nd impression, 1970; E. G. West, *Education and the State*, 2nd edition, 1971; and Ralph Harris and Arthur Seldon, *Choice in Welfare*, 1965 and 1970.

16. *Report of the Committee on the Rent Acts*, Cmnd 4609, 1971.

5 SOME COMMON MARKET HERESIES

1. G. Hallett, 'The Problem of Agriculture in a European Economic Union', *Journal of Agricultural Economics*, vol. XX, no. 3, 1969.

2. M. Miller, 'Estimates of the Static Balance of Payments and Welfare Costs of U.K. Entry into the E.E.C.', *National Institute Economic Review*, September 1971.

3. An exposition of these dangers by a well-known advocate of British membership and former E.E.C. official is given by W. R. Lewis in *Rome or Brussels* (Hobart Paperback, I.E.A., 1971).

6 AN EXCESS OF PRAGMATISM

1. *Constitution of Liberty*, p. 153 (Allen & Unwin, 1960).

2. Beesley, *Economic Effects of National Politics Towards Mergers and Acquisitions*, paper given at a London Conference on Long Range Planning, 18 February 1969, available from London Business School.

10 MORALITY AND FOREIGN POLICY

1. George F. Kennan, *The Realities of American Foreign Policy* (Oxford University Press, 1954), p. 47.

13 FURTHER THOUGHTS ON LEFT AND RIGHT

1. S. Brittan, *Left or Right: The Bogus Dilemma* (Secker & Warburg, 1968).
2. Butler and Stokes, *Political Change in Britain* (Macmillan, 1969).
3. Ibid., p. 192.
4. Ibid., p. 180.
5. Ibid., p. 209.
6. A brief popular account is provided by Eysenck in *Sense and Nonsense in Psychology* (Penguin, 1957), Chapter 7. A full account of the concepts and methods is given in *The Psychology of Politics* (Routledge & Kegan Paul, 1954, reprinted 1963).
7. L. Wittgenstein, *Philosophical Investigations*, 2nd edition (Basil Blackwell, 1958), pp. 31–2.
8. A readable summary of these findings, together with reference to the more technical literature can be found in Richard Lynn, 'Psychology and Politics', *Swinton Journal*, Autumn 1970. I would not, however, agree with all his speculations about, and justifications of, the statistical linkages found on the conservative side.
9. Brittan, *Left or Right: The Bogus Dilemma*, p. 73.
10. Ibid., p. 75.
11. Beckerman (ed.), *The Labour Government's Economic Record* (Duckworth, 1972).

Index

Where a bibliographic source is indicated in the text only by a note reference number, this number is given in the index, in brackets, after the page reference. The note number is also given in brackets where the page number refers directly to the Notes and References.